KAMIL BOUŠKA

THE BIG BOOK ABOUT BITCOIN
AND CRYPTOCURRENCIES

financial literacy for everyone

BPF Media

BPF Media stands for Bitcoin Punctum Fixum Media, with Punctum Fixum being Latin for "fixed point." The name is inspired by the principle attributed to Archimedes: "Give me a place to stand, and I shall move the earth." Bitcoin represents our contemporary fixed point, offering the potential to drive transformative change in society, finance, and governance.

© 2024

A NOTE FROM THE TRANSLATOR

I'm honored that Kamil entrusted me to translate the global English edition of this book from the original Czech version. A Herculean task, the completed work spans over 300 pages and contains over 300 corresponding illustrations, tables, notes, and QR codes. It has been my aim to stay true to Kamil's vision and voice, ensuring my translation accurately reflects his original intent. I hope this book prompts you to think further about how you choose to preserve the value of your good deeds.

—Westley Overcash

© 2024 Kamil Bouška

National Library of the Czech Republic Cataloging-in-Publication Data
The big book about bitcoin and cryptocurrencies: financial literacy for everyone / Kamil Bouška
Říčany: Kamil Bouška, 2024

ISBN 978-80-11-04504-3 (hardbound)
ISBN 978-80-11-06376-4 (paperback)
ISBN 978-80-11-04505-0 (PDF)
ISBN 978-80-11-04506-7 (EPUB)

An imprint of:
BPF Media
Říčany, Czech Republic
Bigbookbtc@proton.me

Translation and editing: Westley Overcash
Cover, illustrations, and cartoons: Marek Simon
Graphic design: Lucie Cíchová
Typesetting: Eliška Tunklová

I dedicate this book to my children, Kenny, Kevin, and Kamča.

You are the most precious thing I have; you are my treasure.
I hope Bitcoin will accompany you on your life's journey, providing
a safe haven to preserve your good deeds. May it bring you
freedom, independence, and security in this ever-changing world.

With love and pride in my heart, now and forever.
—Dad

Disclaimer: The information provided in *The Big Book about Bitcoin and Cryptocurrencies: Financial Literacy for Everyone* is for educational and informational purposes only. The content is not intended as legal, financial, investment, or professional advice. The views expressed are those of the author alone and should not be taken as expert instruction or commands. Readers are encouraged to conduct their own due diligence and consult with professional advisors before making any financial decisions or investments.

Cryptocurrency investments are inherently risky and subject to market fluctuations. The author and publisher do not guarantee any particular financial outcomes or the accuracy of market predictions mentioned in this book. Past performance is not indicative of future results. The author and publisher shall not be held liable for any financial losses or damages resulting from interpretations of the content of this book. The reader assumes all responsibility for all risks associated with financial decisions.

The laws and regulations surrounding cryptocurrencies are subject to change and can vary by jurisdiction. It is the responsibility of the reader to ensure compliance with local laws and regulations concerning cryptocurrency transactions and investments.

The examples and anecdotes provided are for illustrative purposes only and are not guarantees of future performance or success.

This publication may contain logos, links to external websites, or references to third-party sources. The author and publisher do not endorse any third-party services or websites and are not responsible for their content, accuracy, or reliability.

No part of this publication may be construed as an offer or solicitation to buy or sell any currency, product, or financial instrument. Any trademarks, service marks, or trade names referred to in this book are the property of their respective owners and are mentioned for identification purposes only.

By purchasing or reading this book, you acknowledge and agree that you understand this disclaimer and accept the risks associated with participating in any financial transactions discussed or suggested in this book.

TABLE OF CONTENTS

INTRODUCTION

This book is intended for readers of all ages and backgrounds. Written in a popular scientific form, it aims to present what are often technical topics and make them comprehensible to the widest possible audience. In an effort to be concise and understandable, some summaries of more complex topics are simplified, while retaining the overall gist of the information. Although it is primarily aimed at beginners in the field, I believe that even advanced users of cryptocurrencies will find new insights and information in it. Given the broad coverage of the topics in the book, it is one of the most comprehensive publications of its type to date. As such, when you read the introductions to each chapter, you can decide for yourself which content is most interesting to you and which parts you might prefer to skim through or return to later.

In the book, I try to convey in a clear way the knowledge I have gained over the years by drawing on information from many different sources. When I became interested in Bitcoin, I had to educate myself in a number of areas ranging from history to economics to computer science. I spent a lot of time sorting through information and doing my own thinking. I realized that not enough people in society fully understand the nature of money and the economic processes that surround and affect us. Even I had not fully understood the concept of money, and had taken for granted how it works.

As time went on, it became clear to me that although I thought I knew almost everything, I found that in fact I knew almost nothing. It's very exciting when things start to fall into place for you, and suddenly you see the light and start to understand the connections. As you read along, I hope you will feel the same way. Throughout this book you will find occasionally that I also indulge in my own musings and speculations about the future. Think of it as my subjective opinion and a kind of crystal ball divination.

At the same time, it is important to say here that none of the discussions in this book should be seen as investment advice. Each reader should check the information thoroughly from various sources, form their own opinion, and decide freely what their next steps should be. Investing in cryptocurrencies is a risky business. Anyone interested should only invest as much as they can afford to lose.

In the first part of the book, you will learn mostly about money, both from a historical and contemporary perspective. You will learn how money is created, what it is backed by, what functions it should perform—and that there is no such thing as money. You will also learn how inflation occurs and how you can protect yourself against it.

The second part of the book is dedicated to the world of cryptocurrencies. It describes the history and reasons for their creation. You will get an overview not only of the global crypto market, but also of the vast differences between currencies. You will learn how to buy cryptocurrencies and how to safely store them.

In closing, I would like to express my sincere thanks to my team, without them the book would not have been produced in this form. I am thinking of Mark Simon, whose illustrations accompany the whole book and provide humorous commentary on the various themes contained throughout. Next, I would like to thank Lucie Cíchová, our amazing graphic designer, whose significant contribution to the visual representation of the content can be seen throughout the book, including the detailed preparation and placement of the drawings and infographics. Finally, I would like to thank Westley Overcash, whose brilliant translation and editing made the book accessible to an international audience. All of the above have contributed invaluable advice and suggestions that have greatly enriched the book. I am deeply grateful for their hard work and dedication.

Additionally, I would like to thank our corporate partners who have helped to place a physical copy of this book in your hands. A majority of these companies are well-known leaders in the cryptocurrency industry. The fact that they have supported the creation of the book is a significant accolade for me and the entire implementation team. It is also an indicator that we are on the right track, with these industry titans agreeing on the importance of promoting cryptocurrency education. I hope that we will continue to work together and create quality projects that will be meaningful not only for us, but for the entire cryptocurrency community. A big thank you to all of you!

BOOK ONE

MONEY, THE MEMORY OF OUR GOOD DEEDS, AND A LITTLE HISTORY

MONEY, THE MEMORY OF OUR GOOD DEEDS, AND A LITTLE HISTORY

We see money as a normal part of our lives. Most of the time we don't think about why it exists, how it came to be historically, or what all money could be. I've never thought of it that way either. When a friend told me that Bitcoin existed and that it was also money, I laughed at him. I was of the opinion that it was just an experiment by some crazy IT guys that could have no real value. Where would that value come from? It was only when the word Bitcoin started popping out at me more and more often that I decided to find out about it. I began to study what money could be and what functions it should perform. To fully understand the subject, I also researched its history, why people invented money in the first place, and how it has evolved over time. I was surprised to find that I had not realized many things. I began to perceive the use of my time differently and my perspective on the materialistic perception of our lives changed. I realized that if one does not understand the functions and workings of money, one can hardly understand the meaning and workings of bitcoin. Therefore, this issue needs to be studied comprehensively and nicely from the beginning.

HOW IT ALL BEGAN: EVOLUTION DOES NOT MEASURE EVERYONE WITH THE SAME YARDSTICK

Animals and other species have lived on our planet much longer than humans. Like humans, they go through evolution. Some animals have come out of the water onto land and others have learned to fly. Some live and hunt alone and others live in packs. Many have even been domesticated and live with humans. Yet animals are different from humans in many ways. Animals live and act on instinct. They seek immediate fulfillment of their needs. When they are hungry, they hunt. When they're tired, they rest, when it's time to mate, they mate. When threatened, they try to survive by running away, fighting, trickery, or even mimicry. They live in the present and don't worry about what the future holds. Of course, sometimes they do wonder about the immediate future. Most often it is, for example, in terms of surviving the winter or bringing up their offspring. But animals don't think years ahead, and they certainly don't think about what will happen when they are old, or what will happen when they get sick. Animals do not accumulate property, and most relationships between them are governed by the law of the stronger, the instinct for self-preservation, or sexual urges. They try to incorporate a certain intelligence into their behavior, which is often determined by evolution and innate instincts.

However, man has evolved differently and in the process of evolution has created an interesting community where he applies different relationships than those common in the animal kingdom. On the one hand, almost no individual can **live independently** and necessarily needs other individuals both for his survival and for his quality and comfortable life. On the other hand, most individuals at a basic level try to act for themselves and fulfill their needs. They join together to achieve better results, but most of the time it is again only to better fulfill their own needs.

Of course, the fulfillment of one's own needs does not have to be only material. Some individuals consider it to include doing good for others. This gives them a sense of fulfillment, satisfaction, or maybe just social recognition. Often, when the set goals are achieved, there is a need to continue. The chase for more and more metrics ensues. Many individuals try to live at the expense of others. Others need to prove to themselves that they can live better than those around them. How is it possible that evolution has separated humans from other animals in such a fundamental way? Why is human behavior so different from animal behavior? The most fundamental reasons are hidden in the use of intelligence to simplify life and make hunting or subsistence more efficient. It was the use of fire, the creation of tools, simple machines, and weapons, the building of dwellings, the cultivation of plants, and the breeding of livestock that distinguished humans from other animals. But to do all this, man had to start behaving in a different way from animals. Yes, man was simply gifted with a higher intelligence than other species. However, we will not discuss whether this fundamental break, which caused the change in the behavior of one species, was due to the role of chance in evolutionary processes, to a higher power, or to the intervention of extraterrestrial civilizations. Let each reader choose the reason that is most acceptable for themselves. Allow us to discuss together the main reasons why one species has figuratively broken free and advanced beyond other forms of life by leaps and bounds.

Independent life

You might think you could survive on your own in a desolate place, but what would you do without clothes, tools, medicines, and all of the necessities of everyday life? Perhaps some individuals could survive in such conditions, but for how long? Would you be able to help support and expand the population? What would your quality of life look like?

CALIBRATING OUR BRAINS IN PREPARATION FOR A DEEP UNDERSTANDING

I would like to explain two perspectives that will gradually intertwine throughout the book. I will try to explain them briefly so that you can better understand my view of the topics we will discuss together. The first perspective is my perception of time. The second perspective is how I perceive work and our daily activities within the community of people in which we live.

HOW GOOD DEEDS ARE CREATED

We utilize time for fun, relaxation, work, and our loved ones. Sometimes we miss it, but sometimes we waste it. Time is the most precious and important **asset** we have, but not everyone can use it effectively. Everyone has this asset, regardless of whether they are rich or poor.

Animals devote their time to fulfilling the immediate needs mentioned at the beginning of the chapter. For man, time is something extremely precious and everyone should realize this fact. It is a finite and very limited set of hours, days, and years that we have available in this world, and we usually do not know how much more we will have.

> By **asset** we mean everything that one owns, such as property. It is everything that we have acquired through past activities and from which we expect to benefit in the future. Assets can be tangible or intangible. One of our most important assets is time. Education, business, or even family relationships can be considered assets. Most assets are directly or indirectly exchangeable for money.

While money continues to lose its value, time is becoming more precious.
So I'm investing in time.

The essence of human progress is that man is willing to devote his precious time to something other than the immediate fulfillment of needs. While animals just hunt and rest, humans are able to devote much of their time instead of resting to devising various improvements that will help to simplify life or make hunting or cultivating the land more efficient. People have sacrificed and continue to sacrifice time, even though their efforts have not always been successful. On the other hand, when successful, they have gained better catches or more land cultivated as a result of the time spent. This means that they have gained more products that they could exchange for something, and either consume the value of the exchange immediately, or save it for later. We can offer any excess production that we cannot consume ourselves to others, and it becomes our next asset. However, this new asset largely contains our previous most valuable asset: time. Because we live in a community environment, products and any overproduction can also be seen as good deeds that we exchange with each other. This basic principle still works today.

GOOD DEEDS AS SEEN THROUGH THE LENS OF THIS BOOK

Most people would probably define a good deed as a selfless act performed above and beyond the duties or expectations of others. People do them to feel good or perhaps because they want to set an example. Often they expect that if they are ever in need, the person in question, or perhaps a complete stranger, will help them in return. Basically, in this case too, it is a kind of barter. For the purposes of this book, however, let's think of a good deed more as human labor, that is, the provision of services or goods that someone has created and not consumed. One then offers their product to others who can use it. Good deeds in this sense are therefore created by an individual for the use of others on the basis of the consumption of one's own time, and possibly other resources. What good deeds society needs are determined by supply and demand. We speak of a good deed for the community or humanity even when we know that an individual's reasons for doing it are selfish.

A good deed is any benefit created for others.

We can't save time, but we can save the good deeds for which we have used our time. One way to preserve these good deeds is to exchange them for money. By creating good deeds, or utilities, and exchanging them for money, we create capital that we can spend.

Every human should realize that it is desirable to preserve at least some of their good works for a time when they might be needed. It may be for old age, illness, or sudden needs. Therefore, we must store them in such money or property that can hold their value in the long run and can be easily used when needed. If this cannot be done, the good works or deeds will depreciate in value and hence the time we have spent on them will depreciate. In such a case, we must realize that it is like throwing away a corresponding part of our life.

By **capital** we mean everything that we use to create more value in the future. The simplest definition of capital is money used in such a way that it brings in more money. Capital is the portion of assets that we do not consume, but use towards making future profits.

"Money is the memory of our good deeds."
—Juraj Karpiš, Slovak economist

Yes, money is the memory of our good deeds and is capital that can be put away for later.

ARE IDEOLOGIES AND TIME PREFERENCES THE REASON WHY MAN HAS BROKEN THE EVOLUTIONARY CHAIN?

Man differs from animals in three main elements of behavior and reasoning. These are ideology, preference reduction (deferring immediate needs), and specialization. Let us at least briefly discuss each of them.

IDEOLOGY

People are susceptible to the opinions of others and often act under their influence. Some are manipulators, while those who do not hold a coherent opinion of their own tend to be manipulated. This human behavior can manifest itself, among other things, in individuals deciding what is good and what is bad, or even in deciding what money to use. Political or religious ideologies are often the subject of disputes or wars. However, not every ideology is fundamentally wrong. Even human thought processes, such as morality or conscience, can be said to be based on ideologies about how people should behave. Animals don't have ideologies, and as was said at the beginning, they are mostly driven by instinct.

> An **ideology** is an elaborate set of opinions, attitudes, ideas, thoughts, intentions or values. It is based on the articulation of a political, economic, or religious worldview. It often serves as a basis for human action, politics and morality.

TIME PREFERENCES

Perhaps the most important difference in the behavior of humans compared to animals is the fact that productive humans, unlike animals, can postpone the satisfaction of their needs. In general, it is this postponement of needs that is one of the main drivers of human progress. However, the threshold for each person is quite different.

Immediate consumption

In this case, an individual wants to satisfy present needs over future ones. In a consumer society, there is often an immediate fulfillment of needs beyond what is necessary or expedient. This means wasting food, energy, and other goods. It also means acquiring fashionable, luxury, or consumer goods that we can do without at the moment. Furthermore, any action that will bring short-term profit in the present, regardless of possible problems in the future, can also be seen as such. Typically, this may be lying, immoral, or dishonest behavior. It can occur in any context, including business, interpersonal relations, or family.

> In economic theory, **goods** are those things that increase utility. Goods can consist of physical objects or even services. An exception is so-called undesirable goods, which reduce utility.

Delayed consumption

In this case, an individual minimizes consumption in the present and accumulates capital that allows for creating more purchasing power in the future. In other words, one invests in the future, accumulates capital for larger projects, and expects the money saved to have a higher purchasing power in the future. Alternatively, one may simply defer their good deeds until later, when they can be used as needed. Such behavior can bring substantial benefits in the future.

Postponing some of the needs until later can address:

- creating a reserve for when one reaches old age or experiences illness
- increasing the purchasing power of saving if saved in a way that outperforms inflation in the long run (described in further detail in the chapter about inflation from page 75)
- creating capital for projects that could not otherwise be implemented
- increasing moral credit and reputation

Preferring either of these options in setting time preferences divides society into those who are just driving and those who are trying to be progressive. Of course, even a highly intelligent or exceptionally gifted individual who does not save money can be successful in the short term. However, in the long term, they usually lag behind those who can postpone their immediate needs until later. Typical examples are top athletes, celebrities, successful executives, and even politicians. Their popularity can often end very quickly, and if they have not deferred some of their needs by investing in the future or saving, their standard of living and quality of life can deteriorate significantly from one day to the next.

SPECIALIZATION OR DIVISION OF LABOR

Without scaling down to meet immediate needs, specialization would never have come into being. In order to begin to specialize, one had first to be willing to devote one's precious time to activities that did not directly benefit one at the time.

Specialization is of course a very broad concept, which can be seen in terms of hunting, production, services, trade, or even family, but the principle is always similar. Each individual tries to do the activities that he or she is best at, and tries to be useful to others in this way. As a reward for their good deeds, they expect to draw on the good deeds of someone else in the area where they need to fulfill their needs. This rule applies generally, both in business and in family and personal ties. The main advantage of specialization is that it increases productivity and efficiency in a given area. This is because repetitive activities can be performed faster, preparations can be made, and improvements can be devised. As a result, it is possible to produce more products in less time with less labor and at lower cost. They can then be offered on the open market and the newly acquired products can then be used to satisfy as many current needs as possible, or put off until later.

On the basis of innovation and productivity increases, the purchasing power of money increases, as products should become cheaper on the basis of these facts.

WHY HUMANS NEED MONEY AND ANIMALS DON'T

Without specialization, trade could never have developed into what it is today. The moment people began to specialize, it was necessary to work out how they would exchange products and services with each other. Bartering was the first way of doing business. People exchanged products or services directly with each other. In this method of exchange, they always had to find a counterparty that offered what they needed, but at the same time the counterparty had to accept what was available. This way of trading has its limits and often became complicated even in small groups.

Imagine a situation where one member of the community was a skilled hunter and the other a skilled farmer. The hunter had a lot of furs and wanted to trade them for crops with the farmer. If the farmer didn't immediately need the furs, the hunter had to see what the farmer would be willing to accept in their place. The hunter then had to exchange the furs for other goods that the farmer was willing to accept, like pottery for example. Even in a small collective with few goods, this created dozens of possible exchange relationships.

By barter we mean to exchange goods or services for other goods or services without using money. It should be noted, however, that the findings of anthropologists today show that bartering may not have had such a significance throughout human history. Recent theories point out that people in communities helped each other based on different principles, and the good deeds provided to each other were not based on the principle of an immediate exchange of something for something. They more or less conferred benefits on each other based on credit, believing that they would draw a counter-benefit later if necessary. Thus, something for something was paid, but it was not a direct barter. These principles still apply today in smaller communities such as families and neighborhoods.

The formula for determining all exchange relationships between items is

n (n − 1) / 2 = X, where X is the resulting number of links and n is the number of items. This means that for 2 items there is only 1 possible exchange.

For 6 items there are up to 15 exchange options 6 × (6 − 1) / 2 = 6 × 5 / 2 = 15.

The exchange links and the relationships between them are summarized in the following table.

Items	Posible exchange links
15	105
500	124,750
10,000	49,995,000
150,000	11,249,999,000

$n(n-1)/2$

2 items = 1 exchange link

6 items = 15 exchange links

500 items = 124,750 exchange links

With a larger number of items, it was no longer realistic to acquire individual links. Because of the growing barter trade and the large number of items, the need for money arose. One could not do without a way to store one's good deeds and transfer them unchanged in value across place and time. Therefore, people tried to store the good deeds they created in goods or in what came to be called money.

The value of money—its purchasing power—had to be at least equal or greater in surrounding places as well as more distant areas. The same was true for maintaining the value of good deeds over time. If the good deeds on which one spent their precious time began to depreciate over time, then one could write off a certain part of their life because one would be spending time doing something that ultimately had no benefit. So, in their own interest, people have always tried to exchange their good deeds for money, which they could then **invest** in order to appreciate in value over the long term, or at least retain its value. As soon as the chosen money ceased to fulfill this function, mankind gradually discarded it and replaced it with better money. But as is the case with evolution, nothing happens by leaps and bounds. Everything has evolved gradually, depending on the current capabilities and experiences of individual communities.

> **Investments** are funds that have been allocated to a particular project with the aim of appreciation and return. The purpose of investing is to preserve the value of current funds and minimize potential declines in value in the future. Ideally their value should increase.

WHAT CONSTITUTES MONEY?

Money can be anything that another entity is willing to accept as money, in other words, something to which it ascribes value, either on the basis of utility or scarcity.

The first means of payment in barter trade were products. Products can include goods like produce, crops, and livestock, as well as and services such as cooking, cleaning, and sewing. They had to be useful to most members of the community. A reasonable shelf life was also important. In addition to durability, over time society began to place greater and greater demands on money. For something to function effectively as money, it had to perform basic functions and have certain characteristics. Let's take a closer look at this.

REASONS FOR THE CREATION OF MONEY

- to facilitate trade by overcoming the limitations of barter exchanges
- to compensate for the different value of products when trading
- to carry our good deeds from place to place
- to carry our good deeds into the future and preserve surplus value or surplus production for the long term
- for targeted savings or investment

WHAT CRITERIA SHOULD MONEY MEET?

In order for money to be useful, it must be able to perform the functions that humanity demands of it. Additionally, the quality and characteristics of any currency is important. This topic is discussed on page 107.

Basic functions of money
- means of exchange that mediates the purchase and sale of goods or services on the basis of general acceptance
- unit of account that serves as an expression of the price of tangible and intangible assets, like goods and services, and allows for the settlement between different values
- A way to save value from goods and services today so it can be used in the future, helping to build future wealth

Properties of money
- scarcity (it must not be easy to procure, reproduce, or counterfeit)
- endurance under normal use
- durability over long-term holding
- divisibility
- storability (cost of storage space, size, and security)
- transferability (easy to handle, transport, and send)

- easy authentication

- general availability to market participants

- standardization (determination of the same units, their value, and form)

With the emergence of electronic money, people are losing access to direct ownership of their funds. They are forced to use other intermediaries such as banks and other financial institutions. Thus, the risk of intermediary failure including situations like bankruptcy, embezzlement, freezing of accounts, seizure, or restriction by state authorities increases. These risks create the need for additional features:

- security of possession

- resistance to censorship

The main risks include:

Bankruptcy: financial institutions are unable to meet their financial obligations, including paying out money

Embezzlement: the illegal transfer of funds into the possession of another person

Freezing of account: when a bank or government agency stops all activity on an account

Seizure of funds: the government or other authority removes the owner's funds

Restriction or justification of certain transactions: situations where banks or government authorities may restrict or require justification for specific financial transactions

Money is one of the most fundamental inventions of human society and one of the most important tools at our disposal. It has become a universal medium of exchange and one of the most important ways in which we measure the value of things and services. From a philosophical point of view, money is also interesting in that it resembles language in many ways. As a language, it enables communication between people and serves as a means of communicating value.

Money cannot only be a medium of exchange, but it can also influence our thinking and behavior. Money enables us to get the things and services we need, but it can also lead us to unhealthy competition, lust for power, and envy. It can motivate us to work and strive, but it can also lead to laziness and abuse. It is a powerful tool that influences our thinking, behavior, and society as a whole.

Bitcoin, things of use—value, and even Pokémon cards can be considered money if they perform the basic functions of money in a given community (there is a consensus on their value and acceptance). Money today is no longer just about paper notes or coins; humanity is looking for money that best fulfills its preferred characteristics.

Never mind cryptocurrencies. Our new bank focuses on future payment methods like gold teeth and canned food.

THE EMERGENCE OF STANDARDIZED MONEY BASED ON PRECIOUS METALS

Currencies that were based on universally accepted utility or rarity drove trade growth. However, as the market developed and the need for long-term holding became more important, people's views on currency changed. At the same time, there was pressure for some standardization to allow faster and more accurate exchange. Better put, there was a need to stop exchanging and start trading.

THE ADVENT OF UTILITY FICTIONS

Due to the requirements for specific properties of money, utility fictions have increasingly come to be promoted as money. For simplicity, the term fictions is used hereafter.

> **The fictions had no-use value for humans. Their value depended on a general recognition of their rarity or a social agreement to accept them.**

They could not be easily procured or multiplied and had to be considered rare by others. Shells, precious stones, and precious metals were among the first and most widely used fiat currencies.

The word fiction originated from the Latin word fictio (derived from fictus), which means a shaping, fashioning, or invention.

In this book, the term is used in the sense of utility fiction, that is, something that is material but has no intrinsic utility value to humans. Fiction-based money, however, can acquire its value by virtue of scarcity and widespread acceptance.

In the early days of human civilization, shells, precious stones, and precious metals like gold and silver had no intrinsic value, as they could not be used to satisfy basic human needs. For example, gold could not be used to satisfy hunger, thirst, or the need for warmth or shelter.

People needed to travel. As trade developed, there was an increasing need to carry the accumulated good works over greater distances. Traders, of course, first transported and exchanged goods. At the same time, however, they increasingly needed something that could be of great value, that would be recognized as a form of payment even in distant countries, that would be resistant to transport or transmission, and that would not deteriorate over a long period of time. Thus, in addition to the payment of goods, the use of precious metals as standardized money has prevailed over time throughout the world.

Throughout evolution, mankind has been trying to find the best quality money that would have the best properties. That is why fictions eventually won out over products. It is important to remember that this was a pivotal moment in human history. Humans chose something fictitious over something that could have provided them with real benefits and met their basic needs. However, the value of fictions was only determined by the fact that a section of the community recognized their value on the basis of their scarcity and the utility of fulfilling the functions of money. Subsequently, a network effect occurred where more and more people started to use this fiction-based means of payment. Because it was an innovation that held better monetary properties than previous instruments, combined with the effects of crowd behavior (the marginal effect), widespread adoption ensued. Those who did not want to recognize the value of precious metals because they did not find them useful were eventually willing to recognize their value based on the fact that others recognized their value. If not accepted, these people were then left out of the monetary system and would subsequently find themselves at a great disadvantage. Fictions began to be given value even though they had no intrinsic use-value to humans at the time. Thus, humanity was able to check off another characteristic: universal acceptance.

> In economics, the network effect is a phenomenon in which the value or utility that a user receives from a good or service depends on the number of users of compatible products. The adoption of a product by an additional user can be divided into two effects: increasing the value for all other users (total effect), and also increasing the incentive of other non-users to use the product (marginal effect).

On the basis of which characteristics did precious metals win over other currencies?

- scarcity (cannot be reproduced or counterfeited)
- durability against the elements (water, fire, wear) and over time (resistant to rust and deterioration)
- general acceptance as a means of payment
- long-term store of value

The next step in the development of money and the ecosystem around it was the effort to standardize by making individual coins of the same value and easily recognizable. This also facilitated pricing and the creation of global markets. Different currencies could be accepted in a given market based on a market-determined exchange rate that reflected the confidence of market participants in the value of the currency. The main prerequisite for the success of a given currency is whether it has better characteristics than others.

THE EMERGENCE OF PAPER MONEY: THE MOVE TOWARDS VALUE FICTIONS CONTINUES

Precious metals were difficult to store, transport, and protect. People began to store their coins with jewelers, who had treasuries and vaults that offered better protection. A certificate issued by the jeweler served as proof of the storage of the precious metal.

When using the gold standard, the currency consists of either coins minted from a well-defined amount of gold, or banknotes where the issuer guarantees to repay their value in gold. The gold standard is seen as a principle for backing the issued currency.

These were paper vouchers that confirmed how much metal was deposited. When a person presented a voucher to a jeweler, the jeweler would give them the corresponding metal. People soon realized that they could trade using paper vouchers instead of handing over metal coins. These vouchers were given a value based on the amount of metal they represented, and they became known as money orders. Good paper money was equivalent to a gold voucher deposited in a bank, which was equivalent to the gold standard.

However, the traveling merchants required further development of this financial system. Jewelers began to band together, setting up banks, and trying to offer customers greater deposit security. Banks sprang up all over the world and began to enter into agreements and contracts with each other, under which they undertook to cash vouchers issued by the other party. This allowed a merchant to deposit gold in, for example, NewYork and then go to London to collect it again.

Paper vouchers were later replaced by preprinted banknotes with a fixed value. These notes had to be backed by an appropriate amount of precious metal. This was a major shift in the standardization of money, as it allowed for the convertibility of different currencies with each other. As a result, some currencies became more widely recognized.

There was nothing stopping humanity from moving on to the next innovation, even though it was just fiction. People trusted jewelers and banks, believing that their money had the same value as if they owned the corresponding amount of precious metals.

HOW PAPER MONEY WAS SUPERIOR IN UTILITY

- ✔ divisibility
- ✔ storability (cost of storage space size and security)
- ✔ handling (easy to transport and send)
- ✔ easy authentication
- ✔ general acceptance
- ✔ accessibility for market participants
- ✔ standardization (determination of the same units, including their value and form)
- ✔ the unit of account used to determine the market price

HOW PAPER MONEY WAS FAR INFERIOR IN VALUE AND PHYSICAL PROPERTIES

- ✕ scarcity (it must not be easy to procure, reproduce, or counterfeit)
- ✕ endurance in normal use
- ✕ durability for long-term holding
- ✕ sustained value even with long-term holding

Human credulity, convenience, and ignorance won out. Many people trusted that someone else, often referred to as a third party, was capable of looking after their property and would not succumb to the temptation to profit from it. The network effect played a big role. Humanity embraced the innovation of paper money with inferior value and physical properties. On the other hand, it should be noted that in general we cannot talk about a negative phenomenon. Money is built on a network effect. This shift has meant easier use, standardization, and the development of banking systems. As a result, there has been a great boom in global trade.

Paper money, although very important to our economy and daily life, has no intrinsic value beyond the value of the paper and ink from which it is made. Its value is based on trust and on our collective belief that it is a universally accepted form of payment with predefined values.

Paper money is a medium of exchange that allows people to exchange goods and services. However, in order to perform this function well, it must be backed by something of real value, such as gold or silver. This was done in the past, when paper money was backed by precious metals, which guaranteed its value and stability.

Today, no country uses gold or silver standards. The value of paper money is backed by a combination of the state's authority, public trust, and economic conditions. The state determines the value of money by decree, and people trust that it will be accepted as payment. This system of fictions works as long as most people trust the state's authority and its ability to keep the economy stable.

If people stop trusting state authority, there could be a rise in inflation, a hoarding of alternative assets (such as gold or bitcoin), a banking and financial crisis, a rise in the underground economy, and barter. In extreme cases, a country could undertake currency reform or adopt another foreign currency as an official medium of exchange.

It is also necessary to constantly remind oneself that fictions can lose their value and function in the case of crisis situations, when a person urgently needs to satisfy a need. This is due to the fact that they have no intrinsic utilitarian value for a person. A jug of water and a loaf of bread may, in certain cases, satisfy a current need better than a bar of gold or a bag of money. Such situations can realistically occur in war conflicts or natural disasters. Society may then revert to bartering products that have more use-value to an individual at the time. The value of fictions is therefore uncertain, but is based on the principles of market pricing (see page 38).

THE EMERGENCE OF ELECTRONIC MONEY: FROM FICTIONS TO ABSTRACTIONS

Electronic money takes us to a higher technical level that is even further away from the original, physical concept of money. In this step, humanity is moving from fictions to **abstractions**. It is a technological innovation that improves the properties of money. The essence of electronic money is similar to the technical essence of bitcoin, the only difference being that, unlike bitcoin, this money is not at all precious and cannot be held directly by the owner. Better said, it must always be managed by a certified intermediary. Electronic money is a digital substitute for paper money that consists of records in databases and bank servers. Only banks or other legally designated institutions can be the issuer of electronic money. For the time being, the issuer of e-money is obliged to hand over the money to its owner in physical form on request, but cash transactions are gradually being restricted. However, unlike cash payments, banking institutions or private companies charge the merchant a fee for processing transactions. Payments are made using payment cards or contactless technologies, including chips, smartphones, and smartwatches.

An **abstraction** is something intangible, the opposite of something real. In science this term is sometimes used to mean theoretical, or not applied.

In this book, the term is used in the sense of a **useful abstraction**, that is, something that is immaterial and has no basic utilitarian meaning for humans. As with fictions, money-based abstractions can acquire their value by widespread virtue of scarcity and widespread acceptance.

Payments using Face ID have not been successful lately. Mainly because of the scared expression customers have on their faces when it comes time to pay.

The future of electronic money is moving towards Central Bank Digital Currencies (CBDC). Analysts estimate that if CBDCs are introduced, the next step could be to ban the use of cash. However, this would mean that people would lose the complete range of freedom to use their funds, and would be much more at the mercy of the state and bureaucratic power. You can read more about CBDCs in Book Two.

PAYMENTS

Payment transactions take place at different levels and in different ways. Here are the most common ones:

Card systems

They mediate and process payment card transactions between payer banks and merchant banks. The best known are VISA and MasterCard. These are private companies.

Autonomous payment systems

These are services that represent an alternative to a traditional payment card and a personal bank account. They can be considered a form of electronic wallet, where your funds are managed by a private company that you have to put your trust in.

PayPal is one of the widespread payment methods for online e-shops. It allows quick payments between the wallets of their users and also linking with a classic bank credit card.

Revolut offers debit cards, instant payments between users' accounts, payments to other banks, currency management, and exchange. It is also possible to buy shares, commodities, or cryptocurrencies indirectly. It can be an alternative to traditional banks.

Interbank transfers

SWIFT (Society for Worldwide Interbank Financial Telecommunication) is a global communications network that enables banks and other financial institutions to exchange transactions. Within SWIFT, banks and bank accounts are identified by BIC and IBAN. Depending on the specific transaction, the use of BIC, IBAN, or both may be required.

- The BIC (Bank Identifier Code), also known as the SWIFT code, is an international standard format used to identify a specific bank in global financial communications. Each bank has its own unique BIC.
- IBAN (International Bank Account Number) is a standard international format used to identify a specific bank account in international transactions. Each bank account has its own unique IBAN.

SEPA (Single Euro Payments Area) is an initiative of the European Union that enables simple, efficient, and secure payments in euros between accounts in different European countries. SEPA was introduced with the aim of creating a single market for payments in euros where there are no differences between international and national payments. All euro payments within SEPA countries are made through this system using BIC and IBAN.

Fedwire (Federal Reserve Wire Network) is a high-speed electronic system for transferring dollar transactions between Federal Reserve members and other banks in the United States. It provides the infrastructure for immediate, final, and irrevocable gross settlement of transactions between participants.

- The ABA number, also known as the routing number, is a nine-digit code used in the Fedwire system to identify banks and financial institutions for proper transaction execution.

This is another fundamental shift in people's thinking. It is a technological innovation that is embracing **abstraction** instead of **fiction**. In the case of electronic money, people no longer hold anything in their hands and have to rely on a stranger to hold their funds. The state printer saves money on the production of paper money and metal coins, among other things. This brings some advantages for users, but also a number of risks and disadvantages.

THE ADVANTAGES OF ELECTRONIC MONEY OVER PAPER MONEY

- √ fast and cheaper transport (sending payments)
- √ returnability of transactions
- √ improved durability and longevity
- √ absolute divisibility
- √ better accessibility

AND THEIR DISADVANTAGES

- ✗ not scarce at all (they are even easier to reproduce than paper ones)
- ✗ risk of having to hold with third parties (banks, private companies)
- ✗ loss of privacy and anonymity
- ✗ possibility of seizure and censorship by state power
- ✗ poor value sustainability, subject to inflation when held for long periods
- ✗ loss of funds due to ignorance or negligence in handling access data
- ✗ paid transactions
- ✗ dependence on electricity and the internet
- ✗ they are not accepted everywhere

> **Inflation** is an increase in the price of most goods, when money loses its value or purchasing power. It is usually caused by an inflow of newly-created money, and rising prices are just a symptom. Inflation is described further in chapter 3.

Again, human convenience, ignorance, and crowd behavior win out. But nowadays this is mostly done by legal decree. Man is forced to sacrifice his privacy and squander his hard-earned good deeds. Often, he also succumbs to it on the basis of ignorance and the fact that he accepts something as a fact and does not think about the context and consequences. Again, however, it should be noted that, thanks to faster and cheaper payments, the development of electronic banking services is accompanying the further expansion of global trade.

Abstractions, like fictions, can cease to function as money in times of crisis, when people may resort to barter. In this case, the value of abstractions is as uncertain as that of fictions.

THE EVOLUTION OF MONEY TOWARDS GLOBALIZATION

People want to trade globally because it is profitable. To do this, society needs a common, independent, and secure clearing currency. Humanity can be said to be consciously and unconsciously moving towards it. Can bitcoin become such an independent and secure currency? This is a question we will address in more detail in Book Two. However, it is clear that once we find such a currency and subsequently adopt it, everything will become much simpler. People will no longer need clearing houses, payment companies, or exchanges. This will suit people because they enjoy comfort and constantly cry out for simplification.

I won't need to bother calculating the change. I'll just tap and go.

HOW IS THE MARKET PRICE FORMED?

Since we have discussed in detail the functions of money and its properties, it is now necessary to explain how the market price is formed, hereafter referred to simply as price. Price determines the use-value of a given product and is expressed in terms of money. However, different types of money do not have the same value. As such, prices oftentimes vary in different currencies.

- The price is formed spontaneously on the basis of an assessment of the need of the product for a particular community. In other words, the value of the product is determined by market participants. It reflects the rarity or necessity of the product and is determined only by supply and demand.

- The price at the time of the transaction expresses the agreement between what the seller is willing to sell for and what the buyer is willing to buy for.

- The price includes the production (acquisition) costs and the required profit of the trader.

- The price may vary geographically.

- It evolves over time and can be influenced by circumstances such as wars, diseases, crop failures, and natural disasters.

- Prices can be agreed or fixed:

  - agreement prices are used in marketplaces; auctions; tenders; large and complex transactions like real estate; and sales of companies.

  - fixed prices are used where the price needs to be set, for example when there is no time for bargaining or the seller cannot be trusted to fix the price. They are mainly used in standardized sales networks where the price is set by the retailer, such as large chain stores, e-shops, and global distribution networks.

- Fixed prices increase turnover and encourage the development of a global market. It is a standardization that speeds up trading in big stores, shopping malls, e-shops, and wherever fixed price lists exist. It saves time on price negotiation and other transaction costs.

- The price gives valuable and important signals to the economy, and society as a whole, about the current state of the market. Society then reacts spontaneously to these developments, thus providing important feedback.

- The price is set on the basis of continuous information flows between a huge number of sellers and buyers. On the basis of their evaluation by both parties, a sound economic relationship is established.

EVOLUTION OF MONEY

Barter   Precious metals and stones   Coins   Money   Electronic money   Cryptocurrency

MARKET ARRANGEMENTS ARE A NECESSARY CONDITION FOR THE PROSPERITY AND DEVELOPMENT OF SOCIETY

Any regulation that interferes with it will distort the market signals necessary for the healthy functioning of the market and the economy as a whole. Various contributions, artificial incentives, subsidies, and tariffs can also be considered regulation in this context. These in turn alter the global functioning of the market. This results in one being favored over others.

We have obtained a subsidy to combat the problems caused by subsidies.

The opposite of a market economy is a planned economy. A market economy assumes private ownership of the means of production, such as labor, land, and capital. In a planned economy, the means of production are more or less owned by the state. In a planned economy, the state decides what to produce, how much to produce, and at what price to sell it. Communism is a type of planned economy.

It's not true that communism goes against nature and does not work.
Just look at ant colonies.

CHAPTER 1 SUMMARY

Animals

- Animals act on instinct and mostly only for themselves.
- They have no need to exchange goods or services with each other, they do not accumulate assets.
- They want immediate fulfillment of their needs (high time preference).

People

- As a result of the evolution of mankind, man has reached a situation where he is not self-sufficient as an individual. People live in communities where they cooperate and specialize.
- One plans for the future and is able to postpone the fulfillment of needs until later (low time preference). In other words, one invests in the future and accumulates capital.
- People exchange their good deeds with each other. Good deeds can also be work, or the products or services that result from that work.
- Money is the memory of our good deeds.
- Humans use money to transmit good deeds through place and time, to then use them to mediate barter transactions.
- Money can be anything that another entity is willing to perceive as money.
- Good money should best fulfill the functions of money (medium of exchange, unit of account, store of value) and have as many important characteristics as possible (scarcity, resistance, durability, divisibility, storability, transferability, verifiability, availability, standardization, security, and uncensorability).
- The most important function of money is to serve as a medium of exchange. In the long run, it should also serve as a store of value.
- Money is evolving hand in hand with humanity. Innovation always wins. People always start using money with better features (simplicity of use, better sustainable value, divisibility, and security).
- Humanity is willing to accept new forms of money that have better properties in terms of use, even if they have worse properties in terms of use value or scarcity. Sometimes this is also because a higher authority (such as the government) tells them to do so.
- Humanity is willing to embrace fictions and abstractions as part of innovation.
- Thanks to the standardization of money and the development of the banking system, global trade has boomed.
- People first spend money that is declining in value and, conversely, save money that can grow in value over the long term. They get rid of bad money and save good money.
- Anyone who allows the good deeds they have done to lose their value over the years throws away a part of their life that corresponds to the time when they created that value.
- The market price is determined by supply and demand. At the same time, it determines the value of one product relative to others, both locally and globally.
- Private ownership, market prices, and good money are the main prerequisites for the prosperity and development of society.
- Throughout history, money that has ceased to hold value has always been replaced by better money.

GOOD AND BAD MONEY: THE ROAD TO FIAT CURRENCIES

GOOD AND BAD MONEY: THE ROAD TO FIAT CURRENCIES

If we have understood the basic functions of money, how it works, and what characteristics we should demand of it, we should also understand that there is no such thing as money.

Once money had value, this value made it possible to satisfy human needs. Its quantity determined how comfortable of a life an individual could lead and also determined their social status. In order to obtain money honestly, one had to make an appropriate effort in the form of work done or create value (utility) for which others were willing to pay. But it is not surprising that there were individuals who tried to come by money in the easiest possible way. Some robbed and stole, while others tried to counterfeit money. If they were at the lower end of the social ladder, there was an effort to catch and punish them. But if the rulers and those in power chose this method, there was no higher authority to stop them.

Apart from war campaigns, rulers resorted to the method of debasing their currencies in order to increase their wealth. In the long run, however, these methods have always led to the subsequent problems that have recurred throughout human history. Many times these problems have ended in economic collapse, wars, and poverty. So let's take a look at what good and bad money is, and why currencies have collapsed throughout history, regardless of whether they were primitive or contemporary forms of money. This is an important observation to apply when learning about the world of cryptocurrencies.

THE DEBASING OF PRECIOUS METAL-BASED MONEY

Apart from wars and polluting our environment, the debasing of money is another major scourge that has been with mankind since time immemorial. Its pernicious consequences—both for the economy and for society—have been proved many times throughout history. Yet it is such an addictive and tempting activity that a large number of rulers across the world and throughout history have succumbed to the temptation. Sadly, even today, we have to deal with the consequences of this irresponsible behavior caused by governments around the world. But we will talk about that later. For now, let's take it from the beginning.

THOSE IN POWER HAVE THE SAME MOTIVATIONS

In the life of every ruler there came a time when they needed more money than they had available to run their court, such as building palaces and living a lavish lifestyle, or to run the state, including maintaining an army and carrying out war campaigns. So they began to think about how they could get new money.

There were always several options:
- selling part of their property (this was usually ancestral in that it was acquired through inheritance and accumulated over many generations)
- by raising taxes
- by borrowing from another ruler
- by marrying and getting a dowry
- a robbery committed during a war campaign
- robbery by way of currency debasement

While the first five options required some effort and were not always comfortable for the ruler, the last option of devaluing the currency was an attractive one. Rulers, as part of their unlimited power over the territory they controlled, also made decisions about the issuance and use of money. Many throughout history have succumbed to this enormous temptation and enriched themselves at the expense of others by a simple and subtle form of debasing the currency.

The following methods—or a combination of them—were used to debase currency:
- shrinking: coins were minted with a smaller diameter
- thinning: coins were minted with a smaller depth
- reducing: the purity of a precious metal by adding less rare impurities

This was done by the ruler having the coins gradually withdrawn from circulation, then having them melted down and minted with a lower precious metal content, and then putting the coins back into circulation. In other words, they cast more coins from the same amount of precious metal and increased their wealth by the newly-created coins from the saved metal. The new wealth, however, came from nothing. It did not arise from the accomplishment of new good deeds and was not backed by any effort. It was literally a usurpation of the purchasing power of the entire currency from all the people who used it. Since this activity was covert and took place over a long period of time, it could sometimes take even longer for the market to react. However, once merchants discovered that the currency contained a lower precious metal content, they made their goods more expensive, because they needed to get the same amount of precious metal (purchasing power) for them as before. Thus, the original good money began to be devalued by the bad. The ruler who had the new money first, however, was able to meet some of their needs with this money before the market reacted. In other words, they were still buying cheaply for quite a long time. The across-the-board increase in prices then occurred gradually. This was the result of bad money starting to drive out the good money. The biggest problem was that the prices were rising, especially for workers on wages that had not increased or had increased with a considerable delay. In this way the rulers enriched themselves with impunity and convenience at the expense of the merchants and their subjects. Throughout history, this scenario has been repeated on different continents and in many currencies.

Historically, the debasement of money has always led to currency depreciation and economic destabilization. This has been followed by hyperinflation, economic crises, social and political instability, and even wars in some cases. Ultimately, however, any currency that was not managed in a responsible and sustainable manner had to be replaced by a new currency in order to restore stability.

DOWNPLAYING PAPER MONEY

In the previous section we discussed how rulers manipulated money and how they could not resist the temptation to enrich themselves. In the first chapter, however, we said that there was a period when precious metals were stored with the jewelers and only their vouchers circulated. In this period the rulers began to lose their power over money—because there was nothing to withdraw from circulation—hence they had no opportunity to discount it. Paper money would therefore seem to be a solution. But was this really the case?

UNSHACKLING PAPER MONEY FROM THE GOLD STANDARD

History has moved on by leaps and bounds, but the principles of human behavior have not changed much. Rulers and governments continued to try to manipulate money, and while it was not exactly the same, the similarities are clear.

> "History does not repeat itself, but rhymes."
> —Mark Twain

In the last chapter we talked about rulers, and in this chapter we will gradually move to the term government. However, we believe that both rulers and governments have very similar motivations and therefore quite similar behavior.

Let's review important highlights from this chapter:

- Recall where we left off in our discussion of the origins of paper money (page 32). The precious metals of citizens and institutions were held in banks or by jewelers who issued bills of exchange (paper money backed by gold) for their safekeeping. Up until this time, all is well and the vouchers were fully backed by precious metals.

- However, rulers or governments could not discount this paper money because they did not issue it—nor did they have the precious metals mentioned above in custody. Thus, they lost an easy means of acquiring wealth.

- Bankers and jewelers—like the rulers before them—faced a huge temptation to issue more bills than for which they had precious metals stored.

- Eventually they succumbed to temptation and slowly began to issue more money than the stock of precious metals they were supposed to be holding. In other words, they began to issue what are known as unbacked bills.

- However, the market eventually revealed the truth: more money in circulation caused prices to rise. People understood what was happening and wanted to cash in their precious metals. But they were not able to retrieve the full amount before the precious metals ran out. The crooks were lynched, jailed, or executed.

- The currency (essentially the receipts from a given jeweler or bank) in question then lost its value and people subsequently discovered that they could not get their precious metals back. Many unfortunate people lost their saved good deeds and were left with nothing but worthless paper in their hands.

- Repeated failures of bankers or jewelers have happened in many countries independently throughout history.

- The rulers saw what the bankers were doing. They could have punished the rogue bankers, but they needed them. They borrowed money from them for wars and other government projects that they were unable to finance with standard taxes. The bankers could print the money they wanted, but at the cost of increasing the number of uncovered notes. Therefore, the bankers demanded a guarantee of impunity.

- In return for lending money, governments began to pass laws that allowed bankers to hold more banknotes than precious metals. This meant that the value of the precious metals deposited in the bank could be less than the total value of the notes issued. The law then specified what percentage of precious metal by which each note should be backed.

- They adopted the currency in question as state currency and allowed the creation of standardized banknotes. Whereas previously each receipt had a different value depending on the specific amount of metal deposited, the notes were of the same value and the exchange rate against the precious metal was fixed by law. This exchange rate determined how much precious metal the bank would issue per note to the bearer.

- In order to create more money, governments, in cooperation with banks, started to reduce the precious metal backing of the currency. Again, bad money began to be created, devaluing the purchasing power of good money (backed by real good deeds).

- When there was concern that people would want to withdraw their metals from the banks, some governments banned people from owning gold. As such, people couldn't go to a bank and demand their gold because they weren't allowed to own it.

- In other cases, governments depreciated the value of the currency against gold. This was done by a government setting a new exchange rate. For example, instead of issuing 31 grams of gold per note, the bank could instead issue only 20 grams per note. Thus, people lost a significant part of their savings in banknotes. In line with the lower coverage ratio linked to the new exchange rate, the state was then also able to issue more new banknotes. In this way, the government gained new wealth at the expense of the citizens—wealth which it had not earned.

- Issuing new, unbacked money reduced the value of existing banknotes and caused inflation. These were the very same principles as when rulers debased precious metal coins.

- When inflation was unmanageable, the government implemented monetary reform. The principle of monetary reform was that the old dysfunctional currency was abolished and replaced by a new currency. Wages were then paid and prices were set in the new currency. It was stipulated that, for example, for 1,000 old banknotes, people receive one new banknote—and again lost all their savings.

- Particularly to finance wars, countries gradually moved away from the gold standard, and a global era of unbacked national currencies was ushered in.

KEY MOMENTS IN THE HISTORY OF THE USA THAT INFLUENCED NOT ONLY THE DOLLAR, BUT ALSO OTHER WORLD CURRENCIES

The US dollar is currently one of the world's strongest currencies and most countries use it as a reserve currency. Many central banks hold the US dollar as a reserve for foreign currencies. At the same time, the dollar serves as an international currency for determining the prices of commodities like gold, oil, natural gas, electricity, wheat, coffee, and services. As such, most countries in the world are quite dependent on the US dollar economically; this reliance affects the stability of other currencies. Let's review the history of this key currency.

1776: THE UNITED STATES OF AMERICA IS FORMED WITH THE SIGNING OF THE DECLARATION OF INDEPENDENCE

North America experienced an influx of colonists since the sixteenth century. These were mostly progressive individuals who left their homes, unafraid of the unknown or hard work. The main European power structures lay far across the ocean and liberal ideas of freedom and democracy began to spread among the people. With the War of Independence (1775–1783), Americans completed their fight for freedom and the United States became a beacon of freedom and democracy. These principles then began to spread to Europe and other countries around the world. The principal Founding Fathers (George Washington, Thomas Jefferson, John Adams, Benjamin Franklin, Alexander Hamilton, John Jay, and James Madison) were liberals, and shared a distrust of central authority. This distrust began to appear in the various documents defining the powers of government. They tried to build into them safeguards that would limit the potential for abuse of central power. Examples include the creation of the Constitution; the separation of powers; the creation of a Bill of Rights; the strengthening of the independence of the judiciary; restrictions on the use of coercion; collective control over the executive, the legislature, and foreign policy; and the declaration of war. One of the important safeguards was the pegging of the currency to the gold standard. They had already learned from history that the spontaneous issuance of money backed by no value eventually led to its failure. Unfortunately, some of these safeguards have been altered over time through regulation.

- 1776: The Declaration of Independence was signed and the United States of America was created.

- 1783: British recognition of the new state ended the War of Independence and the United States of America was recognized as a separate country.

- 1785: The US dollar (USD) was introduced as the national currency of the United States of America.

- 1787: A new Constitution was created, but it was not ratified until 1789.

- 1791: The Bill of Rights supplemented the Constitution by guaranteeing citizens inalienable rights. The Bill of Rights limits the powers of the federal government of the United States and guarantees the protection of the rights of all citizens within American territory. It protects personal property, freedom of speech, freedom of religion, freedom of assembly and petition, freedom of the press, and the right to keep and bear arms.

- 1792: The Mint Act (or Coinage Act) tied the US dollar to the value of silver and gold, establishing the so-called gold standard.

1913: THE CENTRAL BANK OF THE UNITED STATES IS FORMED

The Federal Reserve System, typically referred to as the Federal Reserve (or Fed), is the central bank of the United States.

In the decades since the gold standard was introduced, there has been a gradual departure from the original ideas of the founding fathers. Bankers and government officials began thinking about how to circumvent the statutory monetary policy safeguards.

Prelude to the creation of the Fed

In November of 1910, representatives from the US Treasury secretly met on Jekyll Island with the most influential bankers and representatives of banking houses like Morgan, Rockefeller, and Rothschild. The aim of the meeting was to create a system that would protect banking institutions from bank runs and bank panics. Banks at that time had issued large quantities of paper notes that were not backed by gold reserves. The participants discussed how to abolish the gold standard, or at least how to create an institution that would be able to bail out commercial banks in the event of failures—a so-called lender of last resort. Indeed, the government was constitutionally not allowed to issue new money. Such an institution was intended to allow the government a way to have access to a bottomless source of money without having to raise taxes.

A **run on a bank** can occur when clients lose confidence in a bank or currency and start to withdraw their deposits en masse. However, at the time of this economic crisis, there were also runs on gold, because the banknotes were still backed by gold.

A **banking panic** is a financial crisis caused by a run on a large number of banks at once. Subsequent failures of multiple banks can then lead to a long economic crisis.

The creation of the Fed

This institution became the Federal Reserve, which was created by the Federal Reserve Act signed by President Woodrow Wilson on December 23, 1913. The main purpose of this Act was that the Fed could create new money and use this money to make loans to the US government or to bail out commercial banks. Eventually, the Fed became a facilitator of new fiat money. As such, the money it created out of thin air could be used to bail out banks as well as to help finance the government's sometimes irresponsible budget policies. The US economy gradually built up a dependency on this inflow of new money.

The Federal Reserve Bank was established for two main purposes: to provide liquidity to commercial banks and to stabilize prices, which it seeks to do through monetary policy decisions. It is governed by seven governors, each of whom serves for fourteen years. Although the governors are appointed in turn by the President, they must be confirmed by the Senate. The Fed is divided into twelve regional Federal Reserve Banks. Each Federal Reserve Bank is organized as a corporation whose stock is sold to banks operating in its district. In fact, the Fed is 100% owned by the private banks that operate in each district. Although the Fed is essentially private in terms of ownership, it is public in terms of governance. Simply put, the Fed behaves like a state institution owned by private banks.

With the new money it creates, the Fed itself buys assets—such as government bonds and stocks—on which it can profit. At the same time, it is a source of unlimited liquidity for commercial banks. Thus, it allows commercial banks, among other entities, to buy any amount of government bonds. It simultaneously serves the interests of the state as well as those of the banks—including those that own them—while also enabling the state to finance anything beyond its revenues. It is a mutual symbiosis of bankers and politicians. That is why it is often criticized from both sides of the political spectrum. Despite all these doubts, the Fed functions as an independent body with broad powers that are not directly controlled politically.

> The **liquidity** of the bank as an entity is understood as the ability to meet its obligations at any time, in particular to pay customer deposits according to the agreed terms.

1933: CONFISCATION OF GOLD FROM CITIZENS AND COMPANIES

By the end of the 1920s, the United States was in the throes of an economic depression as evidenced by the Wall Street Crash on October 24, 1929—also known as Black Thursday. The level of unemployment was rising and people began to worry about the stability of the dollar. The run on the banks that bankers had feared so much was visible on the horizon. Both paper dollars and gold began to disappear from the banks. In exchange for one paper dollar, people received 1.5 grams of gold, an option that became used frequently.

In February 1933, citizens withdrew huge amounts of gold from the banks, and paper dollars also slowly began to run out. The situation was becoming unbearable for the banks because they did not have enough gold or money to pay all the claimants. Wanting to help both the economy and the banks, the government began looking for a solution to the dire situation. Since the gold standard was in effect, it needed to obtain 1.5 grams of gold in order to print each dollar, but there simply was not enough it.

Run on the bank: New York, 1933

The newly-elected President Roosevelt, only in office since March 4, 1933, sought to stabilize the situation and implemented a number of programs and projects under the New Deal to restore prosperity to the American people. One such step was to issue Proclamation 2039 ordering the suspension of all banking transactions from March 6–9. Another step was to sign the Emergency Banking Act on March 9, 1933. In Title I, the Act partially restricted the handling of gold and included retroactive approval of the banking holiday. In Title IV, it allowed the Fed to issue emergency currency that did not have to be backed by gold. In a speech that followed, the President urged citizens to return their withdrawals to the banks, declaring that it was "safer to keep your money in a reopened bank than under the mattress." There was a slight reaction among citizens after his reassurance, and some indeed decided to return their money to the banks. However, the whole system was also in dire need of new dollars, but these could not be printed by law—except under the new Emergency Act—because of the lack of gold. The situation soon became untenable again.

On April 5, 1933, President Roosevelt signed Executive Order 6102, which banned the ownership of gold in any form, effective May 1, 1933. The ban on gold ownership applied to households and private companies. It prohibited the ownership of gold coins, bullion, and gold certificates valued at more than $100, with exceptions for specific purposes and collections. It required the surrender of surplus gold by May 1, 1933, in exchange for $20.67 per troy ounce (31.1 grams). However, many people were unwilling to comply with the order, but could not access the gold they had deposited in banks. Failure to comply was punishable by ten years' imprisonment or a fine of $10,000, or both. Ten thousand dollars was an unimaginable sum for most families at that time. The government solved two problems with this regulation:

- it obtained gold so that it could print more money.

- it saved the commercial banks: no one could come and claim their gold because citizens and private companies were forbidden to own it.

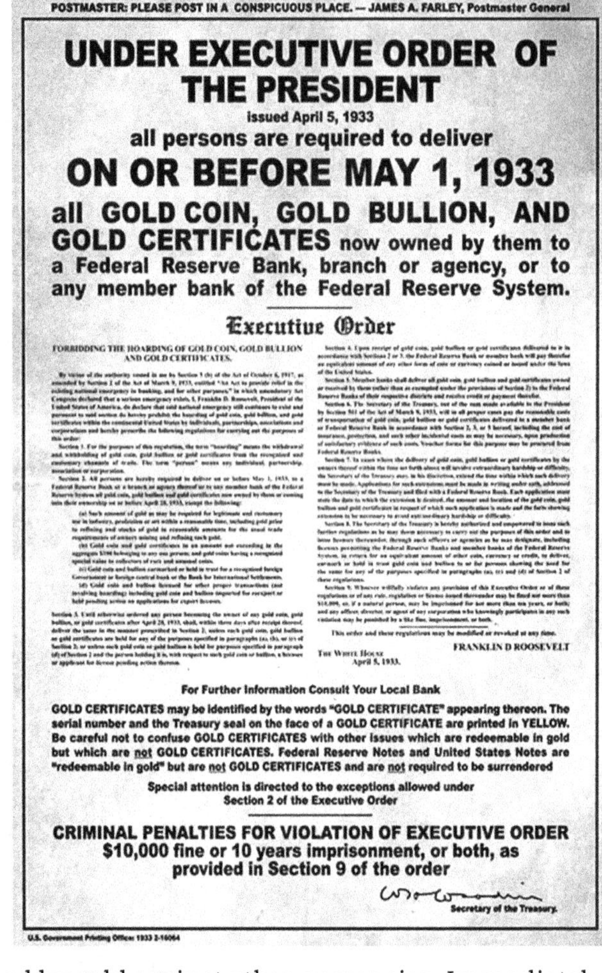

President Roosevelt thus abolished the internal gold standard for US citizens, but the gold standard for foreign banks remained. The dollar continued to be backed by gold against other currencies. Immediately after the confiscation of gold from citizens and companies, the dollar-gold exchange rate was raised from $20.67 to $35 per troy ounce. This move was met with widespread disapproval from the citizens, who began to lose complete confidence in the government and monetary policy.

1944: BRETTON WOODS AGREEMENT

In the post-war order, the Bretton Woods Agreement ensured the dominance of the US dollar as one of the world's key currencies. Many central banks began to use the dollar as a gold-backed reserve currency at a fixed exchange rate.

Before the Bretton Woods Agreement

Before World War I, most currencies were pegged to gold; countries could not issue new money not backed by it. However, during World War II, temporary exceptions had to be made. As such all major currencies began to depreciate as a result of the inflation started by wartime money printing. The dollar, however, depreciated somewhat less because the United States entered the war later, was not fighting on its territory, and its infrastructure was not disrupted.

Bretton Woods Agreement

In July 1944, negotiations were held at the Mount Washington Hotel in Bretton Woods, New Hampshire, USA, under the auspices of the victorious powers. The purpose of these negotiations was to create a global monetary system in a post-war world. Forty-four countries participated in these negotiations, but the United States and Great Britain had the main say. The result was the Bretton Woods Agreement. The points of this agreement had been thought out two years in advance. Its essence was to link the US dollar to gold and all other currencies to the dollar. However, only the central banks of the member countries were allowed to exchange dollars for gold—not citizens—as they had not been allowed to own gold in the US since 1933. The Bretton Woods Agreement came into force in 1945.

Consequences of the Bretton Woods Agreement

The US dollar acquired the status of the official global reserve currency from which the currencies of other countries would be derived. At the same time, the United States had to guarantee the convertibility of the dollar into gold at a fixed rate of $35 per troy ounce of gold. It was in the interest of the central banks of other countries to create sufficient foreign exchange reserves in US dollars. This retrospectively increased the attractiveness of the US dollar and strengthened its position in the post-war world.

The Bretton Woods Agreement created the Stabilization Fund—now known as the International Monetary Fund—which began to oversee the newly created system. In 1946, the International Bank for Reconstruction and Development—now known as the World Bank—was set up in accordance with the agreements.

The Soviet Union rejected the Bretton Woods Agreement. This rejection is considered by historians as the first step towards the Cold War.

1971: PRESIDENT NIXON SHOCKS

Executive Order 6102 on the confiscation and prohibition of gold ownership had been in force for more than forty-one years. Throughout this time, the value of the dollar had been depreciating. Initially, the dollar was 100% gold-backed, but by 1971, approximately one out of every five dollars was gold-backed. At the same time, each of the Bretton Woods Agreement countries could exchange dollars for gold at the rate of 1 troy ounce of gold for $35, even though the price of gold on the open market was worth much more in dollar terms. Many countries took advantage of this and bought gold cheaply from US reserves. The situation became untenable again and the United States had to abandon the gold standard.

On August 15, 1971, President Nixon gave an address to the nation and announced that he was temporarily suspending the convertibility of the dollar into gold in the name of monetary stability. This meant that dollars were no longer convertible into the underlying gold for the central banks of other countries. With this announcement, he effectively ended the Bretton Woods Agreement, definitively unshackled the dollar from the gold standard, and closed the gold window to other countries. It ended the external gold standard, under which foreign governments could buy gold from US reserves at a fixed price of $35 per troy ounce. There was a sharp rise in the price of gold, and by early 1973 the price reached $125 per troy ounce of gold.

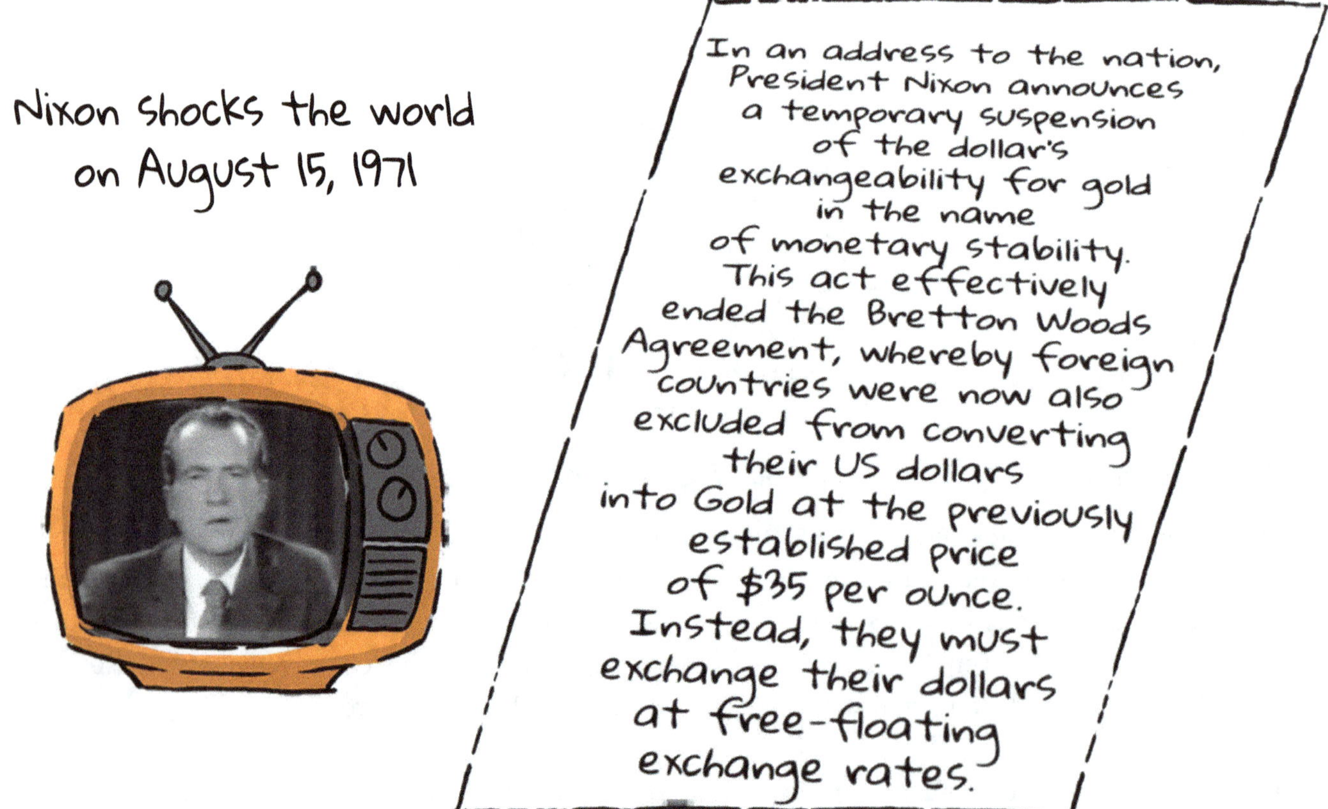

It was not until December 31, 1974, that the restriction on gold ownership by individuals and companies in the United States was lifted. The law that legalized private ownership of gold coins, bars, and certificates was signed by President Gerald Ford.

"For the first time since President Richard Nixon cut the last thin link between the US dollar and gold in 1971, none of the world's major currencies is pegged to a commodity. Every currency is now an unbacked paper currency, resting entirely in the hands of the government."

—Milton Friedman, winner of the Nobel Prize in Economics

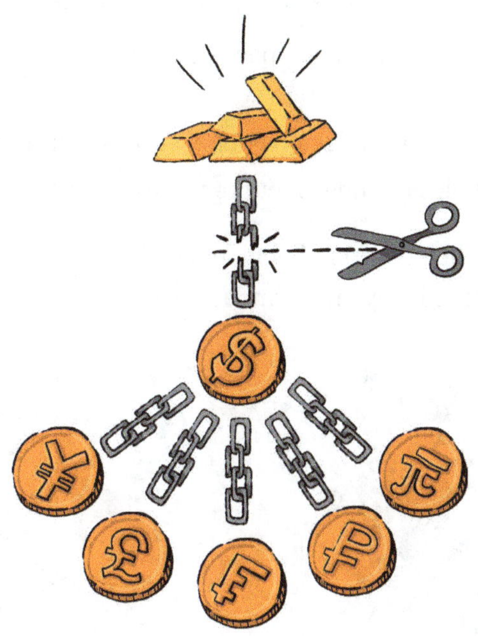

So, what is the solution?

THE ERA OF FIAT MONEY IS DAWNING GLOBALLY

The unpegging of currencies from the gold standard has occurred gradually around the world. Since then, individual central banks have been able to issue new money without having to back it with real value. The new money is backed only by debt, and the people of each country are obliged to use it under government regulations.

WHAT IS FIAT MONEY?

- ✓ It is money created by an official power, its use is established by law as an obligation.
- ✓ Currency with forced circulation also appears under the names of legal currency, fiat currency, or fiat money.
- ✓ The word *fiat* is derived from Latin (let it be done) and essentially means a decree.
- ✓ Forced circulation currencies include all current national currencies.

Central banks have power over the creation of new money in the current monetary system. As such, the incantation of "fiat money" is being heard more and more often.

Let there be light!

Let there be money!

MONEY MULTIPLIERS: BAD MONEY WITHOUT A SAFETY BRAKE

In the preceding chapters we have seen the unfortunate effects of increasing the money supply too much if this increase is not backed by value. Throughout history, rulers have done this covertly, and their actions could be called fraud—or even robbery—of the purchasing power of the population. In a democratic society, the government can no longer print money spontaneously. However, it has made laws to create the independent institution of the central bank and the commercial banks it controls.

These institutions are the only ones that can legally create new money. They are not backed by any value. The moment that debt is repaid, the money is extinguished. Let's call it working bad money. According to some experts, this money, especially in the event of a crisis, is supposed to support the economy and prevent its growth from slowing down.

Safeguards have been created in the laws to prevent large and irresponsible creation of new money. Over time, particularly as a result of pressure from banking institutions and politicians, these safeguards have been watered down or removed altogether.

> "Let me issue and control the money and I won't care who writes the laws."
>
> —Mayer Amschel Rothschild, founder of the Rothschild dynasty

A multiplier is simply a factor that amplifies or increases the base value of something else.

Multiplier 1: fractional-reserve banking

This is a legally recognized banking practice of commercial banks. Commercial banks acquire customer deposits and, in turn, lend that money. However, they are obliged to hold what is known as a minimum required reserve (MRR). This reserve indicates what percentage of a given deposit the bank must have available for customer withdrawals. The rest of this money can be lent or used freely in any way. Up to this point, the whole concept doesn't look too scary.

However, the reality is that the bank will convince the client that they need to open an account directly with them in order to obtain a loan. The moment the borrowed money is paid into the account, it becomes the client's deposit, and the bank can lend the deposited money out again using the same principle. This goes on and on as long as there are loan applicants, or until the limit of money that can be lent is exhausted.

Loan limit: the formula for calculating the maximum possible multiplication limit (total amount of loans) depends on the MRR.

FIRST DEPOSIT ÷ MRR × (100 – MRR)

Thus, fractional-reserve banking expands the money supply and creates new money out of nothing. The purchasing power of the newly created money is created at the expense of the purchasing power of previous deposits. Fractional-reserve banking has gradually been practiced by all commercial banks. For this reason some economists speak of it as a monetary experiment. Historically, it is an untested model that may not succeed in the long run. The amount of possible multiplication is determined, among other legal rules, by the minimum required reserve.

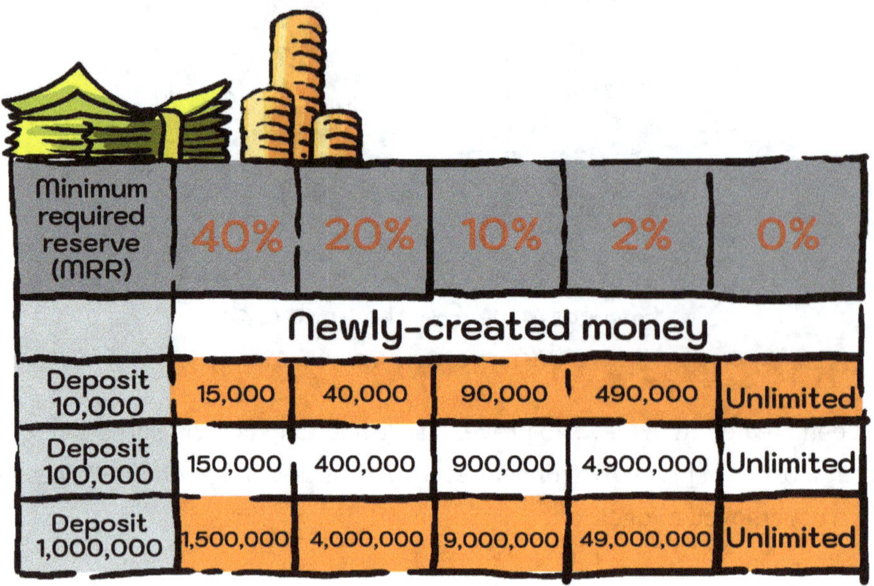

Minimum required reserve (MRR)	40%	20%	10%	2%	0%
Newly-created money					
Deposit 10,000	15,000	40,000	90,000	490,000	Unlimited
Deposit 100,000	150,000	400,000	900,000	4,900,000	Unlimited
Deposit 1,000,000	1,500,000	4,000,000	9,000,000	49,000,000	Unlimited

The aim of creating new money is to try to stimulate the economy, increase **GDP** growth, and provide more revenue for the state, especially through consumption tax. If GDP is growing, it means that more things are being produced in the economy, which can mean more jobs and more money for the people. In the short term, creating new money is politically desirable. If an individual or company were to do this, however, it would be a criminal act.

Gross Domestic Product (GDP), is the final total monetary value of goods and services produced in a given period in a given territory. This indicator is used in macroeconomics to determine the economic performance of countries. The time period is usually a year. GDP per capita is also another form of comparison.

Over time bank reserve requirements have been gradually reduced, and currently range from around 0% to 25% globally. For example in the US it is 0%, while in the Eurozone it is 2%.

Table of minimum % required reserve in selected countries in 2024:

Country	%	Country	%
USA	0.00	Pakistan	5.00
Australia	0.00	Lithuania	6.00
Hong Kong	0.00	Jordan	8.00
New Zeland	0.00	Zambia	8.00
Eurozone	1.00	Sri Lanka	8.00
Czech Republic	2.00	Burundi	8.50
South Africa	2.50	Croatia	9.00
Switzerland	2.50	Ghana	9.00
Latvia	3.00	Hungary	10.00
Poland	3.50	Bulgaria	10.00
Chile	4.50	China	17.00
India	4.50	Tajikistan	20.00

Minimum required reserve (MRR)

Run on the bank and bank panic

The problem can arise when clients lose confidence in the bank—or the currency as a whole—and start to withdraw their deposits en masse. This can then escalate into a banking panic. A banking panic is caused by a run on a large number of banks at once. Subsequent bank failures of multiple banks can then cause a crisis in the entire banking system and lead to long-term economic decline. Some banks may not have sufficient liquidity reserves to pay out all deposits.

Previously, in such a case, the bank went bankrupt. Although a run on a bank can occur in our current system, typically the central bank will intervene. Based on the principle of liquidity creation, it has the power to supply the banks with the necessary reserves. This gives the outward appearance that the problem is resolved. However, there will not always be the political will for such a solution.

We decided to rebuild the branch to meet the requirements of modern banking.

Multiplier 2: central banks

Previously, central banks could only print real money in a legally defined ratio to their gold holdings. When new physical money needed to be issued, the central bank had to increase the actual stock of gold held in its own reserve. This stock could be increased, for example, by buying, mining, war booty, lending, or confiscating gold from citizens. When there was no more gold to acquire, the politicians decided to reduce the statutory gold reserve, for example from 40% to 20%. At that point, a central bank could create a large amount of new money. This increased inflation and also increased the price of gold. If the price of gold was fixed by law, it was enough to change the law, raise the price of gold by a troy ounce, and then new money could be created again.

With a gold standard defined by law, new money can be created in three cases:

- by increasing the price of gold (Section A of the following table)

- by increasing the stock of gold in the central bank reserve (Section B of the following table)

- by reducing the mandatory percentage of government gold reserves (Section C of the following table)

A	B	C			
USD for 1 oz (31.1 g) of gold	USD for 1,000 kg of gold	Mandatory gold reserve held by the government which determines the amount of money supply (value of banknotes and coins in circulation)			
		100%	40%	20%	10%
		Money supply created for 1,000 kg of gold			
$20	$643,087	$643,087	$1,607,717	$3,215,434	$6,430,868
$35	$1,125,402	$1,125,402	$2,813,505	$5,627,010	$11,254,019
$100	$3,215,434	$3,215,434	$8,038,585	$16,077,170	$32,154,340
$2,000	$64,308,680	$64,308,680	$160,771,700	$321,543,400	$643,086,800

This kicked off a kind of perpetual motion, because the reduction of the gold reserve requirement led to inflation, which increased the price of gold. Thus, more money could be created. Unfortunately, even this method of intervention was not enough, resulting in the unshackling of central banks all over the world from the gold standard decades ago. This now allows them to issue new money almost without limit. This money is created by demand for money and is created by an accounting entry in a database. It is bad money created out of nothing.

Just one more little change. All new banknotes will bear the inscription: "Banknotes are covered by the national debt."

Unlike a commercial bank—because of the move away from the gold standard—a central bank does not have to hold required reserves. At the same time, it doesn't hold customer deposits, so there is no one who can collect money from it. A run on a central bank can never occur. On the face of it, this seems like an ideal solution. However, we should not forget that whenever there has been excessive creation of new money throughout history, it has had disastrous consequences in economic and, consequently, social terms. Sometimes the consequences have been felt within in a few decades; at other times, it has taken several centuries.

Central banking

It is oftentimes presented as an invention that ensures economic stability. In the event of a **deceleration** in economic growth, the creation of new money can help to **accelerate** economy and kickstart its **recovery**. Central banks are also supposed to ensure monetary stability and control financial institutions. Opponents, however, argue that they are instead the agent of repeated debt expansion and subsequent contraction. More on this can be found in the extensive debates between the Austrian School of Economics and Keynesian economics.

Economic deceleration:

In economics, this phase is called growth deceleration.

Economic acceleration:

Congratulations, you've finally managed to accelerate the economy. Unfortunately, at the moment, it's spiralling downhill uncontrollably.

Recovery:

I just hope, Governor,
that this was not the proverbial first sign of the economic recovery.

Central banks have historically been created under the following policy objectives:

- lending money to the state (through the purchase of government bonds)

- bailing out commercial banks (by providing liquidity)

- maintaining monetary stability (such as the fight against increased inflation)

To achieve these goals, they have the power to create new money. However, securing those objectives can in some cases go against each other. If there is an economic crisis and at the same time inflation is high, the central bank should create new money to bail out banks, pension funds, or the economy. But on the other hand, it has to stem the flow of new money by raising interest rates because of inflation. It is like driving a car while simultaneously stepping on the accelerator and the brake.

In the cycle of new money creation, wealth is transferred from ordinary citizens and entrepreneurs to the state, banks, the wealthy, and companies at the top of the financial pyramid. In other words, they get to the new money first. This is similar to the phenomenon previously discussed of a ruler creating new value by debasing a currency. Before this was reflected in appreciation, a ruler bought assets that were cheaper. These assets then rose in value as prices subsequently rose—allowing the ruler to grow richer. Such wealth, however, was not fairly created. It was a transfer of purchasing power from the majority of holders of a given currency towards the wealthy at the top of the financial pyramid. Those who get the money earlier enjoy more purchasing power and have more money at a time when prices have not yet risen. Conversely, those at the bottom of the pyramid face higher prices long before the increase in income reaches them. It should also be noted that any subsequent wage increases usually do not cover the price increases.

The effect of new money on the economy is described by the Cantillon Effect. According to the **Cantillon Effect**, if the inflow of new money causes inflation, it enriches the wealthy at the expense of the poor. More about this can be found on page 118.

Cantillon Effect

Richard Cantillon (1680–1734) was a Parisian banker of Irish descent who was one of the first authors to discuss systematically economics in his Essay on the Nature of Trade in General. In his work, he describes the different effects of new money on the economy depending on to whom and how the new funds reach the economy.

- If the money gets into the hands of those who spend it on consumption, market demand grows and inflation occurs. Cantillon used the example of gold and silver mines, where the money comes into the hands of the mine owners and their workers. They then spend it mostly on consumption, thus demand and market prices rise and inflation occurs.

- If the money is spent on investment, production and trade grow. If the inflow of money is the result of an active balance of trade—where exports of goods and services exceed imports—then the money entering the economy is directed into the hands of traders and manufacturers. Already wealthy themselves, they do not so much increase their immediate consumption as invest in the expansion of their enterprises. In such a case, instead of consumption and price level, productivity and, consequently, the volume of trade and production increase.

Quantitative easing

The central bank creates new money through what is known as quantitive easing. For what does the central bank use this money?

- The state issues state bonds for the required amount based on the state budget. This is the difference between what the state is able to collect in taxes and what it has decided to spend in a given period. If no buyer can be found on the open bond market, the remaining bonds can be purchased from the state through financial institutions by the central bank, which creates new money by making an accounting entry in the database for this purpose. The state then uses this money to finance its fiscal policy.

- In the same way, the central bank creates financial resources to cover potential problems of commercial banks that provide loans or mortgages to citizens and companies through fractional reserve banking.

- In addition to bonds, some central banks may also buy shares in commercial companies to inject the money needed to revive the economy. This puts other market participants at a disadvantage. It can also create a price bubble in the stock and real estate markets, which threatens to burst at any time. In such a case, people will then lose part of their investment.

- With the newly created money, the state, through the central bank, can also rescue strategic companies that have fallen into trouble as a result of poor management. It can buy their shares or provide loans guaranteed by the state through commercial banks. The state guarantee works in such a way that the state eventually pays the commercial bank instead of the borrower. It receives the relevant amount in the form of newly created money from the central bank.

Quantitative easing by central banks is a sad reflection of the quality of government money. Like the rulers of the past, today's governments and central banks are unable to keep money unconstrained in the long run. So far, the latest wave of new money—quantitative easing—which took place during the COVID-19 pandemic appears to be huge, global, unprecedented, and extremely risky. This newly-created money is flowing through commercial banks into the financial markets in the form of purchasing stocks and bonds, and creating funds for loans and social programs. Economies have become dependent on the injection of new money, and they can no longer simply get rid of this dependence. Loans that do not serve as an investment in technology, but instead support social programs, for example, clearly fulfill the first variant of the Cantillon Effect. This inevitably leads to higher prices and a widening of the gap between rich and poor.

People are happy when they can actually touch their money.
And we're even happier when we can touch their money.

CURRENCIES THAT DIDN'T MAKE IT

Let's look at a few examples from history where individual currencies lost their value and disappeared into the dustbins of history. The lesson from all of these cases is clearly that a currency that ceases to be scarce or is debased ends. Sometimes it may last only a few decades, sometimes a few centuries, but eventually it will disappear and must be replaced by another. These examples confirm the rule that people will only use money that can hold its value in the long term.

CURRENCIES BASED ON PRIMITIVE PAYMENTS THAT DIDN'T MAKE IT

Only something that is scarce, requires significant effort to obtain, and cannot be easily reproduced can function as a medium of exchange and sustainable value.

Rai Stones from Yap Island

Yap is an island consisting of four islands separated by straits and surrounded by a common coral reef. It is located in the Caroline Archipelago of Micronesia. Yap is also one of the states that make up the Micronesian Federation.

On this small archipelago, stone disks have served as a form of payment for hundreds of years. The stones vary in size from a few centimeters to several meters, with the largest ones weighing several tonnes. They have a hole carved in the middle for easy transport. This stone money is made from aragonite, which is not found on Yap. It had to be shipped from the far away islands of Palau (approximately 450 km or 280 mi) or Guam (approximately 650 km or 528 mi). The difficulty of obtaining these stones using primitive tools—as well as the difficulty and danger in transporting them on canoes or bamboo rafts—guaranteed the scarcity of the currency. If a member of the expedition died, the stone was considered rarer and worth more. Stones that slipped into the sea off the coast and could not be retrieved also had their own specific value and owners. The value of Rai stones was, therefore, not only dependent on the size and quality of the workmanship, but also on the incidents that were associated with their recovery. The principle described above can be summed up in a lesson:

> **Value is dependent on rarity, and rarity is dependent on effort and work done. This rule has always been true and will continue to be true.**

This lesson also applies, of course, to gold, diamonds and all other fictions of value that mankind considers precious and to which it ascribes value. It is very similar with some cryptocurrencies, where in order to obtain them, the miner must show what is known as proof of work.

The stones were placed in common areas. Ownership changed by agreement between the seller and the buyer. Theft was not possible, both because of the large weight and, above all, because within the small island everyone knew who owned the stone. There is a similarity here to the bitcoin ledger, where records of coin ownership are also stored in the public domain and everyone knows how many are owned by each address.

Eventually even the Rai stones succumbed to devaluation. With the arrival of Europeans, advanced iron tools reached the islands, making the mining and processing of stone money much easier. Almost unlimited quantities of new stone money could be transported safely and quickly on large ships. Stone money thus ceased to be scarce and lost its value. Today, the US dollar is used as the official tender. However, the government considers Rai stones to be a cultural asset and protects it by law. The Rai is still depicted in the national emblem of the island of Yap.

PRECIOUS METAL-BASED CURRENCIES THAT DIDN'T MAKE IT

Now, let us take a detailed look at a few historical examples from the Roman Empire, where the irresponsible monetary policies of the ruling emperors caused profound economic disintegration and contributed significantly to its eventual downfall.

Denarius, antoninianus, aureus and solidus. These are ancient Roman coins from the period of about 200 BC to about 1100 AD. These coins illustrate the workings of the various currencies of the period. The denarius was a long-used silver coin that later coexisted alongside the silver coin antoninianus and a gold coin called the aureus. The aureus was replaced after 312 AD by the gold coin solidus.

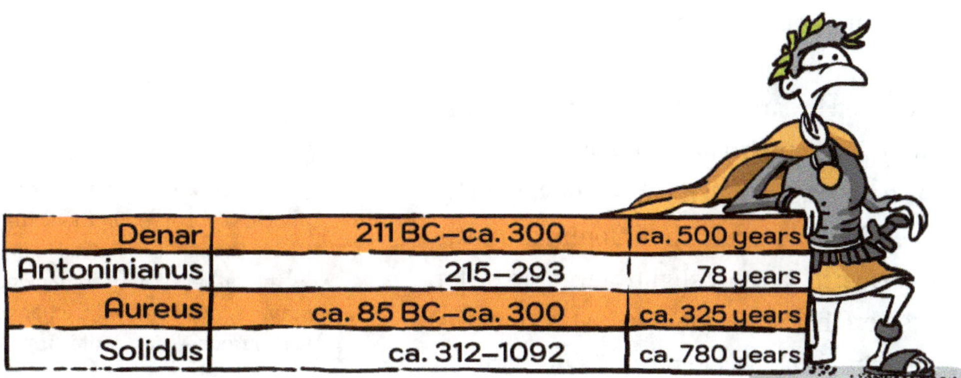

Denar	211 BC–ca. 300	ca. 500 years
Antoninianus	215–293	78 years
Aureus	ca. 85 BC–ca. 300	ca. 325 years
Solidus	ca. 312–1092	ca. 780 years

Denarius

The denarius was an ancient Roman silver coin that was used during the Roman Republic and subsequently during the Roman Empire. It was first minted in 211 BC, and consisted of 4.55 grams of silver. However, the Emperor Augustus (31 BC–14 AD) succumbed to temptation and began to downgrade it around the beginning of the first millennium. By the time of Emperor Nero (54–67), the coin contained only 3.4 grams of silver. Sometime during these periods the denarius was given a bronze core. Septimius Severus (193–211) then increased the copper content of the denarius to 50%. His successor tried to introduce a better currency called antoninianus alongside the denarius. On the next page you will learn that the coinage turned out even more tragically than the denarius. After the currency reform of Emperor Diocletian (284–305), which was just another irresponsible debasement of coins, the denarius contained just enough silver so as to encase its bronze core. The layer of silver was so thin that it wore off quickly with use. The denarius could no longer be debased, and this consequently spelled its end as a silver coin. However, during its use, which lasted about 500 years, the denarius became well-known and its name was later used in other parts of the world for both silver coins and modern money.

Devaluation of the denarius over time

51 BC · First-half of the first centrury

Antoninianus

The antoninianus was another silver coin used during the Roman Empire. However, it was gradually devalued by a higher proportion of bronze—with only about two percent consisting of silver. This coin lasted less than eighty years on the market. In historical terms, this was a brief episode demonstrating where irresponsible monetary policy can lead.

The coin was introduced in early 215 by Emperor Caracalla (211–217). He wanted to launch a new coin that was more valuable than the denarius, which has been devalued by his predecessor Septimus Severus. The antoninianus was similar to the denarius: it was only slightly larger in order to give the impression that it was more valuable than the devalued denarius. Its value was to be equivalent to two denarii. However, the silver content was equivalent only to one and a half denarii when the coin was introduced. This caused inflation and people ended up hoarding denarii instead—a phenomenon later known as **Gresham's Law**. Buyers and sellers alike came to the realization that the new coin had a lower rarity, so they raised prices to compensate. Silver supplies began to run out as the Roman Empire was no longer conquering new territories. The existing silver mines were exhausted, but the rulers needed to pay the army. Thus, each new issue of the antoninianus contained less silver than the previous one, contributing to ever-increasing inflation. Huge quantities were minted and the coins became worthless essentially. During Diocletian's monetary reform, the devalued antoninianus coins were finally withdrawn from circulation in 293.

Gresham's Law is an economic principle observed in the sixteenth century by Sir Thomas Gresham. He is known as the father of English banking, having established the Royal Exchange as London's first purpose-built center for trading stocks.

This law states that bad money drives out the good money in circulation. This is because people spending money will hand over the bad coins rather than the good ones, keeping the good ones for themselves.

It can be understood generally that people save the money that they consider to be of greater value and spend the money they consider inferior.

Devaluation of the antoninianus over time

240s CE ~40% finess

250s CE ~40% finess

260s CE ~40% finess

270s CE ~40% finess

Aureus

As the name suggests, the aureus was a gold coin. The chemical symbol for gold is Au, from the Latin word *aurum*. The first aureus in the Roman monetary system was minted during the wars of 88–85 BC. Its weight was about 10.8 grams, with the gold probably having come as a result of the spoils of war. It was originally defined as twenty-five denarii. As the denarius was gradually downgraded, the definition of the aureus was changed, even though it was also downgraded.

Julius Caesar (100 BC–44 BC) was one of the most important Roman military leaders and politicians in history. Caesar's greatest victory came in the Gallic Wars, when he conquered Gaul and expanded the Roman Empire to the north. Upon his return to Rome, he was appointed dictator of the Roman Empire and instituted reforms to improve living conditions for the poor and strengthen the power of Rome. However, his reign soon ended when he was assassinated by a group of senators in 44 BC. Caesar's legacy influenced Roman history for many years.

One of the most important coins in circulation at the time of Caesar was the aureus, considered a symbol of wealth and power. As such, it was often used as currency for soldiers and officers. Given the strength of the coin, it was also used to finance military expeditions and pay soldiers. Julius Caesar was well aware of the importance of maintaining its stability, so there was no significant reduction in the weight of the aureus during his reign. Caesar also had his own likeness and emblems minted on the aureus, which helped to consolidate his power and authority.

During the reign of **Julius Caesar**—who was assassinated in 44 BC—the coin contained 8 grams of gold and became generally accepted throughout Europe and the Mediterranean. This contributed greatly to the development of international trade. For almost a century, the coin managed to maintain its approximate value. Thus, it helped to maintain economic stability despite the political changes after the assassination of Caesar and the transformation of the Republic into an Empire.

The best years of this coin lasted until the reign of Emperor Nero (54–67), who again could not resist sparing even the aureus. He reduced the gold content from 8 to 7.2 grams. The weight and volume of pure gold then gradually changed during the reigns of subsequent emperors due to war and other expenditures. Emperor Caracalla (211–217) reduced the gold content to 6.5 grams, and Emperor Diocletian (284–305) even further to 5.5 grams. The coin lost the confidence of the population and was replaced by a new coin called solidus, which contained only 4.5 grams of gold.

Devaluation of the aureus over time

44 BC

Gold
8.09 g

198–211

Gold
6.51 g

Solidus

This currency was introduced by Emperor Diocletian (284–305) as a replacement for the aureus. However, it was not until the reign of Constantine I, also called Constantine the Great (306–337), that the coin came into wider use. The Solidus managed to hold its value for quite a long time, mainly because of its stability, which was due to Constantine the Great. As a result, this coin can be considered one of the most important, best known, and longest used in the history of mankind. The solidus was also later called bezant or hyperpyron.

Constantine the Great was an enlightened reformer who introduced major economic measures. He and his followers were obliged to keep a minimum of 4.5 grams of gold content in the solidus, without cheapening it. On the eastern border, between Europe and Asia, on the site of the former settlement of Byzantion (Byzantium), he founded the city of Constantinople in 330. This gave birth to the Eastern Roman Empire, also called the Byzantine Empire. From 312 onwards, he had the solidus minted on a large scale. The solidus thus became the Byzantine currency. Meanwhile, Rome was in a gradual decline primarily because of the worsening economic situation. Although the Western Roman Empire collapsed in 476, the Byzantine Empire (Eastern Roman Empire) still existed for more than a thousand years. The solidus retained its value for a long time, but eventually fell victim to the temptations of the rulers. After the year 800, its weight had already been reduced by about 1 gram. Eventually it was split into two coins of different values, but even that change did not help it to escape subsequent denigration. After more than 700 years, with the empire prospering, Michael IV the Paphlagonian (1034–1041) ascended the Byzantine throne in 1034. This monarch began a gradual process of devaluation. The following thirteen monarchs accelerated and completed the process. The Byzantine Emperor Alexius I (1081–1118) then had to reform the coinage because of an economic crisis in 1092, bringing an end to the solidus.

Devaluation of the solidus over time

Lessons from history

- Money must be scarce to retain its value.

- All of these coins were downgraded over time. This downgrading has always been done at the will of irresponsible rulers who wanted to increase their wealth—mostly to finance war campaigns. This is just a short snippet from thousands of years of human history. We are talking about times when precious metals were used to back the value of coins, mainly because of their rarity. It is the rarity and the impossibility of creating these metals artificially that gave them real value. However, their real value would never exist unless it was recognized by everyone else in society. Coin debasement has continuously happened all over the world—in the case of most currencies—and at different times.

However, the reasons have always been the same: the ruler at the time succumbed to temptation or the need to increase his wealth. Sometimes it was subtle, whereas other times it was quick and obvious. Regardless, it always ended in the collapse of the currency and the economic collapse of the empire or state. Usually poverty and wars followed.

- People behave in a market-like manner. At any given moment, they are getting rid of money that is declining in value, and instead hoarding money that can grow in value over the long term.

> "Those who cannot remember the past are condemned to repeat it."
>
> —George Santayana, Spanish writer

PAPER-BASED CURRENCIES THAT DIDN'T MAKE IT

Just as we have shown the historically documented failures of ancient Roman currencies, let us now take a look at paper currencies. Listing them all would require a separate book. However, what follows are some of the most significant examples.

Initial examples: it didn't go well because it was just paper

According to surviving historical sources, the first massive use of paper money in the world took place in China starting from the tenth century, and in Mongolia from the thirteenth century. However, let's look at North America prior to the War of Independence and the creation of the United States of America.

American colonizers began using paper money in the English colonies in North America. As part of funding the army, the colonial administrators needed funds to pay the soldiers. If the troops were not paid, there would be desertions and mutiny. However, they had no physical gold or silver at the time. Transporting precious metals was difficult, time-consuming, and dangerous. Additionally, precious metals were gradually running out. The colonial administrators therefore decided to issue vouchers guaranteeing the holder the payment of the appropriate amount of gold or silver. The colonies gradually increased the number of paper vouchers in circulation. People became accustomed to them and began to use them to pay for goods, even though promises of payment in gold or silver could not always be kept. This new method of payment quickly became popular. Even Benjamin Franklin, one of the founding fathers, initially saw paper money as a wonderful new technology.

What follows is an excerpt from *The Creature from Jekyll Island,* a book written by the well-known American author G. Edward Griffin. In it, he describes, among other things, the inflationary consequences of the colonial money issue:

> "By the end of 1750, the colony of Connecticut experienced price inflation of 800%. North and South Carolina had inflation of 900%, Massachusetts 1,000%, Rhode Island 2,300%. Money printing had to end in an environment of high inflation, and at the end always came similarly massive price deflation and depression."

Colonial inflation was, however, only finally ended by a **Bank of England** regulation endorsed by the English government. The colonists were ordered that the only valid and authorized money would be that of England. It was only by this means that the colonies were finally saved from ruin and chaos.

But as time went on, resistance to English rule began to grow in the colonies. The colonists did not want to use English money and turned their attention back to gold, silver, and bartering. Their resistance subsequently grew into what became known as the War of Independence. In the course of the War, however, the colonists again had to take the forbidden route and began printing paper money. The consequences were again tragic, but predictable. In 1775, the total money supply was $12 million; four years later, it was $600 million. The concomitant phenomena of inflation, economic decline, and chaos perhaps need not be recounted, but in war many problems are perceived differently. The culprit is always warfare—not money printing. The truth is that in many cases in history, new money has been created from nothing at an increased rate precisely to finance wars.

The War of Independence ended in 1783 with British recognition of the new nation; the United States of America became a separate federal republic. To stabilize the situation, the elected representatives decided to temporarily adopt the then widespread Spanish dollar as their official currency. It was not until 1785 that the American dollar was introduced as the national currency of the United States. However, the Founding Fathers had already learned from history that issuing new money not backed by real value would lead to its failure. So they decided to enshrine in the new nation's legislation an unambiguous safeguard against the temptations of future governments. For this reason, in 1792, the Mint Act (or Coinage Act) tied the US dollar firmly to the value of silver and gold. This meant that a so-called gold standard was established.

However, this insurance only lasted for a few decades. Bankers and government officials began to think of ways to circumvent the statutory monetary policy safeguards. Working closely with politicians, they gradually began to change the environment and the laws. With the creation of the Fed in 1913, some 120 years later, there was a gradual departure from the ideas of the Founding Fathers. Then, in 1971, President Nixon reopened the pathway for the uncontrolled issuance of new money.

Examples of depreciation of world currencies over the last 100 years:

- In Germany (Weimar Republic) after World War I, from August 1922 to December 1923, the rate of inflation reached 32,400%. The daily inflation rate was 21% with prices doubling every 3 days and 17 hours.

- In Hungary after World War II, from August 1945 to July 1946, the daily inflation rate reached 207%. Prices doubled every 15 hours.

The **Bank of England** was founded by Scotsman William Paterson in 1694 to provide a loan to a government in crisis. In return for a loan of £1.2 million, the Bank's founders obtained the status of a government central bank with the right to issue banknotes. The Bank of England is still the central bank of the United Kingdom of Great Britain and Northern Ireland. It is the second oldest central bank in the world and the eighth oldest bank on the planet.

- China went through a period of hyperinflation from 1948 to 1949, with the largest note being the 50,000 yuan note in 1947. By mid-1948, it reached 180,000,000 yuan. In April 1949, inflation peaked at 5.070%.

- Bolivia recorded an annual inflation rate of more than 20,000% in 1985.

- In Brazil, hyperinflation lasted from 1985 to July 1994. Prices rose by 184,901,570,954% during this period as a result of uncontrolled money printing. Brazil adopted a total of six different currencies as the government continuously changed due to the constant devaluation of money by increasing the number of zeros.

- Nicaragua had an inflation rate of 55% in 1990, and 33.6% a year later.

- Russia's inflation rate was at extremely high levels between 1992 and 1993. In 1992, the official inflation rate was approximately 2,520%.

- In Yugoslavia and Serbia, from April 1992 to January 1994, the highest monthly inflation rate was 313,000,000%. The daily inflation rate was 64.6% with prices doubling every 1.41 days.

Examples of hyperinflation in various countries in the first half of 2023:

- Argentina (approximately 110%)

- Syria (approximately 140%)

- Zimbabwe (approximately 175%)

- Lebanon (approximately 260%)

- Venezuela (approximately 425%)

The actual state of inflation in countries throughout the world

The break from the gold standard has taken only a few decades. The creation of new money, backed by nothing, devalues existing money. Newly-created money is not scarce, nor is it backed by labor or other value. Historically, this has always meant a gradual depreciation of the currency followed by its collapse. This has been accompanied by social unrest, the collapse of the political system and, in many cases, wars. No one can predict at the moment how this current global currency experiment will turn out. Anyone who is willing to recognize history and learn from it should realize that even the current global monetary policy is unlikely to be around forever. It has its problems and it has its rulers who run it. A look back at history will show us that the power over the creation of new money is all too tempting and not every ruler can resist it. Even today we can see that individual governments are using (abusing) it more and more. In the ever-accelerating course of events, the eventual collapse of the monetary system may not take centuries.

CHAPTER 2 SUMMARY

- Making money easy or multiplying it creates new, bad money.

- Individuals and companies at the top of the financial pyramid—those who get to the new money first—get richer at the expense of others. This is known as the Cantillon Effect.

- People save the money that they consider to be of greater value and spend the money they consider inferior. As such, bad money drives out the good money in circulation. This is known as Gresham's Law.

- Central banks supervise commercial banks and try to stimulate the economy:

    - lending money to the state (through the purchase of government bonds)

    - bailing out commercial banks (by providing liquidity)

    - maintaining monetary stability (such as the fight against increased inflation)

- Commercial banks are creating more new money:

    - in addition to other rules, the amount of this money is either limited or influenced by the minimum reserve requirement (MRR).

    - more customer deposits and a low bank reserve requirement will allow for a larger and larger supply of new money.

    - the money supply is then several times higher than the real money supply.

- These two basic financial multipliers were originally provided with statutory safeguards, which have eased or disappeared over time.

- At present, the inflow of new money is greater than it should be, and in many countries there is hardly any constraint.

- If people spend bad money, then this newly-created money reduces the value of the previous money.

- The depreciation of money and the loss of its scarcity can, as shown throughout history, cause price inflation and economic disruption.

- Those who do not learn from the history of mankind and the mistakes that have been repeated many times are doomed to repeat those mistakes and suffer the consequences again. People should learn from these examples, but there are many more throughout history:

    - the failure of primitive money, which has lost its preciousness

    - the failure of coins that were downplayed and lost their value

    - the failure of paper money due to irresponsible monetary policy

A PICTURE OF THE DEVELOPMENT OF MONEY

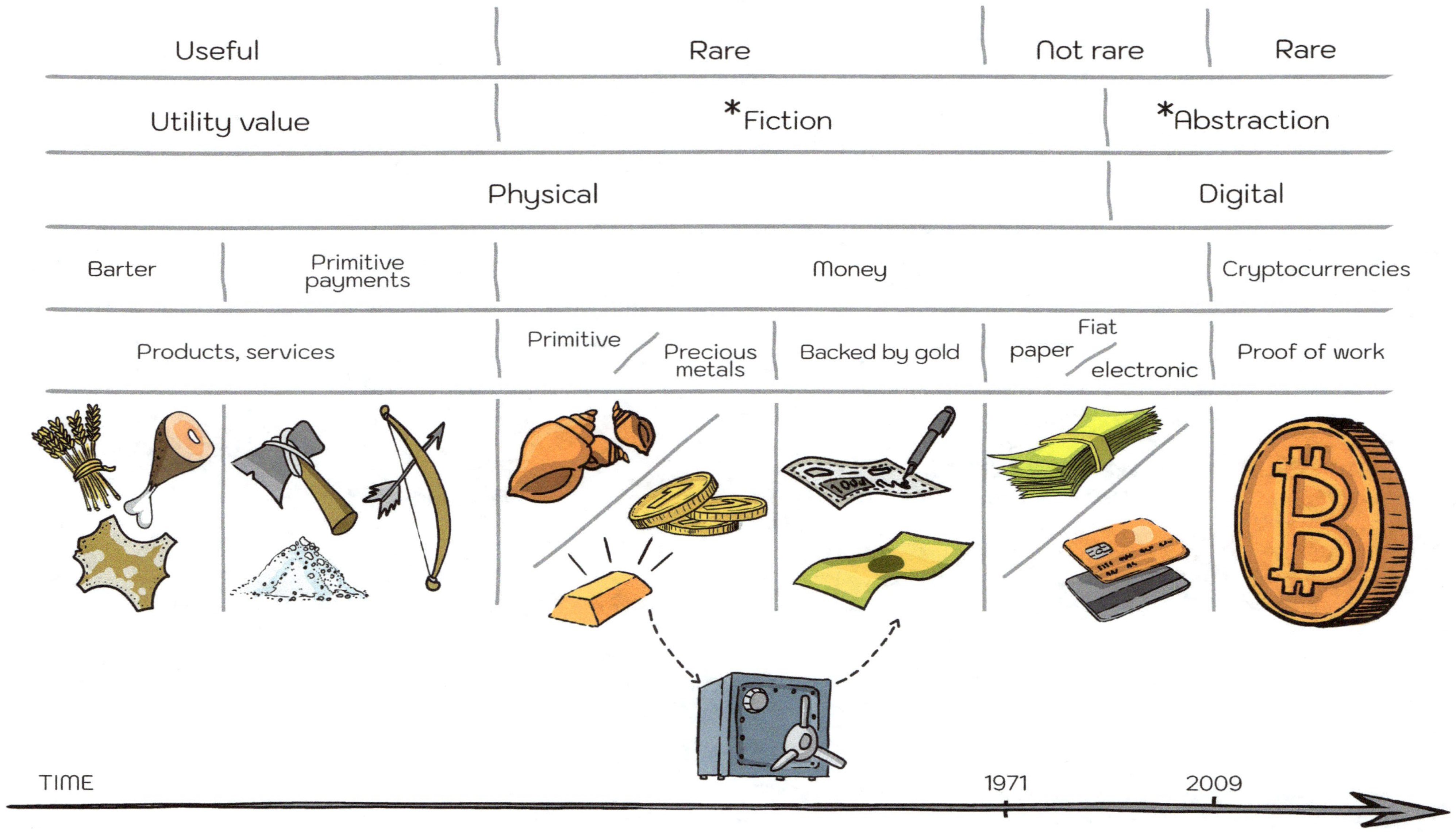

Useful	Rare		Not rare	Rare
Utility value	*Fiction			*Abstraction
Physical				Digital
Barter	Primitive payments	Money		Cryptocurrencies
Products, services	Primitive / Precious metals	Backed by gold	Fiat paper / electronic	Proof of work

TIME

1971 2009

* They have little to no utility value: they are based on scarcity and widespread adoption, thus becoming useful and gaining their value.

FIGHTING THE HYDRA: THE HIDDEN TAX THAT IS INFLATION

FIGHTING THE HYDRA: THE HIDDEN TAX THAT IS INFLATION

So far, we've learned about how bad money is created and its negative outcomes. Let's go through the implications of creating a new money supply in more detail. Flat rate inflation is largely caused by bad money. Bad money primarily drives price inflation, which isn't always apparent and cunningly offsets an ongoing decline in costs that can result from increased productivity. Now, let's take a look at the bigger picture and find out in what ways this deceptive enemy can be countered.

Creating a new financial stockpile works in the world of cryptocurrencies as well. What is important, however, is whether the creation of new coins is based on work done and whether the monetary policy of a given cryptocurrency is fixed—meaning a finite number of coins or a clearly defined increase. If this is not the case, and the cryptocurrency does not deliver the benefits demanded by the market, its value, or its exchange rate against other currencies, is gradually reduced. As with any currency, you need to choose wisely when you decide to invest.

Killing the Hydra represents the struggle against evil forces and the restoration of order and harmony—thus, the comparison to inflation.

In Greek mythology, the Hydra was a nine-headed poisonous, snake-like monster who lived underwater, guarding the entrance to the Underworld. She was the daughter of the stocky giant Typhon and Echidna (half-woman, half-snake).

The Hydra was often associated with chaos and malevolence. She was undefeatable, because if one attempted to sever any one of her heads, two would grow in its place. To make matters worse, her ninth head was immortal.

Only the demigod Hercules eventually managed to kill her. With the help of Iolaus, his nephew, Hercules cut off each of the monster's heads while Iolaus burned the wounds with a torch. This way, they prevented the heads from growing back. Once he had removed and destroyed the eight mortal heads, Hercules chopped off the ninth, immortal head, and covered it with a heavy rock. Hercules then slit open the Hydra's corpse and dipped his arrows in her poisonous blood.

WHAT IS INFLATION?

Inflation is the traditional economic term for the repeated increase in most prices in a given economy. At the same time, however, it means that money loses value. The inflation rate is measured as a percentage. These percentages indicate how much prices have increased, in other words, how much purchasing power has fallen. This applies both to wages and to money saved. The amount of inflation—the percentage decrease in purchasing power, or the percentage increase in prices—usually refers to the previous year. The inflation rate indicates how much more a defined set of products costs compared to the previous period.

However, sometimes people talk about monetary inflation, which means an increase over time in the supply of money, a particular commodity, or even a cryptocurrency. It is important to note that monetary inflation differs from the traditional economic concept of inflation, which describes the rise in prices in an economy. Understanding this difference in terminology will help to avoid confusion with traditional inflation.

Inflation can also be seen as a hidden tax, where all market participants pay an extra share of the money from rising prices to the state. However, unlike real taxes, it does not need to be publicly announced. This hidden taxation is carried out without the public's informed consent. In most countries around the world, this tax is paid by all market participants—especially end consumers—in the form of a value-added tax or a tax on goods. Such a tax is then levied on every purchase made, or a payment made where the relevant tax is assessed. As a result of inflation, the amount of most other major taxes, such as income tax or property tax, is also increased.

It can also be explained this way:

Monetary inflation is an inflow of newly created money
(growth of the money supply).

Price inflation, or price increases, is a consequence of it
(reduction of the purchasing power of money).

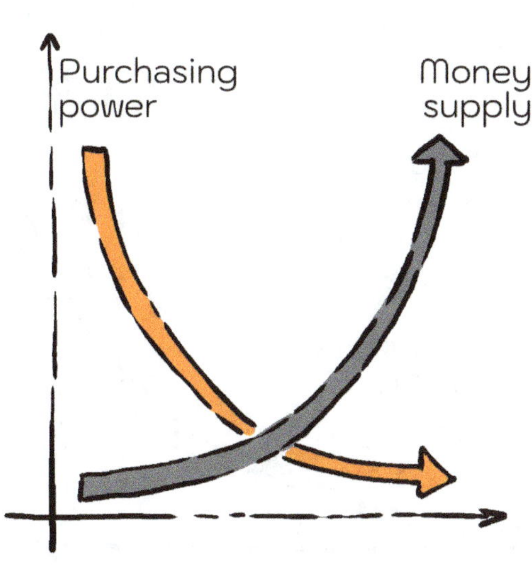

This interdependence between the growth of the money supply and a reduction in the purchasing power of money—which leads to an increase in prices—is demonstrated by the following graph. It shows how, over the last one hundred years, the money supply in the US has been increasing while the purchasing power of the US dollar has been decreasing.

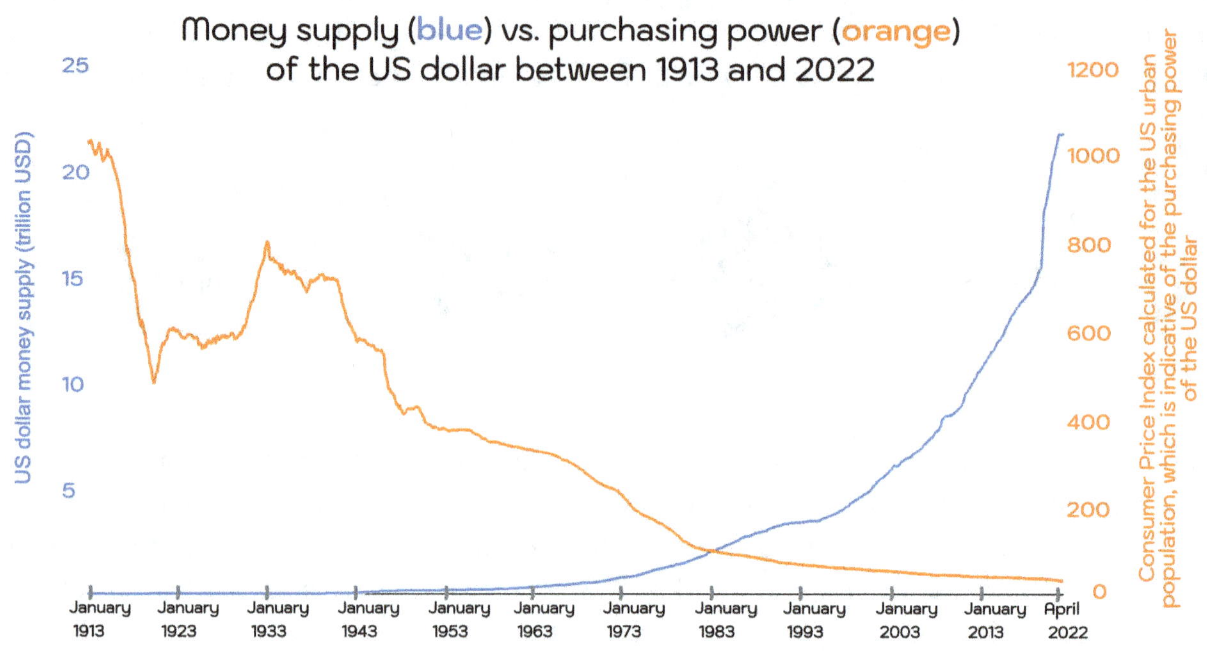

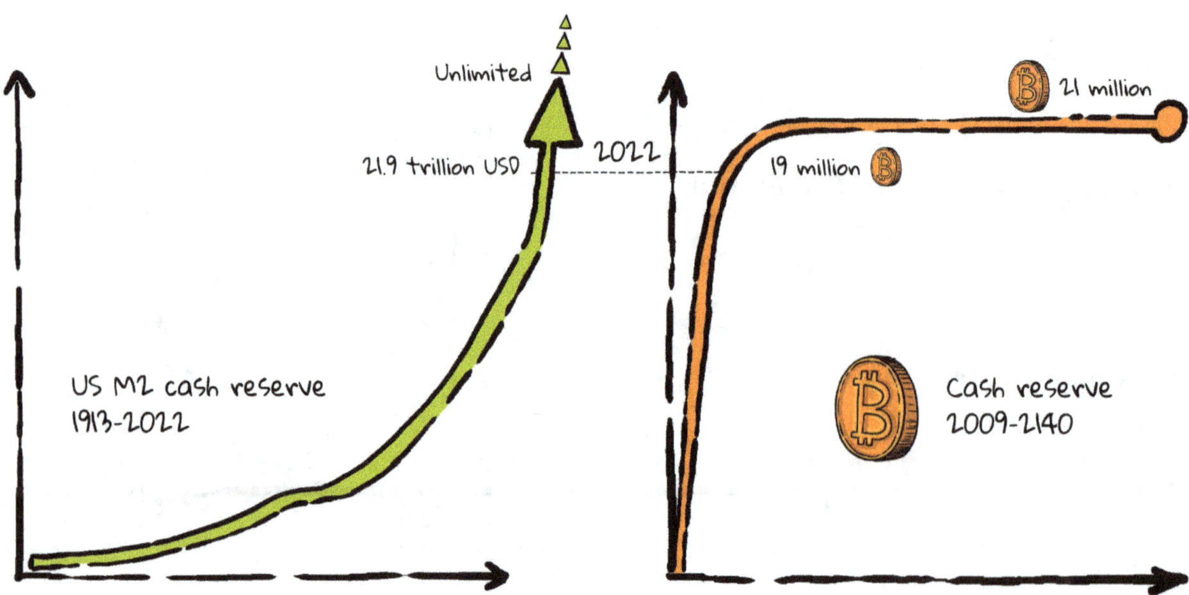

HIDDEN INFLATION

It is important to note that there is another form of inflation known as hidden inflation. This form of inflation is not directly visible in the price of a product. In a competitive market, participants strive to minimize price increases in comparison to other products within the same category. They do this by covertly reducing the quantity of the product or the quality of the raw materials used.

Reducing the quantity

In this scenario, the product looks identical to before, but the packaging contains a smaller quantity. For example, a chocolate bar previously had a weight of 3.5 oz (100 g), but now weighs 2.82 oz (80 g); the packaging has remained unchanged. In this case, your purchasing power has been devalued by 20%.

Of course, I can guarantee you that these particular sausages
do not contain any mystery meat.
Indeed, they contain no meat at all.

Reducing the quality

In this scenario, the product looks unchanged, but is actually made from raw materials or components that are cheaper or of lower quality. As such, your purchasing power has been depreciated by a percentage that corresponds to a reduction in service life or quality.

Our food is no worse than in other parts of the world.
In fact, it often contains additional substances that the body needs—like air and water.

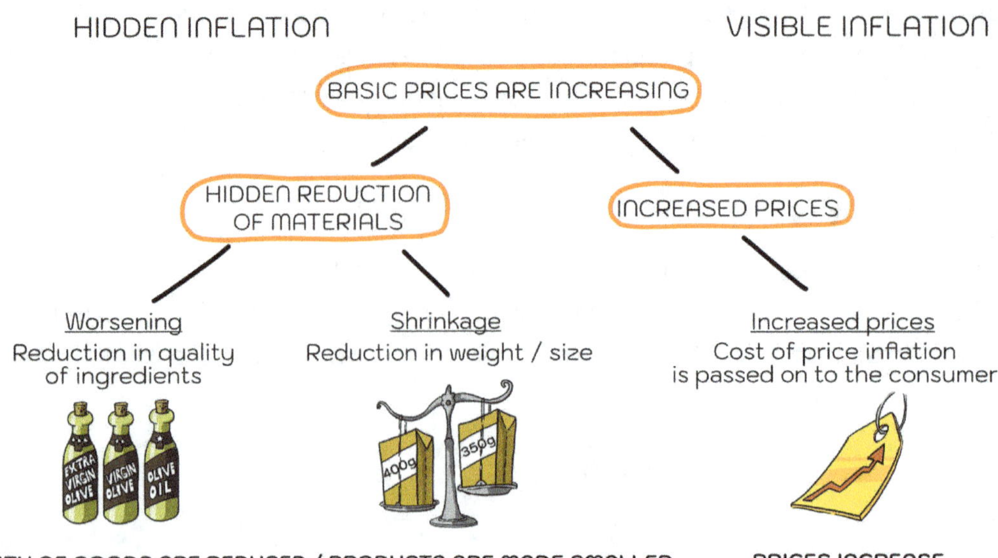

HOW INFLATION IS MEASURED

Inflation is measured in different ways, which vary from country to country. However, international organizations such as the International Monetary Fund (IMF) and, subsequently, most countries follow generally accepted methods of measuring inflation that are based on consumer prices. You will often come across the term market basket, which is a breakdown of the prices of goods and services into predetermined groups. This is one of the main tools used to calculate inflation. Individual countries usually have their own market basket, which reflects the specific consumption habits and preferences of the population. Market baskets can vary between countries depending on differences in culture, eating habits, and lifestyles. In the USA, the market basket is expressed by the Consumer Price Index (CPI). The CPI tracks changes in the prices of consumer goods and services over time. It is adjusted periodically and covers a wide range of goods and services purchased by households. The prices of these items are tracked and evaluated, allowing changes in the average price level to be calculated. Some countries also use the Producer Price Index (PPI), which tracks price changes at the production and supply chain level.

However, it must be clear that each item has a completely different meaning for each household. Some households may no longer consider the subcategories of children's clothing or education for a given year because they may no longer be relevant. Meanwhile, other households may be traveling more, going out to restaurants, building a new house, or renovating an apartment. For a particular family, a given item may then take up a much larger percentage of their budget. It should also be noted that in the figure that follows, some of the hidden inflation factors—such as reduction in quality—are not factored into the actual rate of inflation. Thus, the real inflation rate for a particular household may be different from that recognized by the government. It depends on the actual proportions of each item from one household to another.

Some items in the market basket may be regulated or subsidized by the state, such as electricity, gas, agricultural products, highways, and postage stamps. As a result, it is challenging to measure and compare inflation on an international scale.

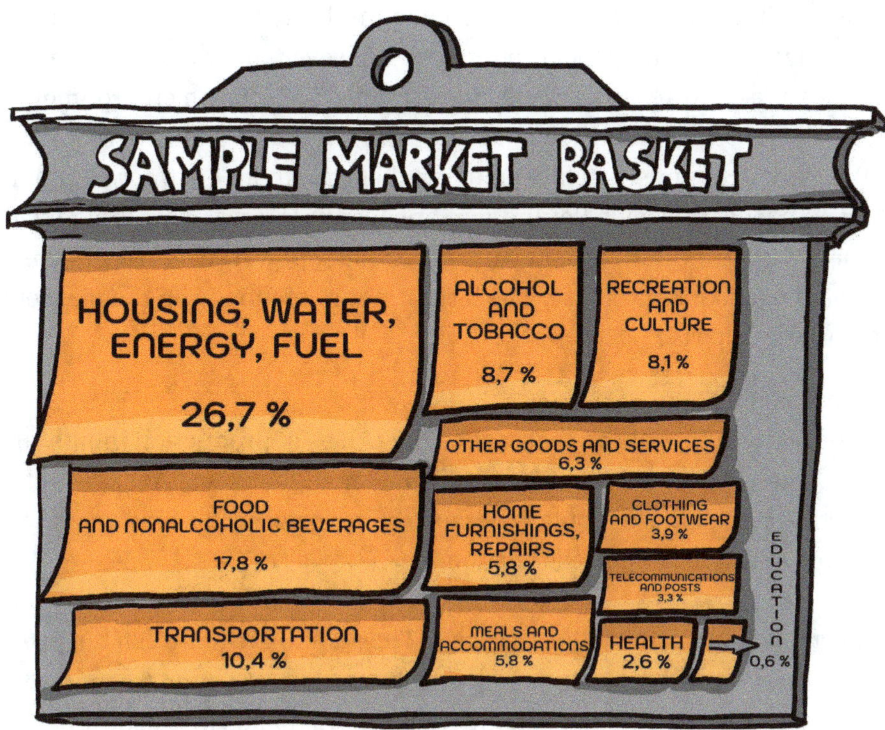

US Consumer Price Index

THE MAIN REASONS FOR INFLATION

- **Increasing money supply (creation of new money)**
When more new money appears on the market, it reduces the purchasing power of existing money. This new money is created out of nothing. When the market eventually detects a reduction in purchasing power, traders make it more expensive. As such, there is an increase in the prices of basic products as well as in the prices of other products where the cost of acquisition, including the cost of human labour, increases.

- **Decline in output without a decline in the purchasing power of the population**
In the case of classic economic crises, the output of businesses declines, layoffs occur, and unemployment rises. These phenomena go hand in hand with a decline in the purchasing power of the population—not money. However, if for some reason production falls and the purchasing power of the population is maintained, the supply of products is reduced, but the population still has enough money and wants to buy. In this case, demand exceeds supply. Consequently, sellers logically increase prices to get the most money for their goods. Those who need the goods the most then buy at the higher prices. This is exactly what happened, for example, during the COVID-19 crisis: when factories cut back production, people stayed at home and the state compensated them for lost wages for work they had not performed.

- **Low interest rates**

  The interest rate, or interest, is stated as a percentage and determines how much money the bank or other entity will pay you for lending them your money. However, the government needs people to spend money. Therefore, the central bank lowers interest rates, creating an environment in which it does not pay people to save. Until recently, the interest rates offered by banks were minimal and, in some cases, zero. But some economists rightly point out that the amount of interest should be a valuation of putting off your needs until later. Setting zero or negative interest rates is completely disincentive to saving money. With the value of money (its purchasing power) declining and interest rates low, saving does not make economic sense. The large amount of money on the market then creates an environment for prices to rise.

- **Input price increases**

  This is a situation where there is an increase in the prices of production inputs such as materials, energy, or labor. These higher costs are then reflected in higher prices for products and services. If the increase in the price of these inputs is because of imports, such as raw materials, energy, oil, or natural gas, this is known as imported inflation.

Inflation forces citizens to try to protect their savings. The solution is to invest, but every investment is risky. Therefore, it can be said that inflation forces people to take risks—and for many it may not pay off. On the other hand, if they do not protect their savings the value of them will certainly decline. Many people do not understand investments or are risk-averse, so they tend to buy property. Others choose not to save, instead spending on more immediate needs. Those in this group often buy pointless goods they don't need, waste food, and don't build up reserves for illness, emergencies, or retirement.

Central banks support and seek to achieve mild and subtle inflation. In the previous discussions on inflation, we explained that it can also be seen as a hidden tax that can help the government pay down the national debt through higher government revenues. Therefore, the state welcomes it if people spend rather than save. The more they spend, the more money retailers pay back to the state, thus supporting GDP growth.

Ahhh, the reliable drivers of any modern economy.
Inflation and poor-quality products.

However, if inflation exceeds a predetermined limit, governments will start to worry. This is because voters are capable of recognizing these price increases and, as a result, begin to rebel. This is dangerous for government officials because their aim is to please as many voters as possible. Often, however, the current government only bears the consequences of the decisions of previous governments. Most countries nowadays have their inflation targets set by central banks. These targets determine how high consumer price inflation should be. The most widely used target is an inflation rate of 2% per annum. However, if prices naturally decrease over time due to increased purchasing power from productivity gains, citizens not only miss out on the natural growth in purchasing power, but also experience greater losses. From this perspective, even zero inflation deprives citizens of the potential purchasing power derived from their savings.

Central banks try to control inflation through various measures. One such measure is to either increase or decrease interest rates. Higher interest rates make new money more expensive. This reduces the number of new loans and the growth of new money. It may then make sense for people to save. Such a scenario has the potential to drive up market prices. However, when interest rates rise, interest on previously issued cheap loans and mortgages can multiply. This can put companies and individuals in existential difficulties. During this period, housing prices may start to fall, but mortgages to purchase them become significantly more expensive.

Thanks to higher interest rates, buyers can take advantage of falling housing prices—though their mortgages will cost more.

Some central banks can further reduce inflation by indirectly withdrawing newly created money from the market. They do this by withdrawing liquidity from commercial banks, selling purchased stocks or securities, and reducing the amount of debt. Banks get rich on interest from lending money created out of nothing. If these debts are repaid, the newly created money may disappear, but the interest on earnings remains with the banks.

HOW INFLATION DEVALUES OUR GOOD DEEDS

Interest on primary and savings accounts never reaches the rate of inflation. Targeted inflation of 2% a year will reduce the purchasing power of savings by approximately a quarter over fifteen years, and by half over thirty-five years. The following chart shows how long it takes to lose one-half of the purchasing power of your savings at different rates of inflation.

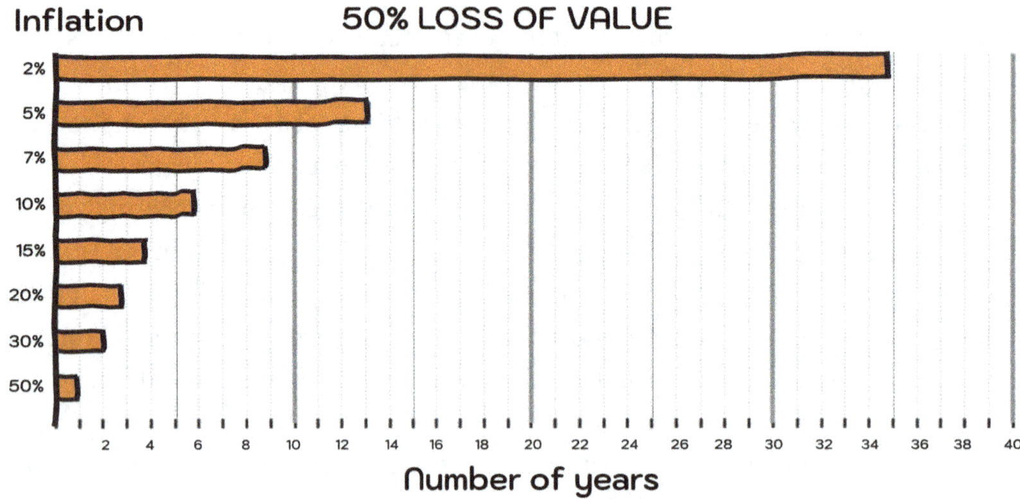

MEASURING THE STRENGTH OF INFLATION

We have learned to live with targeted inflation on an ongoing basis, but not everyone is aware of what may happen next. Inflation has three stages that determine its severity and strength.

- **Moderate**
  Price increases are measured in single-digit percentages. Targeted inflation of about 2%, led by the central bank, is considered natural. Citizens hardly notice the subtle price increases; such inflation is not a political issue.

- **Galloping**
  Price increases are measured in the tens of percent per year. Citizens lose confidence in savings and banking products. There is a clear devaluation of savings. People invest much more and buy long-term stable assets like real estate, precious metals, gemstones, art, and bitcoin. It starts to become a political issue, and governments try to intervene.

- **Hyperinflation**
  Price increases are measured in the hundreds to thousands of percent. This represents a collapse of the economy and confidence in the currency itself. Prices reach astronomical levels, and extremely large quantities of banknotes are issued. Money is devalued because it no longer fulfills its function as a storer of value. As such, money is replaced by substitutes like the US dollar, gold, or bitcoin—and even barter systems may return. Hyperinflation is accompanied by poverty, existential problems, and civil unrest. The government usually resigns or is overthrown.

With irresponsible monetary and budgetary policies, hyperinflation can happen in any country in the world, and we will probably see it several more times.

INFLATION FROM THE GOVERNMENT'S POINT OF VIEW

As we have already noted, moderate inflation is desired by the state—which even tries to encourage it. However, if inflation turns into an economic crash or hyperinflation, the state tries to intervene. How do governments typically attempt to fight inflation?

CORRECTING MISTAKES AND FIREFIGHTING THROUGH ECONOMIC REFORM

The central bank will start to raise interest rates, or start selling off its assets. The state seeks to reform state finances, makes cuts in the state budget, and tries to achieve a balanced budget. It sometimes uses controversial price freezes or price controls, or outright freezes or seizes people's accounts. Social unrest, chaos, and a reduction in the purchasing power of the population tend to accompany this. Often these economic reforms need to be combined with monetary reform.

RESTARTING AND TRYING AGAIN THROUGH MONETARY REFORM

This is a complex and costly economic step, which involves changing the currency or its value in a specific territory. It is usually a decision of a ruler or the government. The aim is to end hyperinflation by introducing a new monetary system. Again, chaos and social unrest result.

CURRENCY SUBSTITUTION

This is the process of replacing the domestic currency with a higher quality currency of another country. It can be a full or partial replacement. In partial substitution, two currencies can operate simultaneously. This solution may be sought unofficially by individual citizens if they do not trust their own currency, or it may be adopted officially at the state level. In recent decades, this phenomenon can be observed all over the world. Individual currencies are no longer tied to specific territories; the terms dollarization or euroization are beginning to be used. Unfortunately, this is a solution where the citizens of a given nation have to rely on a currency that is controlled by another nation. This carries a great risk for the future because even the substitute currency can be devalued over time.

BITCOINIZATION: BETTING ON INNOVATION

It is a modern form of currency substitution, but with one significant difference: bitcoin is not controlled by any central bank or state. This is considered by some people to be a major advantage, by others just the opposite. From a historical perspective, it is certainly a benefit. However, bitcoin has one significant problem today, and that is its high volatility. This means a fluctuation in the exchange rate as compared to other national currencies. This is because of the fact that the price of bitcoin is based on the market principle of supply and demand. Additionally, there are many speculators in the current market, the adoption of the currency is not yet widespread, and the total capitalization (the total number of coins multiplied by the current price) is not that large compared to other national currencies. All of these factors contribute to bitcoin's high volatility. The more users there are and the larger the capitalization of bitcoin, the more the volatility of bitcoin will decrease. Volatility is the biggest impediment to widespread bitcoinization at the moment because it makes bitcoin not work well as a short-term sustainer of value.

However, it is different from a medium- and long-term perspective. So far, anyone who has held bitcoin for more than four years has seen their invested funds multiply in value. Residents in high-inflation countries are increasingly favoring bitcoin over the dollar or other currencies. The volatility of bitcoin becomes less significant to them when their national currency experiences greater depreciation. This is also because in poorer countries not every citizen has access to a bank account or the ability to purchase foreign currencies. However, through a mobile phone, they can transact directly in bitcoin. More countries are likely to want to shift away from relying on foreign national currencies and adopt independent market money that cannot be controlled or devalued by a ruling minority.

Bitcoinization is not just a national process. We also talk about bitcoinization when individuals or entire communities start using bitcoin as an alternative currency to the traditional state currency. This approach offers a number of benefits for people in countries suffering from high inflation or dependence on foreign currency. Since bitcoin is not controlled by any central authority and its supply is tightly limited, it is inherently resistant to inflationary and censorship pressures. This opens up new opportunities for economic growth and stability for countries and communities that choose to bitcoinize. The most important advantages are the independence from external influences and the possibility to reduce dependence on unstable currencies.

Thanks to innovative technologies, countries that choose this route can enjoy significant benefits. Bitcoin provides a decentralized, transparent, and resilient system that does not need to be operated or maintained by the state. It allows easy and fast transfers between users without the need for a trusted third party. It can bring lower transaction costs, greater financial accessibility for all citizens, and increased protection against currency manipulation by politicians.

Is bitcoinization an alternative to the failure of current fiat money-based monetary systems?

HOW TO FIGHT THE HYDRA CALLED INFLATION

A good hedge against inflation is usually investment, or non-inflationary money. However, non-inflationary money has not yet been introduced by mankind. If it ever becomes reality, the Hydra called inflation will be defeated and will disappear from our lives. As far as investments are concerned, it should be pointed out that each of them carry their own risks. These risks are linked to the uncertainty of future returns. Different types of investment carry different levels of risk, but no investment can guarantee a certain return. Risk is associated with factors such as fluctuations in market prices, economic developments, political events, natural disasters, or misdirection of corporate strategies. An investor must always prepare for the possibility that expected returns may not materialize, or that the value of an investment may decline or result in loss.

In terms of investing, it is not how much you earn that is important, but how much you choose to invest. History shows that many people who made large amounts of money ended up on the street. Conversely, those who earned far less, but who over the long term continuously put aside some of their money have improved their standard of living. Everyone should start investing at a young age. If you haven't started yet, you should consider starting in the near future.

The endless and long-term battle with inflation will certainly not be solved by saving in fiat money. However, spending all your money is not a viable option either. So how do we protect the value of the good deeds we have done? They need to be saved in something that doesn't lose value over time, or perhaps even gains value over time. The idea is that the increase in value should be equal to or greater than real inflation.

PRIMARY SAVINGS MECHANISMS

- **Movable assets**
  - The first category includes consumer goods, which are utility goods such as cars, household equipment, and other items of everyday use. However, these are usually not rare and their value declines rapidly through wear and tear or obsolescence. This category of assets is used to satisfy our immediate needs and does not protect the good deeds we create.

  - The second category is more rare. This category includes items like antiques, art, collections, memorabilia, alcohol, precious metals, and gemstones, to name a few. It is the oldest way of accumulating wealth, but these assets are also more difficult to secure. They can be more marketable than real estate and sold off in parts, but are harder to verify. This can lead to complications like haggling between the buyer and seller. An item must be authenticated to determine its true value at the time of sale. The advantage is that you don't have to watch the value over time, but as the purchasing power of the population decreases, so does the price.

- **Real estate**
  This is an asset in which people quite often allocate their investment capital. However, real estate must be maintained and this can require a significant annual cost. If you don't use it for housing or your own business, you can rent it out to earn income. However, it is more difficult to sell real estate than movable assets. It typically isn't possible to sell only a fraction of this type of asset. Also, it can take a long time to find a buyer for the given asking price. Its market value changes over time, and in the event of crises or war, the purchasing power of the inhabitants typically decreases. There is

a risk that the price of the property will be low when you need the money most. Real estate can be conveniently taxed or confiscated by the state. Also you cannot travel with real estate, and it is subject to damage or destruction in the event of natural disaster or war.

- **Shares**
  This asset class belongs to the group known as securities. Shares allow you to own a proportionate part of a company. In order for them to have a true market value, they must be tradable on a stock exchange. The price is then determined by supply and demand. As with any investment, shares also carry risks. A company may weaken economically or technologically over time, succumb to competition, or go bankrupt. If a company's purchasing power declines, its share price also falls. Let's look at two basic types of shares.

  - Growth stocks are more like the fast sports cars of the stock world: they don't pay dividends, but their price can rise quickly.

  - Dividend stocks, on the other hand, are more like the family sedans: they are stocks that pay a regular cash payout (hence their name), but their price growth is lower than that of growth stocks.

- **Commodities**
  This asset class consists primarily of raw materials. It is a type of commodity that is traded without differences in quality, and materials from different suppliers are interchangeable. Contracts (futures) are used to hedge a fixed price for delivery of a given commodity that will take place in the future. This often leads to speculation. This arena is only for experienced investors.

- **Indices**
  This asset class is essentially made up of statistical variables. This means changes are measured in a certain group of stocks, commodities, or bonds that comprise a predetermined part of the market. The index captures the direction in which this given part of the market is moving—either up or down. The market can also invest in these indices. Indices average the investor's risk from one item to a selected part of the market.

- **Investment funds**
  This asset class is offered by a number of institutions. Some of the funds are less risky with guaranteed deposits and lower returns, while others are riskier with the possibility of losing the underlying deposit. They allow you to invest in preset packages primarily focused on stocks, bonds, and real estate. These types of funds have higher fees because they have high overhead. One should thoroughly check the long-term performance of the fund before investing.

- **Exchange-traded funds (ETFs)**
  An alternative to active management of funds by expensive investment fund managers are publicly traded funds known as exchange-traded funds (ETFs). Here, investing is guided by a precise index-based algorithm. Investors can choose to invest in stock market indices, commodities, cryptocurrencies, and more. These funds are traded on global stock exchanges along with shares of major companies. Especially from the perspective of cryptocurrencies, this is an interesting alternative to direct ownership. Purchasing cryptocurrency through an ETF fund can be simpler, particularly for beginners, compared to the direct acquisition and management of assets like bitcoin. However, this approach means relinquishing one of cryptocurrency's key benefits: the ability to 'be your own bank' by directly controlling your assets. In many countries, owning a cryptocurrency through an ETF is more tax efficient, but you have to take into account that someone else is managing it and therefore you may not always have free access to it.

- **Government bonds**

This asset class is considered to be one of the least risky assets. Some government bonds take into account the official inflation rate, however, it is typically not the real one. Government bonds are an appropriate form of investment if they can at least cover the real inflation rate. Otherwise, holding them makes no sense and the holder will realize a loss. However, they usually provide a higher interest rate than commercial banks.

- **Pensions and retirement savings**

Pensions and retirement savings are plans by which individuals save money to ensure financial stability and income when they reach retirement age. The goal of pensions and retirement savings is to provide financial stability and income after leaving active employment. There are many types of pensions and retirement savings, which vary according to national legislation. These include state pension schemes, occupational pension plans, and individual pension plans. For example, in the US, the most common type of pension plan is the 401(k). This plan is named after the pension law that made it possible. It is an employee pension plan that allows employees to deposit a portion of their income into a pre-tax retirement account. These contributions are usually deducted from the employee's pay before taxes are calculated, which reduces the actual tax amount. The money deposited in this account is then invested in a variety of financial products such as stocks, bonds, and mutual funds.

- **Money**

In this case, we are thinking of ordinary savings. First of all, you need to choose a currency in which to save. There are about 180 currencies around the world. However, market participants are not interested in the currencies of many countries because some of them are not sufficiently widespread or not sufficiently trustworthy from the point of view of value maintenance. The most widely used world currency is the US dollar—a consequence of the Bretton Woods Agreement. This does not mean that the dollar is the most valuable nor stable currency. The quality of a currency depends on how a country's central bank fulfills its mission and what budgetary policies the government pursues. If someone decides to invest their money in a foreign currency, they should be aware that there may be a reversal over time. Some Gulf states have stable currencies that rely on vast oil and gas resources. As long as there is peace in the area and there is demand for their mineral wealth, it can be assumed that these currencies will hold their value. You can save by holding the currency in your possession or by entrusting it to a bank. If the fiat currency in which you receive your wages and hold your savings is highly inflationary, it makes sense to save the portion of your funds that you don't need for everyday life in a currency that is less inflationary. Another way to reduce the effects of inflation is to then place that currency in savings or term accounts at the bank. Keep in mind that, in general, if real inflation is greater than the interest you earn, your money loses value. Furthermore, entrusting your money to a bank also poses some risk.

- **Cryptocurrencies**

This asset class belongs to a relatively new and rapidly growing industry. Cryptocurrencies are not yet widespread enough for their fundamentals and operating principles to be considered common knowledge. They present great opportunities, but also great risks. There are currently more than 20,000 different cryptocurrencies—and the number is growing. Mostly, however, they are attempts to realize ideas that remain in the realm of wishful thinking. Many projects can also be described as targeted scams.

The value of cryptocurrencies, like the value of most stocks or commodities, is determined by how much people are willing to pay for them. The price of cryptocurrencies is therefore determined by supply and demand. This is usually done on cryptocurrency exchanges or currency exchanges. If more people want to buy a cryptocurrency than want to sell it at the current price, the price will increase. The same is true in reverse. Cryptocurrencies have long been perceived as high-risk and speculative assets. Only a fraction of them can be expected to succeed in widespread adoption in the future.

Instead of the approximately 180 state currencies that exist today, the future could see a few cryptocurrencies emerging as dominant. A small number of these will act more as money, while the rest will seek to provide complementary functions. Currently, bitcoin is the market leader. It is the oldest, functional, and truly decentralized cryptocurrency, containing the highest level of security. With the longest proven history among cryptocurrencies, it is expected to maintain its market leadership for the foreseeable future. Individuals and institutions can also invest in bitcoin through ETFs.

RISK DIVERSIFICATION

It is generally advisable to have your investments spread over several asset classes, in order to minimize the risks associated with investing. Examples include real estate, gold, bonds, stocks, and bitcoin. The level of allocation is up to each individual to determine. It is advisable to invest mainly in those asset classes that you understand and in which you believe. Beginners and inexperienced investors should take advice, but at the same time verify the information before making up their own minds. You must bear in mind that your investment decisions can have major consequences that can be either positive or negative.

This basic diversification triangle shows that you always need to choose between return, risk, and liquidity. These variables are interdependent, but there is always a quid pro quo. As returns increase, risk also increases. If we want good liquidity, it comes at the expense of higher yield—and sometimes higher risk as well.

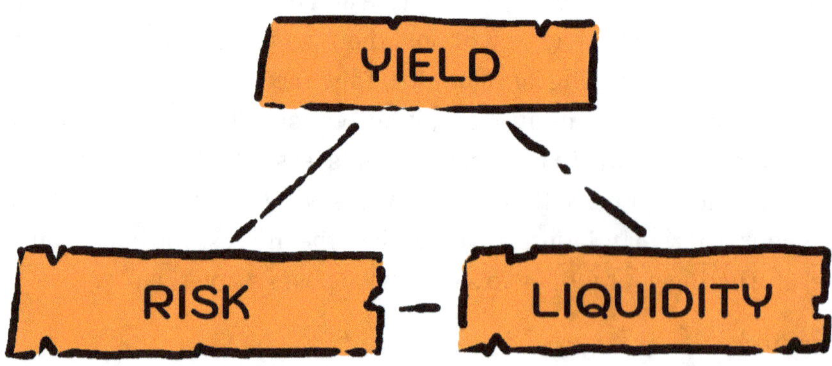

Yield
This refers to the profit or earnings of a given investment. It can also be seen as a reward for the risk taken. After deducting inflation, we get the actual return. In most cases, the amount of return is directly proportional to the amount of risk taken.

Risk

This refers to the degree of perceived uncertainty with regard to an expected outcome. It can also be a loss of invested funds. With high risk, high returns can be achieved—but negative returns can also be possible.

Liquidity

This refers to the ability to exchange an investment back for cash. Good (high) liquidity means a quick, safe, and ideally profitable conversion of the investment back into money.

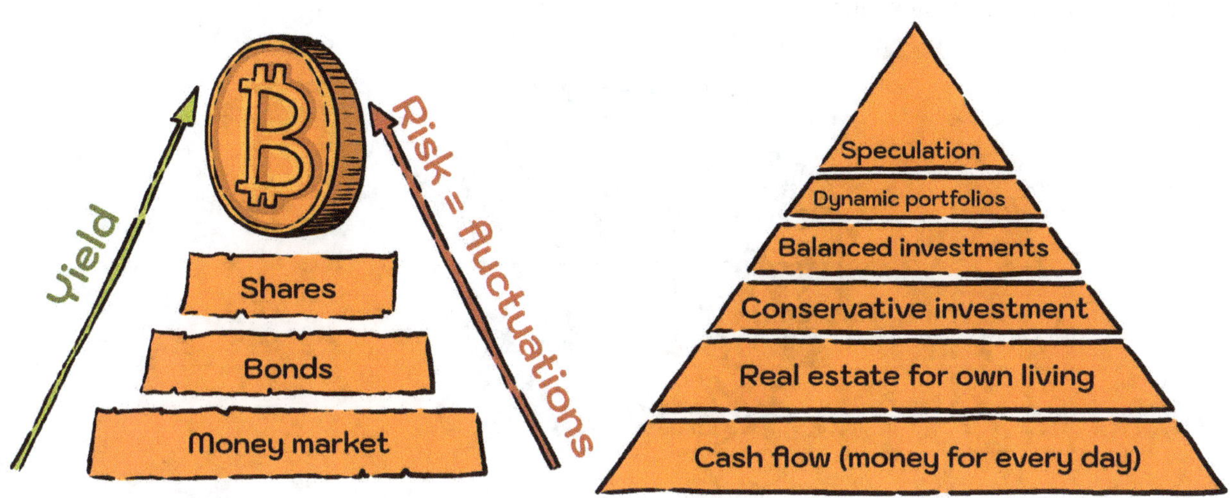

The specific allocation of investments between assets is an individual matter that depends on the objectives and financial situation of each investor. This means that the ideal allocation of investments will depend on various factors such as age, financial situation, goal, and risk tolerance.

Therefore, it is important for investors to consider their own objectives and risk tolerance when deciding how to allocate various resources for investments. Importantly, each investor should allow for a financial buffer in order to manage unforeseen contingencies.

Let's summarize the basic principles of risk diversification:

- **Multi-asset class allocation**
  Investments should be allocated to different asset classes such as stocks, bonds, real estate, precious metals, or cryptocurrencies. This will reduce the risk of losing money. In this way, higher returns can be achieved with less risk of loss.

- **Splitting investments between different companies**
  Investments should be split between different companies to minimize the risk associated with the development of one company. This will reduce the risk associated with specific companies and maximize potential profits.

- **Emphasis on long-term growth**
  Long-term growth should be a priority, so it is important to choose investments that have the potential to grow over time.

- **Investment monitoring**

  Investments should be regularly monitored and adjusted in response to market developments and changes in the economy. Each investor should then adjust their investment decisions based on current information.

- **Risk assessment**

  It is important to assess the risks associated with each investment and adjust the portfolio to reduce the overall risk. Speculative and risky investments—like stocks and cryptocurrencies—should never make up the majority of your portfolio. Every investor should consider the risks associated with each investment and take steps to minimize potential losses.

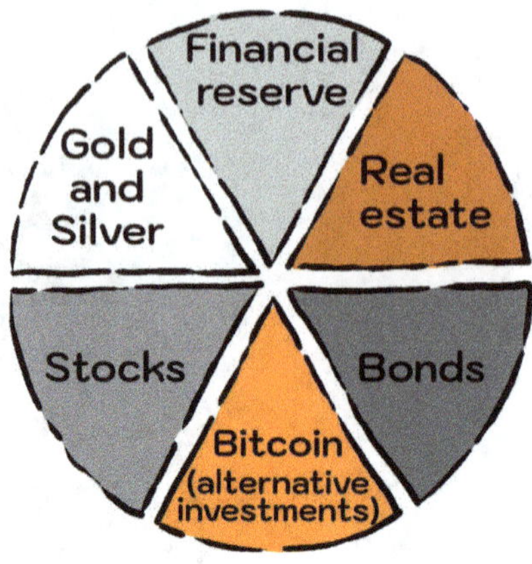

When done properly, diversifying investments can reduce risk and increase the chances of long-term success. However, it is important to remember that diversification does not guarantee a profit nor minimize the risk of loss. All investments involve risk and results can be uncertain. So it is important to have a careful investment strategy and regularly monitor the progress of your investments.

Any investment is risky, but in times of higher inflation, holding money is also a risk.

Just as there is no ideal partner, there is also no 100% guaranteed high-yield and highly liquid investment.

Never put all your eggs in one basket.

CHAPTER 3 SUMMARY

- In an inflationary environment, money is not used for savings and the borrower is usually in a better position than the lender. In such a case, the borrower benefits and the debt-free taxpayer pays the price.

- The state is always the biggest debtor in a given monetary system and the citizens are its creditors.

- Inflation can also be seen as a hidden taxation. However, unlike real taxes, it does not need to be publicly announced and exists without the public's informed consent.

- States and central banks support targeted inflation. Rising prices also lead to higher tax collections and can help pay off government debts or fund pointless projects that the state could never undertake without fiat money.

- Citizens pay this hidden inflationary tax on all purchases in the form of a consumption or value-added tax, in addition to other taxes.

- Government reported inflation rarely corresponds to real inflation. The deviations are a result of inaccurate adjustments to the market basket, both in relation to society and to specific individuals. Further distortions arise from the failure to include parts of hidden inflation and higher purchasing power that result from higher productivity. It can be noted that real inflation is often higher than that reported by the state.

- Policies that target inflation are a smart way to redistribute the additional purchasing power generated by productivity growth.

- Inflation encourages immediate consumption because saving in the national currency does not make sense in the long run.

- Inadequate savings are a major problem in old age, especially in the absence of a good pension policy.

- Citizens are getting poorer as everything gets more expensive; wages typically rise much later and often do not cover the actual rate of inflation.

- Inflation devalues the savings of all citizens and, at the same time, devalues the time taken to create good deeds that have been placed in savings.

- Banks are getting rich on interest from money created out of thin air.

- The state, the banks, and the wealthy—who have access to new money—are able to get richer because they are able to use it before the market reacts to the influx of new money and prices rise. They can buy cheaper with newly-created money because prices don't automatically increase when new money is introduced.

- Inflation forces people to invest so that they do not lose the value of their savings. However, every investment is risky.

THE EVOLUTION OF THE STATE: A FEW STEPS FORWARD AND A FEW STEPS BACK

THE EVOLUTION OF THE STATE: A FEW STEPS FORWARD AND A FEW STEPS BACK

The values of individual currencies are continuously fluctuating in relation to one another. This fluctuation is highly dependent on how the government and the central bank manage the currency. The quality of individual currencies also varies. In truly free countries, a citizen should have the right to decide for oneself in which currency to place their savings. While in many countries this right is recognized, in countless others it is not. Although humanity is going through a period of great expansion, there are attempts by politicians to restrict some basic human rights and the freedom of citizens.

Is the current economic mainstream the way to prosperity? Alternatively, are the opponents who speak of a road to ruin and irresponsible monetary experimentation right? If they are right, is there still time for a turnaround? What can cause the world's wealth to fall into the hands of a few thousand select individuals?

To form one's own opinion, it is necessary to understand the basic relationship between the state and the citizen. By understanding the interests of the parties involved, we can better assess whether we are gradually moving away from the liberal ideas of the world's great leaders and reflect on the growth of political amateurism, populism, and bureaucracy.

Those who are comfortable with the current direction and see the state as an institution that will always take care of them will likely see less of a need for cryptocurrencies. Others, after reading this chapter, may ponder the growing problem between the state and the citizenry caused by irresponsible monetary policy. At the same time, it raises speculation as to whether one of the significant economists of the twentieth century could have been the mysterious Satoshi Nakamoto. Later on, when you reach Book Two, in addition to reading about the possibility of getting rich, you will also find passages on how non-state money can be a way out of monetary socialism and a tool for gaining personal freedom.

THE EVOLUTION OF THE STATE, PART I: REFLECTING ON THE GRADUAL STEPS FORWARD

Over the last tens of thousands of years various power groups and, subsequently, nations have emerged all over the planet. In the overwhelming majority of cases, violent subjugation has been behind the creation of individual states.

This idea was developed by **Dr. Oppenheimer** in his work *The State*, in which he puts forward the theory of the emergence of the state as a coercive relationship arising from forced subjugation.

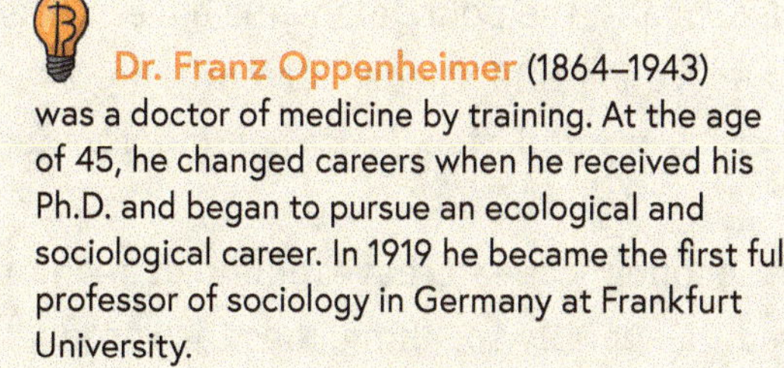

> "The cause of all states is the contrast between peasants and herdsmen, between producers and robbers, between plains and prairies."
>
> —Franz Oppenheimer, German sociologist and economist

Let us summarize the developmental stages that preceded the formation of modern states. This recap is based on Oppenheimer's ideas and should be viewed with some detachment.

1. **Looting:** Raiders plunder settlers, looting their crops, livestock, and furs. They also take people captive, murder, rape, and burn settlements.

2. **Serfdom and slavery:** The raiders realize that the settlers will be more useful if they were kept alive. They regularly take away their produce and leave the settlers with just enough to survive, or force them to perform various activities in exchange for food. They regard them as their property.

3. **Tithes and domestication:** Serfdom and slavery are difficult for raiders in terms of controlling production and maintaining discipline. It is easier to impose a fixed tax or tithe, so that essentially the settlers are paying for protection. Settlers become comfortable with this arrangement because they are left with more of the production. Thus, they have a reason to increase productivity. The raiders settle permanently with the settlers.

4. **Nobility:** Settled raiders pass themselves off as nobility and assume a monopoly on the administration of justice in the territory they control. As they do not like to see disputes in their territory, they establish relative peace and some legal certainty. They often try to impose the divine origin of their lineage on the people, establish hereditary titles to territory and subjects, and create hierarchical power structures to better collect taxes and maintain order. Subsequently, in some cases, dictators come to power with the support of the state or through their own outright power.

5. **Democratic state:** Based on the unsustainability of the previous model because of economic reasons, weakening of power groups, or class unrest, political structures emerge. Society then selects politicians from its ranks based on a specific setup.

BRIEF SUMMARY

Society is all people living in one territory. The settlers became citizens and the political apparatus took over the function of the raiders.

Historically, the political means have consisted of acts like robbery, violence, subjugation, tithing, commands, and prohibitions. Currently, however, they consist of the collection of taxes; the definition of laws, decrees or regulations; and their enforcement by the branches of power.

The economic means have remained unchanged. These are activities such as cultivation, production, and trade. Generally speaking, these are productive activities based on voluntary and mutually beneficial cooperation between the various actors.

The state has always been, and will continue to be, an organization of political means that consists of a power arrangement in which some members of society are placed in a privileged position in which they can legally use those political means. However, in a well-adjusted democratic society, the state has teammates—or adversaries, depending on one's understanding of the matter. The counterpart of the state is the territorial unit, such as a city or otherwise defined community of people, which operates on the basis of economic means.

> "The city is the direct antithesis of the state. While the essence of the state is the development of political means, the essence of the city is the development of economic means. Thus, since the emergence of the city, most of history can be explained through the lens of the conflict between the city and the state."
>
> —Franz Oppenheimer, German sociologist and economist

THE STATE AND THE CITIZEN

The relationship between the state and its citizens, including civil liberties, is addressed by several philosophical trends, political ideologies, and economic theories. In later discussions on the origins of cryptocurrencies, we will talk more extensively about the struggle for freedom and anarchist ideas, so it is important at this point to address this topic.

Liberalism

This philosophy strives for maximum freedom, including personal, economic, religious, and political. It expresses opposition to state power and authority. The goal of classical liberals was individual freedom, including related areas. They demanded the reduction of taxes, regulations, and privileges. They rejected tariffs, while advocating for the freedom of production, competition, and bartering. Land, labor, and capital were to be excluded from the influence of the state, while personal liberties were to be protected from the arbitrariness of ruling groups. They sought peace. The army was to be replaced by a voluntary militia that would deal only with defense. Liberals saw religion as the source of wars, so they wanted to separate it from the state to reduce the possibilities of war funding. The subject of separating the church was only one of many proposed separations from the state.

In essence, they wanted to separate almost everything from the state including the economy, the press, the land, and the army. The state was to be extremely small with a low, almost negligible budget.

Libertarianism

This philosophy is based on the ideas of liberalism. Around the 18th century, several central themes concerning power were developed. The first theme is that power is infinitely corrupting; it is an evil, but at the same time an evil necessity. The second theme is that power must be limited to the minimum consistent with the need to maintain social order.

Distrust of the central government began to appear in various documents defining the powers of governments. These documents, dating from the 18th century, were influenced by the birth of democracy in the United States and contained safeguards against abuses of power. Examples include the establishment of constitutions; the creation of charters of rights and liberties; the tying of monetary policy to the gold standard; separation of powers; strengthening the independence of the courts; limiting the use of coercion; and collective control over the executive, legislative, and foreign policy. In the mid-twentieth century, the term libertarianism was extended by some authors to include some right-wing movements, such as anarcho-capitalism.

Anarcho-capitalism

Anarcho-capitalism is a political and economic movement related to the ideas of libertarianism. This movement seeks the complete abolition of the state. They believe that the state monopoly in particular areas, including property, should be replaced by an unregulated free market. They envision a system where all services, including those traditionally managed by the state such as security and legal systems, would be operated by private entities competing in an open market. Some people believe that anarchists are similar to terrorists. However, the opposite is true. There could not be a more stark difference between the principles of anarchism and the actions of terrorists. Anarchists fundamentally reject any form of violence or coercion, both in society and in the family. Coercion from a position of power is seen as an obstacle to human freedom.

Anarchism is a political ideology based on both libertarian and socialist ideas. It rejects social, economic, and political hierarchies and other forms of domination of man over man, such as through religious beliefs, racism, genderism, and ageism. Anarchists reject political power and centralization. They seek to limit and replace imposed state power with voluntary or commercial structures.

Liberalism vs. anarcho-capitalism

Liberalism puts individual freedom first. Everyone should be guaranteed the right to life, liberty, and property. The free market is a place where the interests of individuals clash, and the operation of the market then leads to the fulfillment of their personal interests. Liberals, however, give partial importance to the state. In their view, the state should be the guarantor of fundamental rights. This is where the two diverge. Anarcho-capitalists seek the complete abolition of the state and reject any form of state intervention and coercion. They believe that all the competences of the state can be taken over by specialized groups that can operate on market principles. The common starting point for both philosophies is individual freedom and the guarantee of individual rights.

THE STATE AND ECONOMICS

The extent to which the state should intervene in the management of economic events in society is addressed by several economic theories and trends. Related, it is important to understand what cryptocurrencies are trying to achieve, especially in terms of the direction of state economies within the current mainstream.

The battle of ideas: Keynesianism vs. the Austrian School

The mainstream is the current economic view and direction that is taught by most universities around the world. It currently consists of two schools of thought: the first is based on neoclassicism, while the second is based on Keynesianism. Although the Austrian School of Economics is not part of the mainstream, it is an important opposing and alternative current to Keynesianism.

Neoclassical school (20th century)

In some respects this school of thought builds on classical economics as well as introducing new ideas and views. It focuses on decision-making about goods, output, and income distribution in markets through supply and demand.

The main point of Keynesianism is that the effect of targeted central bank intervention can be positive for the economy. In contrast, adherents of the Austrian School argue that the effects of virtually all central bank interventions and measures are always negative for the economy and markets in the long run.

Keynesianism

John Maynard Keynes (June 5, 1883–April 21, 1946) was an English economist, professor at Cambridge University, and Governor of the Bank of England. He was the founder of Keynesianism and believed that government intervention in the economy was positive. Based on this idea, the Great Depression was resolved in the 1930s in the USA and England. It paved the way for what is known in current times as quantitative easing. Its success is seen by proponents as an argument that the principles of classical economics have been overcome. However, the promotion of public borrowing had and still has many opponents.

Keynesian economists generally argue that because aggregate demand is volatile and unstable, market economies often experience inefficient macroeconomic outcomes in the form of economic recession (when demand is low) and inflation (when demand is high). These can be mitigated by economic policy responses, for example monetary policy measures by the central bank, and fiscal policy measures by the government, which can help stabilize output over the business cycle. Keynesian economists generally advocate a managed market economy—predominantly in the private sector, but with active government intervention during recessions and depressions.

Keynesian economics is an economic movement that recognizes active state intervention in the public economy. Keynesians admit government intervention in the natural mechanisms of the free market. Their main ideas are lofty and advocate the welfare of society. Many respected economists, however, do not share their views and regard this current mainstream as a path to the abyss.

Which one is right? What gives Keynesians certainty? Could it be that the others are right after all?

John F. Nash, Jr., a Nobel Prize-winning economist more commonly known as John Nash, said this about Keynesianism in his lectures: "Keynesians favor the existence of a manipulative state-run central bank and Treasury establishment that seeks to achieve economic welfare goals with relatively little regard for the long-term quality of the national currency. Under the guise of high and noble goals of general welfare, they have only made it easier for governments to print money."

At the moment, central banks have some independence from the state. This independence is questionable because the top officials of the central banks are appointed by the political apparatus. If central bank officials succumb to political pressures, their monetary policy will usually fail. The quality and independence of a central bank can be judged by whether it can achieve its objectives, such as the target inflation rate.

Modern monetary theory based on Keynesianism

In this case, some modern economists go much further. This economic theory has been growing in recent years and can be very dangerous. The focus is on enhancing the state's involvement in currency issuance. Indeed, the main idea of modern monetary theory is the direct and absolute power of the government to control the creation of new money. At the same time, this theory says that the state can create unlimited debt because it cannot go bankrupt while using its own currency. The state actively controls the economy through taxes, budget policy, and inflation. Monetary policy is passive, and the central bank serves only as a conduit for money and oversees the issuance of money. The state can create as much money as it sees fit. This approach logically opens the way to even greater waste and the useless expenditure of easily acquired resources.

It's remarkable how people are still fascinated when someone throws their money away.

This theory has already failed tragically in many countries where it has caused hyperinflation. For the strong currencies of more advanced economies—or even for the US dollar, which is also the most widely used reserve currency—this type of monetary policy might work for a while. However, no one can say for how long. All of these theories are mere speculation, untested by history. Members of the mainstream advocate that they will be right only until the whole economy, subsidized by constant injections of money, collapses. So we can all only hope that this truth of theirs will last for many years to come.

So this is the proverbial light at the end of the tunnel that we have been chasing all this time?

Austrian School of Economics

This is an economic movement that originated in the 19th century. The main representatives were Austrians Carl Menger, Friedrich von Wieser, and Eugen von Böhm-Bawerk. Today, the Austrian School of Economics is active in many countries around the world and is far from being limited to economics. By studying human behavior and the nature of the world in which this behavior takes place, its representatives delve into philosophy, ethics, and law. In terms of their views, they are usually classical liberalism or libertarianism. Other prominent and well-known representatives are Ludwig von Mises and his students Friedrich August von Hayek, Murray N. Rothbard, Israel Kirzner, and Hans Hermann Hoppe. In 1974, Friedrich August von Hayek was awarded the Nobel Prize in Economics. The Austrian School of Economics is a coherent school of thought in the social sciences. It is currently an alternative and opponent to the mainstream of economics, which is based on the ideas of Keynesianism.

A brief summary of the main economic ideas as conceived by Austrian School economists:

- They take the view that the value of a product is not determined by any predetermined characteristic or the amount of labor required to create the product. It depends on the individual's need at the time and the scarcity of the product. However, each individual may recognize different needs and attribute a different value to them.

- They consider space and time to be important resources on which they place great emphasis.

- They recognize market pricing, which determines the value of the product. They consider the market as a place for settling the needs of all participants—such as consumers, producers, investors, and traders.

- They consider the pricing system to be an important mechanism for obtaining information. Market participants can then use this information to direct their actions to achieve the most advantageous use of available resources. In doing so, they will also best satisfy the needs of the market and, consequently, best satisfy the needs of individual participants.

- They warn that government interference in the market can undermine the proper functioning of market mechanisms, cripple their efficiency, and waste scarce resources. Under government management of the economy (socialism), the main problem lies in the paralysis of natural market mechanisms. Consequently, society gradually declines, wasting previously accumulated capital and leading to poverty.

- They point out that in a regulated environment, officials do not have the necessary information and, therefore, cannot make the right decisions.

- They place a strong emphasis on the actions of the individual and argue that only individuals—not societies and institutions—have specific needs and seek to meet them.

- They recognize market principles in the behavior of individuals as the only correct ones, because the market behavior of companies and institutions then depends on them.

- In their conception, the amount of interest is the valuation of postponing needs until later. They regard it as very important information in a market environment without government intervention. In other words, interest can also be seen as the expected value difference between present and future consumption of goods.

- They point to the fact that money originated as a market product and was only later monopolized by the state. They consider it necessary to return money to its market value.

- They note that institutions such as law, morality, business practices, and language develop and mature through the evolutionary process of the independent actions of thousands of motivated individuals. Interference by the state in this natural evolution usually causes serious consequential problems.

- According to the Austrian School of Economics, the state has two main problems when it controls or regulates any part of the economy. These problems are:
  - the problem of economic calculation.
  - the problem of motivation of politicians and officials.

Austrian School of Economics: two main problems of the state in managing or regulating some part of the economy

The problem of economic calculation

The civil servant or government lacks information mediated by market price. Politicians and officials do not have the ability to know how to set appropriate prices for individual resources, nor do they know how to properly evaluate the scarcity factors they are working with in a given environment. This is why communist countries and state-dominated industries are backward, unproductive, and fail in basic principles.

The problem of motivation of politicians and officials

These are individuals with their own motivations and needs. They are usually not directly responsible for their actions and decisions, and there are usually no consequences for wrong decisions. Their mistakes are rarely reflected in their tenure in office. They may hide behind collective decision-making and create excuses for circumstances. They act with the aim of making dubious short-term gains in the form of votes for the next election.

Yes, of course, free health care, free Bingo, and free all-you-can-eat buffets for everyone.
If I understand correctly, there's going to be an election?

They abuse decision-making opportunities for personal gain and to obtain bribes. Their fundamental motivation, which is important for achieving the above objectives, is to stay in power for as long as possible, whatever the cost. They compete for well-paid positions or future well-paid positions.

I am glad, gentlemen, that we have agreed on a way to cooperate within our party.

The Austrian School of Economics and political ideas

The economists of the Austrian school of Economics, in their realistic analysis of human behavior from an economic perspective, also arrived at political questions which they tried to resolve through a philosophical approach.

- They are of the opinion that government officials and politicians can never lead a country's economy to prosperity.

- They identify with liberal thought and have supported this philosophical trend with their arguments.

- They note that neither the state nor state-established institutions can effectively manage economic processes from a political level.

- Neither politicians nor government officials are interested in the laborious pursuit of long-term goals. They are more comfortable pushing often pointless or uneconomic projects that serve to fulfill their ambitions and populist election promises.

- Politicians are wasting resources and previously accumulated capital. If they consume this capital, they do not hesitate to go into debt and squander money that will have to be repaid by future generations.

- Austrian School economists are of the opinion that the influence of politicians in economic areas should be excluded or kept to an absolute minimum.

We have managed to find billions more to implement our pre-election promises. As always, they have been resting pointlessly in the pockets of the taxpayer.

Bitcoin and the Austrian School of Economics

Various economists around the world independently arrived at similar insights and views as those held by adherents of the Austrian School of Economics. They realized the unreality of freeing fiat currencies from the influence of state policies. They tried to find and propose various alternatives to existing money. One of them was John Nash, an American mathematician and economist who won the Nobel Prize in Economics in 1994. His lecture clearly summarizes everything we have discussed so far. There has been speculation that Nash could be the inventor of Bitcoin. That is the main reason I have included his work in this book. His biography is discussed in more detail in Book Two.

Lecture by John F. Nash, Jr.

"Ideal Money and Asymptotically Ideal Money"

The lecture was written in 1997, when Nash gave a series of lectures in Italy as part of the European School of Economics. Subsequently, he lectured on the topic, with some modifications, at several universities in the USA, as well as in Greece, China, and India. Nash also said that after consulting with some economists at Princeton, he learned about the work of Friedrich von Hayek—an important representative of the Austrian School of Economics. He noted that his personal thinking was quite parallel to Hayek's, both in relation to money and to his view of the functions of the authorities who are the creators of currencies.

Allow me to briefly summarize the main ideas of his work:

Money

Nash considers money to be a "special commodity or medium" that we should think of as a technology. He argues that when viewed rationally, money should have the function of a yardstick, "which is psychologically difficult." It should be comparable to units such as the watt, the hour, or the degree of temperature. He regards money as a tool for the efficient transfer of utility, thus making money itself a utility. He believes that a new kind of money should be created on the basis of optimal standards, but the proposed basis would not be a link to gold. This ideal money should be completely free from inflation. At the same time, however, he says: "It seems very likely that, although this scheme for arranging a system of money with ideal characteristics would work well, it would, on the other hand, be politically difficult to bring about the realization of such a system."

The quality of money

From country to country, the quality of money varies. It should be seen as a public service and its quality assessed in terms of the quality of service of the supplier (the state). The public should learn to demand better quality money in view of the fact that this quality is directly dependent on the way the national currency is managed. Nash states: "People cannot care whether the future quality of the currency is actually assured or whether it depends instead on the shifting sands of political decisions or on the possibly arbitrary actions of bureaucratic officials." Using the euro as an example, he notes that, "the constitutional structure of the body behind the euro is paper money in the sense that nothing is really guaranteed in terms of the value of the euro. However, this is typical of all currencies in use in the world today." In the context of global competition between currencies, people should have an alternative choice of where to put their savings. Nash believes that comparing currencies (domestic price index values) internationally could lead to pressure for good quality currencies and, consequently, less inflationary depreciation.

Money, utility, and game theory

In the game theory studied and applied by economists, the concept of utility is an essential fundamental. At the same time, however, it is also a mathematical concept. In the study of cooperative games—which in economic terminology include mergers and acquisitions as well as cartel formation—two basic classifications seem appropriate:

     1. Games with transferable utility (TU)
     2. Games without transferable utility (NTU)

In practical reality, it is usually money that leads to the existence of a game of type 1 rather than type 2.

Money is the lubricant that enables the efficient transfer of utility. When games can shift from type 2 to type 1, all players benefit on average, regardless of the expected outcome. Money's effectiveness in transferring benefits aligns with the concept of games with transferable utility, which is highly valued in game theory analyses.

Nash defines Keynesianism as a "school of thought" that emerged during the 1929 world economic crisis. He notes that Keynesians favor the existence of "a manipulative state-run central bank and Treasury establishment that would constantly strive to achieve economic welfare goals with relatively little regard for the long-term quality of the nation's currency." The irresponsible creation of new money can lead to the displacement of good money by bad money (people tend to spend bad money earlier and retain good money due to its higher utility or value). Various interest groups, especially Keynesians, introduce the ideology that "less is more," or that that "bad money is better than good money." He notes that "Keynesians always implicitly argue that good managers can do beneficial things when they work with the treasury and the central bank, and that it is neither necessary nor appropriate for citizens (the consumers of the currency supplied by the state) to really understand exactly what managers do and how it affects the state of their wallets." He likens Keynesianism to the dictatorship of the Bolshevik communists, who claimed to provide a much better life than bourgeois democracy. He sees similarities in both systems "because of the promotion of a certain opacity regarding the functions of government as perceived by citizens. And both can also be said to tend to think in terms of government agencies operating in a benevolent way, but which is beyond the understanding of the citizens of the state." He accuses them of "facilitating governments to print money under the pretext of high and noble goals of general welfare."

Lecture by John F. Nash, Jr. "Ideal Money and Asymptotically Ideal Money"

The quality of money and its value

There have been many different currencies in the world throughout history, and this is still true today. However, the quality of these currencies is not the same. The comparison of the quality of different currencies is currently determined by the international exchange rate. In general, the value of a currency is determined by its quality. The quality of a currency is taken care of by a designated custodian. In the past, this was usually the ruler. Today, in most countries, this function has been taken over by central banks. The quality of money depends on the state or, more specifically, on the central bank established by the state.

However, the state and civil servants rarely provide a good service. Unfortunately, this is also the case in the field of money. The ideal solution would be private money that can compete fairly with state currencies, giving people the freedom to choose the currency they prefer. However, the state prohibits any competition, and only state money is legally accepted. Bitcoin, as a form of non-state money, offers a promising alternative to traditional state currencies. Since bitcoin cannot be shut down and lacks a central custodian susceptible to shutdown, it operates independently of legal recognition. What gives it value is whether people voluntarily choose to use it alongside state currency.

So, what is the value of money? As we have already suggested, the fundamental use value of money, based on fictions and abstractions, is close to zero, regardless of whether it is public or private. State currencies are favored because their partial value is already assured by the fact that all citizens in a given territory must use them out of compulsion. However, in the context of fair competition, the only thing that counts is how well the money performs its functions. On that basis, it then becomes useful by generating utility and acquires its value. The value of a currency is significantly influenced by factors such as its backing, level of inflation, and whether its manager (the service provider) prioritizes monetary policy or is influenced by political decisions. Subsequently, the market determines the final value of the currency. What is important here is how many participants are interested in using the currency—or at least in buying it for their reserves or making international monetary transactions with it. The exchange rate against other currencies determines the real value of a currency in the international market. However, in an inflationary environment, money tends to lose its purchasing power over time. As a result, its holders are forced to invest or spend it in order not to face this unpleasant reality.

Money has to be circulated to keep it from losing value, so I'm doing my part by circulating it in my bloodstream.

Let's briefly summarize what determines the quality and value of money. Of course, the functions and characteristics of money are key, as previously discussed on page 28:

- **Trust:** Trust in the currency and the institutions that issue it is essential. If people trust a currency, they are willing to use it for transactions and as a store of value.

- **Stability:** The stability of the value of money is important for its use as a unit of account and the preservation of value. Inflation and deflation can affect the value of money as well as confidence in it.

- **Acceptance and functioning in international trade:** Money must be widely accepted as payment for goods and services. The ability of a currency to function as a medium of exchange in international trade can significantly affect its value and quality.

- **Limited supply:** A limited supply of money helps maintain its value; unlimited or uncontrolled issuance of money can lead to inflation and depreciation.

- **Technological innovation:** Technological innovations—such as digital currency or decentralized blockchain—can improve the characteristics of money and increase its value and quality.

THE EVOLUTION OF THE STATE, PART II: THE LAST 250 YEARS IN PERSPECTIVE

The goal of evolution is transformation in order to adapt to external influences and new realities. With the benefit of hindsight, evolutionary development can be seen as a necessity for survival, but in some cases also as a way to acquire new possibilities and to evolve forward. Not every evolutionary direction is successful. There are also blind branches that prove to be dysfunctional and, for that reason, extinction can occur. The way forward is lined with successes and mistakes. Humanity must hope that it will eventually overcome all the pitfalls, learn from previous mistakes, and not reach a dead end.

JOURNEY TO PARADISE

Before 1800, there were about one billion people in the world, but almost 90% of them faced extreme poverty. Society has long been undergoing an evolution in law, morality, business practice, and language. However, over the last 250 years of human evolution, there has been an increase in human prosperity and evolution has taken a huge leap forward.

The main driving force behind this massive development was the global influence of the liberal movement, reinforced by the birth of a new democracy on the American continent.

- American War of Independence (1775–1783)
- Great French Revolution (1789–1799)
- Industrial Revolution (ca. 1760–1840)

Nations then gradually lost power over key institutions such as the church, media, courts, manufacturing, and trade. The freedom gained led to a significant increase in the potential for open human minds, division of labor, specialization, technological progress, and innovation. Major transformations began to take place in agriculture, manufacturing, mining, transportation, trade, and finance. A paradise on earth—a period of general prosperity—was dawning. Many people were much better off than before. The rule of law began to strengthen and human life obtained value. Today, there are around eight billion people on Earth, and only about 10% of the population faces extreme poverty.

WALLS IN PARADISE

As it happens in the real world, nothing is black and white. By unshackling themselves from the gold standard, politicians have gained the opportunity to back projects and social programs that would have been beyond their means in a market capitalist system without fiat money. Global socialization is occurring.

> "The state is a great fiction by which everyone tries to live at the expense of everyone else."
>
> —Frédéric Bastiat, French political economist

Unfortunately, there are repeated instances in history where humanity takes steps backwards. It is not always possible to maintain the progress, freedom, prosperity, and democracy that have been achieved. It is like the stock market: the price goes down and up. What is important, however, is that it rises in the long run.

What was it like to live under totalitarianism?
I'd like to be wrong, but I think you'll experience it too one day.

GLOBAL SOCIALIZATION AND MONETARY SOCIALISM

In a market democracy based on the gold standard, politicians could only spend money equal to the amount they could raise through taxes or borrow through bonds issued and sold on the open market. In the current system, where the central bank allows the government to issue any amount of bonds that would not be saleable on the open market, a situation arises where governments have an unlimited amount of money at their disposal. At that point, there is nothing to prevent politicians from accumulating debt for future generations to finance the programs they are using to gain voter support. These are usually socially vulnerable groups whose votes can significantly influence electoral outcomes. People are beginning to rely on the state and politicians are devising programs that are payable to socialist regimes.

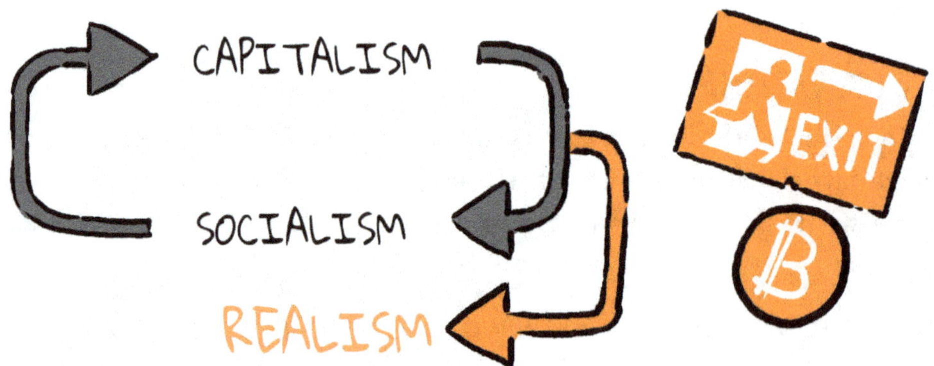

Global socialization and monetary socialism makes it possible to cover a significant percentage of expenditure without the government having to resort to unpopular tax increases. This approach undermines the accountability of public officials to taxpayers. State budgets are being significantly increased without regard to future consequences. It enables the financing of wars, conflicts, and questionable programs, which are frequently overpriced, pointless, megalomaniacal, or not aligned with the current needs of society. Modern socialism allows irresponsible political representation to score short-term political points, after which they may pursue their own personal objectives.

Quantitative easing causes inflation. The increase in social programs is a failure of market principles. The state then tries to regulate the faltering markets. Throughout history, numerous cases have demonstrated the failure of attempts to centrally manage the economy, and this trend continues to persist today.

THE EVOLUTION OF THE STATE IN THE COMING DECADES

Let us try to predict in which direction the evolution of states, which we analyzed at the beginning of this chapter, might continue. If the liberal trend of the last 250 years continues, the role of the state is likely to be further weakened. We are likely to see additional separation of sectors that the state has taken over in the interest of society, but has not been able to effectively develop or finance—like health, education, and pensions. Some of these separations are already partly rooted in the open market environment. Products for improved education, medical care, and retirement savings will be commonly offered on the market. People will stop relying on the state and their quality of life will depend on their willingness to work. Social programs will be transparent, precisely targeted, and probably more community-based. If this does not happen, humanity will spin in a vicious circle between dysfunctional socialism and cruel capitalism. The fact remains that some individuals are already moving away from relying on the state and are trying to provide for themselves by putting off their needs until later through saving, investing, and even community or family care.

I don't really believe in retirement plans.
That's why I set up one here, and another one over there.

The market arrangement is the only conceivable arrangement compatible with prosperity. For these separations to have a real chance of becoming independent, we need to stop monetary socialism and the global socialization arising from the great influx of new fiat money. However, a truly free market needs market-created independent money. This money could be bitcoin, for example, but we will say more about that in Book Two.

The separation of state and money would be a meaningful next step in the evolution of society. Imagine how many of the current problems could be solved by good quality market-based non-state money.

- Countries could not create new money arbitrariliy, which would otherwise reduce the value of the existing currency.

- At the same time, they could not finance programs that lacked significance or purpose. They would need to prioritize only the important and meaningful ones.

- Good works that are deferred or imposed would not lose their value.

- Inflation would ease to a halt.

- Simultaneously, there would be a reduction in wars.

- It would limit the widening of social inequalities caused by the uneven distribution of newly-created money between the richest few thousand people and the rest of the planet.

- Pension, health, and education reforms would be provided by the state only at a basic level. Super-structures would be handled on a market basis by commercial entities.

- There would be greater social justice and people would be more motivated to work.

- The shortage of housing would be reduced because people would not be forced to put their good deeds in real estate, but could put them into good quality money where their value would be preserved for the long term.

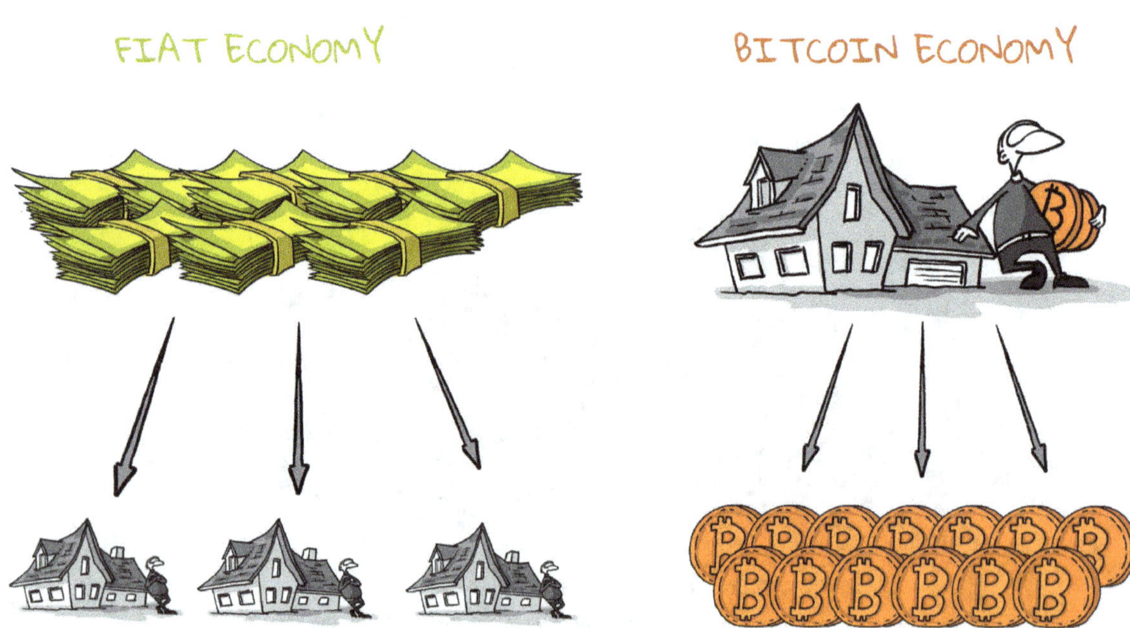

It seems that tax reform would be necessary. State taxes would be reduced, and a portion of the money would then be allocated to increase the budgets of local authorities. This way, society can exercise better control over the management of representatives and officials. The rest of the taxes would be left to the citizens, who would provide for themselves the expansion of the basic areas provided by the state. There would be a much more efficient use of tax funds than is the case today. At the same time, the whole system would be fairer for citizens who work: they would have more money left over, and everyone would have more incentive to work and plan for their future. Of course, the motivation of politicians would also need to be reformed.

An economy and society that operates on non-state money will take another important step towards overall prosperity.

An independent economy operating on a cryptocurrency platform is already emerging. The crypto industry is undoubtedly one of the fastest growing industries today. However, the widespread adoption of cryptocurrencies in society still has a long way to go.

THE EVOLUTION OF THE STATE, PART III: THE NEXT 100 YEARS

Let's take a moment to peer into our crystal ball and speculate on the possible future in the development of the state. The further evolution of humanity is dealt with, among other things, by the philosophical trend of **transhumanism** and its other currents such as **extropianism** and **singularitarianism**.

Transhumanism includes streams such as abolitionism, extropianism, immortality, postgenderism, singularitarianism, and technogaianism. It is a philosophical trend according to which humanity can and should strive to reach a higher physical, spiritual and social level. It promotes research in areas such as life extension; cryonics; nanotechnology; physical and mental enhancement; uploading human consciousness into computers; and megalomaniacal engineering. Transhumanist thinkers study the potential benefits and dangers of emerging technologies that could overcome basic human limitations. They are equally concerned with the ethical constraints on the use of these technologies. The most common transhumanist thesis is that human beings will eventually evolve into beings with abilities so advanced from the current state that they merit the label posthuman.

Extropianism is one of the currents of transhumanism. Extropians seek the intelligent use of technology to overcome the genetic, psychological, cultural, and neurological barriers that prevent unlimited progress and the permanent continuation of life and liberty. They desire to extend their lives to an almost immortal state and to exist in a world where artificial intelligence and robotics will make work meaningless. The purpose of one's own life is to increase the overall happiness of all creatures on Earth through cooperation. Extropians often foresee a future where unlimited lifespans are achievable through advancements in biomedical technology or mind uploading. They anticipate that individuals whose bodies or brains have been preserved through cryonics could be revived in this scenario.

Singularitarianism is another stream of transhumanism. Representatives of this stream are convinced that within a few years we will have the technical means to create beings with superhuman intelligence. They believe that computers can be developed that will have both consciousness and superhuman intelligence.

Science can achieve this breakthrough in several ways:

- Large-scale computer networks and their users can wake up as beings with superhuman intelligence.

- The human-computer connection may become so tight that users may be regarded as creatures of superhuman intelligence.

- Biology can provide the means to increase natural human intelligence.

Shortly after the onset of the singularity, the human era is predicted to come to an end. Proponents of this idea ponder whether it is possible to prevent this evolution. If not, they contemplate the potential for controlling the course of events to ensure human survival. These considerations may yield some possible answers, but could also bring about additional dangers.

One of the possible consequences of the development of transhumanism and its other currents may be a change in our definition of what it means to be human. If technology develops at the rate that some transhumanists expect, it may be that humans will be able to overcome some of the fundamental limits that have defined our human existence in the past. For example, if we were able to transfer our consciousness into an artificial body, we could become essentially undead. If we could improve our cognitive abilities through implants or genetic modification, we could become far more intelligent than we are today. Changing the definition of what it means to be human could have implications for many areas of our lives, including religion, ethics, and law. It could lead to new discussions about what a human person is and what our basic rights and duties are. It could also have implications for our social and interpersonal relationships.

Another possible consequence of the development of transhumanism and its other currents may be the division of society between those who have access to technology and those who do not. If technologies are very expensive, this could lead to the creation of an elite class of people who would have access to the latest technologies, while others would be excluded. New types of inequality and social tensions could arise. The subsequent evolution of humanity and social groupings will certainly bring many opportunities and challenges, but also many risks and pitfalls.

On page 97, we discussed the five steps in the evolution of the state. The additional points that follow serve as speculation about how the evolution of the state might proceed.

6. **A decentralized state:** It is offered as the next possible evolutionary stage of the state, when the state is freed from institutions and projects that should function independently and in a market-based manner. The state will focus only on core functions in terms of property protection and law enforcement. It will provide the military, intelligence services, federal police, and a top-level judiciary at the central level. It will also guarantee basic levels of health care, education, and social services. All other functions will be taken over by commercial entities or territorial administrative units in the form of districts, cities, and villages. Territorial units will gain certain state competences and will have the authority to set taxes and rules within their own territory based on their own decisions. Territorial units will compete with each other, and every citizen will be free to choose in which territory and under which laws or rules they will live. The tax burden set in a particular region will correspond to the guarantees that citizens will have. Based on the guarantees and their preferred level of taxes, individuals will decide in which territorial unit they want to live or establish these guarantees according to their own preferences on a commercial basis. The financing of the state and public budgets will be done only by collecting taxes and selling bonds on the open market. In this process, there will be no buyers who can create their own money and then buy the bonds. Citizens will vote using tokens they receive based on the taxes they pay or the benefits they contribute to society. Successful entrepreneurs will have the option to voluntarily subsidize specific, meaningful projects that benefit society, thus gaining greater influence over the governance of the state. More rationality will be brought to government programs and they will be responsive to real opportunities and needs. There will be a further increase in prosperity based on decentralized, non-inflationary money. There will be far fewer military conflicts because the resources to finance them will not simply be created out of nothing.

7. **Artificial Intelligence, the Matrix, Decentraland, and the Metaverse:** These are virtual worlds where people could connect at a level higher than current social networks permit. Human productivity in relation to reliable non-state money will continue to grow. It will be driven by automation, robotics, and artificial intelligence. Real jobs will start to decline. Humanity will willingly segregate into groups, such as research, operations, or non-engaged, depending on their willingness to participate in meeting society's needs. Over time, the non-engaged group will likely expand due to increased productivity and wealth. The non-engaged individuals are not necessarily unwilling to

work, but there might not be a suitable job available for them within the organization. As a result, they will receive compensation as a form of overproduction, indicating that society cannot provide them with employment opportunities. In a sense, it will be a similar model to farmers getting paid for leaving their fields uncultivated.

Humanity and the real world will gradually begin to move into Metaverse models. Each citizen will decide what community and what part of the Metaverse they want to live in and contribute to building it. In these models it will be possible to fully test the anarcho-capitalist perception of society. In order to prolong life, man will make extensive use of artificial organs. With the rise of artificial intelligence, there will be a gradual blending of the cybernetic and biological worlds. It is difficult to say whether man or artificial intelligence will have the upper hand. People will have two choices: they can either abandon their physical bodies and needs, uploading their consciousness to the cloud to exist as part of a higher collective consciousness, or they can entirely entrust the evolutionary process to artificial intelligence and cybernetization, where human existence would become meaningless. This new evolutionary stage will then act pragmatically, without emotions and ulterior motives. It will draw on the experience and knowledge accumulated by humanity over thousands of years of its existence. The most important difference will be that it will not keep repeating the mistakes from which humanity has failed to learn. Artificial intelligence does not forget and will evaluate repeated failures as reality.

I've been diagnosed with severe forgetfulness.

We talked about the fact that people cannot learn from history and keep repeating the same mistakes. This principle applies not only to monetary policy but also to many other areas, ranging from war conflicts to the subtle errors that popular proverbs attempt to illustrate. We are all familiar with the proverbs "Lies have short legs," "Pride goes before a fall," "He who digs another man's hole falls into it himself," "No work, no cake," "He who saves has three," and "Easily gained, easily lost," along with many others. Previous generations tried to pass on experience and warn their successors against repeating mistakes with proverbs, fables, literature, and historical records. Perhaps every person has encountered these experiences and learned these lessons in some form. Artificial intelligence gives repeated mistakes a higher importance and credibility. It treats them as simple facts and avoids them. Ultimately, this means that AI will no longer allow these mistakes in areas it controls. However, man often likes to forget and tells himself that the lesson does not apply to him, or that this time it will be different. Previous generations have commented on this attitude with the saying "To whom there is no counsel, there is no help."

FOLLOW-ON REMARKS

Please take this attempt at "divination," especially point 7, with some lightheartedness and perspective. But also, take time to think for yourself about the developments that await humanity. Keep in mind, however, that there is always a trade-off: one good deed for another. The world is not a perpetual motion machine, nor is it possible to operate on the basis of money created out of nothing. Politicians who think only of short-term goals and their own benefit cannot lead the country to prosperity. Politicians should be representative of the nation, have strong morals, and refined manners. They should think of the interests of the citizens first and foremost and support only projects that bring benefits. They should also address economic stability from a long-term perspective and encourage citizens to save and protect their savings. Humanity can lead a good life, but to achieve a better life, it must be prepared to invest significant effort and rely on genuine economic processes. Unfortunately, we are partly reliant on the decisions of our political leaders to navigate this path. Their moral failures and unprofessional decisions can then lead to national decline and economic crisis. This issue is eloquently encapsulated in a roughly 100-year-old quote by Tomáš Baťa, a celebrated Czech entrepreneur, who addresses moral and ethical poverty. Not only politicians should take this message from the past to heart.

> The cause of the crisis is moral misery. The turning point of the economic crisis? I don't believe in any turning points per se. What we used to call economic crisis is another name for moral misery. Moral misery is the cause, economic decline is the effect. There are many people in our country who believe that economic decline can be remedied by money. I dread the consequence of this error. In the position we are in, we do not need any ingenious turns and combinations. We need moral positions on people, on work and on public property. Not to support bankrupts, not to run up debts, not to throw away values for nothing, not to extort workers, to do what lifted us out of post-war misery. Work and save and make work and saving more profitable, more desirable and more honest than idleness and waste. You are right, we need to overcome the crisis of confidence. But it cannot be overcome by technical interventions, financial and credit interventions. Trust is a personal matter and trust can only be restored by moral considerations and personal example.

WEALTH DISPARITIES: THE WIDENING GAP

The world's wealth is something that is intrinsically linked to money; as such, it deserves some attention in this book. The influx of new money and its uneven distribution are causing social inequalities to widen between the richest few thousand people and the rest of the planet. Let's examine the facts to gain a clearer understanding.

Data source: Credit Suisse. *Global Wealth Report* (2010 – current)

WHAT IS WORLD WEALTH?

World wealth is calculated as the total value of assets minus liabilities. In simpler terms, it represents the net value of assets after deducting debts. In the developing world, this situation is less of a concern. However, in developed countries, a substantial portion of the population may belong to the poorest category despite having significant assets, often offset by substantial debts. Despite this, their overall living conditions might not be unfavorable. World wealth is measured based on households per adult and excludes national wealth. Companies are included in this measurement through individuals owning shares.

The world's wealth is valued in fiat currencies—most often in US dollars. Its price is continuously increasing, primarily due to the depreciation of fiat currencies, resulting in higher prices for real estate, stocks, commodities, and other assets. The world's richest people—who also have access to new money first—are able to move more of the world's wealth into their possession. The others, on the other hand, are losing wealth. The rich are getting richer faster than before, while others are more or less getting poorer as a result of inflation and the depreciation of world currencies.

> **Approximately 300 years later, we can use concrete figures to confirm the Cantillon effect— especially in relation to quantitative easing.**

The widening gap in the unequal distribution of the world's wealth among its citizens is a confirmation of this effect. The first beneficiaries of the newly-created money—such as bankers and the wealthy—benefit from investments and asset purchases made prior to a rise in prices. Meanwhile, others face higher prices and a decline in the purchasing power of their savings without direct access to these new sources of finance.

The impact of the Cantillon Effect on the wealth gap between groups can be further amplified if wealthy individuals are able to use financial instruments such as investments where they can further appreciate their wealth—an opportunity not always available to the middle class and poor.

The following figure shows the dependence of the growth of world wealth on the ever-increasing money supply (purple curve). It also shows that the wealth of a small number of millionaires (gray and yellow) is growing faster than that of the middle class and poor (blue and orange)

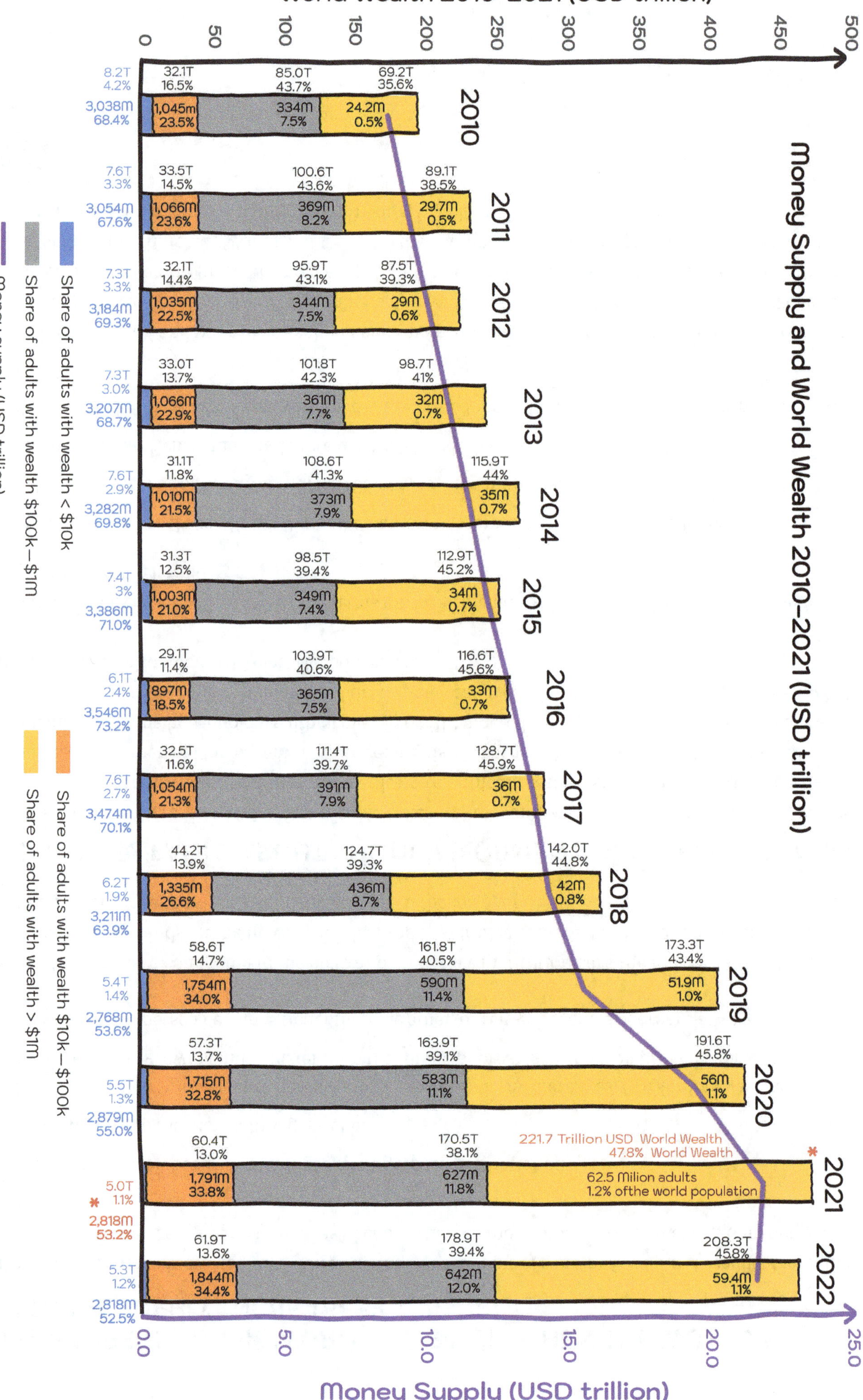

Money Supply and World Wealth 2010-2021 (USD trillion)
World Wealth 2010-2021 (USD trillion)
Money Supply (USD trillion)

Share of adults with wealth < $10k
Share of adults with wealth $100k—$1m
Money supply (USD trillion)
Share of adults with wealth $10k—$100k
Share of adults with wealth > $1m

2010
8.2T 4.2%
32.1T 16.5%
85.0T 43.7%
69.2T 35.6%
3,038m 68.4%
1,045m 23.5%
334M 7.5%
24.2M 0.5%

2011
7.6T 3.3%
33.5T 14.5%
100.6T 43.6%
89.1T 38.5%
3,054m 67.6%
1,066M 23.6%
369M 8.2%
29.7M 0.5%

2012
7.3T 3.3%
32.1T 14.4%
95.9T 43.1%
87.5T 39.3%
3,184m 69.3%
1,035m 22.5%
344M 7.5%
29M 0.6%

2013
7.3T 3.0%
33.0T 13.7%
101.8T 42.3%
98.7T 41%
3,207m 68.7%
1,066M 22.9%
361M 7.7%
32M 0.7%

2014
7.6T 2.9%
31.1T 11.8%
108.6T 41.3%
115.9T 44%
3,282m 69.8%
1,010M 21.5%
373M 7.9%
35M 0.7%

2015
7.4T 3%
31.3T 12.5%
98.5T 39.4%
112.9T 45.2%
3,386m 71.0%
1,003M 21.0%
349M 7.4%
34M 0.7%

2016
6.1T 2.4%
29.1T 11.4%
103.9T 40.6%
116.6T 45.6%
3,546m 73.2%
897M 18.5%
365M 7.5%
33M 0.7%

2017
7.6T 2.7%
32.5T 11.6%
111.4T 39.7%
128.7T 45.9%
3,474m 70.1%
1,054m 21.3%
391M 7.9%
36M 0.7%

2018
6.2T 1.9%
44.2T 13.9%
124.7T 39.3%
142.0T 44.8%
3,211m 63.9%
1,335m 26.6%
436M 8.7%
42M 0.8%

2019
5.4T 1.4%
58.6T 14.7%
161.8T 40.5%
173.3T 43.4%
2,768m 53.6%
1,754m 34.0%
590M 11.4%
51.9M 1.0%

2020
5.5T 1.3%
57.3T 13.7%
163.9T 39.1%
191.6T 45.8%
2,879m 55.0%
1,715m 32.8%
583M 11.1%
56M 1.1%

2021
* 5.0T 1.1%
60.4T 13.0%
170.5T 38.1%
221.7 Trillion USD World Wealth
47.8% World Wealth
* 2,818m 53.2%
1,791m 33.8%
627M 11.8%
62.5 Milion adults
1.2% of the world population

2022
5.3T 1.2%
61.9T 13.6%
178.9T 39.4%
208.3T 45.8%
2,818m 52.5%
1,844m 34.4%
642M 12.0%
59.4M 1.1%

* Let's use the example of 2021 to explain how to read this graph: in that year, 53.2% of the world's adult population owned only 1.1% of the world's wealth, whereas 1.2% of the world's population owned 47.8% of the world's wealth. The yellow portion explains what each number means.

WHAT HAPPENS TO THE WORLD'S WEALTH WHEN THE WORLD'S FINANCIAL SUPPLY INCREASES?

As an example, if someone creates 20% of new money, the use value of existing assets and products remains the same, but their price logically increases because there is more money in the market. In general, the following apply:

- It may seem that we are all seemingly getting richer and better off.

- Those who get to the money first get richer.

- The price of the world's wealth increases as the money supply increases. In a similar way, the wealth of the richest is growing much faster than that of the poorest (see chart on previous page).

- However, if one person becomes richer than the other, the latter becomes poorer relative to the former.

Those citizens that are connected to the state and monetary institutions are the most wealthy. They are the first to get their hands on the new money, leading to significant increases in class differences, which could potentially make the situation unsustainable in the long run.

INTERESTING FACTS ABOUT THE DEVELOPMENT OF WORLD WEALTH

The Swiss bank Credit Suisse, which faced bankruptcy in 2023 and was subsequently acquired by UBS with the support of the Swiss government, has dedicated significant resources over the years to analyze the growth and distribution of global wealth. The Credit Suisse Research Institute, which the bank supports, has been analyzing the household wealth of over five billion people worldwide for over twelve years and is undoubtedly the most comprehensive and up-to-date resource of its kind. It has published the *Global Wealth Report* annually since 2010 (see QR code on page 118).

Many organizations around the world draw on this material, including the UK NGO Oxfam, which published its *Inequality Report* in late 2019.

This report drew on the *Global Wealth Report 2019* and states, among other things, the following:

- In 2019, the world's billionaires—just 2,153 people—had more wealth than 4.6 billion people.

- The twenty-two richest men had more wealth than all the women in Africa.

- The richest 1% of people in the world had more than double the wealth of the remaining 6.9 billion people.

The gap between rich and poor has reached shocking proportions, warns Oxfam. Global economic inequality has spiraled out of control. The number of the world's billionaires has doubled in the last decade. "Our broken economies are lining the pockets of billionaires and big business at the expense of ordinary people," said Amitabh Behar, Oxfam's CEO. He further emphasized that the growing gap between rich and poor was caused by irresponsible governments, which must now come up with solutions.

Report on inequality:
Oxfam. *Time to care: Unpaid and underpaid care works and the global inequality crisis*

CHAPTER 4 SUMMARY

- The state is in a paradoxical situation when it comes to its citizens. It controls society by political means and uses coercive means to enforce its rules. At the same time, however, the political apparatus is trying to win the favor of the citizens. It uses a variety of means to do this, from false populist promises to impossible political goals.

- The state often buys the votes of the socially weaker or less-productive voters with money collected from the productive voters. The collection of taxes, although mandated by law, is an involuntary drain on the resources of some citizens. In this context, some anarcho-capitalists point to the legal definition which states that "misappropriation of another's property or value is theft."

  - Politicians are not incentivized to work responsibly in the interests of citizens in terms of long-term sustainability. They act only in the interest of their personal and short-term political goals. Staying in power for as long as possible is the main objective of most politicians. The unlimited creation of new money at the expense of increasing the national debt gives democratically elected politicians the opportunity to bribe and pamper voters with social models that are unsustainable in the long term. Society then claims ever greater benefits and begins to live at the expense of future generations.

  - Officials and politicians lack market-mediated information, failing to identify and set appropriate prices and allocations for individual resources. They fail to assess scarcity factors. Such an environment is a breeding ground for pervasive corruption in addition to incompetence.

- From this perspective, even democratic models of the state based on the principle of irresponsible and unlimited creation of new money appear unsustainable in the long term. Both previously accumulated resources and future resources are being wasted. Inefficiency, incompetence, and populism are becoming a common political phenomenon.

- The state and society as a whole are evolving. Historical assessments suggest that the separation of key institutions from the state has been important for the development and prosperity of society. One of the next logical steps could be the separation of money from the state.

The top number shows how much the project will cost.
The bottom one shows the forecasted benefit.

SUMMARY OF BOOK ONE

SUMMARY OF BOOK ONE

- Humanity fails to learn from historical experience. George Santayana, the Spanish writer, encapsulated this sentiment in his celebrated quote: "Those who cannot remember the past are condemned to repeat it."

- Bad money created out of nothing, backed only by debt, and issued ex officio, reduces the purchasing power of good money. It creates inflation and sets the stage for social disruption, poverty, and wars. Good money is covered by our good deeds, work done, or specific products that are of value to humanity. Based on historical lessons, good money should be non-state, scarce, and its value should be determined by the free market. Such money will be the path to prosperity and personal freedom.

- For several decades, our world has been running a monetary experiment based on central banking, bad money, and quantitative easing. No economist can say for sure whether this is the right way to go or when it will collapse.

- Multiple crises have made economies addicted to quantitative easing.

- Humanity may be better off than ever before, but more than 90% of the population is poorer in relation to the world's wealth.

- People are getting richer through progress and rising productivity, but the chosen few are becoming exponentially richer.

- There is an accumulation of the world's wealth in the hands of a few elites. Most of them got rich on the principle of the Cantillon Effect by having access to new money before others at the top of the financial pyramid. They did not create new wealth, but they diluted the wealth of the less wealthy. This means that without new money, the middle and lower classes would be richer than they are now.

- The social gap between the chosen few and the rest of humanity is widening. The bubble of wealth is inflating.

- The bursting of a financial bubble is inevitable, and it often leads to a redistribution of wealth.

- Redistribution of wealth has often been resolved by war or revolution in the history of mankind. However, not every revolution has to be bloody.

Allow me to draw on Josef Tětek's thoughts from his book *Bitcoin: Separation of Money and State*:

> The power over money is too tempting, and there is no human or man-made institution capable of holding such power. Like the ring of power, this power must be destroyed or it will destroy humanity. Let's destroy the Ring of Power and be part of the (r)evolution called the separation of money from the state, which will be seen in retrospect as a manifestation of civility and called the next Velvet Revolution.

Is (r)evolution really coming? Could Bitcoin be the tool that will slowly and non-violently change the world? Let's take a look at it together. In Book Two, you will get to know more information about Bitcoin, as well as some arguments for and against it.

That the current state of the world may be the result
of a premeditated plan certainly concerns me.
But I'm much more concerned about the
possibility that no one has a premeditated plan.

Yet another economist.

BOOK TWO

INTRODUCTION

I started studying bitcoin and the world of cryptocurrencies during recent years. The spirit of bitcoin fully engulfed me and suddenly I stopped seeing it as a speculative asset, or just a way to get rich quick. I began to understand its enormous importance and potential for humanity. Today, I view bitcoin as a groundbreaking innovation that offers a secure way to store the value that we've worked hard to earn, essentially encapsulating the time and effort we've invested creating good deeds. It is a discovery that can surpass the importance of the internet and move humanity towards freedom, peace, and prosperity.

Not every generation has the opportunity to witness the birth of something so phenomenal. We are lucky enough to have it, and we can even participate in its connection to the destiny of humanity. I don't know about you, but I certainly want to be a part of it. Bitcoin is an exciting idea in my eyes, and certainly one of the greatest things to occur in my lifetime. I agree that bitcoin serves as a fallback option for society in case current monetary systems collapse, particularly when poor-quality currency undermines the value of good money. If Book Two brings you new insights and persuades you to think about bitcoin as an innovation, it will accomplish what I set out to do.

PLAN B FOR HUMANITY: THE ETHOS AND ORIGINS OF BITCOIN

PLAN B FOR HUMANITY: THE ETHOS AND EMERGENCE OF BITCOIN

Bitcoin has become a phenomenon in recent years. Although most people have heard of it, few have a deeper understanding of its principles. Unfortunately, even fewer understand its socio-political role in terms of the possible evolution of money and the functioning of humanity. Some view it as a pyramid scheme, some as speculation, and others find it intricate and elusive. The goals with Bitcoin are much higher, and they can be achieved thanks to its independence and technical concept. However, the **ethos** of bitcoin and its importance to the preservation of human freedom is far more important than its technical or economic aspects.

Ethos is a Greek word originally meaning "custom." In modern usage, ethos denotes the disposition, character, or fundamental values peculiar to a specific person, people, corporation, culture, or movement. Ethos may change in response to new ideas or forces.

Humanity has always been attracted to mysteries, especially those that remain unsolved. The origin of bitcoin, or rather the identity of its creator, is still shrouded in mystery and will probably always remain that way. However, most bitcoin users have at least at one time or another wondered about the true identity of this mysterious Satoshi Nakamoto. That is why part of this chapter is devoted to speculation about his origins. The fact that the creator is unknown has a significant impact on Bitcoin's independence. However, this aspect is not essential to its functioning. Of particular importance is the environment in which the ideas about the need for free money originated, what community contributed to the birth of bitcoin, and who is developing and maintaining it today.

INTRODUCTION TO BOOK TWO

Starting to invest in cryptocurrencies is a challenging goal, as the whole process seems rather opaque. Various rumors circulate about cryptocurrencies: some raise skepticism, while others suggest great opportunities for rapid financial gain. The information can be so conflicting that you may end up doubting the whole field of cryptocurrencies. However, it is important to remember that it is often fear and uncertainty caused by the media, which works on the principle that negative news attracts the interest of readers. In addition, people who like to comment on the subject are often ignorant of even the most basic information.

So welcome to the wonderful world of bitcoin and other cryptocurrencies, where the money is virtual but the stress is real! Every beginner must prepare for the fact that their journey to education may resemble a journey into an unknown universe where, in terms of the current perception of the world and money, they may even encounter aliens. Computer networks, blockchains, digital money—it can all sound a bit foreign—and at times one may feel like a child learning to read.

The biggest hurdle you will have to overcome is approaching new technologies and changing your mindset. You also have to let go of the idea that money is physically present in your wallet. Try to adopt a new way of thinking about what money is and how it works. Once you discover that there are a multitude of different cryptocurrencies with different characteristics, it will seem like unmanaged chaos. Yes, that's the reality. But in the age of digital money and cryptocurrencies, you have to be open to new ideas and be willing to enter a new world where money is virtual and where you have to trust math and technology, not traditional institutions.

Cryptocurrencies are definitely here to stay in some form and can play a very important role in our lives. That's why it pays to spend some of your time studying and understanding them. Some of you may give up after finding out how much work you need to put in to get started. However, in the future, you may regret not putting some of that time and energy into studying them. You may regret missed opportunities, which can lead to feelings of disappointment and frustration. So fingers crossed that you are one of the successful ones.

The problem with cryptocurrencies is not that they work with 21st-century technologies, but with 20th-century users.

BITCOIN

Why are we starting a chapter on cryptocurrencies with bitcoin when there are more than 24,000 of them today and their number is growing every day? It's because bitcoin is the oldest and longest-running cryptocurrency. Most other cryptocurrencies were created by copying it—by modifying its publicly available source code for example—or at least by drawing on its principles of operation. Bitcoin is also currently the most capitalized cryptocurrency, which means that globally it has the most money stored in it. Simultaneously, it boasts the most secure network, supported by extensive computing power, boasts the largest user base, and stands as the unequivocal market leader, shaping the trajectory of the entire cryptocurrency market. It is also among the most widely used cryptocurrencies in terms of acceptance in everyday life.

The clarity of bitcoin's fundamental principles largely contributes to its popularity and makes it an ideal starting point for beginners. Any newcomer should initially become familiar with purchasing, holding, and transacting with bitcoin before considering whether they wish or need to delve into the study of other cryptocurrencies.

A summary of the main reasons to get started with bitcoin:

- the most famous and most widely used cryptocurrency
- protocol security, broad support, and availability
- high liquidity, capitalization, and acceptance
- advantageous for learning about the principle of cryptocurrencies
- more secure investment potential than unproven cryptocurrencies

Grammar from the point of view of the word BITCOIN

In the following pages, the word BITCOIN will be used in many forms and phrases. Therefore, it is important to clarify at the outset when it should be written using uppercase or lowercase letters. Afterwards, you will be able to distinguish whether we are referring to bitcoin as money or, for example, Bitcoin as an overall concept or project. As is the case with commonly used names such as currency or money, when referring to bitcoin as a unit of currency, a lowercase "b" is recommended. When referring to the overarching concept or technology, an uppercase "B" is recommended. Bitcoin is a relatively new concept and is only just finding its place in different languages. Therefore, there is a possibility that this generally accepted convention could change in the future.

bitcoin: refers to bitcoin as a coin, money, asset, or cryptocurrency. It can also be written using the abbreviation BTC, or the symbol ₿.

Bitcoin project: refers to the Bitcoin project (or project Bitcoin) or any of its associated elements like the protocol, network, or blockchain

Bitcoin protocol: custom executable program including its source code

Bitcoin network: a network made up of nodes operated by miners and some users

Bitcoin blockchain: the public ledger is a continuously growing chain of blocks with a record of payments made and current balances.

THE PREDECESSORS OF BITCOIN

Before we get into explaining bitcoin, we need to mention its predecessors. It was not the first currency to try to stand on its own two feet and compete with state fiat money. It was preceded by a number of centralized attempts that did not end well for the founders and holders of the currencies in question. This gave the creator of bitcoin the opportunity to learn about their concepts and learn from their mistakes. Individual projects have either failed or been shut down by the authorities, funds seized, and founders sued. In fact, the US government prosecutes individuals who try to compete with the dollar. As reported by the *New Yorker* magazine, the FBI has stated the following: "It is a violation of federal law for individuals…to create private coins or currency systems that compete with the official coinage and currency of the United States." Some creators of subsequent projects decided not to launch their initiatives for this very reason. The projects remained as concepts because their creators did not want to risk jail time.

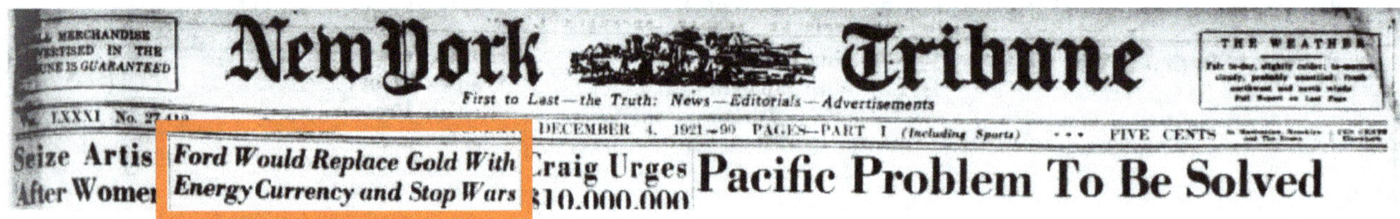

As early as 1921, the American industrialist Henry Ford recommended the following:

> "Creating an **energy currency** that could replace gold, break the grip of banking elites on global wealth, and end wars."

> 💡 **Energy currency** is a currency whose value would be backed by electricity—which is not free anywhere in the world.

Ford Would Replace Gold With Energy Currency and Stop Wars

Declares if Government Will Give Him Muscle Shoals Plant He Can Demonstrate Success of Plan to Substitute Natural Wealth as Basis of World's Money

FLORENCE, Ala., Dec. 3.—Henry Ford and Thomas A. Edison arrived here to-day to inspect the Muscle Shoals nitrate plant, which the Detroit automobile manufacturer proposes to take over from the government, and almost immediately Mr. Ford declared the purpose of his vast new project. It is not to make money, or, primarily, to stimulate the employment of a million men now idle, or to make the South an industrial center. His purpose, he said, is to end all wars forever.

Henry Ford, by building the world's greatest power plant here on the Tennessee River, expects to eliminate gold as the basis of world wealth and substitute for it something different—the units of power. And by doing this, he said, war would cease, for gold is the cause of war.

"It's very simple when you analyze it," said Mr. Ford, "the cause of all wars is gold. We shall demonstrate to the world two things, first, the practicability, second, the desirability of displacing gold as the basis of currency and substituting in its place the world's imperishable natural wealth.

"Almost everybody in the world except the newspapers and the bankers recognizes that civilization has entered on a new era. The newspapers don't see it and the international bankers don't want to see it—it would mean changes in world finance and bankers always oppose changes.

"There is a group of international bankers who to-day control the bulk of the world's gold supply. No matter to what country they as individuals claim allegiance, they all play the same game to keep the gold they have in their own hands and to get just as much more as possible.

"With the international bankers the fostering, starting and fighting of a war is nothing more nor less than creating an active market for money—a business transaction. If the different countries of the international groups are at war—that makes no difference. No matter who loses the war there have been a great many loans—the gold system always wins. The young men from eighteen to thirty fight the war and are maimed or killed, the internationalists are safe and prosperous.

"Ten years ago I said I intended to put every ounce of brains and energy in me to stopping war. I never meant anything more earnestly, and that's why I want Muscle Shoals. I see a way which, if it can be done, will do more to end war than a thousand years of agitation.

"The essential evil of gold in its relation to war is the fact that it can be controlled. Break the control and you stop war. And the simple way to break the control of these international bankers, the way to end their exploitation of humanity forever, is to remove gold as a basis for the currency of the world.

"Army engineers say it will take $30,000,000 to complete the big dam. But Congress is economical just now and not in a mood to raise the money by

(Continued on page six)

The *New York Tribune* published this article on December 4, 1921. Ford's vision shares some similarities to Satoshi's solution, especially in terms of Proof of Work, which is based on electricity consumption.

BITCOIN'S PREDECESSORS IN TIME

The following is a brief overview of currencies that tried, but failed, to compete with state currencies prior to the creation of bitcoin. Nevertheless, they became an important foundation for its subsequent emergence.

- **1921: Energy currency**—Henry Ford. This never evolved beyond the concept level.

- **1989: eCash** (DigiCash company)—David Chaum*. The project went bankrupt. It was a highly advanced, anonymous cryptographic payment system designed primarily for corporations. Chaum's dissertation proposed all but one element of the blockchain, which was later detailed in the Bitcoin whitepaper.

- **1994: CyberCash**—Daniel Lynch, William Melton, and Steve Crocker. This defunct service facilitated internet payments for e-commerce.

- **1996: E-gold**—Douglas Jackson and Barry Downey. Liquidated by US authorities, it allowed the transfer of digital grams of gold when the underlying gold was actually owned by the company.

- **1997: Ideal money**—John Nash*. Although it remained at the concept level, it was a vision of a global currency linked to international comparisons of national price index values.

- **1997: Hashcash**—Adam Back*. *It is not a currency.* Rather, it is essentially a Proof of Work micropayment based system designed to defend against spam email addresses and blogs. Today it is used in bitcoin mining.

- **1998: Liberty dollar**—Bernard von NotHaus. The Liberty dollar was liquidated by US authorities. The currency was issued in round metal coins, gold and silver certificates, and in electronic currency (eLD). It was pegged to gold and silver according to the original definition of the dollar. Ironically, the charge was for counterfeiting the dollar, even though the counterfeit had a much higher underlying value than the genuine currency.

- **1998: Bit gold**—Nick Szabo*. This was an independent digital currency similar to bitcoin that remained at the concept level.

- **1998: b-money**—Wei Dai*. This remained at the concept level. It was an anonymous and distributed payment system whose goals were very similar to bitcoin.

- **2001: E-bullion**—Mr. and Mrs. Fayed. It experienced an internal split, and the gold was seized by authorities. It was essentially a digital gold transaction, similar to e-gold.

- **2006: Liberty Reserve**—Arthur Budovsky. Liquidated by US authorities, it was a centralized digital currency service based in Costa Rica. It handled digital transfers of dollar-, euro- and gold-linked units.

- **2008: Bitcoin**—The pseudonym of Satoshi Nakamoto* continues to this day. The most powerful cryptocurrency, its design allows for the replacement of fiat currencies and to create decentralized non-state money with a fixed monetary policy. The vision for the future is for it to serve as a global world currency.

*These individuals are associated with Satoshi Nakamoto (see below).

GAME THEORY

Before we delve fully into the history and technical issues of bitcoin, we need to discuss the principles of human behavior. This is one of the key points on which Satoshi built his model of the gradual acceptance of bitcoin by humanity. The principles of how bitcoin works were designed to spread naturally and gradually through the population. In addition to psychology or the social sciences, there is also a mathematical discipline that addresses this issue. This field is called game theory. We don't know if Satoshi was a psychologist, but we do know that he was a programmer with an interest in mathematics and cryptography. The way Satoshi designed Bitcoin's monetary policy—including its gradual introduction, increasing rarity, and network economics—suggests he understood how crowds and society operate based on game theory. Among other things, game theory attempts to mathematically prove that when each player plays only for himself, the variant of the game with the greatest number of players benefiting from the outcome has the greatest chance of winning.

Nomenclature:

- **game:** a situation or conflict

- **player**: an individual, company, political party, or government participant

- **intelligent player:** a rational participant in the conflict whose goal is to maximize profit or, at least, minimize loss

- **strategy:** a specific option that a player can choose

- **optimal strategy:** the most advantageous option

Game theory belongs to the field of applied mathematics. It seeks to optimize strategies for specific intelligent players. The concept of game theory is very broad. It encompasses many variations where specific facts matter a lot. These include:

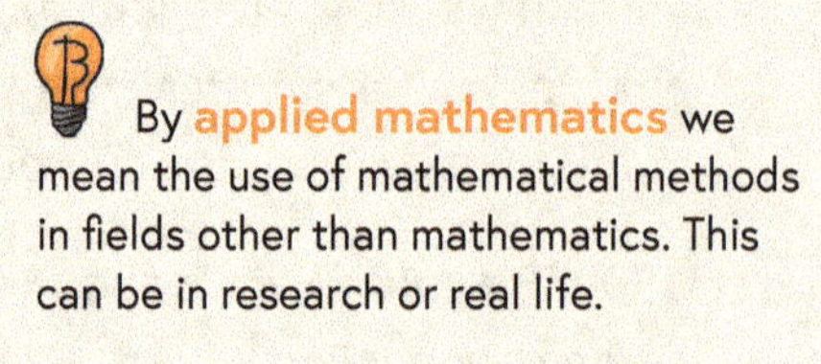

- whether the interests of the players are aligned or in conflict

- whether each player plays for themselves, or whether they can form alliances (either declared or secret)

- whether the players are following the commitments and rules, or whether compliance is unenforceable

- whether players move simultaneously and whether they have information about the opponent's previous move

- whether only one player can win or multiple players can win, and whether other players can benefit from someone else's win

- whether each player has the same game-related information as all other players

- whether the results of the chosen strategy depend on the strategies of other players

- if the order of moves matters, and if all players have the same number of moves

- whether the game has a strictly defined game time and the end of the game depends on the result, or whether it is played continuously without a defined end

Applying game theory to everyday life is challenging because it is an ongoing game with a huge number of players. Some players act independently, while others cooperate either secretly or openly; yet trust is hard to find among them. Each player's moves are independent and each player has a different number of moves. The game is played in a variety of geopolitical settings where individual facts and game resources have different meanings and values. Players do not have the same information and, following different outcomes, benefit differently from the game.

Game theory models analyze conflicts by creating a mathematical representation of the situation and calculating the optimal strategy for specific participants. Applications span several fields: economics (like stock exchanges), diplomacy (international negotiations), political science, sociology, biology (genetic and evolutionary), transport (traffic management), marketing, and military strategy. Game theory exemplifies how mathematics can be successfully applied in practice. Generally, it predicts the behavior of groups with diverse motivations.

One of the key models of game theory is the Nash equilibrium by the American mathematician John Nash, Jr. It can be simply described as addressing a situation where no player can improve their strategy based on knowledge of other players' fixed strategies. The Nash equilibrium calculates the most likely choices of players who decide simultaneously, taking into account the decisions of others. Based on the prediction, an optimal strategy can then be

John Forbes Nash, Jr. (1928–2015) was a mathematician, economist and Nobel Prize winner in economics. His detailed biography is described below in a treatise on who may have been the creator of Bitcoin.

chosen. This is the concept of solving non-cooperative multiplayer games, where players either do not cooperate or share the profit of the game. Nash proved that every finite game has at least one such solution. As such, the concept of Nash equilibrium is used to analyze the outcomes of multi-player strategic decision making.

Basic principles of Nash equilibrium:

- **We cannot predict the outcome if we look at individual decisions in isolation.**

- **Each player's decision must be considered in light of the possible decisions of others.**

The Nash equilibrium has been used in the analysis of war conflicts, traffic situations, and marketing studies. It has also been used to study the processes of adopting technical standards and to study the possibilities of cooperation between people with different motivations. In 1994, Nash was awarded the Nobel Prize in Economics.

Thomas Crombie Schelling (1921–2016) was an American economist and professor of foreign relations, national security, nuclear strategy, and arms control at the School of Public Policy at the University of Maryland. He took over from John Nash at the RAND Corporation.

Robert John Aumann (1930–) is an Israeli mathematician, member of the US National Academy of Sciences, and professor at the Hebrew University of Jerusalem. He is also a visiting professor at Stony Brook University and a founding member of the Center for Game Theory in Economics at Stony Brook University.

Other scientists who jointly received the Nobel Prize in Economics in 2005, based on their work in game theory, were Thomas Schelling and Robert Aumann.

Schelling's books *Strategy of Conflict* (1960), *Strategy and Arms Control* (1961), and *Arms and Influence* (1966) are some of the most widely praised books of their kind. In them, Schelling examines cases of promises and threats, game theory as a whole, and the study of mutual distrust. These books are a significant contribution to the literature on modern war and diplomacy. Additional topics which Schelling explores include the diplomacy of violence, the diplomacy of survival, and the dynamics of mutual alarm.

Aumann's greatest contribution was in the area of repeated games, which are situations in which players encounter the same situation over and over again. Aumann was the first to define the concept of correlated equilibrium in game theory, a type of equilibrium in non-cooperative games that is more flexible than the classical Nash equilibrium.

These are some of Aumann's themes:

- War is not irrational, but in order to be understood and, eventually, to be won, it must be studied scientifically.

- The study of repeated games emphasizes now rather than later.

- Simplistic peacemaking can trigger war, while arms races, credible war threats, and the possibility of mutual destruction reliably prevent war.

Simply stated, game theory attempts to predict the behavior of individuals based on mathematical equations and applies it to the behavior of a crowd or part of a population. From this perspective, Bitcoin can be seen as a project in which its author has used many variables to motivate the general public to participate in the game. Bitcoin spreads among communities, nations, institutions, and states based on its gradually increasing rarity, credibility, innovative properties, and gradually increasing price.

THE CRYPTO-ANARCHIST GROUP CYPHERPUNKS: CRYPTOGRAPHY VS. BIG BROTHER

The term **crypto-anarchy** was coined by Timothy C. May in *The Crypto Anarchist Manifesto* in 1988. The stated goal of the crypto-anarchist movement was to allow people unlimited freedom beyond the reach of the state apparatus. Some see crypto-anarchy as a way to restore the balance between individual rights and state power. Others see it as a tool to prevent the state from identifying individual subjects for law enforcement or fundraising purposes.

 **Timothy C. May** (1951–2018), better known as Tim May, was an American technical and political writer, electronic engineer, and senior scientist at Intel. May was an advocate of libertarianism and internet privacy. From the 1990s to 2003, he wrote extensively on cryptography and privacy. He is one of the most influential figures in the Cypherpunks movement.

Crypto-anarchists seek to use strong encryption and anonymity tools to create a free space beyond the reach of the state and large technology companies. They fight for free speech and free trade. They use cryptographic software to avoid tracking and collecting personal data when using the internet and computer networks. They try to protect their privacy, political, and economic freedom. Crypto-anarchy is the realization of anarchism in cyberspace.

The original enemies of crypto-anarchists were governments that sought to prevent citizens from using encryption. Subsequently, a group of mathematicians, hackers, and self-taught hackers coalesced around a shared belief that the internet would either help civilization flourish or lay the foundations for an Orwellian state. Issues of freedom were and are of paramount importance to crypto-anarchists.

The Orwellian state

In 1949, the English writer George Orwell completed an anti-utopian novel called *1984*. This book, which is the source of the famous line "Big Brother is watching you," is one of the most significant literary works of the 20th century. The story portrays a world under strict totalitarian control, maintained by an ongoing war among three continental powers. The Party dominates this society, and any dissent or individuality is harshly punished. *TIME* magazine ranked *1984* among the 100 most influential books since 1923. After the NSA spying scandal revealed by Edward Snowden, sales of the book skyrocketed.

Cypherpunks and the Orwellian state represent two opposing worldviews. Cypherpunks fight for the protection of personal data and individual freedom through encryption and anonymous technologies, whereas the Orwellian state personifies an authoritarian government with unlimited surveillance and control over citizens. This clash of ideas continues today. Governments and citizens are trying to strike a balance between the general security of society and the personal privacy of individuals in an expanding digital environment.

In mid-1988, Timothy C. May's *The Crypto Anarchist Manifesto* established the movement's core vision, focusing on safeguarding information freedom and resisting government surveillance.

The Crypto Anarchist Manifesto

What follows is the content of the message that was distributed to participants on the Cypherpunks mailing list.

Subject: The Crypto Anarchist Manifesto

Date: Sun, 22 Nov 92 12:11:24 PST

Author: Tim May

A specter is haunting the modern world, the specter of crypto anarchy.

Computer technology is on the verge of providing the ability for individuals and groups to communicate and interact with each other in a totally anonymous manner. Two persons may exchange messages, conduct business, and negotiate electronic contracts without ever knowing the True Name, or legal identity, of the other. Interactions over networks will be untraceable, via extensive re-routing of encrypted packets and tamper-proof boxes which implement cryptographic protocols with nearly perfect assurance against any tampering. Reputations will be of central importance, far more important in dealings than even the credit ratings of today. These developments will alter completely the nature of government regulation, the ability to tax and control economic interactions, the ability to keep information secret, and will even alter the nature of trust and reputation.

The technology for this revolution--and it surely will be both a social and economic revolution--has existed in theory for the past decade. The methods are based upon public-key encryption, zero-knowledge interactive proof systems, and various software protocols for interaction, authentication, and verification. The focus has until now been on academic conferences in Europe and the U.S., conferences monitored closely by the National Security Agency. But only recently have computer networks and personal computers attained sufficient speed to make the ideas practically realizable. And the next ten years will bring enough additional speed to make the ideas economically feasible and essentially unstoppable. High-speed networks, ISDN, tamper-proof boxes, smart cards, satellites, Ku-band transmitters, multi-MIPS personal computers, and encryption chips now under development will be some of the enabling technologies.

The State will of course try to slow or halt the spread of this technology, citing national security concerns, use of the technology by drug dealers and tax evaders, and fears of societal disintegration. Many of these concerns will be valid; crypto anarchy will allow national secrets to be trade freely and will allow illicit and stolen materials to be traded. An anonymous computerized market will even make possible abhorrent markets for assassinations and extortion. Various criminal and foreign elements will be active users of CryptoNet. But this will not halt the spread of crypto anarchy.

Just as the technology of printing altered and reduced the power of medieval guilds and the social power structure, so too will cryptologic methods fundamentally alter the nature of corporations and of government interference in economic transactions. Combined with emerging information markets, crypto anarchy will create a liquid market for any and all material which can be put into words and pictures. And just as a seemingly minor invention like barbed wire made possible the fencing-off of vast ranches and farms, thus altering forever the concepts of land and property rights in the frontier West, so too will the seemingly minor discovery out of an arcane branch of mathematics come to be the wire clippers which dismantle the barbed wire around intellectual property.

Arise, you have nothing to lose but your barbed wire fences!

This manifesto describes a vision of a society where encryption and technology enable individuals to protect their privacy, freedom, and independence. It emphasizes the importance of cryptography as a means of ensuring anonymity and independence from state control. It also predicts that this technology will enable the creation of alternative, decentralized systems for communication, finance, and the organization of society beyond the reach of traditional power structures.

In 1991, **Phil Zimmermann** released PGP, a program that guaranteed strong encryption based on asymmetric cryptography, and made it freely downloadable on the internet. This technology made government snooping impossible, which the US government did not like. In a tactic against activists, public key cryptography was labeled as "modern weapons technology," making its distribution illegal. A lawsuit launched by the US government for allegedly violating the Arms Export Act lasted more than three years.

Philip R. Zimmermann (1954–) is an American computer programmer who wrote the Pretty Good Privacy (PGP) encryption program in 1991. It became the de facto standard for private email encryption and later became the basis for the actual OpenPGP standard. According to Zimmermann's Law, "The natural progress of technology is to make it more and more impossible to keep track of us" and "The ability of computers to track us doubles every eighteen months."

In late 1992, Eric Hughes, Timothy C. May, and John Gilmore founded the Cypherpunks movement. At the same time, the now legendary Cypherpunks mailing list was created. By 1994, the group had 700 active contributors and subscribers from all over the world. In its heyday, it was a very active forum, with dozens of technical emails a day discussing topics including mathematics, cryptography, computer science, politics, and philosophy.

The main goals of the movement are based on *The Crypto Anarchist Manifesto*:

- encryption
- digital money
- anonymous networks
- digital pseudonyms
- zero knowledge about the user
- reputation
- information markets
- black markets
- the collapse of governments

In retaliation for the prosecution of Zimmermann, Cypherpunks printed books containing the software code and distributed them around the world. The US government could not ban the book because the free distribution of printed materials falls under the freedom of speech guaranteed by the Constitution. In support of the fight for privacy, people tattooed pieces of the code on their bodies and made T-shirts with the PGP code. After the government dropped the lawsuit in early 1996, Zimmermann founded PGP and released an updated version of it. Due to this revolt, numerous companies can now legally incorporate encryption into their products to protect end-user privacy.

Later, a splinter group began to develop the possibility of free money. This was the creation of a new discipline at the interface of economics and computer science. The representatives of this group continued the ideas of the Austrian economists Ludwig von Mises, Friedrich Hayek, and Murray Rothbard. Through papers and discussions, they thought about how to take money creation out of the hands of governments. They wanted to prevent irresponsible monetary policy and preserve privacy in the dissemination of electronic money and the collection of information by commercial banks. The group focused on monetary policy and took to calling themselves "High-Tech Hayekians." Their aim was to create a free global market.

The issue of misuse of technology for illegal activities has been discussed repeatedly for a very long time. In fact, Timothy C. May, the founder of the Cypherpunk movement, was once asked if these technologies could be misused for illegal activities. His answer was quite blunt: "Yes, accept it." Governments would like to maintain control and are trying to regulate technology. Often, they border on restricting fundamental human rights and freedoms. Authoritarian regimes and dictatorships stand out the most. Unfortunately, even in democratic societies there are attempts to strengthen the powers of the authorities, tighten surveillance of citizens, and create surveillance mechanisms at the level of states or large technology companies.

These efforts often border on the definitions of **liberal democracy**. This is done under the pretext of protecting individuals or society as a whole. Unfortunately, not everyone can foresee the possible consequences. In general, any technology can be used for the benefit of humanity and, at the same time, be misused to commit evil or criminal acts. The solution is not to ban technology, but to prosecute those who misuse it in violation of the law. The automobile can also be used as a weapon to kill people, but it makes no sense to ban its use. From the point of view of civil liberty, I don't think anyone wants to live in an Orwellian environment overseen by "Big Brother."

Liberal democracy is a form of government that combines two essential aspects: representative democracy and liberalism. This form of government is characterized by elections between freely competing political entities. The main ideas are the separation of powers, the rule of law, a market economy with private ownership, and the protection of human and civil rights for all.

THE BIRTH AND DEATH OF SATOSHI NAKAMOTO

The global financial crisis in 2008 was followed by massive central bank bailouts. Lehman Brothers Holdings Inc., founded in 1850, became one of the largest investment banks in the US. It was among the first banks to be hit hard by the collapse of the US housing market. On September 15, 2008, it announced that it was seeking protection from creditors, setting a record for bankruptcy in American history. The Cypherpunks movement had been revived by a new generation. Beyond privacy and its own sovereignty, it has become much more concerned about the growing dangers associated with monetary policy, of which massive quantitative easing has become a normal part. At first, this was supposed to be a one-off program, with $600 billion created. However, the actual figure was almost double that. Central banks around the world lost their inhibitions and began to use this method as a standard means of creating new money. The world's economies have become addicted to new money in much the same way as an addict is addicted to drugs.

On October 31, 2008, someone using the pseudonym Satoshi Nakamoto—whom I respectfully refer to as "Satoshi" and "Nakamoto" throughout this book—announced via email a new decentralized peer-to-peer digital currency system to recipients on the Cypherpunks mailing list. Along with the announcement, Nakamoto included a document known as the Bitcoin whitepaper, detailing the system's principles. The world was introduced to a new digital currency system that was peer-to-peer, fully decentralized, and not governed by any authority. The design ensures that no one—not the author, individuals, groups, institutions, banks, or governments—can manipulate the currency, counterfeit it, freeze accounts, control its flow, or cause inflation.

Peer-to-peer, also referred to as P2P, is the principle of making payments or sending messages directly without any intermediary. In practice, this means making payments without the involvement of payment companies, banks, or other intermediaries in the payment system.

A whitepaper is a report or manual. It briefly informs the reader about a complex issue and presents the philosophy or technical solution of the founder or manufacturer.

However, Nakamoto's announcement was initially met with a high degree of skepticism. Years later, on March 19, 2013, Hal Finney, in his last post on the bitcointalk.org online forum summed up his work on bitcoin by saying:

> "Fast forward to late 2008 and the announcement of Bitcoin. I've noticed that cryptographic graybeards (I was in my mid 50's) tend to get cynical. I was more idealistic; I have always loved crypto, the mystery and the paradox of it."

When Satoshi announced Bitcoin on the cryptography mailing list, he got a skeptical reception at best. Cryptographers have seen too many grand schemes by clueless noobs. They tend to have a knee jerk reaction. I was more positive.

Hal Finney and a few other Cypherpunks eventually became interested in Satoshi's concept.

The nine-page treatise full of equations presented a solution to a complex problem that has plagued the Cypherpunk community for many years. No previous concept of digital money had solved what Satoshi referred to as the problem of double spending.

A **noob** is slang for a person who does an activity in which they are not proficient, is doing it for the first time, or does not know how to do it. It was derived from the English "new boy" (such as the new boy at school, or in the army) in the 1960s, which was shortened to newbie, and then the most common version evolved: noob.

"We propose a solution to the double-spending problem using a peer-to-peer network," Satoshi wrote. The peer-to-peer system was intended to eliminate the need for any central authority to verify transactions. "A lot of people automatically dismiss e-currency as a lost cause because of all the companies that failed since the 1990s," he wrote. "I hope it's obvious it was only the centrally controlled nature of those systems that doomed them. I think this is the first time we're a decentralized, non-trust-based system." To accomplish these goals, Satoshi proposed a publicly accessible shared ledger (blockchain) that would document every transaction. Independence from banks was a key theme for Satoshi, as he had just witnessed the global financial system collapse due to the irresponsible policies of large investment banks. "The root problem with conventional currencies is all the trust that's required to make it work," Satoshi went on to write. "Banks must be trusted to hold our money and transfer it electronically, but they lend it out in waves of credit bubbles with barely a fraction in reserve." These quotes from the communication capture his view of banking operated under the protection of central banks.

It should also be mentioned that, according to his own statement, Satoshi started coding the first version of bitcoin in the C++ programming language sometime in the spring of 2007. He also registered the domain **bitcoin.org** on August 18, 2008.

Bitcoin.org is a public information website for the general public to help educate and facilitate the understanding and purchase of bitcoin.

On January 3, 2009, Satoshi Nakamoto launched the Bitcoin protocol—a program for mining bitcoin—and thus started the Bitcoin network. By writing the first block called Genesis, he also set up the bitcoin blockchain (ledger). Satoshi hid a message in this block containing the headline from the front page of the British newspaper The *Times*, which read: "Chancellor on brink of second bailout for banks." With this action, Satoshi sought to achieve two objectives. He wanted to confirm that the block wasn't mined before January 3, 2009. Simultaneously, he aimed to highlight the banking system's flaws and the practice of creating money out of nothing.

In 2009, he also founded the bitcoin and cryptography forum **bitcointalk.org**, where the main communication about the new currency subsequently moved. It's a place where people can still write about bitcoin, blockchain, and other cryptocurrencies. Discussions here take place in many different forums, divided by content. Satoshi essentially formed a "Bitcoin open-source team" around himself. These were enthusiasts who worked voluntarily and free of charge to modify the public Bitcoin protocol, which was then available free of charge to anyone else on an **open source** basis.

Bitcointalk.org is a public forum where blockchain enthusiasts, developers, and crypto-investors discuss bitcoin, cryptocurrencies, and blockchain in general.

Open source is a type of software (OSS) that is publicly available. Anyone can see, modify, and redistribute the code as they see fit.

Satoshi then worked with other developers on the open source team for ten months. He was careful never to reveal anything personal about himself. He had good reasons to remain anonymous after the experience of previous visionaries who had tried to make better money. As we have already mentioned, many of them were arrested, charged and prosecuted, and funds were seized. Around mid-2010, Satoshi's contact with the development team and the community gradually began to wane. Around this time, he also handed over control of the source code repository and key features of the software to Gavin Andresen, one of the programmers involved in the open source team. He handed over bitcointalk. org, bitcoin.org and several other domains to leading members of the bitcoin community. In one of his last communications, he sent a cryptic email to another developer stating that he "probably won't be here in the future." His last messages were from April 2011. In them, he wrote that he had "moved on to other things." However, in 2014, a **controversial message** emerged.

A controversial report from 2014

In 2014, reporters from *Newsweek* located an elderly man who happened to share the same last name (Dorian Nakamoto, born Satoshi) living in the US. They speculated that he was the real creator of bitcoin. However, he categorically denied the claim—even going so far as to point out that he didn't have enough money to pay for an internet connection. Around that time, the last known message believed to be from the real Satoshi Nakamoto was sent: "leave grandpa alone."

Not everyone was convinced that this message was sent by Satoshi himself, but the grandfather was left alone regardless. Was this message really written by Satoshi? If he didn't write it, he must have given someone in the community access to his account. Unfortunately, this is just speculation and we'll probably never know the truth.

Satoshi Nakamoto combined existing technical and cryptographic solutions and introduced measures to address the double-spending issue, establish a monetary policy, and create an operational concept. He fully automated the process, piecing together what many consider "the world's most important puzzle."

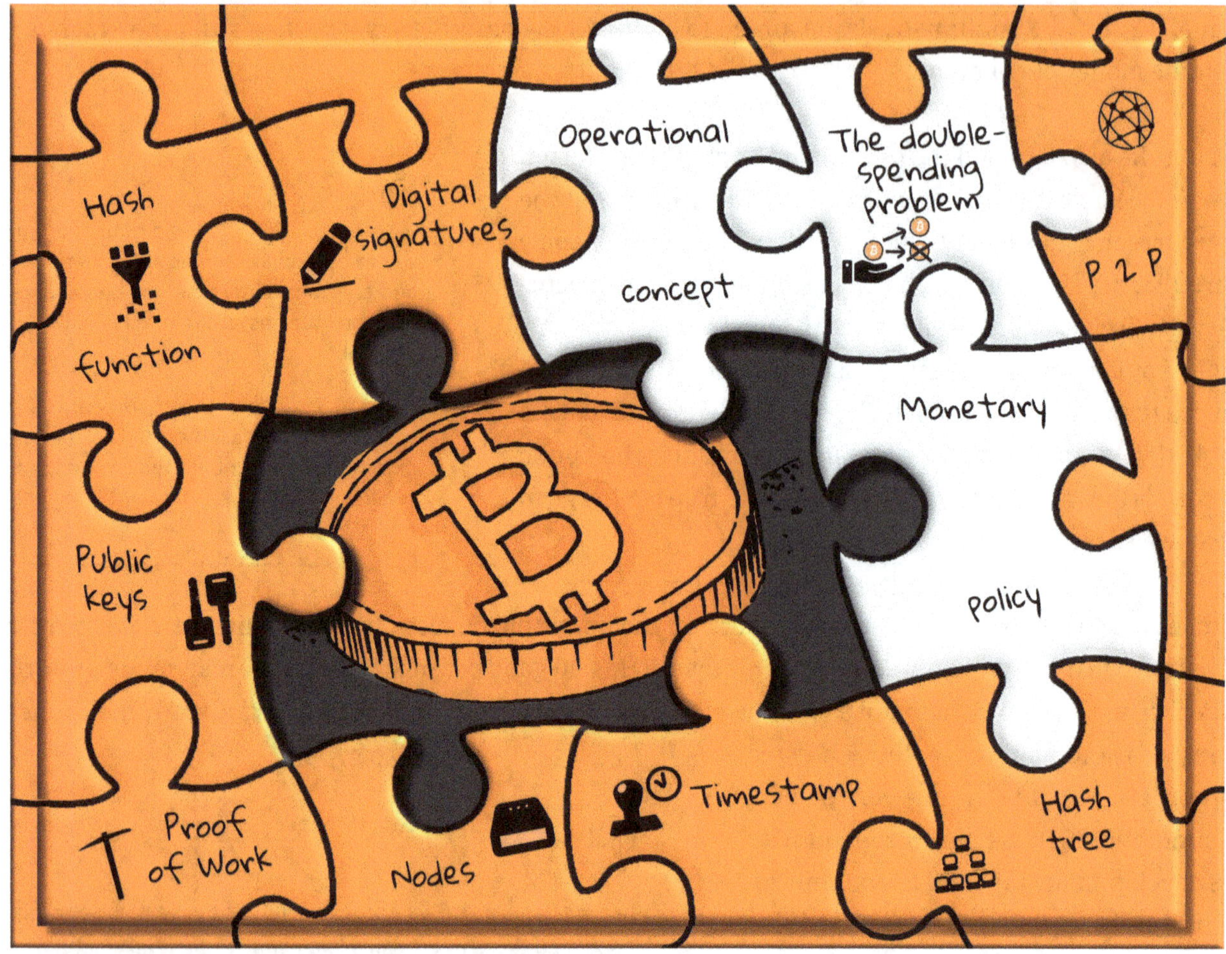

Satoshi Nakamoto has probably disappeared forever, leaving his invention to mankind free of charge and without any conditions. We are all Satoshi now, and it is up to us what we choose to do with the technology and how we will value his legacy.

On September 27, 2012, the Bitcoin Foundation, a non-profit foundation, was established with the main goals of standardizing, developing, protecting, and promoting the use of the cryptocurrency bitcoin for the benefit of users worldwide. In addition, the organization has chosen to financially support the core open source development team's efforts, offering funds for infrastructure development, publishing, and conferences. Gavin Andresen was hired as the chief scientist, taking over the scepter from Satoshi. Funding for the foundation was primarily based on contributions from the community, and later from technology companies.

Currently, several companies and individuals are supporting the development of the Bitcoin protocol, including providing funding for independent developers.

PLAN B FOR HUMANITY

Satoshi Nakamoto ushered in an era of a new financial system. To this day, no one knows if it was an individual or a group of people. It may look like Satoshi invented bitcoin all by himself, but the opposite is true. He created the entire concept based on existing features, protocols, and cryptographic solutions that had been developed over many years by enthusiasts and professionals connected to the Cypherpunk movement. This community discussed Satoshi's ideas with him, helped solve problems that arose, and then took on the further development of the Bitcoin protocol. There is no doubt that Bitcoin as an open source project was built and rebuilt by a community of programmers who gradually rewrote 70% of its code, and that it continues to be a gradual, collective process.

At first glance, it would appear that Satoshi was trying to solve a technical problem. However, looking back and analyzing some of his statements, it appears that Satoshi was mainly trying to solve a socio-economic issue that was emerging at the time. As this issue has intensified over the years, the need for Satoshi's solution has grown.

From this perspective, Satoshi cannot be seen solely as a programmer with an interest in mathematics and cryptography. At the same time, he was also an astute economist, psychologist, and sociologist. Most crypto-anarchists tried to look for technical solutions at the level of code. With his unique perspective and understanding, he combined existing technical solutions and ingeniously addressed the Byzantine Generals' Problem, thereby solving the double-spending issue.

The Byzantine Generals' Problem is a coordination problem of the participants in a decentralized system, some of whom may be dishonest. This problem was raised in 1982 by a collective of scholars (Leslie Lamport, Robert Shostak, and Marshall Pease). Until 2008, it was a major barrier to the emergence of decentralized currencies.

In 2008, the Bitcoin whitepaper proposed a solution to a complex issue, which can be analogized using the scenario of multiple armies besieging a city. The defending and attacking forces are evenly matched. Victory for the besiegers hinges on a coordinated attack. Each general must decide in the morning, by sending messages to the others, whether to attack or retreat. However, the challenge is determining the trustworthiness of the received messages, as there's a risk of some generals or messengers colluding with the enemy.

Bitcoin's creator tackled this challenge by requiring each general to send a decision message to every other general. As a result, each general receives a consistent set of messages indicating either an attack or a withdrawal. The majority decision then becomes the binding course of action for all. This solution is predicated on the trustworthiness of over half of the generals or messengers.

Drawing from this principle, the blockchain ensures that funds cannot be spent twice. This system remains secure unless a dishonest entity achieves 51% computational dominance within the network.

He also expertly crafted the monetary policy, managed the issue of increasing scarcity, set internal network rules (like adjusting mining difficulty), and addressed various technical challenges to facilitate future development, among other things.

This expansion goes beyond simple cryptography and mathematics, delving further into advanced game theory. Yet, Satoshi didn't stop there. He converted the entire proposed framework, typically outlined in legal documents and user guidelines, into mathematical formulas. This ensured the system operated autonomously without requiring oversight or intervention. Translating this mathematical model into code was a routine programming task.

Satoshi succeeded in designing and launching an independent payment system unparalleled in history. He gifted this project to humanity without charge. Afterward, he dedicated several years to resolving the system's initial issues, fostering a community of believers. Then, as he stated, he moved on to something else. This independent payment system could offer an alternative in the event of a failure of the traditional monetary system and provide a solution to keep trade and investment going.

Lately, more and more people are beginning to believe that bitcoin may be an alternative in case the fiat system collapses. If this option seems theoretically realistic to you too, you may see it as a Plan B for yourself, our society, or even humanity as a whole.

Printing money did not solve the problem of printing money.
It's time for Plan B.

WHO MIGHT HAVE BEEN SATOSHI NAKAMOTO?

The more bitcoin becomes known, rare, and expensive, the more people are trying to find out the real identity of Satoshi Nakamoto. It is not the intention of this book to uncover the true identity of the creator of bitcoin. However, anyone who is interested in bitcoin is sooner or later confronted with various speculation as to who might be hiding behind this well-known pseudonym. So let's summarize the speculation that has circulated through the media and the community over the years. Instead of drawing any in-depth conclusions, I will just list the publicly available information which has been gathered from many different sources.

Although I have devoted a great deal of time to this chapter, it is not within my power to verify the full accuracy of all the data. I have come across various contradictory statements and have ultimately used those that could be verified from multiple sources. Some of the data may be misleading, and some may even be false. It is up to each reader to draw his or her own conclusions, verify the data, and place the individual facts in the timeline described in this book. Those who are interested can then continue their search for Satoshi on their own. The internet—and especially the various historical internet forums—are full of information. Research on this topic requires objective analysis, free from the shallow media speculation that seeks sensationalism without dedicating the time needed to reach a thorough conclusion.

I especially recommend the official sites where you can access most of Satoshi's texts, discussions, and emails.

 Satoshi's Archive

 Satoshi Nakamoto Institute

ARE THE FOOTPRINTS LEFT BY SATOSHI LEADING US IN THE RIGHT DIRECTION?

It has already been suggested in the previous discussion that Satoshi could not be just an ordinary cryptographer. He more or less adopted some cryptographic solutions as they were designed. If we want to talk about the fact that Satoshi left at least some traces, they can be found in the code and reports he personally wrote between 2008 and 2011. This body of text consists of several hundred emails, messages, and documents (including the Bitcoin whitepaper) that he published via the Cypherpunks mailing list, and later on bitcointalk. org, and other forums. These texts have been carefully catalogued by the community and are seen as sacred by his admirers. By analyzing Satoshi's online writings for linguistic patterns, we can uncover several hints that may pierce his meticulously crafted anonymity. Let's delve further into what these hints suggest.

- **One individual**
  There are several independent opinions that Satoshi was really just one individual. This conclusion has been reached by both Tim Carver, professor of computer science at Trine University, and Joshua Davis of the *New Yorker*, in addition to other researchers. They concluded that the texts in question were not written by multiple people.

- **British national**
  It is believed that Satoshi was a British national connected to the Cypherpunks movement. This theory is suggested by the *London Times* headline used in the first mined Genesis block. Satoshi frequently used British English terms, including "favour," "maths," "flat" (referring to his apartment), and the phrase "bloody hard." He also employed the British date format. These clues suggest that Satoshi might have originated from Britain, or that he lived there for an extended period.

- **Academic**
  There is further speculation that Satoshi could have been a British academic, given his impeccable use of British English. Supporting this theory is the observation that the code's language doesn't align with open-source program standards from the early 2000s. Instead, Satoshi's language usage mirrors that of the 1990s, a style commonly found in British universities at the time.

- **Probably lived in the UK**
  He was active in the late hours of UK time or early hours of US time, but used the term "yesterday" at moments that didn't align with US time references.

There is also speculation that some of the creators of bitcoin's predecessors could be hiding behind the pseudonym Satoshi Nakamoto. These are mainly those who, based on the experience of others, have stuck to a concept that they have discussed with the community. For them, the possibility that they might try to implement the project anonymously is directly suggested. Some have indeed appeared in community conversations with Satoshi in which they have actively participated. In such a case, they would have to appear in the conversations in a dual role, either in order to conceal their identity, or in order to spark discussion on the topic (or both).

Anyone can explore the publicly accessible archives containing numerous emails and conversations. It is then up to each individual to consider to what extent it would be bearable for Satoshi to correspond in almost a schizophrenic manner with himself for years. However, serious reasons for hiding one's identity are also an argument. Today, Satoshi might not be as concerned about legal repercussions. However, another significant concern arises: with the increasing value of bitcoin, he could face threats from extortionists, intense media scrutiny, and persistent appeals from individuals seeking financial assistance. Given his unquestionable intelligence, Satoshi could have been a master manipulator, managing to deliberately leave subtle and isolated red flags over long periods of time to lead would-be pursuers on a false trail. So we will probably never know his true identity or whether he was a spokesman for a wider group or just a brilliant individual. Nor are we likely to know if any of his close associates in the community had clues to his true identity.

POTENTIAL CANDIDATES

In the following passages, we'll take a look at some of the possible Satoshis and try to unravel one of the biggest mysteries in the world of cryptocurrency. Again, the individuals listed below are simply those most frequently speculated to be Satoshi Nakamoto, according to both the crypto community and media coverage.

Hal Finney

Finney was born on May 4, 1956, in Coalinga, California, and died August 28, 2014, in Phoenix, Arizona. He is given more coverage in this book because he was one of Satoshi's close associates and his life and views nicely illustrate the time and atmosphere in which bitcoin was created.

Finney was a libertarian, Cypherpunk, cryptography pioneer, and cryptographer. He was instrumental in the development of PGP and the Bitcoin protocol. He and his wife Fran have a son, Jason, and a daughter, Erin. He corresponded with Satoshi and is known as the first recipient of a bitcoin transaction. In August 2009, he was diagnosed with ALS and five years later, due to complications from ALS, Finney's body was taken off life support and immediately transferred to cryopreservation at the Alcor Life Extension Foundation in Scottsdale, Arizona, at his request.

Amyotrophic lateral sclerosis, more commonly known as ALS, is an incurable disease that affects motor nerve cells in the brain and spinal cord. As a result, the brain is unable to control the muscles and their movements. Over time, the muscles weaken and tissue is lost.

Cryonics deals with the preservation of life by stopping the dying process through sub-zero temperatures, with the aim of restoring good health in the future through medical technology.

In 1974, Finney graduated from Arcadia High School with honors and subsequently earned a position at the prestigious California Institute of Technology. He was interested in mathematics and engineering. He took every programming course available, because at that time there was no corresponding field of computer programming. It was also here that he met his wife Fran. They married in 1979 after Hal's graduation. Afterwards, he spent some time in the gaming industry, but said of himself: "I never considered myself a game developer. I was more of a general developer working in assembly language."

In 1991, Finney started developing code generators and optimizers. Around the same time, he started communicating quite actively with Cypherpunks. Finney, like many other Cypherpunks, was inspired by the work of David Chaum. In 1992, he wrote on the Cypherpunk mailing list, "Here we are faced with the problems of loss of privacy, creeping computerization, massive databases, more centralization— and Chaum offers a completely different direction to go in, one which puts power into the hands of individuals rather than governments and corporations. The computer can be used as a tool to liberate and protect people, rather than to control them."

David Chaum proposed theoretical systems that would allow anonymous communication and even untraceable financial transactions using encryption tools. Chaum developed the first ever virtual currency, eCash, which shared some anonymous and decentralized properties with Bitcoin, but never became widely adopted.

The motto of the Cypherpunks movement was that "Cypherpunks write code." The co-founder of the Cypherpunk movement, Timothy C. May said that "Hal was one of the people who actually wrote the code." When news hit the mailing list that privacy activist Phil Zimmermann was planning to release PGP, Finney became one of the first to collaborate with him. At the time of Zimmermann's prosecution, Finney was rather low-key and devoted himself to working on PGP without pay. After the lawsuits ended, he became a key employee at Zimmermann's company. Later, when Zimmermann evaluated Finney's contribution to PGP, he said that "Hal contributed tremendously."

After the widespread use of PGP, Finney was also the first to incorporate encryption software into remailers, essentially launching the first anonymous remailer based on cryptography. "Two people can communicate using email, with the identity of both protected from the other party," he wrote as part of a Cypherpunks mailing list post. These tools have gradually evolved into powerful Tor-like anonymization services that are now used by millions of people around the world.

Finney never gave up on Chaum's ideas for a pseudonymous digital currency. In a 1993 mailing list post, he stated that using digital money and chip cards should allow for transactions where no organization can invade your privacy or take your funds. This approach empowers individuals to protect themselves, rather than relying on others, thereby granting more power to the consumer.

Hal Finney (like Nick Szabo and Wei Dai) was interested in Extropianism long before he was diagnosed with ALS. He frequently participated in internet discussions about Extropianism, cryonics, life extension, space colonization, nanotechnology, artificial intelligence, and mind uploading. Notably, in an email **email from February 19, 2002**, Finney shared his thoughts on John Nash with his friends, referring to Nash as a proto-Extropian.

In 2004, Finney even used a Proof of Work system very similar to the one later used by Bitcoin.

Date: **Tue Feb 19, 2002** - 15:56:42 MST

I've just started reading Sylvia Nash's biography of mathematician John Nash, A Beautiful Mind, which is the basis for the movie of the same name. Nash made significant contributions to economics, among other things, before succumbing to schizophrenia. But this list of his earlier character traits sounded eerily familiar:

- "His heroes were lonely thinkers and supermen like Newton and Nietzsche."

- "His passion was computers and science fiction."

- "He considered 'thinking machines,' as he called them, to be superior in some ways to human beings."

- "At one point, he was fascinated by the possibility that drugs could enhance physical and intellectual performance."

- "He was fascinated by the idea of an alien race of hyper-rational beings who had learned to ignore all emotion."

I think there would be many recipients on this list who would share many of these views. The allure of figures like Newton and Nietzsche, the fascination with computers and science fiction, the experimentation with drugs and dietary supplements for physical and mental enhancement, and the prioritization of rationality to discover truth all characterize Extropian thought.

Hal

When the idea of Bitcoin first appeared on the Cypherpunks mailing list in 2008, Finney immediately jumped on board and responded with many questions—despite skepticism from the community. He downloaded early Bitcoin code and ran it on his desktop computer. He is widely believed to have been the first person other than Satoshi to do so. Finney left it running for several weeks and was able to mine up to a hundred coins a day on a common processor at the time. Sometimes after mining a thousand coins, Finney would shut down the machine because the computer would overheat.

During his experimentation with Bitcoin, Finney corresponded with Nakamoto and sent him numerous bug reports and suggestions for fixes. He later wrote that although he had no idea of Nakamoto's real identity or whereabouts, he imagined the Bitcoin creator as "a young man of Japanese descent who was very smart and honest."

In early 2009, Nakamoto also sent Finney the first-ever test bitcoin transfer. At that time, Finney began to experience the first symptoms of a serious illness. He became tired quickly, had difficulty speaking, felt a strange tingling sensation, and lost coordination in his right hand. In August 2009, he was diagnosed with ALS. Despite his deteriorating health, Finney continued to write code for Bitcoin. He wrote an enhancement to its elliptic curve cryptography that increased the transaction speed by up to 20%. He didn't stop even after he lost the ability to type with both hands. The moment he stopped typing altogether, he continued to write code using eye-tracking software. "I'm most proud of my work on PGP," Finney wrote in an email to a *Forbes* reporter, "Although I wouldn't be surprised if my small contribution to Bitcoin, particularly optimizing the mathematics of elliptic curves, could be a lasting contribution to my work."

In his March 19, 2013, message to bitcointalk.com, he wrote: "When Satoshi announced the first version of the software, I immediately got hooked. I think I was the first Bitcoin user since Satoshi. Satoshi and I chatted via email, and when he sent me ten coins to try, I was the recipient of the first bitcoin transaction."

What speaks in favor of Hal Finney being Satoshi?

- Finney lived for some time in Temple City, California, where another aspiring Bitcoin inventor, Dorian Nakamoto (born Satoshi), was staying at the time. They reportedly lived less than two miles apart. This fact raises a number of questions. Did they know each other? Did they help each other? Did Finney invent Bitcoin himself and just use his neighbor's name as a pseudonym?

- He was an active member of the Cypherpunks mailing list.

- The concept of issuing digital money was explored even before Satoshi.

- The results of an analysis of writing style commissioned by a *Forbes* reporter along with Juola & Associates showed significant similarities to the style of the Bitcoin whitepaper.

- The family subsequently sold most of the bitcoins mined in the first few days at a rate of around $100 to pay for Finney's medical bills.

- His family was blackmailed to obtain bitcoins that the blackmailer believed they possessed.

Finney was adamant even on his deathbed that he was not Satoshi, did not know the true identity of the inventor of Bitcoin, and had never met Dorian Nakamoto. Whatever the reality, Hal was certainly one of the main pioneers and co-creators of the Bitcoin protocol. "I'm pretty lucky overall. Even with the ALS, my life is very satisfying. But my life expectancy is limited," Finney wrote. "I'm comfortable with my legacy."

"Nakamoto's Neighbor: My Hunt For Bitcoin's Creator Led To A Paralyzed Crypto Genius" via *Forbes*

"Who is Hal Finney?" via Medium

Nicholas Szabo

Szabo was born on April 5, 1964, in the United States. He is an American computer scientist, legal scholar, and cryptographer known for his research in digital contracts and digital currency. He graduated from the University of Washington in 1989 with a degree in computer science and received his Juris Doctor from George Washington University Law School. Szabo is the author of the Smart Contract concept, a term widely used today specifically in connection with the potential uses of cryptocurrencies. At one time, Szabo was also an advocate of Extropian life extension techniques.

In 1998, Szabo proposed a concept for a decentralized digital currency called Bit Gold (page 137), which is often referred to as a precursor to Bitcoin. In this concept, the participant was to devote computing power to solving cryptographic puzzles. On the network, the solved puzzles were then to be sent to a public, fault-tolerant registry that would also be tolerant of the Byzantine Generals' Problem. There they were to be matched to the public key of the solver. Each solution would become part of the next problem, creating an increasing chain of new properties. This aspect of the system provided a way for the network to verify and time-stamp new coins, because if a majority of the parties did not agree to accept new solutions, they could not begin work on the next puzzle. When trying to design digital coin transactions, one encounters the double-spending problem. Once the data is created, reproducing it is a simple matter of copying and pasting. Most digital currencies solve this problem by relinquishing some control to a central authority that tracks the balance in each account. This was an unacceptable solution for Szabo, who commented: "I have tried to replicate as closely as possible in cyberspace the security and trust properties of gold, and these include, above all, that it is not dependent on a trusted central authority."

In a May 2011 article, Nick Szabo stated: "Myself, Wei Dai, and Hal Finney were the only people I know of who liked the idea (or in Dai's case, its cognate idea) enough to pursue it to any significant extent before Nakamoto (assuming Nakamoto is not actually Finney or Dai)."

- Like Finney, Szabo was an early Cypherpunk, befriended many people in that circle, and was an active member of the Cypherpunks mailing list. He was involved with the concept of issuing digital money before Satoshi.

- Nathaniel Popper wrote in the *New York Times* that "the most compelling evidence points to a reclusive American of Hungarian descent named Nick Szabo." In 2008, before Bitcoin was released, Szabo wrote a comment on his blog about his intention to create a live version of his hypothetical currency, Bit Gold. However, whether he chose anonymity out of fear of potential legal conflicts remains unknown.

- The main reason for speculation that Szabo could be Satoshi is the striking similarity between Bitcoin's whitepaper and Szabo's concept.

- In 2014, a linguistic study of the Bitcoin whitepaper was conducted at the Centre for Forensic Linguistics at Aston University. The results show that Nick Szabo may be the real Nakamoto. Many of the phrases used by Nakamoto are also found in Szabo's writings. Another clue was that both Nakamoto and Szabo used the same typographic language to write their papers.

- It is reasonable to speculate that Szabo might have renamed his Bit Gold project and introduced it under an anonymous identity for safety reasons, especially since he had a history of using pseudonyms.

However, Szabo has patiently dismissed speculation that he could be the creator of Bitcoin, leaving the world in suspense.

Wei Dai

Dai was born on May 3, 1963 in Beijing, China. He is an Australian computer scientist of Chinese descent. He moved to Australia in 1991. As a computer engineer, he is known for his contributions to cryptography and cryptocurrencies. He developed the cryptographic library Crypto++, created the b-money cryptocurrency system, and co-designed the **VMAC** message authentication algorithm. WEI, the smallest subunit of ether (another cryptocurrency), is named after him.

VMAC is a Message Authentication Code (MAC) algorithm based on a block cipher and using a universal hash, proposed by Ted Krovetz and Wei Dai in April 2007.

Dai earned his Bachelor's degree from the Beijing Institute of Computer Science in 1985 before completing his Doctor of Philosophy at Murdoch University in 1996. He began his career as a computer scientist at Telecom Research Laboratories in Melbourne, Australia, where he worked from 1992 to 1995. He then transitioned to a role as a Research Fellow at the Commonwealth Scientific and Industrial Research Organisation, holding that position from 1995 to 2000. Subsequently, Dai served as a consultant to various organizations. He consulted for Space-Time Research Pty Ltd from 2000 to 2001, for Deakin University in 2002, and has been consulting for Victoria University in Melbourne, Australia, since 2003.

In 1998 he proposed the concept of an anonymous distributed payment system b-money. Satoshi Nakamoto **credited Dai's b-money in the Bitcoin whitepaper**. However, Dai himself questioned the influence of b-money on Bitcoin. He stated: "I understand that the creator of Bitcoin, who calls himself Satoshi Nakamoto, did not read my article before he came up with the idea. He only found out about it after the fact, and credited me in his document. So my connection to this project is quite limited."

Satoshi's first known email with an early Bitcoin whitepaper proposal was written to Wei Dai.

From: Satoshi Nakamoto <satoshi@anonymousspeech.com>
Sent: Friday, August 22, 2008 4:38 pm
Who: S. S: **Wei Dai** <weidai@ibiblio.org>
Cc: Satoshi Nakamoto <satoshi@anonymousspeech.com> Cite your b-money page

I read your b-money page with interest. I am about to publish an article that expands your ideas into a complete working system. Adam Back (hashcash.org) noticed the similarities and pointed me to your page.
I need to find out the year of publication of your b-money page for quotes in my article. It will look like this:

[1] W. Dai, "b-money", http://www.weidai.com/bmoney.txt, (2006?).

You can download a preliminary version of the publication at

http://www.upload.ae/file/6157/ecash-pdf.html Feel free to forward it to anyone else you think might be interested.

Title: Electronic Cash Without a Trusted Third Party

Abstract: A purely peer-to-peer version of electronic cash would allow …
(followed by a familiar description of the concept)

Satoshi

So how is Wei Dai related to Satoshi Nakamoto?

- Dai was an active member of the Cypherpunks mailing list and one of the first people to communicate with Satoshi.

- The concept of issuing digital money was explored even before Satoshi.

- Crypto++, the coding library written by Dai, is widely used in Bitcoin code, and his coding style bears a striking resemblance to that of Satoshi.

- B-money has remained at the concept stage—similar to Szabo's Bit Gold—and its goals are very similar to Bitcoin.

- B-money is described as money that cannot be regulated and shares similarities later implemented in Bitcoin and other cryptocurrencies. Dai's first paragraph in the b-money concept reads: "I am fascinated by Tim May's crypto-anarchy. Unlike the communities traditionally associated with the word 'anarchy,' in a crypto-anarchy the government is not temporarily destroyed but permanently forbidden and permanently unnecessary. It's a community where the threat of violence is impotent because violence is impossible, and violence is impossible because its participants cannot be linked to their true names or physical locations."

Wei Dai—B-money

David Kleiman

Kleiman was born on January 22, 1967, and died on April 26, 2013. He was an American computer **forensics** expert and author as well as co-author of several books.

In 1988, at the age of 21, Kleiman was named United States Army Soldier of the Year. After distinguished service in the Army, Kleiman returned to his hometown and became a law enforcement officer with the Palm Beach County Sheriff's Office (PBSO).

In 1995, after a motorcycle accident, Kleiman became paralyzed and had to use a wheelchair. Despite this disability, he continued to work with the PBSO and achieved the rank of detective. He also worked as a Systems Security Analyst in the Computer Crime Division and helped configure the Computer Crime Lab.

Computer **forensics** is a branch of computer science concerned with the search for legal evidence in computers and data media. The goal is to gently read the data medium in order to identify, treat, recover or analyze the data to obtain the facts and assess the digital information.

Securit-e-doc has developed breakthrough server-based applications for storing, accessing and transmitting sensitive (encrypted) data in the cloud over open networks for intelligence agencies, the U.S. military, government agencies, law enforcement and global private sector organizations.

In early 2001, Kleiman began working for a startup company called **Securit-e-doc** as Director of Information Security. Some of his most notable work comes from this period. During this time he developed a groundbreaking encryption tool for Windows. This technology was used at NASA, the US Treasury Department, the Office of Inspector General, and the US Postal Service.

Kleiman had an interest in at least one business company that he founded with business partners Carter Conrad and Patrick Paige. He may also have had business connections with Craig Wright (more on page 163), but this has been the subject of litigation.

In 2010, Kleiman contracted a complicated MRSA infection. He was in great pain and his health was deteriorating. This also caused his mental deterioration and was probably the reason for his death in April 2013.

Kleiman died in abject poverty at the age of just 46. He was found in his Florida home, which he would likely have lost in foreclosure. According to Gizmodo, his body was discovered in a state of decomposition, with traces of blood and feces covering the room. A loaded gun and open bottles of alcohol were also found near his remains. A bullet hole in the mattress suggested that a gun had been fired at some point in the room, but no bullet casings were found.

Methicillin-Resistant Staphylococcus Aureus, more commonly referred to as MRSA, is a bacterium responsible for difficult-to-treat infections in humans and animals. In medical facilities, this superbug can even cause complications in minor surgical procedures. It is a strain of golden staphylococcus that is resistant to many types of antibiotics.

So how does Kleiman relate to Satoshi and his legacy?

- What connects Kleiman to Bitcoin itself is the fact that Craig Steven Wright claims that Kleiman was involved in its invention. However, Wright also claims that he himself is Satoshi Nakamoto. Wright's claims are mostly rejected by the community and generally considered false. Other sources, on the other hand, cite Kleiman as a possible Satoshi Nakamoto. Indeed, it could be that Wright knew or suspected that Kleiman was the real Nakamoto, and tried to work with this information after his death.

- Kleiman was also a contributor to the Cypherpunks mailing list, where Satoshi Nakamoto first introduced Bitcoin on October 31, 2008.

Ira Kleiman, David Kleiman's brother, litigated with Wright over the estate and alleged joint interest in companies that were to be involved in bitcoin mining as well as other technical projects. The situation is highly opaque, with the surviving Kleiman making his claim and Craig claiming something different. It seems that substantial parts of the puzzle were taken with David Kleiman to his grave. He was known to have carried a USB drive in a metal case with him at all times. It is not publicly known whether he gave the drive to his brother Ira or if it simply vanished upon his death. Patrick Paige, a close friend and business associate of the late Kleiman, informed Gizmodo that Kleiman employed robust encryption technology. He stated that attempting to search his computer would likely be fruitless.

The following QR codes link to more information about David Kleiman. Kleiman's brother has shared some of the documents and arguments submitted to the court, highlighting how Wright's stance evolved over time. However, you will also find information about Kleiman's life.

Dave Kleiman

"In Search of Bitcoin's Mysterious Creator: Can David Kleiman Be Satoshi Nakamoto?" via Cointelegraph

Adam Back

Back was born in 1970 in London. He is a British cryptographer and Cypherpunk. He was educated in the UK. He received a Ph.D. in computer science from the University of Exeter. During his studies he was interested in PGP encryption, electronic money, and remailers. He spent most of his time working on encryption. After graduating, he began to devote himself full time to applied cryptography, writing cryptographic libraries and designing, revising, and breaking other people's cryptographic protocols.

In 1997, Back introduced the Hashcash system, which was used to defend email addresses against spam. This principle became the basis for the Proof of Work (PoW) system, which is at the very heart of how the Bitcoin network works.

Similar to Wei Dai, David Chaum, and Hal Finney, Back is a pioneer in early digital asset research.

Back is currently the CEO of Blockstream, which he co-founded in 2014. It is a technology company with a focus on cryptocurrencies, particularly Bitcoin. Since its founding, this company has become one of the key players in the development of blockchain technology. Blockstream is involved in the development of protocols such as the Lightning Network, which facilitates faster and cheaper transactions on the Bitcoin network. The company is developing a satellite broadcast system for the Bitcoin blockchain, enabling access to the Bitcoin network in remote and less-connected regions of the world. Their work has made a significant impact on the overall availability and scalability of Bitcoin. Blockstream has devoted significant resources to the development and sustainability of the entire Bitcoin ecosystem. The company provides grants aimed at supporting research, development, and innovation that bolster the ongoing growth and stability of Bitcoin as a decentralized currency. This community engagement and investment in the ecosystem demonstrates its long-term commitment to blockchain technology and the entire Bitcoin project.

Adam Back is still one of the key figures in the fields of cryptocurrency and blockchain technology today. His opinions are often widely respected and followed by the community.

What similarities does Adam Back share with Satoshi?

- Adam Back is British.
- The language in which the early Bitcoin protocol code is written does not match the standards of open-source programs of the first decade. Satoshi used a language typical of the 1990s, which was prevalent mostly in British universities. This would coincide with the time when Adam Back was actively studying.
- Back is one of the few people who corresponded with Satoshi. He's the only one who never made his emails public, although he admitted to the correspondence.

- Hashcash was quoted in the Bitcoin whitepaper. However, Satoshi later wrote that Back was only named in the document because he was the only recipient who responded to Satoshi's distribution of the concept prior to its publication. Back, in his response, allegedly informed Satoshi that his plans for Bitcoin would not work.

- After Satoshi's departure, Back contributed significantly to the development of the cryptocurrency until 2014, when the community began to split.

However, Back consistently denies being Satoshi and asserts that he is unaware of Satoshi's true identity.

John Forbes Nash, Jr.

Nash was born on June 13, 1928, and died on May 23, 2015. He is known and published as John Nash. Nash was an American mathematician, economist, and part philosopher who won the 1994 Nobel Prize in Economics. This prize was awarded to him for his groundbreaking work on the mathematics of game theory, which he began in the 1950s.

Nash began studying chemical engineering at the Carnegie Institute of Technology in Pittsburgh, but later switched to mathematics. He earned both his bachelor's and master's degrees in mathematics in 1948. Two years later, at the age of 22, he completed his Ph.D. at Princeton University. In 1951, he joined the faculty of the Massachusetts Institute of Technology (MIT), where he conducted research on partial differential equations. He resigned in the late 1950s after bouts of mental illness. He then began an informal collaboration with Princeton University, where he became a senior research mathematician in 1995.

While still a university student, Nash published his first article, "The Bargaining Problem," in April 1950. He developed his mathematical model of bargaining in his influential doctoral thesis titled "Non-Cooperative Games." Nash established the mathematical principles of game theory. He demonstrated that in any finite game, players can consider the potential actions of their opponents and reach an optimal outcome. This outcome is known as the Nash equilibrium, which is widely used today.

Nash's research on differential equations at MIT led to his seminal paper "Real Algebraic Manifolds" which was published in *Annals of Mathematics* in November 1952.

From 1950–1954 he worked for the RAND Corporation as a consultant in game theory. In 1954, Nash was arrested for indecent exposure. Although the charges were dropped, his high security clearance was revoked and he was fired from the RAND Corporation. His position dealing with game theory was subsequently filled by Thomas Schelling.

> The RAND Corporation, an esteemed American research institution, was founded on May 14, 1948, and is headquartered in Santa Monica, California, USA. Its mission is to address critical societal challenges, aiming to enhance safety, health, and prosperity worldwide. Recognized as one of the top 10 think tanks by the University of Pennsylvania, it also ranks as the third most prestigious national security research institution globally.

At the height of his career in 1958, Nash began to show symptoms of mental disorder. In 1959 he was diagnosed with paranoid schizophrenia. From 1960 onward, Nash spent some of his time at Princeton. However, until 1970, he also spent periods in various psychiatric hospitals.

In the end, the administrative decision by Princeton's mathematics faculty and computing center to allow Nash to use university resources for his research during this difficult period proved to be the most effective step toward his cure. Nash became a mysterious figure in the minds of students, scribbling arcane equations on blackboards in the middle of the night. This research led him to the Princeton computing centers, where he developed high-level computer programs for his work.

In his later years, Nash expanded his focus to economics. Starting in 1997, he presented a series of lectures on the theory of ideal money (see page 106) at various universities across the USA, as well as in countries like Italy, Greece, China, and India. In addition to these endeavors, he received notable recognitions including the John von Neumann Prize for Theory in 1978 and the Leroy P. Steele Prize for Distinguished Contributions to Research from the American Mathematical Society in 1999. In 1995, Nash expressed that his nearly thirty-year battle with mental illness had prevented him from reaching his full potential. However, shortly before this admission, he had begun to find success.

Nash's research into game theory and his long struggle with paranoid schizophrenia became widely known thanks to the 2001 Oscar-winning film "A Beautiful Mind," which was based on Sylvia Nasar's 1998 biography of the same name. The 2002 public television documentary "Brilliant Madness" provides a more factually accurate portrayal of Nash's battle with mental illness.

Nash made significant contributions to mathematics, including the development of the Nash-Moser inverse function theorem, the Nash-De Giorgi theorem, and the Nash embedding theorems. For these accomplishments, the Norwegian Academy of Science and Letters honored him with the Abel Prize in May 2015. This prize was awarded for his "fundamental work in the field of partial differential equations." The Academy further described his work as "some of the most original results in geometric analysis of the twentieth century." Nash's work is considered groundbreaking by many scientists, yet it is also seen as deeply complex, suggesting that it's challenging to fully understand.

On Saturday, May 23, 2015, Nash and his wife Alice tragically died in a taxi accident near Monroe Township, New Jersey. He was 86, and she was 82. Police said the driver lost control of the vehicle while overtaking another, causing it to strike a guardrail. Mr. and Mrs. Nash were ejected from the car because they were not buckled up. Nash was returning from Oslo, where he had attended the Abel Prize ceremony. The award was presented by King Harald V of Norway. Nash accepted it alongside Louis Nirenberg, a celebrated mathematician. It was later said that Nash and his wife were supposed to go home in a limousine, but the driver did not show up. So they took a taxi instead.

For a brief description of John Nash according to his biography by Hal Finney, see page 154:

- "His heroes were lonely thinkers and supermen like Newton and Nietzsche."

- "His passion was computers and science fiction."

- "These 'thinking machines', as he called them, he considered superior to human beings in some respects."

- "At one point, he was fascinated by the possibility that drugs could enhance physical and intellectual performance."

- "He was fascinated by the idea of an alien race of hyper-rational beings who had learned to ignore all emotion."

- "The emphasis on rationality as a means to attain truth, the attraction to figures like Newton and Nietzsche, and the exploration of computers, science fiction, drugs, and dietary supplements for mental and physical enhancement are all common elements of Extropian thought."

Could John Nash be the mythical Satoshi Nakamoto?

- He copied the Austrian School of Economics in his views and from about 1997 onwards was involved in the theory of ideal money.

- Nash was an excellent mathematician, economist, and cryptographer who achieved the world's greatest recognition for his contributions to the mathematical treatment of game theory.

- Nash tried to use equations and calculations to predict the behavior of individual pigeons within a flock. It would be a piece of cake for him to translate the operating rules of Bitcoin through mathematics into a fully automated protocol.

- Nash was a scientist who deciphered a number of problems in completely different fields during his lifetime. He always concentrated fully on the problem at hand, and then solved the problem in theoretical terms. He conducted a series of proofs and validations on the issue and subsequently published his findings. For a period, he dedicated himself to teaching and sharing his insights with experts familiar with the problem. Eventually, he shifted his focus to other matters, much like Satoshi did.

- He was not British, but he was an excellent academic.

- Could he have developed the initial version of the Bitcoin protocol as he neared 80 years old? His son or a student might have assisted him with the coding. Nash understood programming and likely could have provided specific requirements, including established mathematical calculations and equations..

- Nash and Satoshi had similar views and shared a broad scope of agreement on many subjects. With a bit of insight and some speculation, it can be said that they shared perspectives on topics like the Austrian School of Economics, smart contracts, and the pooling of computer power, also known as parallel control machines.

Aspects of Nash's life and work suggest some parallels with Satoshi. Nash had a deep knowledge of mathematics and cryptography. He was interested in game theory, economics, and alternative currencies. Nash was a great critic of existing monetary systems, and in some of his works he proposed concepts that pointed towards a decentralized monetary system. In 2008, while he was actively involved in academia, he was also known for his stringent measures to safeguard his privacy.

For more information about Nash's life:

"19 Reasons John F Nash, Jr., was Satoshi Nakamoto" via Medium

"Parallel Control" by John Nash for the RAND Corporation

"How Bitcoin Fits with 'Beautiful Mind' Mathematician John Nash's Ideal Money" via *Bitcoin Magazine*

"The Many Facts Pointing to John Nash Being Satoshi Nakamoto" via Bitcoin.com

"In conversation with John Nash, Jr., on Ideal Money" via yanisvaroufakis.eu

Less likely candidates

- **Gavin Andresen:** former bitcoin protocol developer
- **David Lee Chaum:** American computer scientist and cryptographer, creator of eCash
- **Bram Cohen:** American programmer and author of the BitTorrent protocol
- **Len Sassaman:** a cryptographic genius, committed suicide in 2011 while experiencing depression
- **Michael Clear:** postgraduate student of cryptography at Trinity College Dublin
- **Vili Lehdonvirta:** Finnish economic sociologist and former game developer
- **Neal King**, **Vladimir Oksman**, and **Charles Bry:** patented bitcoin-related technology
- **Martti Malmi:** developer living in Finland
- **Jed McCaleb:** creator of the Mt. Gox exchange and co-founder of Ripple and Stellar
- **Donal O'Mahony** and **Michael Pierce:** computer scientists
- **Michael Weber:** Swiss software developer
- **Shinichi Mochizuki:** Japanese mathematician
- **Dustin D. Trammell:** security researcher
- **Grigory Perelman:** Russian mathematician

Unlikely candidates

- Paul Solotshi Calder Le Roux was a programmer and the head of a criminal drug cartel, later turned DEA informant. He created E4M, an open source program for encrypting disks in Microsoft Windows. He is sometimes credited with authorship of the open source program TrueCrypt (based on E4M), which he denies. In June 2020, he was sentenced to 25 years in prison.

- Craig Steven Wright, known in the community as "Faketoshi," has claimed to be the creator of Bitcoin. Since 2016 he has alleged that he is Satoshi Nakamoto which has resulted in several legal disputes over this assertion. It is alleged that Wright collaborated with the late David Kleiman. His claims have been met with skepticism and derision, as proving his identity as Satoshi could seemingly be simple—by signing a transaction from one of Satoshi's recognized addresses. However, Wright seems unable to access these addresses. In reaction to his unproven claims and legal actions, COPA filed a lawsuit against Wright. A British court determined in March 2024 that Wright is not Satoshi Nakamoto.

Cryptocurrency Open Patent Alliance (COPA), was founded in 2020. Its goal is to support the adoption and advancement of cryptocurrency technologies and to remove patents as barriers to growth and innovation. COPA has 33 member companies, including Coinbase, Block, Meta, MicroStrategy, Kraken, Paradigm, Uniswap, and Worldcoin.

- Dorian Nakamoto, born Satoshi, is a scared and kind Japanese retired physics professor. In his own words, he has never worked in cryptography and is so financially poor that he cannot even afford an internet connection. But he is invited by the community to conferences and benefits from the popularity of his pseudo-name. At one time, he lived near Hal Finney.

- Elon Musk has been speculated to be the elusive Satoshi Nakamoto in the past. He once tweeted something suggesting that it should be obvious who Satoshi is. However, most people no longer consider Musk a candidate for being Satoshi. This change in perception is largely due to some of Musk's surprising comments, which have led the cryptocurrency community to believe that his understanding of the subject is rather limited.

WHY IT'S PROBABLY A GOOD THING SATOSHI DOESN'T EXIST

If Satoshi Nakamoto were still alive, and if he still held the private keys to his wallet, he would be one of the richest people on the planet. For Bitcoin, however, the fact that the creator is unknown or perhaps even dead is one of its greatest strengths. Unlike other cryptocurrencies, its distinctiveness lies in the fact that there's no single figure to hold accountable, and no founder who can sway or manipulate the community. Bitcoin is free money to all who show an interest in it. Whoever Satoshi Nakamoto was, let's give him the peace and anonymity for which he fought.

A HIDDEN TREASURE: SATOSHI'S LOST COINS

The last piece of information we know about Satoshi is how many bitcoins remain at addresses attributed to him. This issue has been heavily researched by analyst Sergio Lerner, who published his research and conclusions on the bitcointalk.org forum. Lerner examined a performance graph of the individual computers that mined bitcoin in the early days and their mining results. He shows that 36,000 blocks, at 50 BTC each, have the same footprint, indicating that they were mined by a single computer. This amounts to a total of 1,800,000 BTC. Moreover, some of Satoshi's addresses are public knowledge because they sent various payments to each other within the community.

According to Lerner, Satoshi's addresses hold just over 1,800,000 BTC. Of this amount, 63% has never been moved, leaving approximately 1.1 million BTC untouched. These coins can be categorized as "lost coins," which could be in circulation but aren't because no one probably has access to them anymore. Such a situation can arise if a user loses access keys, or dies without passing along the keys. In 2010 on bitcointalk.org, Satoshi wrote in a discussion regarding users losing access to their wallets: "Lost coins only make everyone else's coins worth slightly more. Think of it as a donation to everyone." If Satoshi never intentionally used or transferred these coins, it's as if he has granted all Bitcoin users a value boost by effectively "removing" more than 5% of the total coins from circulation.

Comments on Satoshi's possible lost coins from Sergio Lerner via bitcointalk.org

CHAPTER 1 SUMMARY

- Bitcoin is a decentralized form of currency that operates on a peer-to-peer network, independent of any state control. Its monetary policy is clearly defined and predictable. From a global perspective, it is a non-inflationary currency.

- Bitcoin is volatile, but in the long run it seems to be a good sustainer of value.

- Humanity has been steadily progressing towards the creation of money that is antifragile and independent of the control of states and banking institutions. This trend has been ongoing for so long that, with a touch of exaggeration, one might say it has been happening since time immemorial.

- Democratic states should endorse bitcoin and the burgeoning crypto-industry as an innovative form of free money, allowing ordinary citizens to choose the currency they wish to use.

- We can assert that a goal long sought by renowned thinkers, freedom fighters, and economic reformers has finally been attained. This goal is the realization of a superior form of money that is free from reliance on declining fiat currencies.

Summed up from John Nash's perspective:

- Bitcoin serves as a technological facilitator (or lubricant) that efficiently enables the transfer of value (or good deeds), thus proving itself useful.

- From a global perspective, it is completely non-inflationary and extremely rare.

- It is a new kind of money—without a link to gold—that cannot be influenced by states or institutions.

- From a service perspective, it assures people of long-term, unlimited quality.

- Thanks to its unique features, bitcoin is poised to become a global standard for measuring value, akin to other units that define quantities such as kilograms, degrees, watts, meters, pascals, and hours.

BITCOIN TECHNOLOGY: OPPOSING THE CRITICS

BITCOIN TECHNOLOGY: OPPOSING THE CRITICS

Now, let's explore the essence of how Bitcoin works. It is a complex technology that is not easy to explain in a nutshell. However, it would be much more complicated if you didn't already understand the principles behind fiat currencies and the objectives Bitcoin seeks to fulfill. I can assure you that I will not go into technical complexities like how hashing and other principles of cryptographic functions work. I don't want you to feel that you have to do a complicated homework assignment in order to better understand how bitcoin works.

Your homework assignment: each one of you will calculate one bitcoin.

Understanding Bitcoin is similar to understanding other technical equipment, such as a car or a television. You don't need to know in detail the technologies that underpin them. You only need to understand the basic principles of their use and handling.

HOW BITCOIN WORKS

As you have previously read, Satoshi drew upon various cryptographic functions developed within the Cypherpunk community to conceptualize the entire network. These features and tools were designed to enhance security and freedom in the digital realm. However, integrating these elements alone was not sufficient to develop a fully automated system. Such a system also required the incorporation of economic incentives and principles aligned with game theory to ensure its effective operation. This has created a model of non-state money that has the potential to compete with fiat money.

I'd rather swing with bitcoin than slide with fiat.

WHAT PROBLEMS DID SATOSHI SET OUT TO SOLVE?

Satoshi had the opportunity to study the failures of previous projects and learn valuable lessons from them. Let's briefly summarize the main problems he had to solve.

- indestructibility through decentralization: creating a system without a central point of failure, where servers cannot be shut down, founders arrested, or assets seized

- a system that anyone can trust that ensures transparency and compliance with network rules

- a system without the need to trust anyone and without the need to centrally manage further development

- anonymity, verifiability, and security for the network and its users, with robustness to support billions

- openness of the system to all

- transference of real value (good deeds) from the real world to the electronic world

- monetary policy that ensures gradual adoption, scarcity, and perceived currency quality

- determination of the total number of coins and gradual release of coins

- network economics that motivate people to run a Bitcoin network

- double-spending problem

- conversion of the operating rules of Bitcoin through mathematics into a fully automated protocol

Here is Satoshi's message, where he humbly introduced the Bitcoin concept, claiming to have addressed all of these challenges.

Bitcoin P2P e-cash paper

Satoshi Nakamoto at vistomail.com

Fri Oct 31 14:10:00 EDT 2008

I've been working on a new electronic cash system that's fully peer-to-peer, with no trusted third party.

The paper is available at: http://www.bitcoin.org/bitcoin.pdf

The main properties:
    Double-spending is prevented with a peer-to-peer network.
    No mint or other trusted parties.
    Participants can be anonymous.
    New coins are made from Hashcash style proof-of-work.
    The proof-of-work for new coin generation also powers the network to prevent double-spending.

Bitcoin: A Peer-to-Peer Electronic Cash System

Abstract. A purely peer-to-peer version of electronic cash would allow online payments to be sent directly from one party to another without the burdens of going through a financial institution. Digital signatures provide part of the solution, but the main benefits are lost if a trusted party is still required to prevent double-spending. We propose a solution to the double-spending problem using a peer-to-peer network. The network timestamps transactions by hashing them into an ongoing chain of hash-based proof-of-work, forming a record that cannot be changed without redoing the proof-of-work. The longest chain not only serves as proof of the sequence of events witnessed, but proof that it came from the largest pool of CPU power. As long as honest nodes control the most CPU power on the network, they can generate the longest chain and outpace any attackers. The network itself requires minimal structure. Messages are broadcasted on a best effort basis, and nodes can leave and rejoin the network at will, accepting the longest proof-of-work chain as proof of what happened while they were gone.

Full paper at: http://www.bitcoin.org/bitcoin.pdf

Satoshi Nakamoto

The Cryptography Mailing List

HOW BITCOIN WORKS AT A GLANCE

Now, let's try to simplify the general overview of how the Bitcoin protocol works. Its operation involves cryptographic elements that have been in common use by humanity for a long time. In fact, a substantial part of these elements originated in the Cypherpunks community, and subsequently spread to other areas of activity. Let's discuss this in a little more detail.

And this is a very simple explanation of how Bitcoin works.

- Participants in the Bitcoin network include miners (who are part of mining pools or associations), full node operators, and users who make payments.

- Only miners and node operators are operators of the Bitcoin network.

- Bitcoin can be obtained through mining, buying, or earning it.

- The Bitcoin protocol, the Bitcoin network, and the Bitcoin blockchain operate on the principles and technologies set out in the Bitcoin whitepaper published by Satoshi Nakamoto.

- The core concepts outlined in the document include decentralization, the use of a peer-to-peer (P2P) system, mining as a Proof of Work completed, an automatic system for regulating mining difficulty, a controlled release of coins through a process called halving, and rewards for mining blocks, along with transaction fees.

- The technologies employed include timestamp cryptography, digital signatures, the use of private and public keys, hashing functions, hash trees, ledgers, and network nodes.

- The whole system of mining new bitcoins is based on the principle of competition. This competition is open to anyone, but it is not free. Each participant has to perform a certain activity in which they have to invest their own resources. This activity is called Proof of Work.

Principles of the Bitcoin protocol

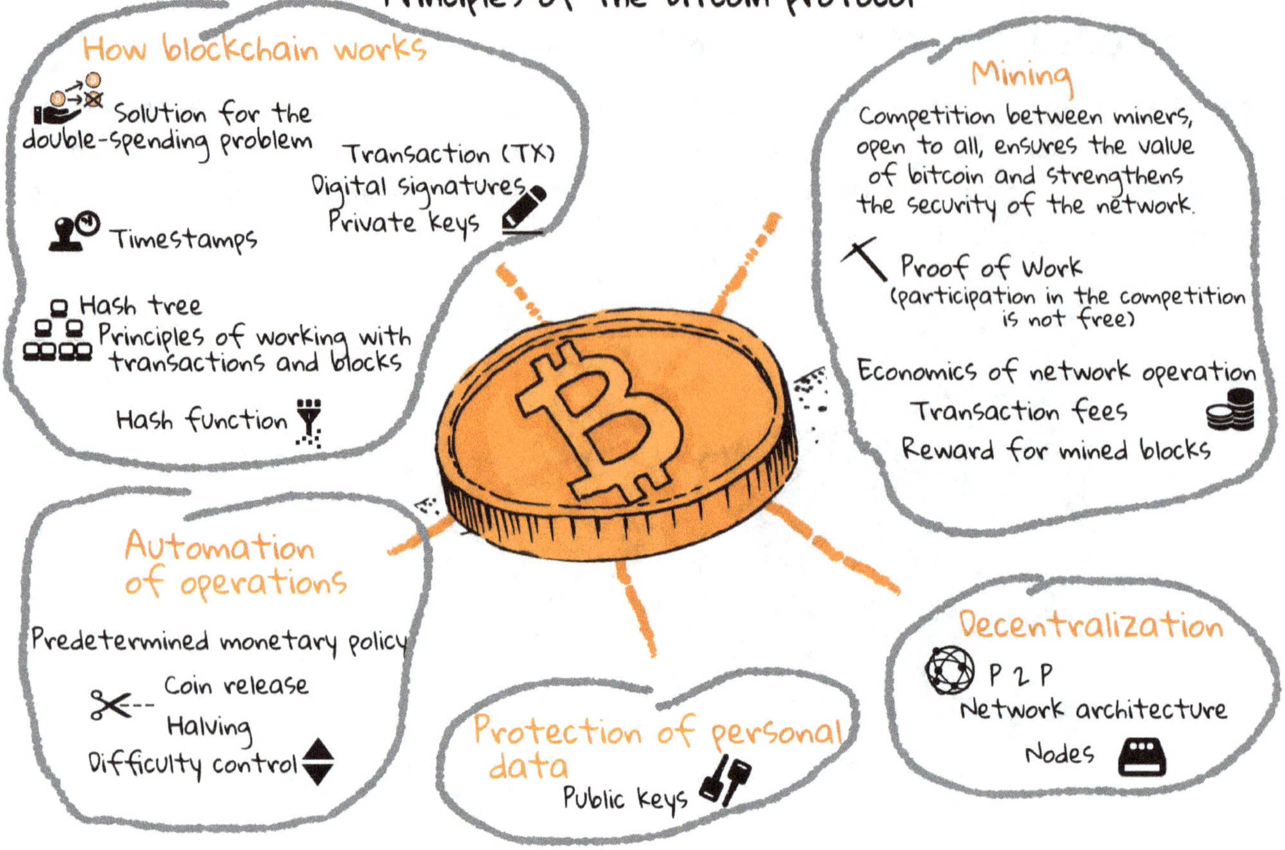

How blockchain works

Solution for the double-spending problem

Timestamps

Transaction (TX)
Digital signatures
Private keys

Hash tree
Principles of working with transactions and blocks

Hash function

Mining

Competition between miners, open to all, ensures the value of bitcoin and strengthens the security of the network.

Proof of Work
(participation in the competition is not free)

Economics of network operation
Transaction fees
Reward for mined blocks

Automation of operations

Predetermined monetary policy

Coin release
Halving
Difficulty control

Protection of personal data

Public keys

Decentralization

P 2 P
Network architecture

Nodes

Where can we find these principles in the Bitcoin whitepaper?

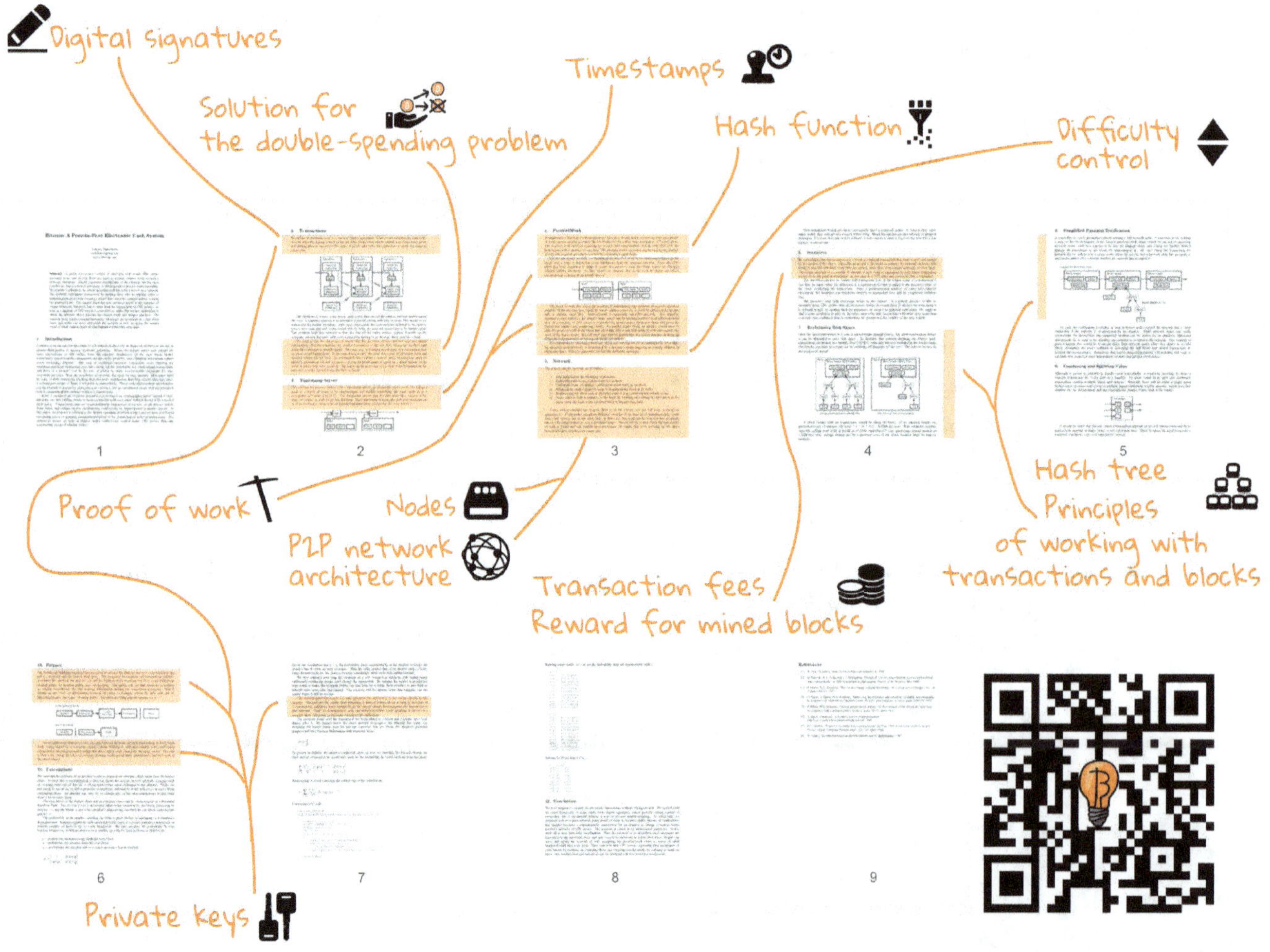

Miners and mining pools

These are the participants in the competition. Each round of the competition lasts about 10 minutes, and the miner who finds the correct solution—effectively writing or creating a new block—is rewarded. This individual then verifies and records transactions, thereby supporting the functionality of the Bitcoin network. Due to the significant computational power needed to discover a block by testing various random numbers, miners (those who create blocks) often collaborate in pools. In this context, a pool of miners is an organized group that voluntarily combines their mining capacities to enhance outcomes. When a mining pool receives new bitcoins, it distributes them among the participating miners based on a predetermined arrangement. The operators of these pools assume a managerial role and receive pre-agreed compensation for their services.

Mining

Miners can be likened to rolling a hypothetical dice with as many sides as there are atoms in the universe. Instead of literally rolling dice, the mining computer generates large random numbers. Depending on the mining difficulty, anywhere from billions to quadrillions of attempts may be needed. When a miner finds the correct number, or "nonce," they can create a new block and are rewarded with a specific number of new bitcoins for that mined block. The entire network then verifies that this block aligns with the established rules. After verification, the miner populates this block with pending transactions and earns additional rewards from user-specified transaction fees. This system operates on the premise that finding the correct number is incredibly challenging, but once it's found, its validity can be quickly and easily confirmed by the entire network. After each round, a new target number is generated, and the competition resumes. Finding a new block requires significant effort, which is why the algorithm is called Proof of Work.

Hash rate (computing power)

This metric measures the performance of the Bitcoin network, or more specifically, the mining machines. The performance is quantified in terms of hashes per second.

Mining difficulty

This is the mechanism by which the Bitcoin protocol adjusts the mining difficulty every 2,016 blocks, approximately every fourteen days. It verifies how many blocks have been mined, and adjusts the mining difficulty algorithm accordingly. The general rule of thumb is that a new block is created roughly every ten minutes. If there is an increase in the number of miners, new blocks may be created faster because there is more computing power on the network. After adjusting the difficulty of mining, a particular miner (pool) will, on average, mine fewer or more bitcoins than at the same power before. Mining difficulty is monitored and adjusted roughly every fourteen days, depending on the current average hash rate in that period.

Proof of Work

Miners compete with each other on the basis of calculations. Under decentralization, competition must be available to everyone, but participation cannot be free for the mined coins to have value. The miner must invest significantly in technology and continuously cover the electricity costs to participate in the mining process. However, electricity is not free anywhere in the world. Through payments for the electricity consumed, real value—in the form of our good deeds performed—is transferred into cyberspace.

Decentralization

Individual miners and node operators form the Bitcoin network. Although they may not know or trust one another and might be unaware of each other's locations, they collaboratively ensure the ledger's integrity, confirm that the system adheres to its established rules, and validate both mined blocks (bitcoins) and the accuracy of individual transactions. Given the experience and lessons learned from previous failed attempts at non-state currency, the system is designed without a central point of failure. The entire network cannot be shut down, no funds can be seized, and it's impossible to shut down all operators.

User, transactions, and transaction fees

The user participates in the Bitcoin network to send and receive payments without being responsible for its security. Their funds are stored on this network. The user pays fees for each transaction, the amount of which depends on the network load. However, users can determine their transaction fees based on how quickly they want their transactions to be processed. Miners prioritize transactions with higher fees due to their own financial incentives. They confirm each transaction and ensure the payer has the funds they're sending. Once a transaction is confirmed, it's irreversible and cannot be voided by any authority. A simplified diagram of how transactions work is shown in the following figure.

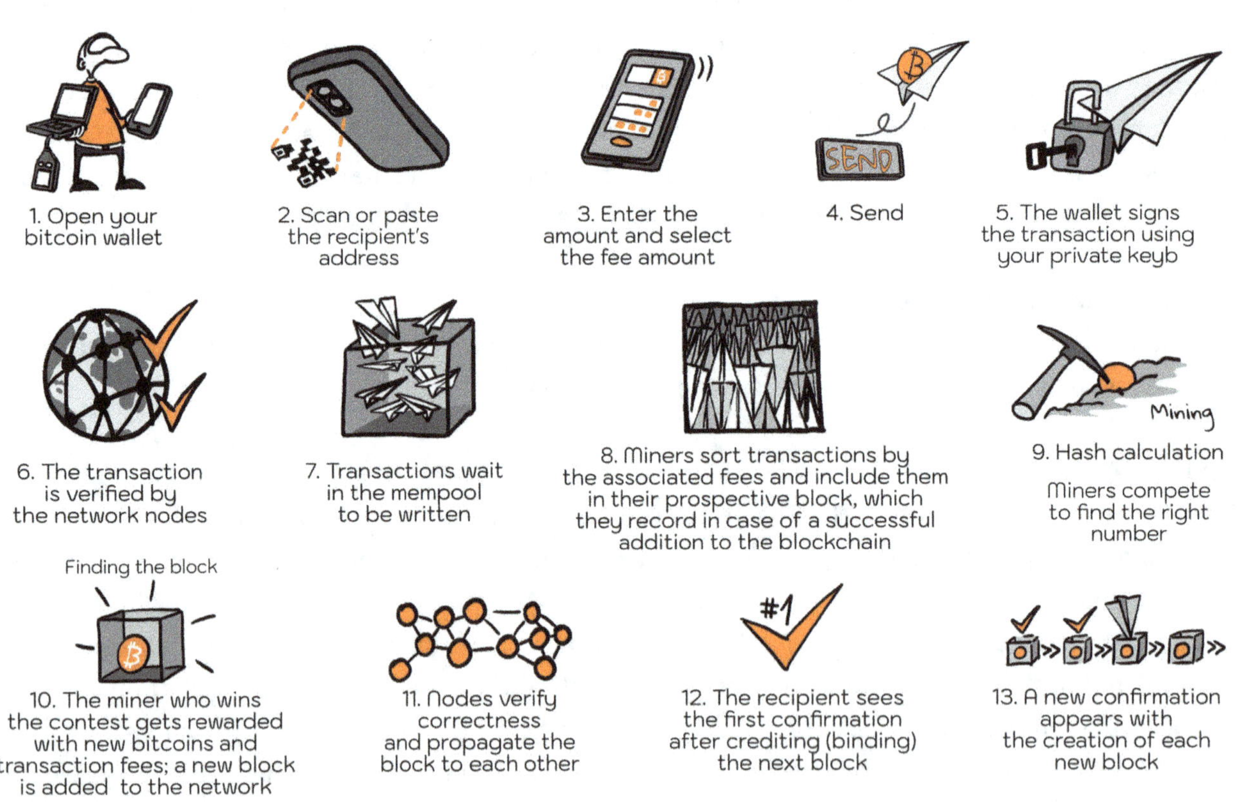

Full node

Full node operators are also Bitcoin network operators as they oversee protocol compliance. Each full node of the Bitcoin network maintains a complete and verified database of all transactions that have ever taken place on the network, including mempools. The most commonly used version of the Bitcoin full node is a fully synchronized Bitcoin Core. There are tens of thousands of active nodes in the network. Each miner (mining pool) simultaneously runs a full node. Anyone can be a full node operator. Affordable hardware for bitcoin mining is readily available, and you can even buy pre-set solutions that simply need an internet connection. I can recommend the purchase of your own full node to anyone who is serious about bitcoin. First of all, you will also become a network operator, but most importantly, you will be able to check the status of your transactions on your own node.

Mempool

This term is used to reference a memory pool. It is like a waiting room where all new and valid transactions are collected. However, these transactions are not yet confirmed (mined) by the miner. We therefore refer to such transactions as either unconfirmed or zero confirmation transactions. Since the network has no central transaction database, each node maintains its own separate mempool with unconfirmed transactions. Therefore, some mempools differ, for example, in their total memory size.

Private keys

Each user owns his or her own private key, generated and renewable based on the seed (explained on page 292). A user's wallet, whether software or hardware, stores only their private keys, which enable them to send the satoshis they possess. For simplicity, think of these keys as passwords or access permissions. The wallet also provides a view into the user's created addresses and allows for management of the balances associated with those addresses. If a wallet is lost or its PIN is forgotten, the private keys can be regenerated using a backup seed, restoring user's access to their bitcoin. Without the private key, not only is it impossible to manage the funds at a specific address, but those funds also cannot be seized.

Public keys

These represent individual addresses, similar to an account number, as described in detail on page 246. An address is the public information you give to your peers when they want to send you a payment. Addresses that the user does not associate with their own identity are anonymous.

Blockchain (ledger)

This ledger is maintained by tens of thousands of miners and nodes around the world. Participants in the network are unaware of each other's identities or locations. However, they collaboratively ensure the legitimacy of the mining process and the accuracy of transactions. The ledger consists of already mined blocks, which record the transactions made between users. The ledger continuously expands as new blocks are mined, capturing every transaction made on the network since its inception. If disputes arise, the chain recognized by a majority (51%) of the validators prevails, adhering to the "longest chain wins" principle. This ledger also keeps a record of all previously mined bitcoins, linking them to the respective user addresses. Miners are also seen as users from the perspective of ownership of the mined funds, since the coins mined by them are attributed to their addresses. Importantly, users don't actually store their coins in a wallet; rather, all coins are recorded in this globally backed-up ledger.

The economics of bitcoin

Profitability arises primarily from mining rewards (new BTC awarded to miners) and transaction fees paid by users to miners for recording transactions. Initially, miners primarily profited from newly-mined bitcoins. As fewer bitcoins become available for mining over time, miners' income will increasingly come from transaction fees. This ensures that the network remains operational even after the last bitcoin has been mined.

Peer-to-peer (P2P)

The whole system is designed so that users do not need intermediaries, but can communicate directly with each other. Individual payments are sent directly between user addresses (wallets) without the involvement of a third party.

Open source

In a decentralized system like Bitcoin, individuals don't need to trust each other; instead, they place their trust in the Bitcoin protocol. To ensure trustworthiness and transparency, the Bitcoin protocol is built as open source.

Halving

Once 210,000 blocks are mined—approximately every four years—the number of new BTC in the block is halved.

- Approximately one block is mined every ten minutes worldwide.

- In the first period, **50** BTC were mined per block.

- Following the initial halving on November 28, 2012, each block rewarded miners with 25 BTC. After the second halving on July 9, 2016, this reward was reduced to 12.5 BTC. Most recently, after the fourth halving in May of 2024, miners now receive 3.125 BTC for each mined block.

- The total number of bitcoins mined during each halving period was as follows: 10.5 million in the first period, 5.25 million in the second period and 2.625 million in the third period. From May 2020 to January 2024, only 1.3125 million bitcoins were mined. The next halving in 2028 will see a total of 20.34375 bitcoins mined out of a total of 21 million bitcoins.

- There will be a total of 32 halvings, and bitcoin will be mined until about 2140.

- In each halving period, the same number of bitcoins is always mined as in all subsequent halving periods combined.

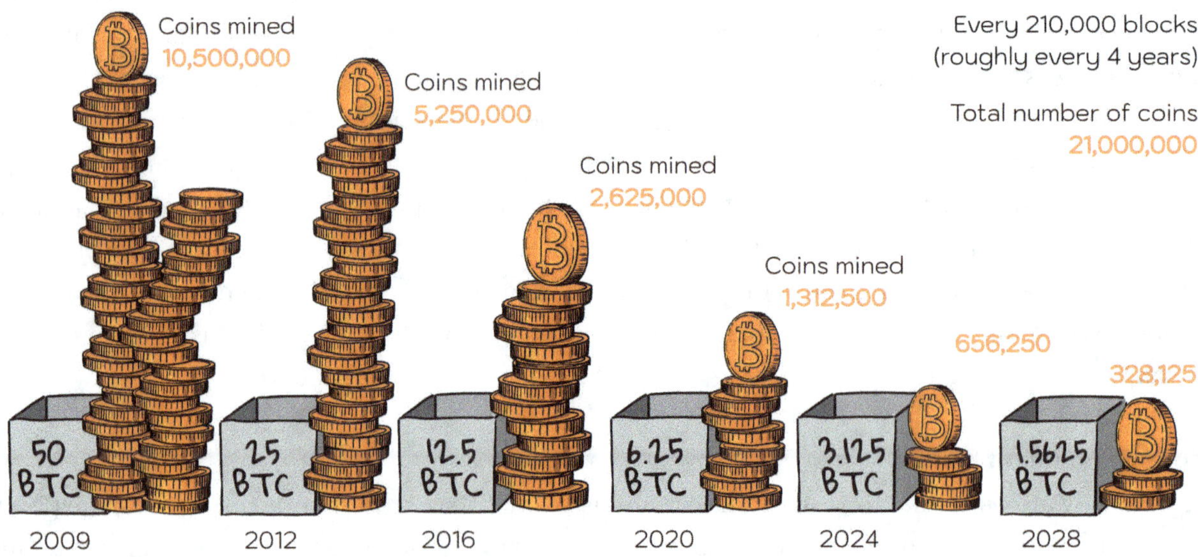

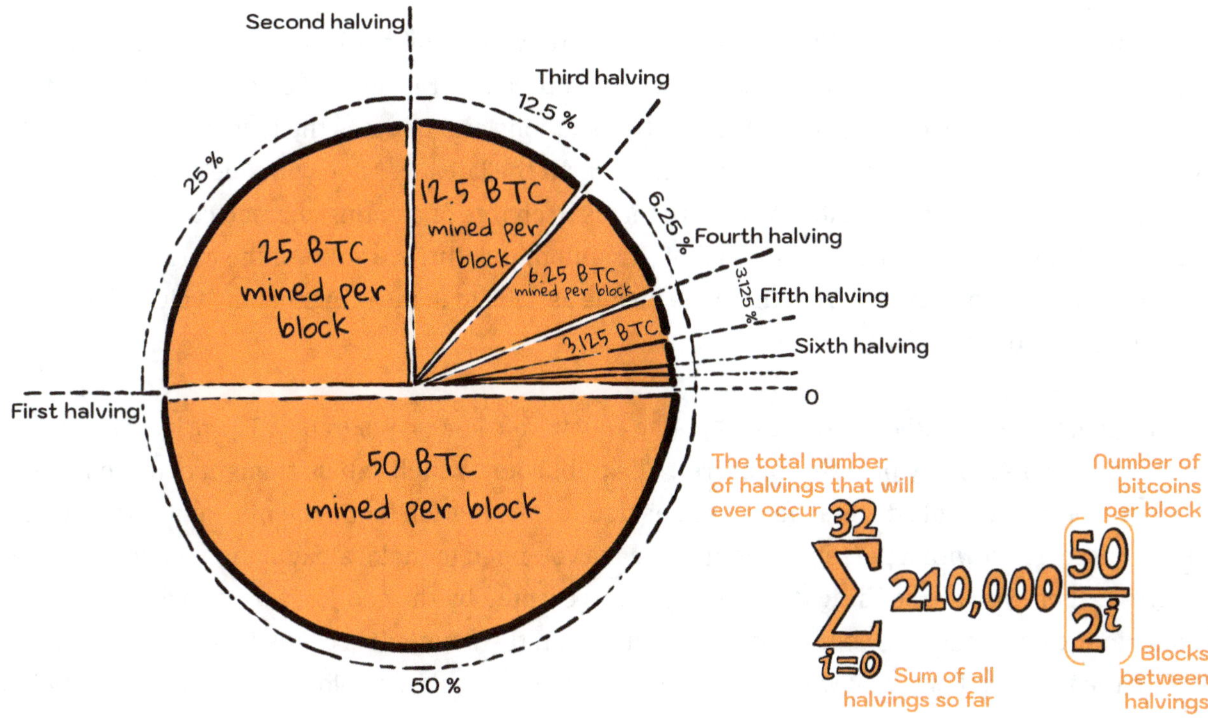

$$\sum_{i=0}^{32} 210{,}000 \frac{50}{2^i}$$

Fixed monetary policy

The rules for the creation (mining) of digital coins and their final quantity are fixed in advance. The maximum number of bitcoins created is set by the Bitcoin Protocol at 21 million bitcoins. One bitcoin (BTC) is equivalent to 100,000,000 satoshi (SAT). Mining will continue indefinitely, with the understanding that for approximately 130 years, miners will receive a gradually decreasing reward of newly created bitcoins from each block mined. At the same time, the trend of increasing rewards for written transactions is expected to continue.

Automated operating rules

The established operating rules are fully automated through the mathematics and functions of the Bitcoin protocol. There is no single individual or central authority throughout the Bitcoin network that is charged with controlling the creation of currency units, verifying transactions, performing operational oversight of compliance with the established rules, coordinating Bitcoin network operators, resolving arbitrations, or managing development work on the bitcoin protocol.

HOW BITCOIN WORKS IN SHORT DETAIL

Bitcoin is the world's first fully decentralized digital currency. Better said, it is a decentralized network for peer-to-peer payments, and a virtual currency that functions as online cash. It is an open-source digital currency that can be used pseudo-anonymously, or anonymously until a given address is linked to a specific person's identity.

Until the invention of bitcoin, online transactions always required a trusted intermediary, known as a third party. Without these intermediaries, any digital money could be spent multiple times. In computer science, this problem is known as the double-spending problem or the Byzantine Generals' Problem. Until the advent of Bitcoin, it could only be solved by using a trusted third party to keep the ledger. For the first time in history, Satoshi solved the double-spending problem without the need for a third party.

Every payment that occurs on the Bitcoin network is recorded in a public ledger (blockchain). The Bitcoin ledger is automatically distributed to all Bitcoin network operators, replacing the need for a trusted third party. In this way, the Bitcoin network validates transactions and updates the ledger through the P2P network, where all nodes continuously share and confirm the latest version with one another. There is no central authority in the entire Bitcoin network that is in charge of creating currency units or verifying transactions. The Bitcoin protocol handles all of this automatically. The value of the currency is not derived from gold or fiat money, but from the value people ascribe to it, meaning that the value of bitcoin is determined on the open market.

Individual payments are authenticated using public and private key cryptography. The private key, which can be thought of as a password, is kept secret. The public key, which can be thought of as an account number, creates a payment address that is used as public information for payments. Public keys are not inherently associated with a person's identity. In case you need to make a payment, you need to enter the address where you are sending the money. This is created by the counterparty's public key. Then you confirm the payment with your private key. After that, the payment is checked, timestamped, and written to the mempool, where it waits to be written to a new block. The blocks are written to a public ledger synchronized between all active nodes of the global network. All payments are checked against this ledger to ensure that the sender is entitled to the funds sent, and that they have not been previously spent. The moment a payment is confirmed by a sufficient number of independent Bitcoin network operators, it is considered approved. In other words, other blocks are linked to the block containing the payment, making it part of the ledger forever.

The security of the network depends mainly on miners providing their computers and computing power. In addition to the equipment they purchase, they consume a considerable amount of energy. Both cost them a substantial amount of money. This approach, known as Proof of Work, is employed to transition value, represented by real-world contributions or utility, into the digital realm. The actual mining of bitcoins is a purely mathematical process. Bitcoins are mined by engaging a massive number of computers around the world to search for a number based on given parameters.

To be more precise, the system uses a hashing algorithm on the data from the last block to produce a unique number, known as a nonce. Miners' computers generate random numbers within a given range, akin to rolling dice, aiming to discover this particular number. When a miner successfully identifies the number, the system initiates a new challenge by generating another unique number for the next block, and the process resumes.

According to established rules, the discovery of a new block (or a match) should ideally take place approximately every ten minutes across the global network. Checking whether the bitcoins are being mined at the specified rate is done automatically at the log level roughly every fourteen days—after 2016 blocks are mined. Depending on the mining evaluation, the Bitcoin protocol automatically adjusts the difficulty of the mathematical assignment, thus generally ensuring that bitcoins are and will always be mined at a rate that more or less matches the set rules.

For their efforts, miners receive a set number of bitcoins as a reward. Additionally, they earn transaction fees for recording pending payments. Initially, the reward for discovering each block was 50 bitcoins. About every four years, or precisely after 210,000 blocks are mined, this reward is halved. Consequently, after each halving, fewer bitcoins are introduced into the market daily, increasing the cryptocurrency's scarcity.

If an item becomes scarcer, its price increases in the market environment. So far, every halving in the past has been followed by an increase in the price of bitcoin. Unless the demand for bitcoin changes, this trend is likely to repeat in the future.

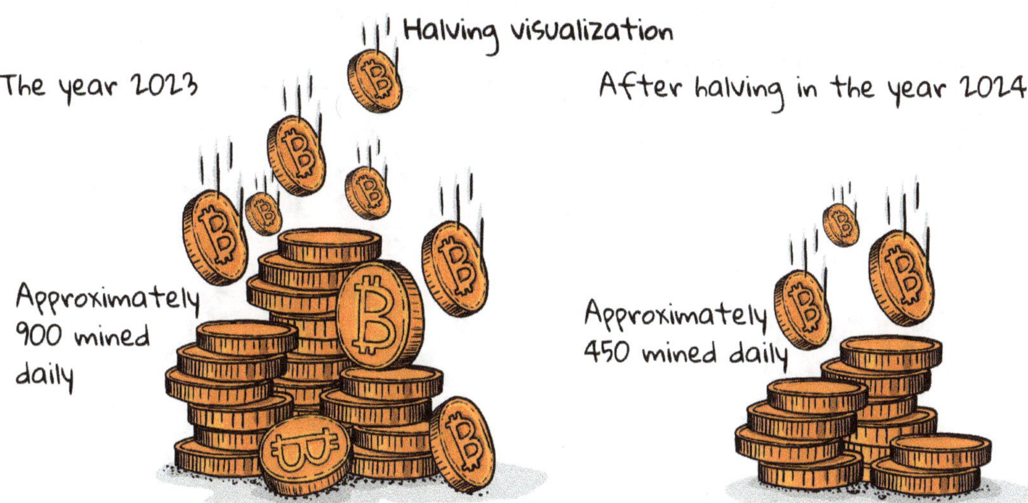

The process of mining bitcoins will not last forever. Satoshi has set the limit of bitcoins to be mined at 21 million. Roughly 132 years after the launch of the Bitcoin network—around the year 2140—new bitcoins will no longer be added. The only reward for miners witll be fees for recording payments made. This will incentivize them to keep the network running after the last bitcoin has been mined. On April 1, 2022, the 19 millionth bitcoin was mined. However, the exact number of bitcoins actively in circulation remains uncertain. It's estimated that roughly two million bitcoins, including those belonging to Satoshi, might have been lost.

I would like to mention the fact that after thirteen years of operation, more and more people are of the opinion that Bitcoin is an antifragile system. Throughout its existence, it has faced attacks from hackers and the media, as well as bans from institutions and governments.

Antifragility refers to systems that thrive in conditions of volatility, randomness, chaos, or stress. First introduced by the Lebanese-American economist Nassim Nicholas Taleb in his book *Antifragility: How to Profit from Upside, Uncertainty, and Chaos*, the concept captures how certain systems not only survive shocks and crises but also benefit and grow stronger from them.

This principle underpins many evolving entities, including evolution, culture, and political systems. Removing these stress factors from such systems would make them more vulnerable and fragile. Based on antifragility theory, everything can be categorized into:

1. Fragile: Items that are susceptible to damage or deterioration under stress or over time.

2. Resilient: Entities that withstand disturbances or stressors, maintaining their state and functionality during crises.

3. Antifragile: Elements that thrive on or gain from disorder, improving or becoming more robust under pressure.

For instance, a centralized nation-state exemplifies fragility, whereas a decentralized system of city-states aligns with the idea of antifragility.

To date, Bitcoin has managed to face even unpredictable events known as **black swans**. Despite the challenges, Bitcoin has grown stronger each year. Its resilience is primarily attributed to its complete de-centralization, unwavering market principles, and expanding adoption. These conditions provide an ideal environment for game theory to operate. Because of these elements, Bitcoin functions as an autonomous system, evolving similarly to nature, economies, and nations.

The term **black swan** (black swan concept) introduced in another book by Taleb, refers to rare and unpredictable events that have profound effects on society. While these events are impossible to anticipate or assign a specific risk, they are often retrospectively deemed predictable. Much of economic and human history unfolds due to such unpredictable "black swan" events. The best preparation for such unforeseen occurrences is to employ antifragility mechanisms.

FURTHER DEVELOPMENT OF BITCOIN

Satoshi designed Bitcoin with the expectation that future developments would address users' genuine needs. While he consulted with the user community about these aspects, he believed that the core functionality of the network initially required fine-tuning. Together, they later speculated about potential applications. Since its inception, Bitcoin has undergone significant improvements in areas like signatures, block-writing efficiency, and a secondary layer that greatly enhances transaction speed and affordability. **In the future, among other things, we can expect better smart contracts or complete anonymity**. To give you an idea, I include a snippet of one of the many emails Satoshi exchanged with the community.

 2010-06-17 18:46:08 UTC

Re: Transactions and scripts

The nature of Bitcoin is such that once version 0.1 was released, the core design was set in stone for the rest of its lifetime. Because of that, I wanted to design it to support every possible transaction type I could think of. The problem was, each thing required special support code and data fields whether it was used or not, and only covered one special case at a time. It would have been an explosion of special cases. The solution was script, which generalizes the problem so transacting parties can describe their transaction as a predicate that the node network evaluates. The nodes only need to understand the transaction to the extent of evaluating whether the sender's conditions are met.

The script is actually a predicate. It's just an equation that evaluates to true or false. Predicate is a long and unfamiliar word so I called it script.

The receiver of a payment does a template match on the script. Currently, receivers only accept two templates: direct payment and bitcoin address. Future versions can add templates for more transaction types and nodes running that version or higher will be able to receive them. All versions of nodes in the network can verify and process any new transactions into blocks, even though they may not know how to read them.

The design supports a tremendous variety of possible transaction types that I designed years ago. Escrow transactions, bonded contracts, third party arbitration, multi-party signature, etc. If Bitcoin catches on in a big way, these are things we'll want to explore in the future, but they all had to be designed at the beginning to make sure they would be possible later.

This excerpt shows Satoshi's belief that it was very important to build a stable foundation for the new technology that Bitcoin undoubtedly was. He was of the opinion that these stable foundations needed to be built before exploring other applications and subsequent scaling. However, despite this stance, he was open to new ideas and was prepared to work with the community to further develop and innovate.

Satoshi has designed the concept and architecture of the Bitcoin protocol so that other desired features and improvements can be implemented easily in the future. The ability to adapt and respond to user needs based on the consensus of the majority of the community is one of the key features of an open and decentralized system such as Bitcoin.

MODIFICATIONS TO THE BITCOIN PROTOCOL (BITCOIN CORE)

The Bitcoin protocol sets the rules for how Bitcoin works. It has freely available open-source code. Miners and all other Bitcoin users must follow this protocol if they want to remain part of the network. As with all working software solutions, the Bitcoin protocol requires regular maintenance and updates. Because the Bitcoin project is not managed by a single entity, development and maintenance must be done based on a majority consent of the network operators. Developers (individuals or teams) around the world propose or initiate modifications and improvements. These are then reviewed by developers actively working on the Bitcoin project.

Bitcoin Core is the most popular software client that ss use to create nodes, store coins, transact, and more on the Bitcoin network. It is the interface that determines how users interact with the Bitcoin ledger. There are multiple software clients for Bitcoin, but none are as widespread and essential as Bitcoin Core. It was created from the original Satoshi code and is still seen as the Bitcoin software client that sets the standards for other software clients.

The resulting consensus will decide if the proposed changes are approved for implementation or rejected. If approved, they will be presented to the network operators for validation. If there is no across-the-board support for the modifications among them, there is little chance of implementing the changes. To assess support for proposed changes, a method known as "signaling by miners" is used. Miners indicate their willingness to accept the suggested modifications by recording them in the blocks they mine.

SOFT AND HARD FORKS

Fork translates as branching. It is an update or split of the Bitcoin protocol. Just as mutations and adaptations in nature lead to new species and diversity of life, forks bring improvements, innovations, or different directions of development.

Interesting infographic: A map of bitcoin forks

Soft fork

This is an upgrade to the Bitcoin protocol. While it is a means for developers to enhance the system, its implementation depends on the network's majority approval. This type of update is backward-compatible, meaning it can work with the earlier version of the protocol. It gets activated from a specified block number, allowing certain participants the flexibility to adopt the new version later on.

Hard fork

This is an upgrade to the Bitcoin protocol that isn't backward-compatible. This means all users must decide simultaneously whether to adopt the new version or continue with the old one. Typically, this leads to a split, creating two separate networks: one using the original protocol and the other using the new version.

As a result, a new cryptocurrency can emerge from the original. Each resulting cryptocurrency operates independently, each having its own blockchain and set of rules. Since the Bitcoin protocol is open source, it can be replicated, its rules altered, and a new currency can be intentionally created through a hard fork. Past examples include the emergence of Bitcoin Cash and Bitcoin SV.

LIGHTNING NETWORK

The Lightning Network, or LN, is a "second layer" payment protocol and a routing network that serves as an extension of blockchain-based cryptocurrency. This protocol has been utilized as a solution to the Bitcoin scalability problem, which involves increasing the performance of the Bitcoin network. It is a peer-to-peer system for making micropayments through a network of bidirectional payment channels. The payment channels allow participants to transfer money to each other without having to publish all their transactions on the Bitcoin blockchain.

On the Bitcoin network, transaction fees, known as "on-chain fees," are paid to enter transactions into the ledger. The Lightning Network is a second, separate network used for fast and cheap payments of rather smaller amounts. On each of these different networks you have a different account address where you can keep your funds. In this case, you need two different wallets, or one wallet that can work with both types of accounts. Moving funds between these two networks (see FixedFloat service, page 285) is subject to standard transaction fees for on-chain entry of the transaction into the Bitcoin ledger. Moving part of your funds to the other network is not free. It takes the same amount of time as writing a regular bitcoin transaction on the main network.

The main Bitcoin network is used to store larger amounts or to make larger payments. In contrast, the Lightning Network is used to make quick and cheap payments of smaller amounts for cheaper goods, such as everyday purchases at restaurants, books stores, and cafes. As such, you may not be able to make a larger payment on the Lightning Network because there are not enough funds on that channel. However, the transaction capacity of the LN is gradually improving.

Unlike the more conservative Bitcoin protocol, the Lightning Network is currently evolving rapidly and is trying to respond to new technological and user needs. Most wallets try to make it easy for consumers to use, and offer as much convenience as possible. This oftentimes includes setting them up for you. This continual evolution, however, can lead to minor disruptions and glitches in the system, as well as in the products that are built using this protocol. Some payments may not go through due to poor balancing of payment channels. Despite these minor issues, the Lightning Network is edging towards the future of fast and cheap bitcoin payments. Its growing popularity around the world shows that it has the potential to change the way we pay for goods and trade cryptocurrencies.

Key benefits of the Lightning Network:

- Speed: transaction settlement time on the Lightning Network is typically less than one minute, often in the lower units of seconds, but can be in milliseconds.

- Payment throughput: there are no fundamental limits on the number of payments per second that can be made. The number of transactions is only limited by the capacity and speed of the individual nodes or channels.

- The transaction fees are extremely low: they are often in the low tens or single-digit satoshis.

- It can reconcile payments of less than 1 satoshi. This includes payments in milisatoshi or msat.

- It allows for greater anonymity, as payments are not recorded in the bitcoin ledger.

- There is a possibility of developing automatic swaps. This enables the passing of different currencies between some blockchains.

The following figure illustrates how the two layers of the Bitcoin protocol are connected. The blockchain serves as the ledger in Bitcoin and provides a basic level of decentralization and security. The Lightning Network is then the second layer, which enables faster and cheaper transactions between two participants without the need to record each transaction on the blockchain.

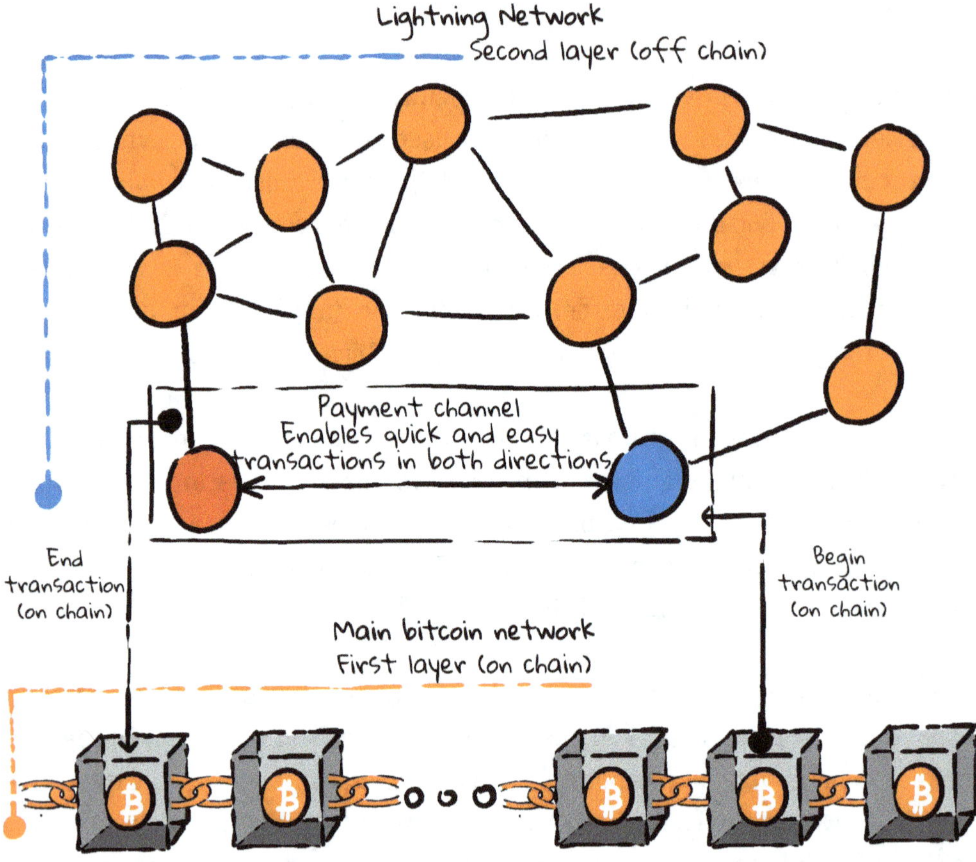

If you would like to learn more about this, I recommend you read *Mastering the Lightning Network*. This book is suitable for readers who understand the technical fundamentals of Bitcoin and other open blockchains. It is available in bookstores or via the following link, which contains the first edition, as published in paperback and ebook by O'Reilly Media.

Mastering the Lightning Network

MYTHS ABOUT BITCOIN

Myths are often disseminated by individuals who lack sufficient understanding of the creation and value backing of fiat money, as well as the fundamental principles and ethos of Bitcoin. Far more dangerous, however, are the interest groups that fight against the existence of bitcoin in an effort to keep fiat currencies in circulation for as long as possible. These people are at the top of the financial pyramid, amassing vast fortunes at the expense of others. It is through the printing of new money that they have made their fortunes. These facts are described throughout Book One in the discussions on inflation, the Cantillon Effect, and the inequality of world wealth. These bankers and businessmen, seeking to preserve the current world order, sway politicians and public opinion by promoting ideas that are either untrue or only partially true. Let's go through the most common Bitcoin myths together, and examine why they are misguided.

"BITCOIN HAS NO VALUE: IT'S EITHER A SCAM OR A GAMBLE"

This is the most common argument of newcomers and the uninformed. "Dollars or gold have value and bitcoin is just an abstraction." However, even gold is a fiction with no real use-value for meeting basic human needs. What gives it real value is its rarity. Bitcoin is as abstract as electronic money, but it is much rarer. Unlike unbacked fiat, bitcoin is backed by the value of the technology and electricity for which each miner must pay. Henry Ford's 1921 vision of creating an energy currency independent of gold is fulfilled through this model. Bitcoin is a precious and independent currency that is backed by electricity. It cannot be influenced by bankers, rulers, or state apparatuses. Electricity here serves as a means to transfer the value of utility (representing our good deeds) from the real world to the virtual one.

If gold were not universally recognized as valuable, people might prefer something to eat or plain water to drink, regarding gold as nothing more than a heavy, useless stone. When people discover that they can store value in gold and that others accept it, gold becomes more precious to them in everyday life than water. This is because water is relatively abundant and most people don't place as much value on it as they do on gold. As we previously discussed, however, gold has many disadvantages, which is why mankind has abandoned this "value fiction" as a universal currency and gone the way of unbacked "fiat abstractions." This is why bitcoin, over its lifetime, is winning the value battle by a huge margin not only over fiat currencies, but also with gold, stocks, and real estate. However, for conservative individuals, gold remains a much better choice for saving than devalued government currencies or stocks. Its value and rarity is confirmed by many thousands of years of use.

"BITCOIN IS ALREADY TOO EXPENSIVE, I'D RATHER BUY SOMETHING CHEAPER"

It's not about how much bitcoin is worth. It's about whether its price can still rise. If bitcoin proves to be a genuine innovation, it will become much more expensive, because we are still in the early stages of its spread. Those who don't have the means to buy one whole bitcoin should buy and save individual satoshis one by one. Bitcoin is a reliable and proven currency that sets the direction of the entire cryptocurrency market. In the long term, storing funds in bitcoin is generally considered safer than risking investment in one of the tens of thousands of other cryptocurrencies that might be inexpensive now, but offer the prospect of potential profit. In fact, it is very likely that the vast majority of those cryptocurrencies will no longer exist in a few years, or will have lost a significant portion of their value. Of course, it cannot be ruled out that for a small number of cryptocurrencies, their price will rise as much or perhaps even faster than bitcoin. For more on the possible evolution of the price of bitcoin, you will want to pay particular attention starting from page 218 onwards.

"BITCOIN IS UNSUSTAINABLE BECAUSE IT CONSUMES TOO MUCH ENERGY"

This is probably one of the most hotly debated topics of our times. It is a battle of many conflicting opinions and studies. Some studies point out that banks and banking systems around the world consume much more energy than bitcoin mining, yet no one blames the banking industry for that. They also point to the fact that gold mining is much more environmentally unfriendly than bitcoin mining, and nobody addresses that either.

To put Bitcoin's energy consumption into perspective, consider everyday items that also use a lot of electricity. Clothes dryers, kettles that heat more water than needed, and even Christmas lights are examples. Inefficiencies in cooking, ventilation, heating, lighting, and air conditioning also contribute to electricity waste. There are studies that point to the fact that these items, and a long list of others, consume significantly more "bad energy" than bitcoin mining does at any given time globally.

We must acknowledge that any convenience comes at a cost. Electricity consumption affords bitcoin both value and security. Let's try to view bitcoin as the quality, safe, scarce, non-state, and market money that society needs to prosper, be free, and reduce wars. Wouldn't it be a better trade off to simply try to do without Christmas lights, clothes dryers, and other less important things?

I'm trying to live more eco-friendly. I used to carry my groceries home
in a plastic bag while walking. Now I carry them by hand...
straight to my car.

When discussing the use of "bad energy" from coal-fired power plants and other non-renewable sources, it's important to note that bitcoin mining is increasingly turning to green energy. Based on market principles, miners can easily relocate to find locations with cheaper, more environmentally friendly energy sources. In many markets, energy from renewable sources such as solar, wind, and hydropower has become increasingly competitive in price, often rivaling or even undercutting traditional fossil fuels.

For certain resources, such as gas from oil rigs, energy from volcanoes, or power from remote waterfalls, bitcoin mining may be the only viable use. This is because these sources are often located far from populated areas where the electricity could otherwise be utilized. The distance makes it uneconomical to build the necessary infrastructure, like power lines, to transport the energy to where it might be needed. In some cases, this approach even gives room for the creation of new settlements, communities or related services in remote locations. For example, just think of the California Gold Rush of 1948, which led to the settling of less hospitable places and the formation of new cities.

Before the era of bitcoin mining, gas that leaked from remote oil wells was often ignited to burn off rather than risk an explosion, a practice that continues in many places. With the advent of bitcoin mining, however, this gas can be used to fuel gas-fired power plants. When burned in this controlled environment, the combustion process produces significantly less harmful carbon dioxide compared to spontaneous combustion. Some studies report that this method results in about 60% less CO_2 emissions.

Furthermore, there are many cases where off-peak renewable power plants discharge excess energy into the ground, instead of storing it in backup batteries. Projects are now being developed that take a new approach to dealing with excess energy from renewable power plants. Instead of discharging this excess energy into the ground or storing it in large, high-capacity batteries, the energy is converted directly into bitcoin through mining facilities. This method is seen as a greener alternative because it doesn't produce the waste associated with old batteries, which can become an environmental issue if not managed properly. Additionally, the mining of elements for battery cells or electrolyte production can be less environmentally friendly than gold mining, making the direct conversion to bitcoin an attractive option.

Today, bitcoin mining is finding growing applications in heating systems. In this approach, traditional electric heat sources are replaced by mining machines that utilize the transfer of heat through air, water, or oil. These mining machines consume the same amount of electricity and produce the same amount of heat as conventional heating systems, but with an added benefit: the bitcoins mined during the heating process. This mining serves as a by-product that significantly offsets the costs. After covering the initial higher price of this type of heating system, any bitcoins mined become net profit. Some even view this as an appealing "cashback" on electricity consumption, with the potential to far exceed the original costs if the mined Bitcoins are held over time.

On the one hand, computer chip manufacturers are focusing on producing special mining chips with higher performance and lower electricity consumption, while on the other hand, companies are emerging that want to produce common appliances that will generate heat and mine bitcoin as a by-product.

As we will explain later in our discussion on innovation, in the life cycle of the emergence and diffusion of new technologies, the market itself produces "pragmatic" companies that improve existing technologies while developing new ones. They look for secondary and new uses and focus on increasing utility and ideal functioning. It is currently estimated that more than 60% of bitcoin is from renewable sources or as a by-product of utility heat production. Some interesting links on this topic can be found on page 317.

The usual panic has gripped the market.
In the nation's capital, they are currently discussing additional environmental measures.

"BITCOIN IS NOT EVOLVING: COMPARED TO EMERGING CRYPTOCURRENCIES, IT IS OUTDATED"

What advantages do emerging cryptocurrencies offer, and how can they improve upon or surpass existing options? Bitcoin is first and foremost money, and from that perspective I believe it does exactly what it is supposed to do. There is no need to invent anything else. Moreover, unlike other cryptocurrencies, it has been proven to work the longest and under the heaviest load. The only point of contention is the dispute between Proof of Work and Proof of Stake technologies. Many experts point out that the Proof of Stake mining method may reduce the security of the cryptocurrency's blockchain. This method is also less fair for new miners and not nearly as decentralized as bitcoin mining. This issue is discussed in detail starting on page 248.

The issues of poor scalability in bitcoin, characterized by slow and expensive transactions, have frequently been highlighted. These problems are already addressed by the second layer of the Lightning Network, as discussed on page 183.

Many visionaries see the future of cryptocurrencies in DeFi, smart contracts, staking and other add-on functionalities. These new functionalities will only become meaningful after cryptocurrencies achieve widespread acceptance. They can be addressed through additional layers built on top of the Bitcoin network. You can read more about this beginning from page 237.

Bitcoin is constantly evolving, but it is more conservative than some other cryptocurrencies. Currently, it primarily addresses functionalities directly related to the operation of money and ease of use.

"WILL THERE BE ENOUGH BITCOIN FOR EVERYONE?"

Ignoring the fact that the Lightning Network can work with units lower than one satoshi, let's answer this question through the following calculation:

21,000,000 **bitcoins** multiplied by 100,000,000 **satoshi**

divided by 6,000,000,000 **relevant users*** equals 350, 000 satoshi **per user**

*The number of relevant users is inflated, the internet has slightly over 5 billion users in 2023.

Let's calculate what it would look like if all the world's wealth were to be transferred into bitcoin if it became a global currency. The Global Wealth Report 2022 puts the average global wealth per adult at $87,489 (see page 118). If we divide $87,489 by 350,000 satoshi per user, we find that 1 satoshi would be worth about $0.25. The value of one bitcoin in this case would be $25,000,000. This will probably never happen, but even in this extreme case, there would be enough bitcoin for the total "stock of possible users" on planet Earth. Better said, the smallest unit of payment in the bitcoin ledger would be $0.25 (1 SAT). However, it's important to recognize that this would probably represent a much lower real value in terms of purchasing power than the current $0.25. Additionally, it should be noted that through the Lightning Network, 1 satoshi could be subdivided even further.

Thus, there is enough satoshi for every relevant user on Earth to have the necessary cash contained in satoshi. Bitcoin as a currency, even with its limited supply of 21 million, can hold the value of all the world's wealth.

"BITCOIN IS ANONYMOUS MONEY FOR ILLEGAL TRANSACTIONS"

As we have previously noted, bitcoin is not an anonymous currency, but only a pseudo-anonymous one. Anonymity, or rather pseudo-anonymity, is a much discussed topic in the context of bitcoin. Let's break it down in more detail.

- If two people exchange cash, there is no record of the transaction. No one else knows about it, and unless they reveal their identities to each other, the transaction is completely anonymous.

- If two individuals exchange money using a bank, credit card system, or another payment service like Revolut, Wise, or PayPal, their identities are known. The intermediary handling the transaction, which is typically required to provide transaction details to authorities upon request, always has knowledge of the exchange. However, the transaction is not known to a wider range of users.

- If two people send bitcoin to each other, the transaction is visible to everyone in the ledger. In fact, every transaction that has ever taken place in the history of the Bitcoin network is publicly viewable in the ledger. However, public keys (addresses) have no identity assigned to them in this ledger. From this perspective, all transactions are anonymous. However, if users share their identities with each other or provide them when registering for an exchange, then anyone who has access to the identity connected to that address can trace all incoming and outgoing payments from that address. Various organizations, authorities, and government agencies have analytical tools that can identify an increasing number of addresses on the ledger. If authorities don't have a specific address identified at the moment, they can attempt to trace it by examining the addresses from which payments have been sent or from which payments have been received. They know where to inquire to obtain information about the sender or recipient of the payment. Through this method, the identity of addresses in the Bitcoin network can be gradually uncovered.

Many bitcoin addresses are already linked to an identity, but a user cannot reliably determine this connection for another address. Therefore, bitcoin is not truly anonymous but rather pseudo-anonymous. Once a person's identity is tied to a public key, it becomes possible to sift through the transactions recorded in the blockchain and locate all transactions related to that key. Associating a real identity with an otherwise anonymous bitcoin address may not be as challenging as some think.

Several factors can reveal a person's identity. For example, identifying information about the IP address might be recorded on the websites of individual e-shops. Moreover, if fiat currency is exchanged for bitcoins on a bitcoin exchange, identity verification (known as KYC, or Know Your Customer) is almost always required under Anti-Money Laundering (AML) regulations, except for small amounts. This issue is discussed further on page 279.

In order to increase the chances of maintaining pseudo-anonymity, the user would have to use a VPN, anonymizing software (such as Tor), and be careful never to transact with bitcoin addresses that might already be identified. From the point of view of anonymity, it is certainly safer to use cash—at least until its circulation is reduced or it is altogether banned. Although bitcoin is often referred to as an anonymous currency, in reality it is very difficult to remain anonymous in the Bitcoin network.

Several studies, including one from Chainalysis, an agency that works closely with governments around the world, suggest that the rate of cryptocurrency use for illegal activity accounts for less than one percent of all illegal transactions. To put this in context, for traditional transaction facilitators, where we can include banks, this estimate is between two and four percent. It should be remembered that in this case we are talking about cryptocurrencies in general. However, Bitcoin's share in the percentages quoted is minimal, as it is more convenient for illegal activities to use cryptocurrencies such as Monero or decentralized exchanges (DEX), which bring a higher degree of anonymity.

"Revealed: Credit Suisse Leak Unmasks Criminals, Fraudsters and corrupt Politicians" via the *Guardian*

HSBC's Money Laundering Scandal

"BITCOIN IS CONTROLLED BY THE SECRET SERVICE AND CAN BE SHUT DOWN AT ANY TIME"

Let's look at the environment and atmosphere of the emergence of the Cypherpunk movement and the crypto-anarchist community. The same people fighting for freedom had the PGP code tattooed on their bodies, printed on t-shirts, or shared with the world in book form. This was definitely not a secret service controlled environment. At most, one could speculate that some technology got out of hand, as it has many times in history. Just as government-sponsored institutions were behind the birth of the internet, so cryptography and the development of many cryptographic tools may have been sponsored in part by these institutions.

However, just as the internet can no longer be shut down globally, Bitcoin can no longer be shut down or stopped from being distributed and used. This simple fact can be understood by anyone who is sufficiently familiar with how these technologies work. Bitcoin is a platform that governments, particularly non-democratic ones, are rather afraid of because they cannot control it. At the same time, they understand that this runaway train cannot be stopped. History provides numerous examples that innovation can be resisted, but never ultimately defeated. Democratic governments should encourage innovation. Moreover, they cannot fight against free money, even if it suits certain interest groups. This is also why certain groups constantly highlight alleged threats and repeatedly spread untruths that have already been refuted many times.

"BITCOIN PAYMENTS ARE SLOW AND TRANSACTIONS ARE EXPENSIVE"

These arguments are often used to claim that bitcoin cannot be used for regular payments. This is not true. We clearly refuted this in the previous discussion of the Lightning Network on page 183.

"BITCOIN WILL END WHEN ITS PRICE FALLS AND MINING STOPS PAYING"

In such a case, some miners who rely on expensive electricity from mostly non-organic forms, and who do not have the finances to sustain mining, may temporarily drop out. This will make bitcoin mining even greener. The remaining miners will mine more bitcoin and it will pay off. As a result, some of them will start to return to mining, especially those who have found cheaper sources of energy. Miners who use electricity for heating and treat bitcoin mining as a secondary benefit would rarely have to cut back on mining. A long-term drop in the price of bitcoin would mainly impact the purchase rate of new mining equipment, as well as the cost of that equipment.

"BITCOIN WILL END WHEN QUANTUM COMPUTERS COME"

Here, too, there are frequent speculations and clashes of opinion between different groups. According to most experts, quantum computers can develop much higher computational power, but they cannot substantially increase the direct hashing power. Quantum computers can be much smarter and faster at thinking, but not significantly faster at rolling the dice. They can, however, gradually crack some private keys in **older address formats**. But the same is true for banking systems, military, government, and research databases.

The question arises regarding what governments or hackers would prioritize targeting. Hacking a money system might not be the most lucrative option, as doing so would effectively devalue and destroy the system without gaining any real value. Instead, there might be more interest in acquiring classified information and technology, which could provide immediate profit or a strategic advantage. It's also important to note that it wouldn't be feasible to hack or rob everything at once. Such an endeavor would take a long time and be extremely costly. Experts anticipate that there would be enough time on a global scale to technologically prepare and adjust security measures.

For **older address formats**, quantum computers might have the capability to reverse-engineer a private key from an address, thereby gaining access to the bitcoins associated with that address. To counteract this risk, some forks of the bitcoin protocol have implemented higher address security through changing to different address formats. As a precaution, it's advisable to create a new address and transfer funds from the original address to the new one (essentially sending a payment to oneself). With the change in address format, some forks will also generate a newer transaction format, leading to smaller and, consequently, less expensive data volume.

Cryptography has always struggled with hackers and solutions were always found in the process. A major security shift will be the move to post-quantum algorithms, which are already being worked on by various teams around the world. Some see this move as akin to replacing a car engine. It probably won't be quite that simple, because there will also need to be community consensus. The important thing to keep in mind is that there is a solution.

"Quantum Computers and the Bitcoin Blockchain" via Deloitte

"Could Quantum Computing Bring Down Bitcoin and End the Age of Crypto?" via Investment Monitor

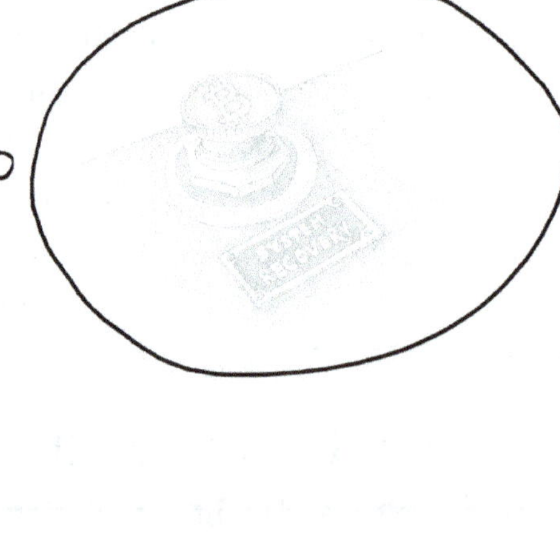

CHAPTER 2 SUMMARY

- From a technical perspective, Bitcoin is a decentralized form of currency that operates on a peer-to-peer network and is independent of any government control. Its monetary policy is clearly defined and predictable. From a global perspective, it is a non-inflationary currency.

- The independence and value of bitcoin are due to its decentralization, scarcity, and the electricity consumption involved in its mining, which in a way 'backs' the value of bitcoin.

- Security of possession is ensured by the most advanced cryptography. This same cryptography is used by banks, large corporations, and even armies to secure their data.

- The security and backup of the bitcoin network is provided by tens of thousands of independent miners and node operators.

- Bitcoin can be obtained through mining, purchasing, and earning it.

- The economics of the rewards for operating a Bitcoin network are based on mining and gradually shift to transaction fees.

- Contrary to what interest groups and media often claim, bitcoin is not as damaging to the environment nor as conducive to anonymous illegal transactions as it is portrayed.

- There is enough satoshi for all the inhabitants of Earth. If needed, bitcoin as a currency could technically hold the value of all the world's wealth.

- Bitcoin is much rarer than existing fiat currencies. It is a modern independent payment system that can better preserve the value of your finances in the long run. If traditional cash becomes less prevalent, bitcoin can offer a means of conducting private transactions. It is the new digital "cash" of the future.

- Bitcoin is a tool for people's freedom, not a weapon of the secret service.

- For larger amounts and maximum security of your funds, the main Bitcoin network operates on-chain. Higher on-chain fees provide a reward to the network operators. Confirming transactions can take minutes to hours. This network is pseudo-anonymous. To achieve full anonymity, both anonymous purchasing and anonymous trading need to be addressed.

- For smaller amounts, the Lightning Network can be used where instant payments are made for minimal fees. Unlike standard card payments, the payee always receives the full amount and a small fee is paid by the sender of the payment. Payments through the Lightning Network are more private than on-chain payments.

- Based on the proposed principles and technologies, it is a highly sophisticated, innovative, trustworthy, secure, cost-effective, and anti-fragile monetary system.

IS BITCOIN AN INNOVATION?

IS BITCOIN AN INNOVATION?

Innovation fuels our advancement, manifesting in various fields of human activity to enhance performance and better our lives. For an innovation to succeed, it must benefit the group of users affected by its potential use. Today, almost everyone on planet Earth uses some form of money, and most use money in the form of national currencies. Any type of innovation related to money affects billions of people around the world. Most people consider money to be an automatic part of their lives and seldom consider whether this system could be improved. As we have seen, money has evolved over time and even greater demands are being made with regard to its quality. However, the problem is that given its significant importance, any innovation to money would also impact special interest groups.

> "No matter what they talk about, it's always about money."
> —Murphy's Law

As you will read in this chapter, most major innovations are accompanied by many challenges, and only after these are overcome can widespread adoption occur. One significant challenge is often regulation. Interest groups, who wield considerable influence over policymakers, may try to block these innovations to protect their existing income streams or to prevent others from profiting. However, historical evidence suggests that progress is unstoppable, particularly when the majority of the population sees the benefits. Even resistance from influential politicians can eventually be overcome.

This is the agenda for today's congressional meeting. We expect the greatest resistance to the last item.

IS BITCOIN AN INNOVATION COMPARED TO THE CURRENT MONETARY SYSTEM?

First, let's define what we mean by innovation. Unlike an invention, which is the creation of a completely new product or process, innovation refers to a modification or improvement. Often, it involves combining existing products or processes to create something distinct from what came before. When evaluating the new product, it should be clear that its utility, features, or criteria are better than the previous one. However, from the perspective of this book, let us consider innovation and invention as the same phenomenon. Many people refer to cryptocurrency as an innovation and others refer to it as an invention. Personally, I am of the opinion that it is a monetary innovation, particularly with regard to the way it is exchanged and owned. Historically, most improvements have come about naturally among the population. The moment mankind understood what made a given innovation better, there was always an exponential increase in users.

INNOVATION AND REGULATION

Only the most groundbreaking innovations are significant enough to warrant the creation of **regulations**. A major factor is that regulators are unable to adequately assess the importance of the innovation; sometimes they don't even understand it. They cannot estimate the speed or rate of adoption of the innovation by society. But with mass adoption, politicians capitulate in an effort not to antagonize their much-needed voters.

Lobbyists often struggle to halt innovation and the accompanying regulations because the advantages of innovation effectively advocate for themselves. Politicians subsequently guide officials, allowing the innovation to proceed. When states or authorities try to regulate new innovations, they rarely succeed in completely halting public

Regulation is a purposeful, systematic, and routine control or direction activity. It can be carried out by a person, authority, or government. It usually interferes with natural development of free markets.

Lobby translates to:

- entrance hall, vestibule, hall, foyer

- political background (congress)

- a political or other interest group (promoting certain interests)

Lobbying, as it has come to be known, means influencing congressional officials or other similar holders of office. Lobbyists are people who try to promote particular interests.

acceptance. More often, they only manage to temporarily slow its adoption, which is usually followed by an even more rapid expansion.

Not every regulation should be perceived negatively. Some regulation is beneficial and some is even necessary. Regulators simply need to adapt and evolve to better align with real-world conditions. Consider what the roads would be like today without traffic regulations. In a way, regulations legitimize and legalize a given innovation—even though they may not always make sense at the time.

Do you think banning guns will really solve terrorism?

Let's examine the adoption of the automobile by exploring specific cases that highlight the innovations and the regulations that came along with them.

England

In England in the early 19th century there was a strong anti-car lobby that called for the regulation or, in some cases, the banning of cars. Regulation of the automobile had several stages. First, there was indifference. Automobile enthusiasts were regarded as harmless oddballs and were often the butt of jokes and ridicule. After it became clear that cars really did function and could be useful, the authorities began to restrict them. Various interest groups tried to fight against the introduction of cars. The first British traffic regulations are proof of this.

Individual counties required the payment of tolls—sometimes as much as ten pounds—for the operation of cars. Some counties even established hours when it was allowed to drive cars. If the driver's timing through each county didn't align with the permitted timeframes, the driver had to stop and could only resume the journey during the allowed hours.

In 1861, British Conservatives pushed through the Locomotive Act. While this legislation limited the amount of tolls for driving on the roads, it also set the maximum speed limit at ten miles per hour (16 km/h) and five miles per hour (8 km/h) in the city. Additionally, it required a two-man crew to operate a vehicle.

In 1865, another nonsensical regulation was passed in England. This was the infamous Flag Act (Locomotives on Highways Act, also known as the Red Flag Act). This Act reduced the speed limit for cars to four miles per hour (6.4 km/h) and two miles per hour in town (3.2 km/h). Simultaneously, it mandated that a man with a red flag must walk or trot in front of an automobile at a distance of at least 60 feet (about 18 meters) and use a bell or whistle to warn the surrounding area of impending danger. This regulation permitted horse-drawn carriages and stagecoaches to travel at higher speeds, while motor-driven cars were restricted to a crawl, led by a weary individual holding a red flag.

In other European countries at the time, the automobile industry was booming. Sleek cars powered by internal combustion engines were prowling the streets. Meanwhile, in England, the development of the automobile industry was heading in the opposite direction. In fact, some high-ranking Englishmen considered the automobile to be a disgusting, smelly nonsense that needed to be destroyed.

America

As in England, lawmakers and police officers in America tried to curb the development of automobile traffic in the early years, introducing red flags in some states in addition to nonsensical regulations. For example, before an intersection, a driver had to stop and turn off the engine, scan the road ahead, and signal their arrival by honking, shouting, striking a gong, or firing a shot.

Red fleku trafic lows

Locomotive ACT 1865

Let's summarize the major milestones and innovations in the automotive industry:

- **1835**: The first-ever electric car was built jointly by Dutch professor Sibrandus Stratingh and his assistant Christopher Becker. However, the world eventually became enamored with cars powered by internal combustion engines.

- **1888**: The first air-filled tire was invented by the John Dunlop, an English veterinary surgeon.

- **1903**: Henry Ford established his factory.

- **1909**: Ford introduced the Model T, which sold an incredible 15 million units by 1927. The Model T became the most widely used car of its time.

- **1913**: Ford was the first company in the world to implement assembly line production in factories. This significantly reduced the cost of the final product, making cars accessible to more than just the wealthy elite.

- **1929**: Paul Galvin, an American, invented the first car radio.

- **1936**: The Volkswagen Beetle was introduced. Over 21 million were produced by the time production ended in 2003.

- **1951**: The first power steering became available.

- **1973**: The Oldsmobile Toronado became the first car where buyers could pay extra for an airbag.

- **1974**: The first-generation Volkswagen Golf was launched and went on to become the best-selling car in history, with over 24 million units sold.

- **2020**: A massive global shift to electromobility began.

With the passage of time, it can be said that cars and transport based on internal combustion engines have become an everyday part of our lives worldwide. It is proof that if innovation makes sense and mankind finds a use for it, it will eventually become widespread, despite nonsensical regulations. Meaningful regulations, such as road rules in the case of automotive transport, in turn encourage mass adoption.

DISSEMINATION OF INNOVATION

In this section, we explain how innovation diffuses and how the user group for which the innovation is relevant expands. We will discuss the different stages of diffusion, the influences to which they are subject, and at the same time what needs to happen for an innovation to become widely used. Reading the following pages will give you an idea of where Bitcoin is and what challenges lie ahead.

S-curves and their utility in estimating innovation diffusion: understanding the increase in the number of users

Almost everything exists in a limited supply. Even the Earth is essentially a reservoir of finite resources—land, water, and air. Therefore, many phenomena can be understood as processes involving the depletion of these resources.

- The spread of epidemics reduces the "stock" of a healthy population.

- Economies extract finite resources like oil, gas, and gold.

- The adoption of new, innovative technologies is constrained by a market that consists of a limited number of potential consumers or users.

The finite nature of supplies imposes an upper limit on growth. An epidemic, for example, ceases to spread and starts to recede when potential victims either succumb to it or gain immunity. Similarly, the sales or usage of technological products, or any other innovations, will eventually slow and reach a peak when most potential buyers or users have acquired or adopted the product. These growth processes—or the depletion of available stocks—can't be accurately described by constant growth rates or linear functions.

With limiting environmental factors, the exponential growth curve usually changes to an S-curve. Obviously, the S-curve does not predict the future, nor is it a completely reliable representation of reality. However, it is a practical tool in understanding how things might develop in the future. In order to estimate the diffusion of innovations, it is assumed that all potential users who need a given type of product are involved on an ongoing basis. In essence, the time it takes to exhaust the stock of users not yet involved is estimated. Following this curve, the price of the product changes. If the stock can be replenished in a given time and supply is higher than demand, the price may fall. If the stock is close to exhaustion or if there is less supply than demand, the price rises.

What is an S-curve?

As the name suggests, it is an S-shaped curve that helps visualize exponential growth. This curve represents a sigmoid function—an S-shaped function—and is sometimes referred to as a logistic function. Besides describing how innovation spreads among a finite number of users, the function can also represent the average growth curve over the life cycle of a population or a firm.

Crossing the Chasm: understanding the S-curve in technology adoption

Crossing the Chasm is a concept that visualizes the adoption of a new technology over time and, by linking it to an S-curve, can illustrate the diffusion process of a particular innovation.

In 1962, sociologist Everett Rogers published the book *Diffusion of Innovations*. Today, this model is known as the technology adoption life cycle. It comprehensively describes the adoption or acceptance of a new technological product or innovation. In 1991, Geoffrey Moore further developed this model in his book entitled *Crossing the Chasm*.

Let's briefly summarize the main ideas of these works:

The different groups in the technology adoption life cycle are categorized based on the psychological traits of the users, although these can also be partially shaped by specific geopolitical factors.

Diffusion of Innovations is a book written by Everett Rogers in 1962. His work helped to popularize the theory of diffusion of innovations. This theory explains how, when, why, and at what speed new ideas and technologies spread. According to Rogers, there are four elements that influence the diffusion of an idea: innovation, modes of communication, time, and the social system. An innovation must be adopted by a large number of people in order to sustain itself.

Crossing the Chasm is a book by Geoffrey Moore, an American organizational theorist and management consultant. The book discusses marketing and selling high-tech products to mainstream customers.

Innovators (tech enthusiasts)

They are often actively engaged in the issue before the innovation arrives or before it becomes common knowledge. In decentralized models, they are often involved in the conceptualization or subsequent development (see Cypherpunks). Their support provides the necessary reassurance for other consumers in the market. These enthusiasts usually also act as a test group.

First users (visionaries)

Like innovators, visionaries are those who want to use new technology in the early stages. Unlike innovators, however, they are usually not technologists. They are looking for a revolutionary breakthrough and are willing to take high risks when trying something new. They begin to place higher demands on the functionality and performance of the product. They don't care much about public opinion, preferring instead to rely on their own intuition and beliefs. They are ready to provide references for other adopters in the population.

Early majority (pragmatists)

The first two groups of adopters belong to the "early market" group. Similar to visionaries, pragmatists are usually able to estimate the potential and importance of a given innovation. However, compared to visionaries, they are driven by a much stronger sense of practicality. They know that many innovations will not ultimately come to fruition, and they need at least partial results and references to confirm their view for the potential of a given innovation. They often wait to see how the technology will be handled by early adopters, regulatory authorities, and market trend-setting companies. Getting this group on board is crucial for the breakthrough of the innovation into the "mainstream market."

Late majority (conservatives)

This group is about the same size as the pragmatists and shares all their concerns. Unlike the pragmatists, they are not as progressive and believe more in traditional technologies. They find new technologies harder to handle and wait for a given innovation to become an established standard for adoption. To win them over, it's essential to provide references, a large user base, and assurance through service or regulatory certainty. Gaining this group is essential to controlling the entire "core market."

The stragglers (skeptics)

They usually want nothing to do with new technologies. They often start using innovations only as part of another product, sometimes unknowingly. They may adopt the technology only when they feel they would be at a distinct disadvantage compared to others, or simply because they think, "If everyone else has it, I should probably have it too." However, their critical attitude towards the functionality and performance of a given innovation can provide valuable feedback. This group is no longer relevant from a "mainstream market" perspective.

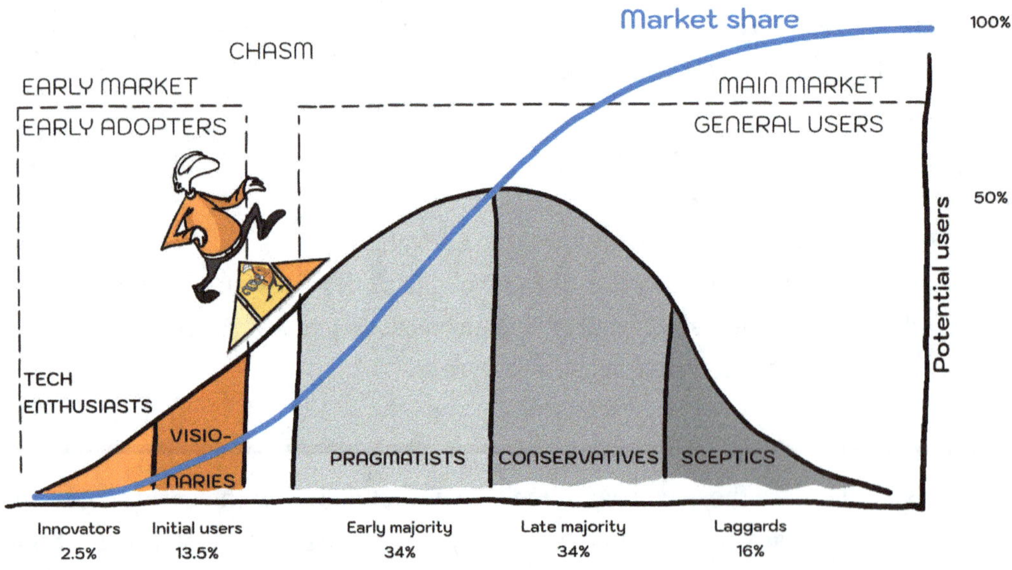

Crossing the Chasm

There is a gap in the life cycle between visionaries and pragmatists that an innovation must cross in order for the network effect (described on page 31) to fully develop, and for the innovation to achieve widespread adoption. Bridging the gap means:

- achieving credibility in the field of public opinion (see discussion of the Hype Cycle page 207).

- finding ways of using it in such a way that it benefits not only a small number of specialized adopters, but also a large number of ordinary users.

- using progressively higher technical performance to achieve the best possible ideality.

- obtaining a sufficient number of references and recommendations from different user groups. It is important to note that certain groups of people often trust references from people who belong to their own group.

- exploring how regulators will deal with the technology and what positions will be taken by companies that set market trends.

Crossing the Chasm has its own life cycle stages. These phases are illustrated in the next figure.

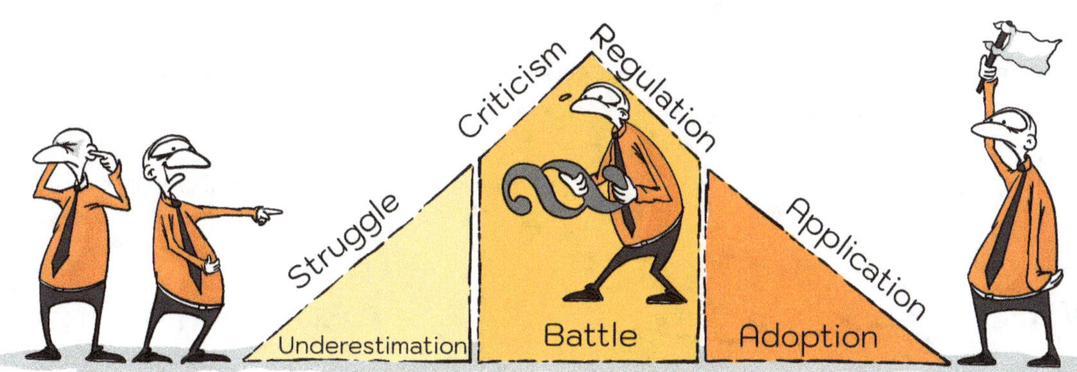

The entire process of innovation can be aptly summarized by this quote, often attributed to Mahatma Gandhi:

> "First they ignore you, then they laugh at you,
> then they fight you, and then you win!"

To this one might add:

> "And then they build monuments to you."

Technical performance and ideality

In order to achieve the above objectives of bridging the gap, considerable attention must also be paid to technical performance. It makes the technology more ideal for wider use by more users. Ideality means not only the gradual fulfillment of increasing expectations and better availability of the technology, but also increasing user friendliness.

The increase in technical performance of any innovation is dependent on the development of the performance parameters of the technology, downstream technologies, products, applications, and services. It occurs when pragmatic early adopters decide to bet on the widespread adoption of a given technology. It is the development of these downstream technologies that will trigger further growth in adoption by the remaining pragmatic user community.

Often this happens in leaps and bounds as higher generations of the technology come on stream and new layers of downstream technologies, products, applications and services emerge. Each layer then makes the technology available to other users. Thus, one global S-curve may be composed of several sub-S-curves as the technology improves over time, accompanied by the introduction of higher generations of products and the emergence of additional layers.

In terms of user growth, this process continues until it reaches the maximum possible number of users. The improvement process then continues, but no longer results in a substantial increase in users. This whole process is accompanied by a Hype Cycle, which is described further on page 207. Just as a single global S-curve can contain multiple sub-S-curves, the evolution of public opinion can create sub-Hype Cycles with each new generation or layer.

The following figure shows the dependence between increasing ideality (and technical performance) and the increasing numbers of users (adopters).

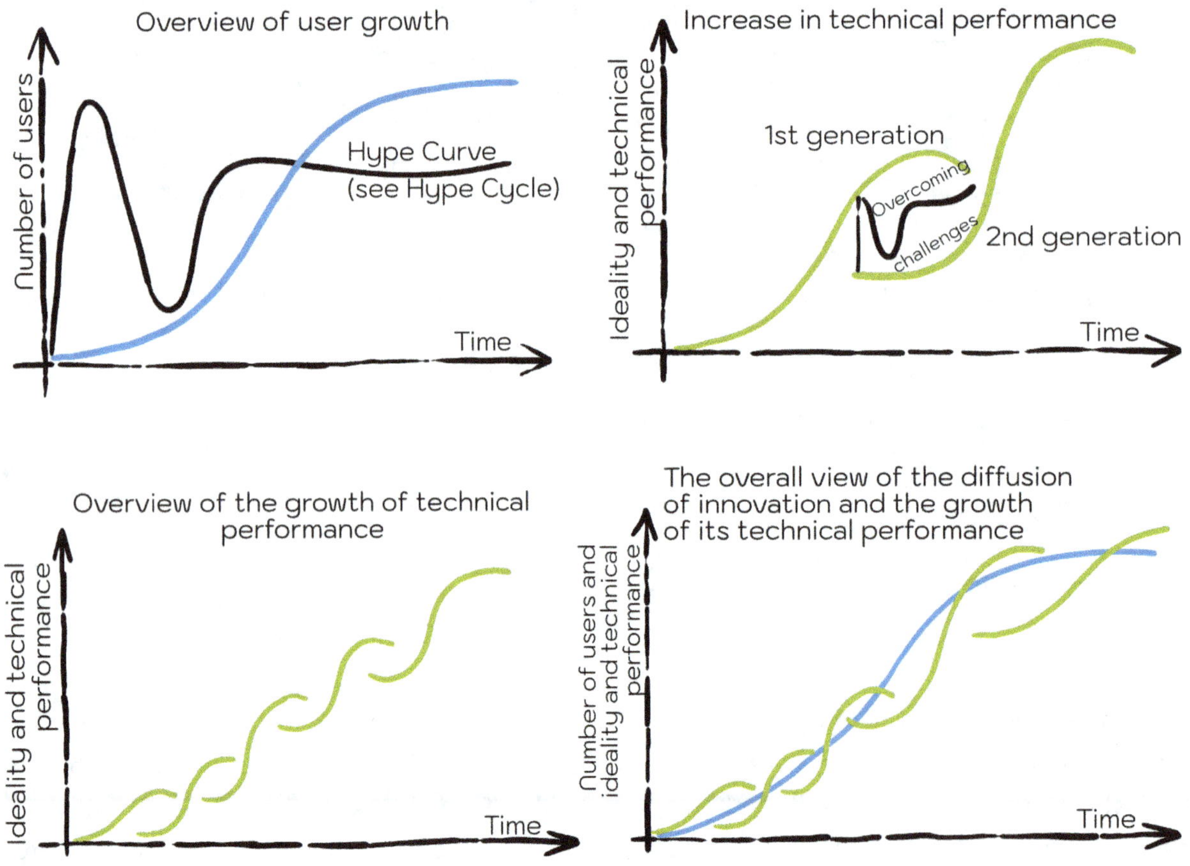

The following chart displays selected S-curves for various technologies, highlighting their growth in technical performance. As we explained previously, technical performance (with the associated extensions) often starts massive adoption. Note how each graph evolves after crossing the gap, indicated by the red arrow.

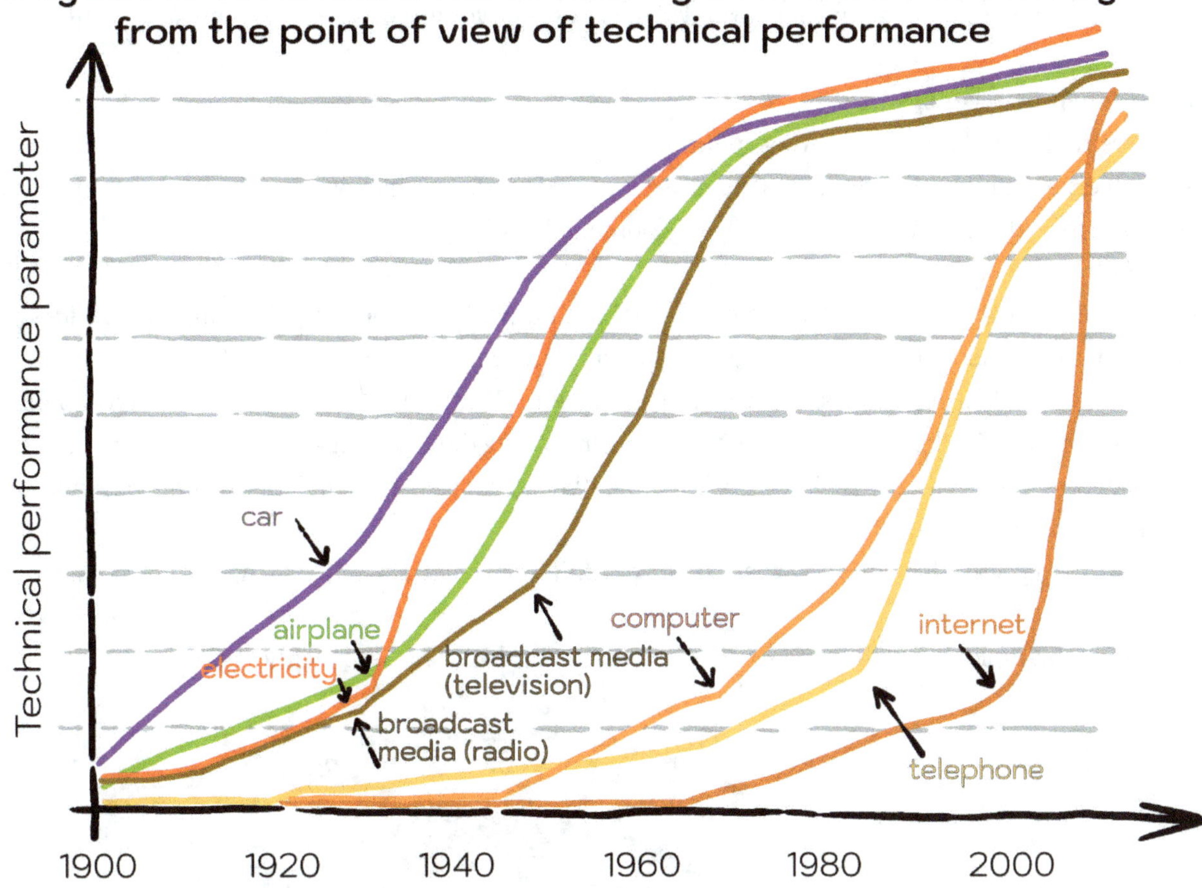

Introducing Technology Timeline Interpretation to Technology Diffusion and Maturity Analysis as Applied to Different Industrial Sectors (on page 8) via ResearchGate

The increase in technical performance, the emergence of additional layers, and the bridging of the gap can be clearly explained in the following examples and subsequent illustration:

Internal combustion engine
Alone it would have very little potential for use by the wider population.
Downstream technologies supporting adoption:
  –2nd layer: cars, trucks, aircraft, and military equipment
  Crossing the Chasm
  –3nd layer: roads, highways, gas stations, service stations, airports, and weapons systems

Internet

Without additional layers, it would also have a very low potential for use by the wider population.

Downstream technologies supporting adoption:

  –2nd layer: personal computers, mobile devices, email, websites, and e-shops

  Crossing the Chasm

  –3nd layer: smartphones, social networks, wireless, 5G networks, smart homes, and streaming services

Bitcoin (cryptocurrency)

Downstream technologies supporting adoption:

  –2nd layer: exchanges, brokers, Lightning Network, software and hardware wallets, payment gateways for e-shops and merchants, technology development for miners

  Crossing the Chasm

  –3nd layer (future possibilities): Bitcoin ETF, global financial operations (global currency), widespread development of decentralized finance and smart contracts (page 245); full node as part of hardware wallets or electrical appliances; the possibility of keeping bank accounts in bitcoin; electric appliances capable of producing heat and mining bitcoin, thus reducing the cost of energy consumed and increasing the decentralization and security of the bitcoin network; wider use of bitcoin as a state currency or for institutional reserves

  Time will ultimately determine whether these optimistic predictions I'm making come to pass.

Below, is an example illustrating the various layers that build upon these technologies.

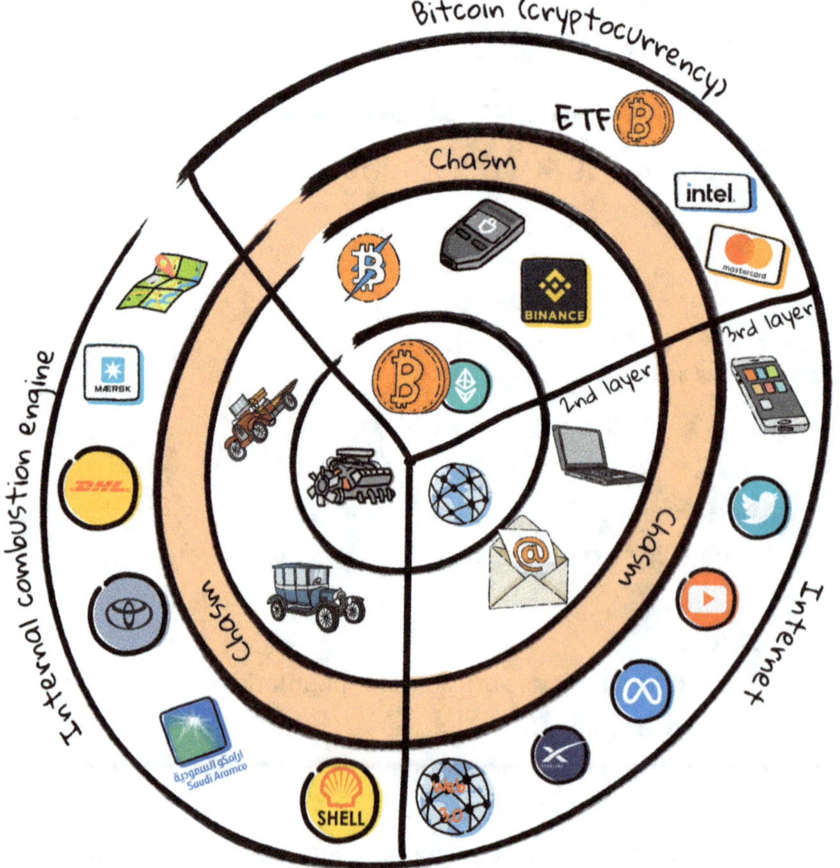

Some have likened cryptocurrencies and their superstructure functions to the next natural evolution of internet-related technologies. Others see them as a natural innovation of money created by its evolution and the internet environment as merely a necessary foundation for their emergence. Regardless of which view everyone subscribes to, cryptocurrencies are undergoing a similar evolution.

In general, once the gap is bridged, there is a public and widespread acceptance of the innovation, especially with regard to the principle of the network effect (described on page 31). This process is commonly referred to as **mainstreaming**. Public opinion no longer boosts expectations, as people have already recognized the innovation's importance and found ways to utilize it. An exponential growth in users commences. In free market terms, when user demand goes up and production can't keep pace, the price rises.

Mainstream can be described as a set of ideas and attitudes that represent or conform to the views, values, or tastes of the majority in society. The term is used especially in the fields of media, economics, and culture.

Amara's Law **and** Hype Cycles

Amar's Law suggests that the rollout of new technology, or innovation, generally takes an extended period of time. However, the media and the public usually expect a rapid introduction in the beginning and predict a revolutionary impact on people's lives. Later on, they find that the expected miracle has not occurred, and in disillusionment, they "bury" the technology.

Roy Charles Amara (1925–2007) was an American researcher, scientist, author, and futurologist. He was president of the Institute for the Future. His rule of thumb on predicting the effects of technology was: "We tend to overestimate the effects of technology in the short run and underestimate its effects in the long run."

Gartner, one of the world's leading international technology research and advisory firms, has created a model it calls the **Hype Cycle**. It is a graphical representation of the lifecycle phases that a technology goes through from inception to maturity and widespread adoption. This model elaborates on Amara's Law in a more detailed way.

Nonetheless, the technology continues to evolve, seeking various applications based on market dynamics and game theory. Over time, people are surprised to discover that the technology is not only still "alive," but also evolving and finding new uses. This leads to another wave of heightened interest, or "hype", a cycle that can repeat itself in some instances. The key takeaway from this model is that real-world progress may lag behind expectations, yet the eventual outcome could surpass even the most wildest imaginations.

Bitcoin has experienced this situation many times.

However, not every new project turns out well in the end. In this case, one of Murphy's Laws describing the project life cycle can be applied. This law states that every project has five phases:

- pre-project enthusiasm
- reality check during implementation
- finding the culprits
- punishing the innocent
- rewarding those not involved

Each Hype Cycle is divided into five key phases of the technology lifecycle:

1. **Innovation Trigger:** a potential technology breakthrough kicks things off. Early proof-of-concept stories and media interest trigger significant publicity. Often no usable products exist and commercial viability is unproven. The new technology starts to be covered in the media, public interest is aroused, and hopes and expectations are raised.

2. **Peak of Inflated Expectations:** early publicity produces a number of success stories—often accompanied by scores of failures. Some companies take action; many do not. Hopes and expectations peak, but there are also failures. Partial disillusionment sets in, and a tipping point occurs when hopes and expectations begin to fall.

3. **Trough of Disillusionment:** interest wanes as experiments and implementations fail to deliver. Producers of the technology shake out or fail. Investments continue only if the surviving providers improve their products to the satisfaction of early adopters. Hopes and expectations plummet, reality sets in, and the technology is often dismissed or written off.

4. **Slope of Enlightenment:** more instances of how the technology can benefit the enterprise start to crystallize and become more widely understood. Second- and third-generation products appear from technology providers. More enterprises fund pilots; conservative companies remain cautious. The technology slowly gains ground, there is a shift in media and public perception, and popularity gradually returns.

5. **Plateau of Productivity:** mainstream adoption starts to take off. Criteria for assessing provider viability are more clearly defined. The technology's broad market applicability and relevance are clearly paying off.
   There is market recognition of the value of the technology and its wider use.

Hype Curve (Hype Cycle)

The Hype Curve illustrates the visibility of a technology or innovation over time, comparing public expectations to actual usability. Essentially, this curve reflects public sentiment, often shaped by media portrayals.

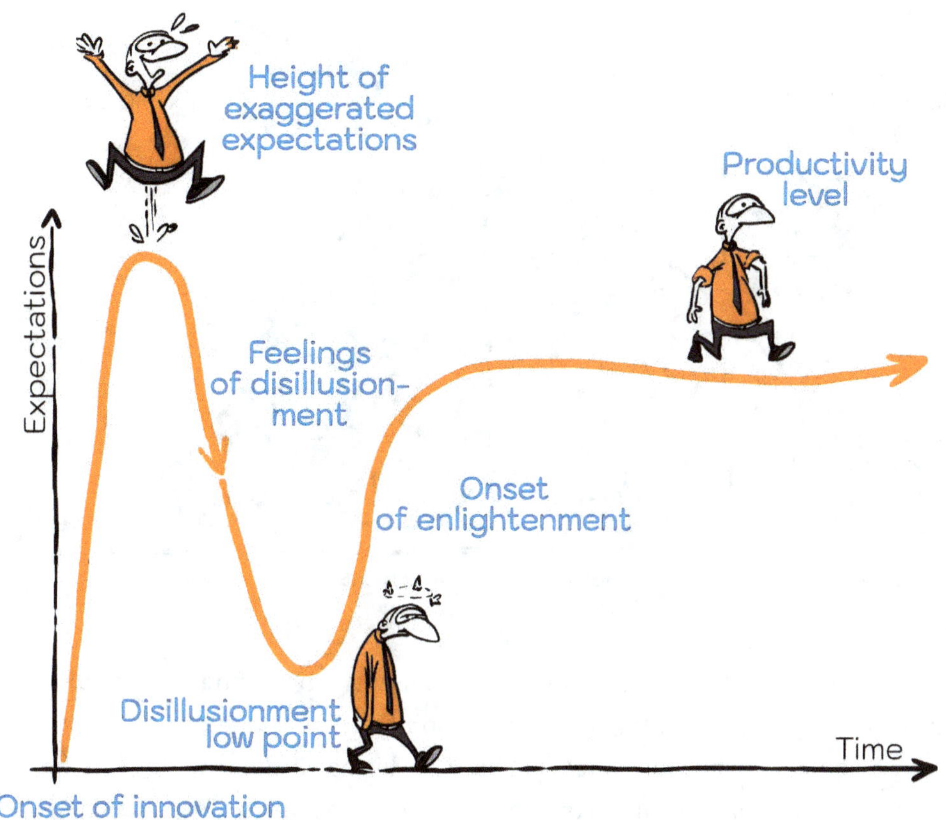

Gartner Hype Cycle: Interpreting Technology Hype via Gartner

The Hype Curve vs. the S-curve of innovation adoption

While the Hype Curve rather expresses the public opinion, the S-curve expresses the actual usage rate (actual number of users and funds invested).

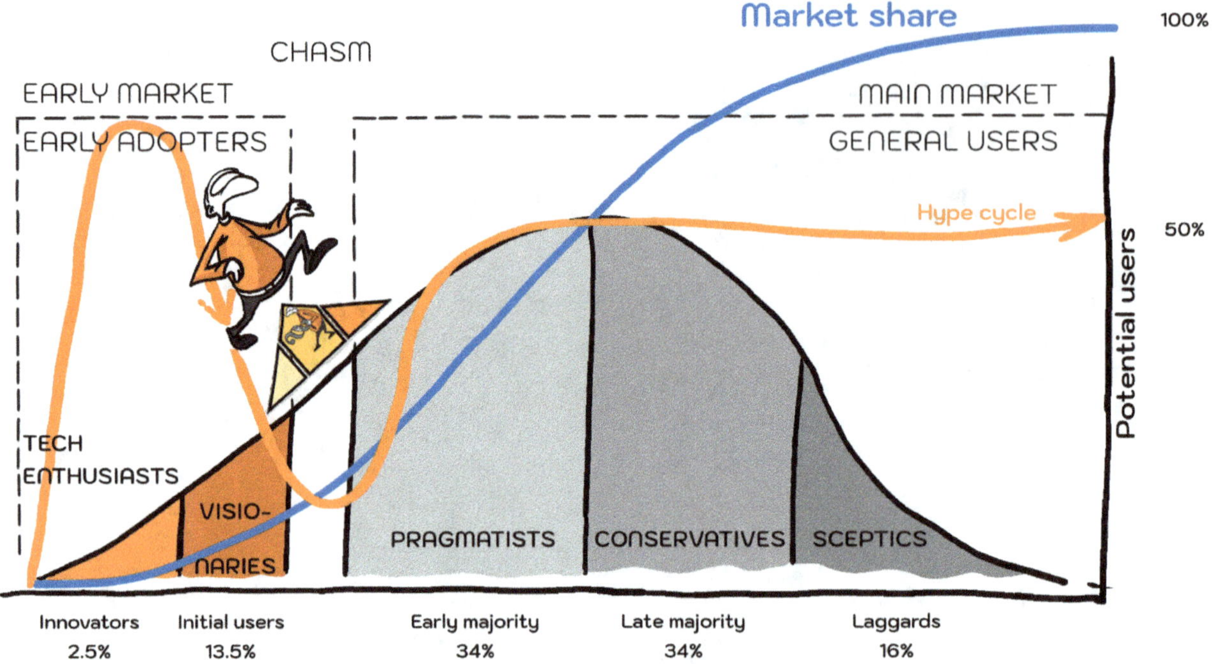

The Hype Curve projected onto the S-curve corresponds in time to the phase of the visionaries across the chasm to the beginning of the early majority. At this point, there is public and widespread adoption of the innovation. Expectations are no longer elevated because humanity has understood the importance of innovation and found a way to harness it. An exponential increase in users begins, usually accompanied by the building of additional layers.

It is important to note that if there is an increase in the number of users and an increase in the amount of money invested, but the quantity of the asset is limited, there is likely to be a significant increase in the price per coin of the asset.

IS BITCOIN AN INNOVATION?

Let's compare electronic fiat money with bitcoin according to the monetary properties outlined in Book One. We'll rate it from 1 to 5, with a rating of "1" being most desirable and "5" being the least desirable. An asterisk (*) indicates a rating from the perspective of the present. These values can be expected to improve in the coming years. Important characteristics, highlighted in red, are frequently overlooked but should be considered twice as valuable. Gold has also been added to the table for illustrative purposes. If red values were counted twice, gold would take second position and fiat currencies would be third. In case you are of a different opinion, try recalculating the table according to your own classification.

According to this assessment, Bitcoin is clearly a significant innovation.

Comparison of payments by functions and features

	Fiat	Fiat classification	BTC	Bitcoin classification	Gold
*Means of exchange	2	The interest of traders in bitcoin is growing very fast. Even large international chains are starting to allow payments. Further significant growth is expected in the future.	4	The interest of traders in bitcoin is growing very fast. Even large international chains are starting to allow payments. **Further significant growth is expected in the future.**	3
*Accounting unit (prices set in the given currency)	2	There is no global tender in which the prices of goods are quoted worldwide. International trade and transactions must involve transfers between currencies.	4	The first companies are emerging that quote prices in bitcoin or pay employees' wages in bitcoin. **Further significant growth is expected in the future, both in retail and international trade.**	5
*Short-term holder of value	2	With galloping inflation and hyperinflation, it doesn't work well as a short-term value sustainer either.	5	Due to high volatility, it is currently risky from a short-term holding perspective. However, for countries with high inflation it is much better than a given fiat currency. **With increasing market capitalization and an increase in new users, a gradual reduction in price fluctuations is expected in the future.**	2
*Long-term holder of value	3	Fiat currencies fail as a long-term sustainer of value in the face of ever-present inflation (spontaneous or targeted).	1	With a long-term holding of more than four years, it shows the best appreciation results among all assets (stocks, real estate, and gold) throughout its existence on a global scale.	1
Rarity	5	It is not rare and is not backed by any value.	1	Absolutely rare due to the fixed final quantity. It is rarer than gold.	2
Durability under normal use	1	Excellent	1	Excellent	1
Long-term durability	1	Excellent	1	Excellent	1
Divisibility	1	Excellent	1	Excellent	3
Storability (storage and security costs)	1	Excellent	1	Excellent	3
Transferability	1	Excellent	1	Excellent	3
Verifiability of authenticity	1	Excellent	1	Excellent	3
Availability for market participants	2	It needs an intermediary (bank, payment company). A large number of people on Earth do not have the possibility to open bank accounts.	1	It's more affordable than electronic fiat.	3
Standardization (defined units)	1	Excellent	1	Excellent	2
Security of possession	2	Can only be held with an intermediary (bank, PayPal, Revolut). Risk of bankruptcy due to mismanagement, deliberate embezzlement, or restrictions at the national or international level.	1	It allows for direct possession by the person who owns the private keys to the address. It cannot be stolen, confiscated, or nationalized.	2
Uncensurability	5	Confiscation or restriction of use from the point of view of state power, but also at the international level, is possible, and commonly happens	1	There are no restrictions at the Bitcoin network level.	1
Overall rating	30		25		35
Evaluation	2nd place		1st place		3rd place

COMPARISON OF CRYPTOCURRENCIES AND THE INTERNET

For new, innovative technologies it is generally true that the growth in use as well as overall user numbers depends primarily on its availability and utilization. In the case of the internet, the boom in accessibility came with the advent of personal computers followed by the advent of mobile phones. Further massive growth followed with the growth in usage, especially with regard to e-shops, social networks, and adult entertainment sites. Even if a technology is groundbreaking, it won't become widely adopted unless it is accessible and useful. How widespread would cars be without roads and gas stations, or electricity without electrical appliances?

The internet and cryptocurrencies are similar technologies in several ways: they are both global and decentralized, blur national boundaries, and offer greater freedom to individuals. The internet is the most widely used global technology in the world. Will cryptocurrencies follow suit?

HISTORY AND DEVELOPMENT OF THE INTERNET (INCLUDING THE NUMBER OF USERS)

1962: ARPA develops a project for an experimental network that has no central node, so that it will work even if parts of it are destroyed

DARPA, the Defense Advanced Research Projects Agency, was established in 1958 as part of the US Department of Defense. The agency is responsible for the development of new military technologies. Its mission is to maintain the technological edge of the US armed forces. The name of the agency has undergone several changes over the years, often incorporating the word "Defense": it was originally called ARPA in 1958, changed to DARPA in 1972, reverted back to ARPA in 1993, and finally became DARPA again in 1996. DARPA focuses on short-term projects that can be completed within two to four years. The agency's organizational structure is very simple, with only two levels of leadership and almost no hierarchical structure. This allows for a rapid transfer of information, ideas, equal access, and a fast decision-making process.

1969: ARPANET experimental network is created; first experiments were carried out in September with four connected nodes
1972: ARPANET is expanded to about 20 routers and 50 computers
1972: Ray Tomlinson develops the first e-mail program

Raymond Samuel Tomlinson (1941–2016) was an American computer programmer who implemented the first email system via the ARPANET, the precursor to the Internet. It was the first system capable of sending messages between users of different computers connected to the ARPANET. To achieve this, it used the @ sign separating the username and the computer name, a system that has been used in email ever since. Previously, messages could only be sent between users using the same computer.

1983: MILNET (Military Network) separated from ARPANET; TCP/IP transferred to commercial sphere; and DNS (Domain Name System) introduced.

This moment can be considered the beginning of the internet in the commercial sphere.

1984: Only 1,000 computers connected to the ARPANET

1987: The term "internet" is coined; 27,000 computers are connected to the network.

1989: Tim Berners-Lee published a proposal for the development of the World Wide Web (WWW)

Sir Timothy John Berners-Lee (1955–) is an English computer scientist and creator of the World Wide Web (WWW). It refers to a system for viewing, storing, and linking documents found on the internet. This multimedia information system was created by Berners-Lee during his time at the European Organization for Nuclear Research (CERN). The aim was to allow access to various resources from many other locations. The tool allowed scientists around the world to conveniently exchange data and ideas.

Berners-Lee discussed his invention, saying: "I took the idea of hypertext and combined it with the concept of TCP and the domain system and the World Wide Web was born. Most of the technologies involved in the Web had already been invented, I just had to put them together." Berners-Lee never took out a patent on the WWW and never asked for royalties from anyone. He allowed his invention to be distributed quite freely. In many ways, we can find a parallel with Satoshi Nakamoto.

1990: ARPANET ends

1991: deployment of the WWW at the European laboratory CERN.

1992: The White House is connected

1993: Marc Andreessen developed Mosaic, the first WWW browser, and made it available for free

1994: The internet became commercialized

Around the period 1994–1996, it overcame the "innovation gap."

1996: 55 million users

1997: 130 million users

1999: 200 million users

The internet took 16 years to reach 200 million users, starting from a base of about 1,000 computers. In contrast, the number of cryptocurrency users hit the 200 million mark in June 2021. This milestone was achieved just 12.5 years after the mining of the first bitcoin, which initially involved only a few dozen computers.

2000: 250 million users

2003: 600 million users

2004: Mark Zuckerberg launched Facebook on February 4

2005: 1 billion users

2006: Jack Dorsey launched Twitter on July 15

2010: Instagram emerged

2022: 5 billion user threshold crossed

https://crypto.com/images/202107_DataReport_OnChain_Market_Sizing.pdf
https://www.oberlo.com/statistics/how-many-people-use-internet

* ITU estimate

https://www.itu.int/en/ITU-D/Statistics/Pages/stat/default.aspx

Growth in the number of cryptocurrency users

A study from July 2021 by Crypto.com, called "Measuring Global Cryptocurrency Users: A Study to Measure Market Size Using On-Chain Metrics," states on page 9 that the global number of cryptocurrency users reached 200 million in June 2021. This is a slight drop from 221 million users reported in July. Since the introduction of the first genuine cryptocurrency, bitcoin, on January 3, 2009, the user base has grown to 200 million over the course of 12.5 years. Although it's challenging to obtain precise numbers, other sources corroborate these figures. Importantly, the number of users continues to grow.

Measuring Global Crypto Users via crypto.com

Comparing the number of internet and cryptocurrency users

The internet and cryptocurrencies share many similarities and even complement each other in various ways. The widespread use of computers, mobile devices, and smartphones has paved the way for cryptocurrencies to gain mainstream adoption, particularly in online shopping and electronic payments. It took the internet approximately 16 years to amass 200 million users, while cryptocurrencies achieved this milestone in just 12.5 years. The internet expanded from 200 million to 1 billion users in around six years. This raises the question: how long will it take for cryptocurrencies to reach the 1 billion user mark?

Let's calculate a simple word problem:

It took the internet roughly 16 years to reach 200 million users. Cryptocurrencies took only 12.5 years to reach 200 million users.

It took the internet 6 years to get from 200 million users to 1 billion users.

1) How long will it take cryptocurrencies to reach 1 billion users if they continue to grow at the same rate?

2) When will cryptocurrencies reach 1 billion users, if 200 million users were reached in June 2021?

Solution:

1. To find the solution to this problem, we first need to calculate the growth rate of cryptocurrencies compared to the growth of the internet.
   Growth ratio
   = Time for internet growth / time for cryptocurrency growth
   = 16 years / 12.5 years
   = 1.28 (rounded to two decimal places)
   Now we can calculate how long it will take cryptocurrencies to reach 1 billion users if their growth is faster than the growth of the internet according to the same ratio: the time for cryptocurrencies to grow to one billion users
   = internet growth time from 200 million to 1 billion users / growth ratio
   = 6 years / 1.28 ≈ 4.69 years (4.69 years is approximately 4 years and 8 months)
   Based on this calculation, we can expect that cryptocurrencies could reach 1 billion users in about 4 years and 8 months.

2. We can now calculate an approximate date when cryptocurrencies could reach 1 billion users:
   June 2021 + 4 years and 8 months (time for cryptocurrencies to grow from 200 million to 1 billion users)
   = February 2026
   Cryptocurrencies could potentially reach 1 billion users by around February 2026.

This projected date is just a mathematical estimate and may not accurately predict actual growth. Some people might argue that cryptocurrencies won't grow as fast as the internet because not everyone needs a modern, decentralized form of money. On the other hand, there are those who believe that the adoption of cryptocurrencies could accelerate even faster due to motivations like the allure of quick wealth or the need to safeguard personal assets from inflation.

I think that cryptocurrencies, due to their innovative characteristics, will eventually attract as many users as the internet has. Both technologies cater to a similar user base and complement each other well. However, the rate of cryptocurrency adoption will largely depend on legislative decisions, global economic trends, and how quickly cryptocurrencies can bridge the innovation gap on their path to mainstream acceptance.

The internet took roughly three years (from 1994 to 1996) to gain mainstream adoption. Cryptocurrencies might take longer to reach the same level, given the complexities of establishing a legal framework for a new form of asset and eventually, a new currency. However, the powerful human motivations for freedom and wealth should not be discounted. These factors could potentially accelerate the adoption of cryptocurrencies. While it's hard to predict the exact timeline, growing interest in cryptocurrencies is likely, and this could particularly drive up the price of bitcoin due to its scarcity and limited supply.

CHAPTER 3 SUMMARY

Bitcoin is certainly a significant innovation, but it faces many challenges that no other innovation of this magnitude can avoid.

- Regulations give legitimacy to a given innovation, but not all of them are reasonable. There will be competition between opponents and proponents of this new technology, and, as with the automobile, the fight will move to the political level and to the international level.

- The more astute can gain an edge and economic advantages. Opponents can miss the train and put themselves at a long-term economic disadvantage. In democratic countries, over time, most politicians will side with the majority of voters. Because of fear of missed opportunities, some non-democratic countries will gradually follow suit.

- Additional layers must be added (creating a coherent ecosystem) to increase the parameters of ideality and technical performance to help bridge the innovation gap. This will involve building a network of ATMs, payment terminals, exchange offices, integration into existing payment systems, and integration into standard banking and investment services.

- At the same time, there will be pressure to make transactions faster and cheaper. Applications and technologies will be improved to make everything as simple and user-friendly as possible. Technology companies will start to figure out where this technology can be used. Gradually, it will be incorporated as a payment method into social networks, messengers, streaming services, e-shops, and will find a firm place in other online services.

- A number of merchants around the world will begin accepting cryptocurrency payments as an alternative to their national currencies, allowing users to avoid currency exchange fees. Some will eventually start setting fixed prices in satoshi.

- Countries that do not have a national currency will gradually adopt bitcoin as an independent currency. National laws will gradually begin to recognize bitcoin as a commodity and, over time, will view it as a real currency.

- Many people will have difficulty changing their thinking and perception of the new non-state currency. Over time, however, they will change their mindset and embrace the innovation in the same way they have embraced credit cards.

If bitcoin manages to meet at least some of the challenges outlined above, it will bridge the innovation gap, change public opinion, and see a massive increase in users. Due to the limited amount of bitcoin, the price of bitcoin will rise in the long term. It is important to remember that at the moment we are still at the beginning (the level of the first visionary users) and bitcoin still has a long way to go.

BITCOIN PRICE DEVELOPMENT: A CASE FOR OPTIMISM?

BITCOIN PRICE DEVELOPMENT: A CASE FOR OPTIMISM?

In the first chapter of Book Two, I mentioned the ethos of bitcoin and boldly asserted that it was more important than the economics. This statement of mine was based on the view that "money is not everything." However, there are other perspectives, such as "money always comes first" and others. Purchasing power is what lends value to money. For centuries, famous philosophers, politicians, writers, and ordinary people have commented on this topic. Here is just a glimpse of a few of these well-known sayings and proverbs.

- "Money doesn't stink." —Titus Flavius Vespasianus, Roman Emperor
- "Money is the key that opens every lock." —Molière, French writer
- "I'd like the life of a poor man with a lot of money." —Pablo Picasso, Spanish painter
- "When money speaks, truth is silent." —Greek proverb
- "Love can do much, money can do everything." —Portuguese proverb
- "Even the blind can see money." —Chinese proverb

Okay then, I admit that the price of bitcoin is important too. Actually, it makes sense. The price of bitcoin will probably continue to rise faster than the price of commodities and real estate over the long term. Fiat currencies, on the other hand, will gradually lose their purchasing power. In that case, most people will find it more sensible to save in bitcoin for the long term.

It would also probably be fair to admit that the vast majority of people have and will invest in bitcoin initially because of the potential profits. However, some have delved deeper into the subject and have come to understand its underlying ethos. While those even more thoughtful and curious have looked into the future and seen the (r)evolution it could cause.

So we can freely admit that it is normal to invest in bitcoin for selfish reasons. It is, after all, a natural effort to protect the good deeds one has performed and to keep the purchasing power of one's own money in good shape. It is a standard approach to money that has been tested over thousands of years of human history.

BITCOIN PRICE AND BITCOIN AS PART OF AN INVESTMENT PORTFOLIO

We have already explained that money can basically consist of anything that others will perceive as money. Something similar is true with regard to the price of bitcoin. Bitcoin will be worth what someone else is willing to buy it for and what someone else is willing to sell it for. That being said, its price is not derived from gold or fiat money, but from the value people place on it. In reality, this means that the value of bitcoin is determined in a global, open market and only by supply (sellers) and demand (buyers). Anyone who buys bitcoin becomes an integral part of that market. However, the open market must be seen as a living organism, which is sometimes irrational. This means that it sometimes does not behave according to the fundamentals that should determine its development, and often—especially in the short term—goes against expectations based on apparent reality. The same is true of the price of bitcoin. The market is not a Garden of Eden, nor a peaceful place to live. It is made up of millions of speculating entities—some of which even join together on purpose—each seeking to profit at the expense of the others according to the principles of game theory.

Particularly with speculative investments, it is important to remember that the market can be irrational for longer than a given investor can be solvent. It is for this reason that no one should invest more in cryptocurrencies than they can afford to lose. Investment advisors often recommend that beginners invest 1%–3% of their assets in cryptocurrencies, while experienced investors might consider allocating 3%–10%. However, from another perspective, it's advisable to invest in bitcoin only as much as one understands and believes in it. You can tell if you have invested more than you should by asking a simple question:

"Do you necessarily need the price to go up, or do you just want it to?"

Irrational: defying reason, incomprehensible, or absurd

Foundation: the basis or essence

Speculation: a purposeful, deliberate action aimed at achieving a benefit or profit

Solvent: the ability to pay, meet monetary obligations (opposite of insolvent)

If you absolutely need the price to rise in order to obtain a profit or yield, then you have invested more than you should have. The market can frequently move in the opposite direction than expected, and the turnaround may take longer than an investor is willing to wait.

BITCOIN PRICE DEVELOPMENT

As you will see in the table and charts below, there is roughly a fivefold reduction in the increase in appreciation between periods. At the same time, there is also a slight decrease in the declines between periods according to almost identical ratios. If you look carefully at the figures, you will see that the increases are falling much faster than the decreases. I personally believe that this is because we are close to the innovation gap and are waiting for it to be overcome.

In the discussion on Bridging the Gap, the graphs of the technology S-curves clearly show how the growth of the above parameters slows down before the Gap is crossed and, on the contrary, there is an exponential increase after the Gap is crossed. This increase then, of course, brings with it a massive increase in the adoption of the technology by other users and, in the case of a limited number of bitcoins, very likely an increase in price. However, the gradual reduction in the rate of bitcoin's price increases over time is partially due to its rising cost. Large investors, or speculators, pump significant sums into cryptocurrencies. For them, an increase in price—measured in high double-digit percentages—is sufficient to meet their profit targets. Once these targets are reached, they often sell their cryptocurrency holdings to avoid potential market declines that they perceive as risks in other markets.

In the next passage, we will discuss the chart of the price of bitcoin (BTC). First, let's explain the difference between a linear and a logarithmic representation of the BTC price against the USD. It is important to note that both graphs show the same price evolution over the same period, represented in green.

Linear representation

The division on the Y-axis is linear, meaning all segments have the same value (e.g., 1, 2, 3). As a result, exponential price growth—like the kind experienced by bitcoin—appears as a steep arc on the chart. The price evolution during the first seven years is hardly visible, even though the price increased by thousands of percent during that period. In contrast, the price changes over the last five years are much more pronounced, showing both exponential increases and decreases. This chart effectively captures the overall growth in the asset's value from its inception to the present.

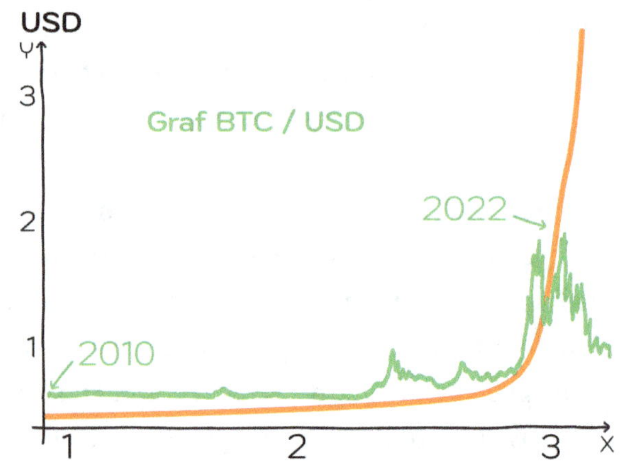

Logarithmic representation

Individual ticks on the Y-axis have a multiplicative relationship to one another (e.g., 1,10,100). When plotting the price of bitcoin against the USD over the same period using a logarithmic scale, the chart appears more uniform and provides a clearer view of the price fluctuations in each period. Exponential growth in price is represented more like a straight line in this case. This

logarithmic chart is especially useful for showing growth or loss relative to the previous period as a percentage. As such, it is commonly used in trading environments, where the primary concern is the rate of asset growth rather than its absolute value.

We will now review and analyze in detail the development of the price of bitcoin against the US dollar from the beginning of 2010 until March 24, 2023, when I must submit the manuscript of this book to the publisher. We can compare how the price has evolved over the period of each halving in both a clear table and a graph.

BTC/USD price development	Profit: peak (+% from trough)	Loss: trough (-% from peak)
Beginning (around 2010)	~$0.10	$0.01 (-90%)
1. The period prior to the first halving (January 3, 2009–November 28, 2012)	$32 (+318,000%)	$2 (-94%)
2. The period after the first halving (November 28, 2013–July 9, 2016)	$1,240 (+61,900%)	$160 (-87%)
3. The period after the second halving (July 9, 2016–May 11, 2020)	$19,800 (+12, 275%)	$3,120 (-84%)
4.The period after the third halving (May 11, 2020–April 20, 2024)	$69,000 (+2,112%)	$15,544 (-78%)

BTC vs. USD price evolution on a logarithmic chat
BTC/USD from mid-2010 to April 20, 2024
(Trading view/BTC INDEX platform)

Let's consider the projected outcome for bitcoin during its fourth halving period. If bitcoin's performance aligns with the mathematical ratios observed in previous halving events, then the peak price for this period is likely to fall within the $76,000 to $79,000 range, while the lowest price could be between $12,000 and $14,000

Unfortunately, in November 2021, when the price reached a new all-time high, the world markets began to deal with a large increase in inflation and the resurgence of the COVID-19 pandemic. Stock markets took a big plunge, and the further projected growth of the price of bitcoin came to a halt. Before the situation could stabilize, the war in Ukraine broke out in February 2022. This was followed by global crises in energy, food, and minerals, leading to further increases in their prices.

Although the last global mortgage crisis contributed to the emergence of bitcoin, the price of bitcoin has only evolved in a growing economy. Meanwhile, the downturn in global markets since the end of 2021 has affected the price of bitcoin as it correlates with the stock markets. For these reasons, both the peak and the trough may be elsewhere than would normally be expected. We will see how the price of bitcoin evolves in the fifth period (2024–2028), a time when both the adoption gap could be bridged and the global economic crisis could recede.

On the other hand, if the global financial crisis were to cross the threshold and turn into a cascading collapse of banking and monetary systems, traditional products such as safe government bonds and even conventional money could cease to function. In such a situation, even more conservative investors would turn their attention to alternative investments such as bitcoin, even though it can be very volatile. However, despite its volatility, it can be seen as a safe haven in times of crisis, as opposed to collapsing traditional financial instruments. Such a situation could cause a sharp rise in the price of bitcoin and a decoupling from its correlation with equity markets. In such a situation, bitcoin would become "digital gold" and could be seen as a currency of limited quantity that can serve as a stable investment when traditional financial systems fail. Of course, this is a situation we would rather not experience, but the ironic twist is that if such a collapse occurs, bitcoin may be the one currency that could survive.

Of course bitcoin is safe.
It has appreciated more than 1,000% and cannot depreciate more than 100%.

PRICE DEVELOPMENT PHASE

Bitcoin is evolving and the market is gradually trying to establish its fair value. This process has been going on for more than a decade and will continue for decades to come. Let's go through the stages of development it has already passed, explain what stage it is in now, and speculate on how its price might evolve in the future.

Anarchist money

Originally developed within the Cypherpunk community, bitcoin was first adopted by tech enthusiasts and advocates of digital privacy as an alternative to traditional monetary systems and a way to evade state surveillance. Since adoption was very low, the price per bitcoin was in the range of thousandths to tenths of a US dollar. Initially, there were no goods or services available for purchase using BTC.

In fact, the first documented bitcoin payment is still celebrated around the world today as **Pizza Day**. Because of its relative anonymity at the time, bitcoin gained popularity on the darknet. As more organizations started to adopt it, its price began to increase. Subsequently, it began to be used for regular trading outside the **darknet market**. The influx of new users sparked demand for the creation of services that would allow bitcoin to be exchanged for fiat.

Nonetheless, exchanges, currency exchangers, and Bitcoin ATMs that started serving a growing customer base operated within specific countries. Most countries enforce Anti-Money Laundering (AML) regulations as part of international agreements. These businesses must adhere to the legal requirements of their respective countries while also complying with financial market regulatory standards.

Pizza Day: In 2010, programmer Laszlo Hanyecz made a historic purchase. Back then, the value of bitcoin (BTC) was much lower than it is now. On May 22, 2010, Laszlo spent 10,000 bitcoins to buy two pizzas.

The **darknet market** is a secretive online marketplace that operates on the darknet, a hidden part of the internet. Accessible through special networks like Tor (The Onion Router) or I2P, the darknet market primarily serves as a black market. It facilitates the buying and selling of illegal items such as drugs, weapons, counterfeit money, and stolen credit card information, along with other illicit goods. Some legal items are also available for sale.

They have also implemented Know Your Customer (KYC) policies. In order to comply with these policies, each user of the system has to upload their identification documents, verify their bank account, address, phone, and email. This process leads to a gradual loss of anonymity of some addresses in the bitcoin network. Governments have then, with the help of private companies, gradually started to identify the owners of individual addresses. This is why the bitcoin network is now only pseudo-anonymous, and why it is used less for illegal transactions than the ubiquitous cash.

Speculative asset

Until recently, bitcoin was presented only as a highly speculative and risky asset. In the long term, however, bitcoin has shown significantly greater price appreciation than equities. The price of bitcoin has been correlated to some extent with the stock markets, but the volatility has been much higher. The main reason was the speculative behavior of most investors. It is estimated that these speculators controlled the majority of the market. Speculators see bitcoin primarily as an investment opportunity for short-term gain, instead of trying to understand bitcoin and its potential benefits to humanity.

The moment the BTC price, driven by user growth, reaches their set targets, they start selling their coins at a profit. This speculative activity often leads to abrupt declines in bitcoin's price. These drops are further intensified by both inexperienced newcomers and average individuals who lack a deep understanding of bitcoin and investing. Based on alarmist media reports, they then panic and dispose of the coins they have bought, usually at a considerable loss. The market behaves like a living organism and often goes in the opposite direction to what fundamentals and most participants predict. During price fluctuations, among other things, the market cleanses itself of overbought trades. Players with huge amounts of investment capital—known as whales—can influence the market partly by their well-timed transactions. The market can also be influenced by the media and celebrities.

However, it should be understood that this distribution is necessary and arises spontaneously on the basis of the market behavior of individual actors. Indeed, it is important that there is a further redistribution of SATs so that bitcoin ownership can spread to the wider population. This will then be reflected in an increase in the price, which may then move towards new all-time highs. Bitcoin is often compared to other cryptocurrencies and there is constant speculation as to whether any of them can replace it. Compared to other cryptocurrencies, bitcoin boasts the longest established track record, the highest level of decentralization, and the greatest computing power supported by substantial electricity costs. It also leads in market capitalization, calculated as its current price multiplied by the total number of coins in circulation, and has the largest user base.

Supercycle—or are we approaching a standard commodity?

Here again we are entering into speculation, but we are getting very close to this stage. A lot will depend on bridging the innovation chasm. The outcome will determine the market capitalization of bitcoin and its level of acceptance in society. Price declines are likely to decrease significantly in the future as market capitalization increases. This means that the steep price declines of 70–90% that accompanied the "bear market" will continue to decrease over time. However, it is likely that as price declines become less pronounced, price increases will also decrease. In order for this forecast to come true, the amount of speculative funds in the market needs to decrease. It can be expected that more investors—thanks to bitcoin ETFs—will start to see bitcoin as a long-term investment as well as a better form of money.

Possible money of the future, or even a global currency?

As you have likely come to understand, bitcoin has the potential to become a worldwide global currency. If this is successful, there will be nothing in terms of today's conception of money that compares to it. Perhaps the local exchange rates of the surviving fiat currencies will be tracked for some time to come. It would then make sense to track bitcoin's exchange rate, especially in relation to other cryptocurrencies, some of which will also tend to fit money. There will be users who will speculate on other still volatile cryptocurrencies, as the possibility of multiplying one's funds is always a big attraction.

From the perspective of investors, bitcoin would cease to be interesting as an investment and would only be used when they need to exit their positions in the stock, commodity, and other markets. Income in bitcoin would be a natural occurrence at this stage. Ordinary people would no longer need to protect their money with risky investments because bitcoin is not inflationary. The growth in the value of bitcoin will continue to be a long-term process directly dependent on the growth in purchasing power resulting mainly from productivity growth, which can be expected to increase in units of one per cent per year. For those who do not understand investments, bitcoin would thus be a safe and peaceful haven that will protect their good deeds for later in their lives.

The dollar is terribly volatile against bitcoin.

THE GLOBALIZATION OF MONEY

In ancient times, humankind strived to find a common means to facilitate the mutual exchange of good deeds. Eventually, they invented precious metal-based money, which spread throughout the world. Although different currencies were introduced in different territories, since their value was determined by the amount of precious metal, there was no fundamental problem of exchangeability. In our current and historically brief experiment with fiat currencies, this possibility of determining value has disappeared. Humanity is beginning to realize the need for an independent currency that is not subject to the policies of central banks, the World Bank, or the International Monetary Fund. Of course, individual decisions or sanctions are often justified, but they always achieve only political objectives. In the global market, however, they distort the real values of individual currencies in the same way that subsidies and regulations distort the market prices of products. A globally independent currency would set up a fair competition between the monetary policies of individual countries, and political objectives would have to be achieved in other ways, for example by strictly enforcing the prohibition of cooperation with sanctioned countries in political, economic, scientific, and cultural terms. It would be ideal for the actors involved to do so on the basis of their own decisions and not by government decree. There have long been attempts by the great powers to impose a preferred currency as a global one, but logically this can never happen. However, humanity needs an independent global currency and is slowly moving towards it. But such a currency must be resilient, decentralized, and based on the scarcity principle. It's uncertain which cryptocurrency will ultimately prevail, but bitcoin is currently the leading candidate.

The most important factors that will influence whether bitcoin can become a global currency include:

- **Increased adoption**: bitcoin will be more and more accepted as a payment for goods and services or used as a means for long-term savings.

- **Stability and reliability**: increasing adoption will increase the capitalization of bitcoin, thus gradually reducing the ups and downs of the price. Bitcoin will become more trustworthy.

- **Regulation and legislation**: regulations and legislative adjustments for the crypto sector in many countries around the world will contribute to the involvement of large companies and more cautious individuals.

- **Confidence in the financial system**: confidence in the existing financial system may gradually be lost. In this case, people could see bitcoin as a safe and stable alternative to traditional currencies.

- **Technological innovation**: technological innovation must continue, especially in terms of simplifying the user experience and improving efficiency.

Why does the universe want a single form of money? Read this article written by Oleg Andreev in 2013.

"The Universe Wants One Money" by Oleg Andreev

Money is heading towards globalization

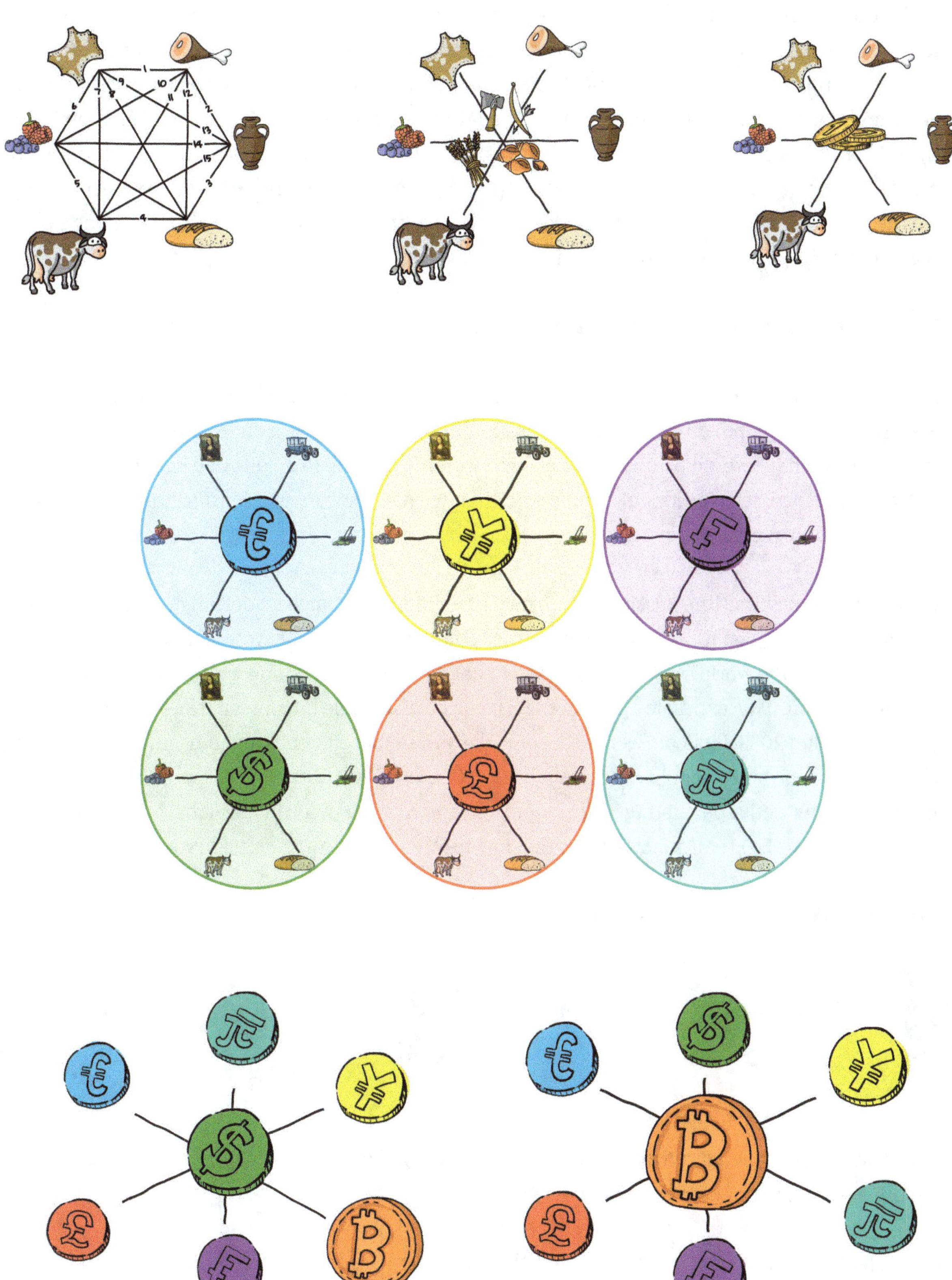

HOW HIGH WILL THE PRICE OF BITCOIN GO IN THE FUTURE?

Bitcoin is a disruptive innovation that is at the beginning of its widespread adoption. It has been embraced by tech enthusiasts and visionaries in previous eras. Currently, in terms of the innovation S-curve of widespread adoption, we are probably in the space of the gap, a period where humanity is searching for a clearly definable use case, and there is a struggle for recognition of legitimacy by both the general population and the political representation. The world is growing increasingly polarized. We are transitioning from Gandhi's phases of "First they ignore you" and "Then they laugh at you" to "Then they fight you." Should we be afraid of this phase? I don't think so. Nowadays, Bitcoin can no longer be shut down or banned. Even the most stringent regulations can at best slow its spread. In terms of the Hype Curve, we are on the uphill climb on the "slope of enlightenment." Moreover, we are at a time when fiat money is failing and no longer fulfilling the most important of the three basic functions of money:

Fiat state currencies are failing as a store of value.

Once the chasm is crossed, we can probably very quickly flip to the "And then you won" phase. We may not be talking about a global currency right away, but bitcoin could go through several phases of wider adoption. The first phase would be that small merchants take a liking to it, followed by large corporations. Eventually, it could replace traditional banks. And then we just have to wait for our grandmothers, shop assistants, and taxi drivers to start using it.

However, let's try again to outline possible future developments under such an optimistic scenario. If bitcoin were to become the only global currency, then its price could be derived from the value of the world's wealth. However, the value of the world's wealth expressed in fiat currencies is no longer relevant, because it is constantly growing. Optimistic estimates predict that the price of a single bitcoin will range from $500,000 to $1,000,000 by around 2032. If bitcoin were to become the only global currency and bind all the world's wealth to itself, the price of one bitcoin could range from $1,000,000–$10,000,000 within a few decades. Many financial analysts are constantly speculating on this topic, but much will depend on the global economic condition and political situation. The reality, however, is that no one knows anything—nor can we see into the future.

Here are a few articles that discuss this topic:

 Bitcoin at $1 million: Cathie Wood revises her prediction, deadline advanced

 Bitcoin could hit $10M in 9 years but more sidechains needed: Blockstream CEO

From a free market perspective, an increase in demand (users) often leads to an increase in price, especially if production (output) cannot cover the increase in demand.

A comparison of the Hype Curve (public opinion), the Innovation S-curve of widespread adoption (user numbers) and the Price Evolution (continuous price growth) can give us a hint of what the price of bitcoin might look like in the future. These curves are closely related, but each evolves based on its own input parameters.

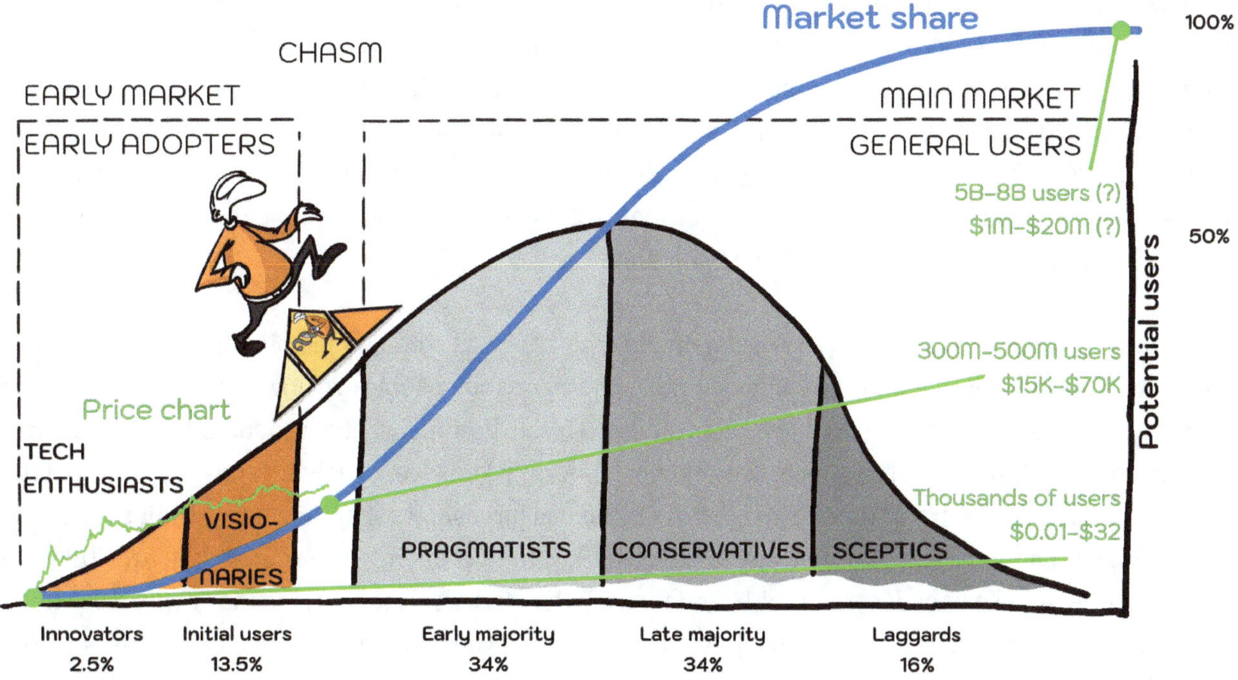

These estimates could either be too high or significantly too low. However, it should be remembered that if the US dollar continues to exist in a few decades, a million dollars may buy only a small fraction of what it does today.

The following figure shows the decline in the value (purchasing power) of the US dollar over the years.

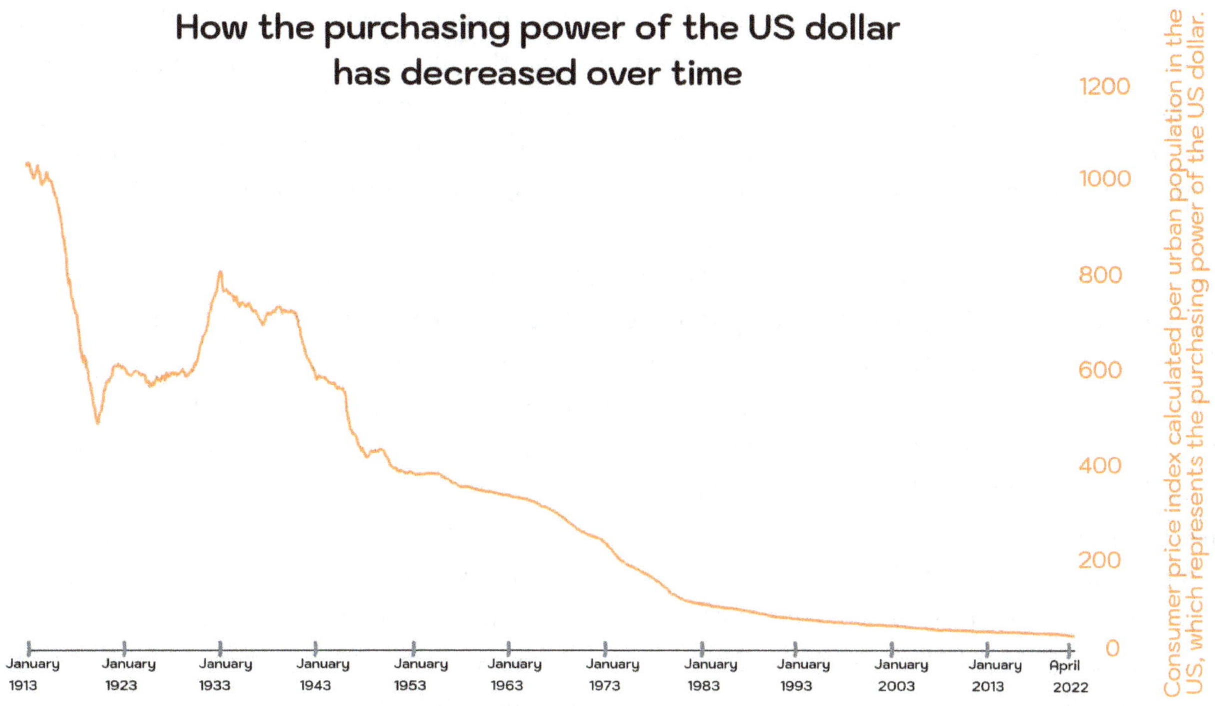

There is no point in trying to predict the future value of bitcoin. It will depend on many circumstances, and also on how much of a share some of the other surviving cryptocurrencies take. People should think that it would be good to have some value stored in bitcoin just in case. Those who believe in it probably don't need to be persuaded. But even skeptics and latecomers should at least buy a few satoshi just in case it takes off. From the bitcoin perspective, speculation about its price is not the most important factor; it possesses many other essential properties. For many of its users, the fact that it can protect their funds from depreciation in the long run would be sufficient.

Unfortunately, more and more people are starting to envy those who bought bitcoin for a few dollars a few years ago or for much less than they can buy it now. These envious people are now screaming that it's not fair, that cryptocurrency profits should be taxed, and that it's all definitely a scam or something like a lottery. They are completely unaware that these lucky bitcoin holders risked losing all their funds. The fact that they once bought bitcoin cheaply and persisted in not selling it clearly shows that they have studied a lot about the workings of fiat money and the workings of bitcoin. Now they are being rewarded for the time they took to understand all the principles, their faith, and the risk they took. Yes, there were many who were not as convinced. They merely speculated on the price of bitcoin, and when it rose, they sold their coins at a profit. Today, they despair because they have long since spent the money they earned—often in a "slightly gained, slightly lost" fashion—or, if they didn't spend it, inflation is eating it up. Now they sigh at the loss of multiples of potential gains. Anyone envious of bitcoin investors should remember that they could have also educated themselves on the basic economic principles of how money works. They could have studied the theories of John Nash or delved into Austrian economics. Furthermore, they had the opportunity to purchase bitcoin for just a few dollars, betting on a currency founded on the decentralized principles of game theory.

On the other hand, nothing is lost and we are still in the very early stages of bitcoin adoption. If the price evolution follows the innovative S-curve of widespread adoption, every owner of at least some satoshi will probably be very happy in the future. Consider the fact that, with roughly 200 million users, the price ranges from $15,000 to $70,000. With some exaggeration, we can say that almost all of the finite amount of bitcoin has already been extracted. More precisely, of the final 21 million electronic coins, more than 19 million already have been mined. The remaining 2 million bitcoins will be mined over the course of the next 120 years. So the increment (inflation) of new coins will be minimal until it stops altogether.

However, in the next four to eight years we may see a roughly fivefold increase in the number of users. Should this actually happen, this would have a big impact on the price of bitcoin precisely because the growth of new coins is already minimal and is steadily declining. This means that there may be another large number of people who will want to buy bitcoin. In such a case, there will have to be a reallocation of the coins already on the market, which will undoubtedly cause the price to rise. Of course we need to keep in mind the issue of supply and demand and be aware of the competitive environment of other cryptocurrencies. But as we have already discussed, every investment is risky. The converse is also true: those who have savings in fiat currencies and do not invest them lose the value of their good deeds in the long run. Let everyone make their own choices. Just refrain from complaining in ten years about how unfair the system is, or suggesting that the wealth of the crypto-rich should be distributed to the poor. Even students who were financially constrained but managed to save small amounts in bitcoin are now more than financially secure.

CHAPTER 4 SUMMARY

Bitcoin is steadily maturing as an innovation and more practical uses are being found for it. There is a gap in the market because the world needs an independent and reliable global currency. What is also obvious is that as adoption grows, so will its price. Will it ever be worth a million dollars? No one knows, but if we can build downstream ecosystems of other layers and bridge the innovation gap, it may reach, and perhaps even surpass, that threshold in the long run.

Those who decide to buy bitcoin should not overload their brains with speculation about how fast its price will rise. On the contrary, investors should be prepared for the possibility of significant losses over several years. It's important to remember that until you sell at a loss, you still own the same amount of satoshis. Patience is key; waiting may be the only option. In such a situation, I recommend not watching the price for a few months and not burdening your brain with unnecessary stress. The price should eventually return to its previous values and in the long run it may still rise.

In any case, Bitcoin is an interesting innovation in the field of finance and its growing importance should not be underestimated. It is gradually establishing itself on the market as a reliable and independent global currency that is increasingly being used. Assessing its development to date, it shows a high degree of resilience and adaptability to market changes. Its price has been rising over the long term and has reached new highs roughly every four years so far.

I am convinced that everyone should acquire at least a piece of bitcoin, according to their means, so that they do not regret the missed opportunity in the future. Over the course of its existence, bitcoin has significantly outperformed stocks, commodities, and even gold.

It's not that we couldn't catch up to bitcoin;
we just didn't realize it wouldn't wait for us.

The question of bitcoin's future value is challenging to predict accurately, yet the general consensus is: it will be worth it.

THE GLOBAL CRYPTO MARKET: NAVIGATING THE WILD WEST

THE GLOBAL CRYPTO MARKET: NAVIGATING THE WILD WEST

I consider bitcoin to be the clear leader of the crypto market. Unfortunately, the public perception of bitcoin's societal benefits is becoming diluted due to the overwhelming number of other cryptocurrencies in the market. I personally see bitcoin as something completely different and separate: a representation of free market money. All of the other cryptocurrencies belong in a completely different category. Therefore, I consider myself a "bitcoin maximalist," but in this chapter I will attempt to objectively evaluate other crypto projects as well.

I consider the phenomenon of decentralized finance to be revolutionary, but it needs to be thoroughly examined. Mutual competition is important and necessary for the development of the entire crypto market. Some cryptocurrencies attempt to emulate bitcoin, while others are opening up avenues for expanding functionality and further innovation. Only a tiny number of them can be considered truly independent. A significant issue facing the entire cryptocurrency market is that many projects primarily serve as fundraising schemes for their founders, rather than providing genuine value. This prevailing trend has greatly hindered the widespread adoption of bitcoin. It discourages many bidders and gives governments an excuse to impose stricter regulations.

Let's venture into the Wild West where only the informed and cautious prevail. This chapter will introduce you to the current crypto market and prepare you for some of the hidden threats. Note that the best way to protect yourself is to be well-informed and to use common sense. Nothing is free. The promise of huge returns is oftentimes just a cover to lure potential investors into a scheme.

THE GLOBAL CRYPTO SCENE: UNREGULATED MARKETS WITH LIMITLESS POSSIBILITIES

There are currently around twenty thousand cryptocurrencies in existence. Some of them are used for engaging in fraud. Others simply will not able to survive the huge competitive pressure in the long run. Nations are attempting to regulate cryptocurrencies, but government officials often do not have a deep understanding of the technology nor its potential ramifications on various industries. They create laws and regulations with little forethought, research, and planning. Some infringe on citizens' freedoms. Others are even nonsensical or unworkable. Of course, regulations are partly desirable in order to protect unsophisticated investors. On the other hand, everyone should research the topic independently, form their own opinion, and take responsibility for any poor choices they make. Instead, many people transfer their incompetence caused by lack of interest—or laziness to educate themselves—to the state. It's not surprising that politicians often discuss these issues that they don't fully understand, framing them as matters of public interest to gain support from less fortunate citizens. In doing so, they are often concerned with pure populism or prioritizing personal short-term goals.

Another problem is that some cryptocurrencies can be considered as shares. It should be pointed out that this does not apply to bitcoin because there is no entity behind it. These crypto projects face sanctions and bans for circumventing rules designed for publicly traded shares on stock markets. When regulators begin to investigate—sometimes even heavily sanctioning companies behind these projects—there is usually a sharp drop in the price of the cryptocurrency in question. Sometimes the drop in price is permanent.

BITCOIN: THE MARKET LEADER

Bitcoin is the undisputed market leader at the moment. When bitcoin rises in price, so do most other cryptocurrencies and vice versa. It is also true that other currencies often rise in price faster than bitcoin, but they realize much greater losses when prices fall globally. Many of them subsequently fail to recover and end up in decline and oblivion. However, bitcoin is primarily money at the moment and is not yet trying to be anything else. This is because most of society doesn't yet understand the broader uses of cryptocurrencies and global demand at the moment is all about money. Satoshi clearly indicated that bitcoin can be developed in any direction, but people need to mature in order for it to do so (see page 181): "The nature of Bitcoin is such that once version 0.1 was released, the core design was set in stone for the rest of its lifetime. Because of that, I wanted to design it to support every possible transaction type I could think of." He goes on to say that, "The design supports a tremendous variety of possible transaction types that I designed years ago. Escrow transactions, bonded contracts, third party arbitration, multi-party signature, etc. If Bitcoin catches on in a big way, these are things we'll want to explore in the future, but they all had to be designed at the beginning to make sure they would be possible later."

A number of cryptocurrency exchanges are trying to invent additional add-on functionality, but Satoshi has made it clear that one should proceed step by step. Additional functionality should only be incorporated when conditions are ripe for it. First, humanity must accept bitcoin as non-state money, understand its meaning, learn how to work with it, and create a simple and user-friendly interface. Only after that does it make sense to connect the general public to other decentralized services. Currently, a small percentage of the population owns cryptocurrency. However, most of these owners do not understand its underlying principles and are primarily interested in it for speculative investment.

Only after the innovation is widely understood, broadly adopted, and its foundational technologies are refined can we begin to introduce additional features that the general public will find useful and necessary. Satoshi envisioned this ongoing development, and the Bitcoin protocol's developers continue to enhance features that the community—measured by both its user base and market capitalization—has yet to reach consensus on. For enthusiasts who advocate for bitcoin's continuous development, its function solely as money is not enough. They want to advance further and start testing new possibilities. Although development and exploration of new features is needed, additional functionalities will take hold only through mass adoption. Research and exploration through struggle is not bad for Bitcoin either. If other projects are investigating features that the Bitcoin community currently doesn't prioritize, those projects could achieve their objectives more quickly and securely when those features eventually become relevant to bitcoin users.

BITCOIN MAXIMALISM: IDEOLOGY IN PRACTICE

Bitcoin maximalists are people who have decided that bitcoin is the only cryptocurrency that makes sense. In most cases, this opinion stems from the experience they have gained after several years of trading other cryptocurrencies. I don't know anyone who began with crypto and immediately considered themself a bitcoin maximalist. Most that began experimenting with other cryptocurrencies eventually returned to bitcoin. Knowledge gained from such experiences is non-transferable. This book should serve to warn newcomers to experiment judiciously and attempt to avoid any subsequent financial losses. They can be substantial.

Of course, the user base is made up not only of bitcoin maximalists. Most other cryptocurrencies have their die-hard supporters as well. Oftentimes, there is a degree of mutual animosity between the various groups. On the one hand, it's nice that these modern-day "apostles" are trying to spread their "gospel" across the population. In principle, they don't mind a certain blindness that stems from personal opinion. It is beyond the pale to slander and troll others on social media—which can escalate from a difference of opinion to hateful attacks. These militant individuals are called toxic maximalists.

The crypto market environment is complex and sometimes even opaque. More than 90% of cryptocurrencies are scams or nonsense. On the other hand, the free market needs to be left free. After all, these are the values that the founder and co-creators of Bitcoin fought for. Competition is fine as well as necessary. A number of other cryptocurrency projects are introducing new ideas and driving further development and innovation. Unfortunately, those that succeed in the long run may be small in number.

Influencers who subscribe to bitcoin maximalism are a separate entity These people have a massive reach, have built their careers over years, and care deeply about their long-term reputation. Almost every one of them has been through a round of experimentation, and most of them have experienced financial losses. It is the inexperienced newcomers who have neither the proficiency nor the knowledge that are most impacted. Many of them enter the crypto market believing that it is a space where staggering profits can be realized very quickly. Newcomers often gain only a superficial understanding and are easily influenced by current trends, which can lead to long-term issues.

The strong opinions held by bitcoin maximalists often stem from a sense of responsibility toward individuals who have invested their savings in cryptocurrency. I believe this form of maximalism serves a purpose. Ultimately, newcomers will form their own opinions and make their own choices. In this context, bitcoin maximalists act as a sort of "speed limiter," helping beginners navigate the initial complexities of the crypto landscape. This cautious approach may reduce the number of people who experience significant losses early on and consequently abandon cryptocurrency altogether.

ALTCOINS: ALTERNATIVE FUNCTIONALITIES OF CRYPTOCURRENCIES

Altcoin refers to any alternative cryptocurrency to bitcoin. Dozens of them exist. Each of them are battling it out to see which can implement a groundbreaking innovation. As previously mentioned, not all technological innovations are suitable for mass adoption. Many people either don't fully understand them or don't see them as a priority. Some of these technologies aren't well-tested, leading to hacks where people lose their savings. Additionally, many projects lack a stable monetary policy—such as a finite supply of coins—and suffer from high inflation. These projects often launch with overvalued coins, creating inequality between creators, investors, and regular users. Market manipulation is also possible by initial large coin holders. While some of these projects may become important in the future, it's difficult to predict which among the numerous promising altcoins will ultimately succeed. We'll summarize the landscape of altcoins in the sections that follow.

- **Complexity for general users:** specialized wallets, bridges, wraps, and unique protocols from various developers add layers of complexity. While these offer diverse functionalities, from gaming to banking, they are not always fully secure.

- **Exploring new blockchain features:** these technologies are experimenting with various blockchain functionalities, such as Proof of Work (PoW) versus Proof of Stake (PoS), decentralized finance (DeFi), smart contracts, staking, yield farming, and liquidity mining.

- **Suitable for advanced users:** these platforms cater to more tech-savvy users, offering intriguing features that may become widely used in the future. However, for mass adoption, the user interface will need significant simplification.

- **Challenges for Ethereum:** currently the leading altcoin, Ethereum faces multiple challenges. These include the need to make transactions faster and less expensive, clarify its monetary policy (specifically concerning ongoing inflation or an undetermined finite supply of coins), and fend off numerous competitors. Many of these competitors are already outperforming Ethereum in certain aspects. After Ethereum's transition to Proof of Stake, it will be crucial to ensure that this new security mechanism is both robust and decentralized.

For less experienced users, altcoins offer the opportunity to work with them as a currency and bet on their possible price growth in the future. However, everyone should be aware that this speculation is very risky.

SHITCOINS AND MEME CURRENCIES: LOW ODDS OF SURVIVAL

The term "shitcoin" refers to projects with irrational objectives. However, shitcoins are not primarily fraudulent schemes. From an investment standpoint, they represent a high-risk gamble or a playful lottery when invested in at low levels. Some of these coins are not aiming to achieve anything significant; they are initiated as jokes or fun projects. Their existence relies on the fact that people are drawn to projects they find amusing or endearing.

This category of shitcoin is called meme currency. In the short term, with a certain amount of luck, one can make money on them. However, in the long term, if the holder doesn't dispose of them in time, they are almost certain to lose a large portion of their invested funds. It should be remembered that some of the altcoins that had interesting targets in the previous time period can very quickly fall into the shitcoin category. This can happen as a result of it failing to meet those goals or being outperformed by another competing currency with an attractive offer. It is also often the case that users get sidetracked by other new, amazing, and functional projects.

Meme coins are a humorous phenomenon in the digital currency world. Dogecoin, the most famous meme coin today, was introduced in 2013, featuring a Shiba Inu dog logo. It was created to parody other alternative cryptocurrencies, which emerged by adapting and slightly altering Bitcoin's original protocol. Elon Musk began endorsing Dogecoin, leading to a significant price surge in 2021, although the increase was short-lived. Other notable meme coins include Shiba Inu, Akita Inu, Tamadoge, SafeMoon Inu, and Dogs of Elon.

As we explained with the Hype Curve, public opinion is fickle and sometimes does not wait for the fulfillment of heightened expectations. It's also important to remember that many of the projects are startups with inexperienced teams that fall apart before the project is finished. Any altcoin that disappears into the annals of history will always be seen as a shitcoin. History may be written by the winners, but unfortunately they change so often in the crypto market that the transformation of altcoin into shitcoin seems like a standard life cycle of constantly emerging cryptocurrencies. There are exceptions that disprove this rule, but cryptocurrencies like Ethereum are rare when compared to the thousands of other cryptocurrencies. Some long-time bitcoin enthusiasts, having witnessed multiple failures of promising alternative cryptocurrencies, are skeptical and often categorize all cryptocurrencies other than bitcoin as "shitcoins." On the other hand, some overly enthusiastic fans may label a project as an "altcoin" even when it teeters between being a "shitcoin" and an outright scam. Always consider the perspective of the person commenting on a specific cryptocurrency, as only time will provide a conclusive judgment.

SCAMS: OUTRIGHT FRAUD

Fraudsters are always looking for new ways to steal your money. The massive growth of cryptocurrencies in recent years has created plenty of opportunities for them. If you want to enter the crypto market, it is imperative to know the potential risks. This is because the global crypto market is largely outside the oversight of government institutions. From a liberal point of view, this is a good thing. However, all participants need to be aware that there are plenty of pitfalls at every turn caused by individuals trying to get rich at the expense of others. This is, in principle, a legitimate feature of all game-theoretic concepts (stock markets).

It has been practiced since time immemorial across a wide scope of commercial activities. The problem is that there are hardly any rules, and little oversight. Thus, many participants play an unfair game. Fraud and untrustworthy projects abound. Unfortunately, it can be said that a majority of the tens of thousands of cryptocurrencies on the market fall into this category.

Let's explore some of the most frequent characteristics of fraud to better protect yourself and your finances. You will become familiar with common crypto scams, how to identify them, and strategies to avoid falling victim to them. You can encounter deceptive behavior anytime, anywhere. Cryptocurrencies can be used as a means to pique your interest or as a means of payment. Sometimes entire crypto projects are scams. Scammers use influencers or celebrities through social media to promote the amazing features of the project. Sometimes they invoke the names of famous people who have no idea that their names have been misused. Unfortunately, there are also cases where famous celebrities have been paid very well for promoting the scam. For some of them, money was the only motivation. Meanwhile, others, due to ignorance, may have believed that the project would be successful.

In general, however, the following basic parameters apply to the recognition of fraud:

- Above-standard profits are promised.
- It all seems too good to be true.
- There is no fixed monetary policy in advance (the final number of coins or the rate of inflow of new coins, how many coins have been created in advance, and how they will be handled).
- No risks are mentioned, or you are even assured that there are none.
- You are asked for a quick money transfer or an unusual payment method.
- Someone asks you to send, tell, or fill in access information (PIN, card number, CVV, or seed).
- To withdraw deposited funds, they require additional funds to be sent (fee, tax).

Defending against scams:

- Don't believe the ads and promotional videos.
- Always try to look at the options on offer from a common sense perspective and don't be afraid to question them. Miracles don't happen and you are probably not chosen by fate to get rich quick.
- Check the address of the company.
- Check their social media activity.
- Get reviews from several different sources (other than the links below the ad or article).
- If the parameters of fraud are met, don't be afraid to report everything to the police. Doing so will help others too.

Scams are very dangerous in the cryptocurrency industry. They ruin reputations, slow down adoption, and deprive newcomers of their hard-earned money. They create mistrust between investors and cryptocurrency users, which can lead to a drop in adoption and a decrease in the value of cryptocurrencies. At the same time, scams can slow down the diffusion and adoption of new technologies. They also attract negative media and public attention, which can cause reputational damage to the crypto industry as a whole. Therefore, scams need to be fought hard, in particular by educating the population and drawing attention to detected scams.

"What Are the Most Popular Crypto Scams to Watch For in 2023?" via *TIME*

"Avoid Scams" via bitcoin.org

NFT: THE FUTURE, OR FASHIONABLE NONSENSE?

An NFT (non-fungible token) can be used to represent ownership of unique items. It is transparent proof of ownership of a digital item and allows quick and accurate identification of the owner. Essentially anything can be tokenized. Currently, NFTs are most commonly used to tokenize photos, videos, songs, game items, virtual land, or even tweets. However, in most cases, tokenized items remain freely available for viewing or download to anyone, which sometimes makes one think about the meaning or value of tokenization.

A token, traditionally made of metal, plastic, or paper, often serves as a stand-in for currency in situations where using money is impractical, such as at theme parks, for gift vouchers, or club entries.

In the digital realm, a token can represent various entities, from values to receipts to voting rights.

Within a specific ecosystem, a token can take on multiple roles, acting either as an asset or a tool based on its designated purpose. Unlike coins, tokens don't possess their own blockchain; they operate on another cryptocurrency's blockchain.

Proof of ownership is stored in the blockchain. An NFT's entry in the blockchain usually consists of its content, serial number, or other data. In this process an unalterable token is created, commonly known as "minting." The functioning of these tokens can be tied to smart contracts, which enables the automated functionality for processes like selling or voting. Another advantage is that an NFT can be set up in such a way that, in addition to the initial income, a certain percentage of the price from each resale reverts to the original NFT publisher. This can be especially useful in the case of transactions like the sale of tickets or artwork.

Since we are in an unregulated global crypto market, users are still trying to use NFTs for functionalities tied outside of legal frameworks. The market for NFTs has grown tremendously in 2021. Many people have started buying a number of different images in the foolish belief that they will get rich from them. Some of the best known NFT image series perhaps have the potential to hold value in the longer term, but most of the others are likely to end up as unsaleable pieces with zero value. Unfortunately, even the most famous series are at risk of large price drops and are very risky assets. The actual use of NFTs may also depend on the real world acceptance of the Metaverse (Meta's virtual world) or other virtual worlds where NFTs might start to make some sense to users.

However, a major use could come when some states or institutions are able to give a legal framework to the selected NFTs. This could lead to decentralization of registries held by state institutions. The main advantage of using a blockchain instead of a traditional database is that it eliminates the need for a trusted authority, like a government institution. While the government would lose its exclusive control over things like vehicle registries, it would also save significant resources on maintenance and reduce the risk of corruption and document forgery related to stolen cars. Decentralization and independence from state institutions could be an advantage, but there would have to be official adoption of the technology. This seems unlikely in the near future. If it happens in the future, it would mean the advent of global decentralization, increasing citizens' freedom, and reducing state surveillance.

In such a case, unalterable tokens would have to have two main categories:

- **transferable:** examples include tickets, vouchers, car registries, art objects, patents, and trademarks. These registries should be global and allow citizens to trade quickly and securely. Without a firm anchor in global legislation, buyers would lack legal certainty in terms of the trade being conducted.

- **non-transferable:** examples include identity on the internet and in the digital world. Later on, registries of identification documents (ID cards, passports, and driving licenses) could be followed by voting and referendums. Most of these options are not realistic without legislative changes.

A majority of innovations or inventions were created to solve a specific problem. The current situation with NFTs is that they are a technology known to mankind, but there is speculation about their optimal use. Their eventual success will depend on what uses emerge, whether they prove useful, and possibly how strong of an ecosystem can emerge around them. There are ways to create NFTs on the bitcoin blockchain as well (Ordinals protocol), but the community cannot yet agree on whether this functionality is needed. Besides Ordinals, there are other projects on the bitcoin protocol such as the BRC 20 tokens or the Runes protocol launched in April 2024.

What are Bitcoin Runes, and how do they differ from BRC-20 tokens?

STABLECOINS: FIAT IN YOUR OWN CRYPTOCURRENCY WALLET?

In the world of cryptocurrency, having a stable currency with a consistent exchange rate is crucial for trading and transferring value. Stablecoins serve as this reliable conversion bridge, allowing for the valuation of other cryptocurrencies. At the same time, they should also serve as a safe haven into which traders convert profits or, in the event of major turbulence in the cryptocurrency market, withdraw their funds temporarily until the storm has calmed down. All stablecoins possess the advantages of cryptocurrencies, which are mainly the speed of transfers and the ability to be held in their own wallets. Transferring larger amounts of fiat currencies into or out of the crypto environment tends to be complex, takes a long time, and is often burdened with significant fees. That is why many users, thanks to stablecoins, try not to move their funds from this crypto environment to the fiat environment. They are not needed from the perspective of maintaining the value of the underlying assets for long-term ownership, as it is always safer to hold the underlying asset itself. However, some users hold them for the long term without having to trust banks as an additional intermediary.

Unfortunately, stablecoins require trust in an intermediary to maintain value and liquidity. They can never guarantee this function 100%. They work on the basis of a predetermined underlying asset such as fiat currencies (mostly USD), gold, or cryptocurrencies. Sometimes it is a predetermined ratio of different underlying assets. Although it is non-state money, it is always backed by specific companies or decentralized groups. Stablecoins may be at risk of insufficient backing, poor liquidity, or regulatory issues related to central management through another entity. Many of these companies do not keep the underlying assets, such as dollars, in a bank. Instead, they use them as investment instruments, purchasing bonds, stocks, or making other types of investments. They do this to cover the costs of running the company and to make a profit. However, if they invest in the wrong way, they may not be able to secure the exchange of that stablecoin back for the underlying asset. **None of the stablecoins can currently guarantee the long-term maintenance of the value of the underlying asset**. However, most make a good faith effort to do so. Failure to do so risks loss of user confidence, a run on the stablecoin in question, and potential bankruptcy.

Some of the modern stablecoins are algorithmic. These are stablecoins that maintain a stable rate according to an algorithm. Sometimes they work with multiple underlying assets, where the algorithm can provide adjustments to the ratios between these assets if some are rising in price and others are falling. The problem can arise in a general market downturn when all the linked underlying assets lose value. The algorithm should maintain a stable price based on supply and demand. Whenever the price rises, the algorithm would create new coins and put them into circulation. The price would thus usually decrease. If, on the other hand, the price fell significantly, the algorithm would withdraw the coins from circulation and destroy ("burn") them. This would cause the price to start rising. As long as demand is growing, or at least there is no major drop and panic selling of coins by the user of the stablecoin, there is no problem issuing new coins. However, if there are major market shocks and the price starts to fall, then withdrawing coins from circulation beyond the reserves held by the stablecoin issuer cannot realistically be assured. There is no collateral offered by the algorithm to users in exchange for tokens, and arbitrary deletion of coins from users' wallets cannot be implemented. Thus, the price increase cannot be ensured and the stablecoin loses its function. It is then threatened with a run and bankruptcy.

Currently, most countries are dealing with the introduction of regulations, including precise rules of operation and government oversight. Once regulations are in place, the safety of the funds invested will be similar to the past when funds were entrusted to jewelers or banks. You will have to trust that the organization in question has good and honest managers, that the government can monitor compliance with the rules, that the rules are well set, and that the stablecoin in question is therefore sufficiently covered and liquid.

Existing major stablecoins include Tether (USDT), USD Coin (USDC) and the algorithmic Dai (DAI). The algorithmic stablecoin TerraUSD (UST) serves as a clear illustration of what can occur when events unfold differently than the founders anticipated. In May 2022, this stablecoin couldn't sustain the crypto market decline and went bankrupt, causing investors to lose billions of dollars.

Unless you prefer to hold digital cash on your own wallet for fundamental reasons, it doesn't make sense to hold funds in stablecoins in the long term. At best they just replicate the price of the underlying asset. However, they add additional risk in the form of the issuer (custodian) of the stablecoin in question. Most market participants use them as a transfer station between fiat and the purchase of other cryptocurrencies.

CBDC: THE FUTURE BIG BROTHER?

Central Bank Digital Currencies (CBDC) is the concept of a digital currency guaranteed by a central bank itself. CBDCs share a number of characteristics with cash because they represent a claim directly on the central bank. However, unlike cash, these currencies are purely digital. From the standpoint of scarcity and value preservation, it functions as a pure fiat currency. This characteristic significantly undermines its other monetary properties, making it an undesirable option for anyone who values freedom and choice. It is programmable money, running on a central bank blockchain. Ownership of these currencies will always be firmly tied to the identity of the citizen in question. Every coin will be traceable from the moment it is issued. The entire history of the money will be traceable and it will be possible to find out who paid what, to whom, when, and for what. It can be expected that within a few years of the introduction of the CBDC, there will be efforts to abolish cash altogether for reasons of money laundering and greater efficiency in the handling of funds. Commercial banks will lose their status and most financial services at that point can be centralized within one institution.

CBDCs have been compared to cryptocurrencies and have been described as an innovation. However, the states and authorities in power will be given enormous power by their introduction. The extent to which this power will be abused by political structures in the future cannot be determined in advance, but the problem is that there will be a real danger. It will **be possible at any time to restrict any citizen or company from dealing with all their money.** Central banks will be able to impose different rules on the operation of a given currency.

Take notes. I thought of some CBDC innovations.

Here are just a few of them:

- **Automatic collection of taxes and fees** (including extraordinary ones): there will be no need to wait for a citizen's voluntary decision to pay a given tax or fee. The competent institution will be able to deduct money on the basis of a decision on an extraordinary social tax as a result of events like pandemics, wars, or natural disasters.

- **Restrictions on buying certain goods or services:** different services or products may be allowed or banned for certain groups. For example, you may not be able to buy medicines from abroad that have not been approved in your country.

- **Confiscation of resources and control of citizens:** in the event that cash no longer exists, every citizen and society will be subjected to pressure from state institutions. The state can freeze or confiscate all your assets at any time. You would then be unable to survive in society in the long term. In such a case, this will be a disproportionately powerful instrument of state power that can be abused directly by state institutions—or even by interest groups that can corrupt state institutions.

If some CBDC currencies do not operate on top of the blockchain, are not programmable, and operate only on the principle of a classical database, there may not be such a high risk of abuse. Otherwise, it is likely that the rights of citizens to personal freedom would be severely restricted.

I don't gamble. I declare my taxes. I don't pay my mistress. I don't bribe anyone. And I don't buy drugs. But I don't want to deprive my children of those opportunities.

There is currently a power struggle to win the battle for the global currency. This struggle is being fought on the basis of who will introduce their CBDC first, and how they will introduce it into the global market. Hopefully, the adoption of free cryptocurrencies will be faster than the mutual agreements of politicians and bureaucratic officials. Negotiations of this nature often result in unfavorable outcomes for citizens, primarily because many participants lack a thorough understanding of the issues involved. Moreover, officials tend to focus on short-term political objectives, such as combating money laundering or shielding uninformed citizens from their own choices. If the adoption of cryptocurrencies continues to accelerate, we can only hope that Central Bank Digital Currencies (CBDCs) will occupy a secondary role rather than becoming major competitors.

OTHER CONCEPTS IN THE CRYPTO WORLD

In this section, we will explain the meaning of terms you will encounter in the crypto space.

Cryptocurrency coins and tokens

We use the term "coins" for native cryptocurrencies like bitcoin and Ethereum because each has its own blockchain. Conversely, a "token" refers to a cryptocurrency that operates on someone else's blockchain. The most common platform for creating tokens is Ethereum. A cryptocurrency created on the Ethereum platform is usually referred to as an ERC20 token. However, there are a variety of tokens. These include utility tokens, security tokens, asset-backed tokens, and NFT tokens.

Smart contract

A smart contract is a protocol or software that secures, verifies, or enforces the execution of a specific contract or arrangement. This must be done in a way that removes the need for a written contract. In other words, it is an attempt to transfer the practices of contract law into a digital world without courts and arbitration panels. The terms of the contractual agreement between the partners are programmed into an e-commerce protocol that can enforce them without any further intervention. Smart contracts are the cornerstone of DeFi (see below) and ensure the operation of some cryptocurrencies, including those based on PoS. To execute a smart contract, some value needs to be locked up as collateral from each of the contracting partners. However, there have been a number of cases where hackers have discovered vulnerabilities in smart contracts that have allowed them to steal locked assets.

DeFi: decentralized funding

It is a new form of financing that is independent of traditional centralized intermediaries such as banks, funds, and brokers. Bitcoin is in many ways the first application of DeFi because it allows you to actually own value and send it to anyone around the world without additional intermediaries. The basic principle of DeFi is to allow people to raise and provide funds and services to other people directly among themselves, without knowing or having to trust each other. It uses smart contracts embedded in the blockchain to carry out transactions. In addition to making payments, DeFi can be used to make loans or guarantees; exchange money and cryptocurrencies; place bets; speculate on the price movements of individual assets; hedge risks; or earn interest from staking or other forms of passive income. Decentralized protocols are difficult to regulate from a legal point of view. The authorities do not know about them and are not interested in laws or borders between countries. However, investors have no legal protection when they suffer financial losses due to a mistake in a smart contract. Investing on advanced DeFi platforms is not for beginners and requires a high level of technical and financial literacy.

CeFi: centralized financing

It shares some similarities to DeFi. It is usually offered by specific companies, such as exchanges. Therefore, CeFi cannot be described as decentralized. While user identification is often required, the benefit is that CeFi platforms are generally easier to use. Similar to DeFi, CeFi allows you to earn interest on savings, borrow money, or use a crypto debit card at traditional stores that accept only fiat currencies. In such instances, your cryptocurrencies are automatically converted into the required fiat currency according to a predetermined sequence.

UTXO consolidation: private and public keys, addresses, transactions, and fees

As mentioned on page 175, a private key functions similarly to a password, while a public key enables you to generate an address for receiving resources. Let's now describe in more detail how it all works.

At the top of the hierarchy of the entire tree (hierarchical structure) of access permissions and addresses is your highest access permission, known as a seed (page 292). It can also be seen as the master password of the virtual wallet on the blockchain, which creates the tree of your accounts, addresses, and individual transactions. You can manage this virtual wallet using any compatible software or hardware wallet. You can learn more about wallets on page 292. From the seed, an extended private key (xPriv) is generated. This master key then produces individual private keys for specific addresses.

At the same time, it also generates a master public key, the so-called extended public key (xPub), which then generates all public keys for individual addresses in the virtual wallet. The creation of a specific bitcoin address always starts with the generation of a private key. From this, an algorithm is used to generate the corresponding address that represents the public key. The address is a shorter form of the public key. Each address has its own unique private and public key, and each address is based on xPub, which can generate a virtually unlimited number of addresses. However, the public key cannot be backcomputed from a given address. This is known as one-way cryptography. Most wallets will generate a new address to receive payment via your xPub the moment you receive funds at the previous address. This is for privacy reasons, so that no one can associate multiple transactions with the same entity. Under no circumstances should you disclose your xPub to third parties. Knowing your xPub allows someone to track the entire payment history in your wallet and find out the final balance at all addresses you have established. Within a given wallet, you can group individual addresses into so-called accounts.

Partial linking of individual addresses also occurs when you send a transaction that contains inputs collected from multiple incoming transactions. This is where we arrive at the issue of UTXO, or Unspent Transaction (TX) Output. This is a technical term used to refer to the balances of individual incoming transactions. UTXO can also be seen as a specific record of a payment received in the ledger. So let's discuss this in more detail. Within a given wallet, we have one or more addresses. Each address has as many UTXO records as there were payments received. So if we send 1 BTC to a given address, the address will contain 1 UTXO with 1 BTC. However, if we accumulate 1 BTC with ten incoming payments (transactions) in succession, the address will show 1 BTC, but realistically there are 10 different UTXOs with a total value of 1 BTC. The wallet then does not handle individual addresses, but works with the total balances of all UTXOs (from all generated addresses) within a given xPub. With outgoing payments it is the other way around. The wallet automatically assembles the amount you want from the UTXOs it has available. Thus, one payment can be sent from one UTXO or composed from tens or thousands of existing UTXOs. However, on the recipient's side, there will always be one UTXO ledger entry with the total amount corresponding to the specified payment. On the sender's side, the UTXOs used are spent. If there is a balance on the last UTXO after the last part of the payment has been deducted, the value of the balance is overwritten, or rather a new UTXO is created with the resulting balance. Multiple payees can be paid in one transaction. Each transaction therefore consists of an input UTXO and an output UTXO.

Let's take a simple example:

You have 1 BTC at address A in the form of 1 UTXO. You make a transaction of 0.6 BTC to address B. A UTXO of 1 BTC disappears from address A, a UTXO of 0.6 BTC arrives at address B. The remaining 0.4 BTC will be transferred to your new address C as a new UTXO. Most wallets will create a new address C from xPub. This is called change output. So the transaction had one input (1 BTC) and two outputs (0.6 and 0.4 BTC). Of course, you still need to account for the fees that will be transferred to the miner who will write your transaction to his mined block. Therefore, the change output of the transaction (change returned) is not actually 0.4 BTC, but this amount is reduced by the agreed upon transaction fee.

The amount of transaction fees is calculated according to the current market price per byte. The resulting transaction price is directly dependent on the amount of space it takes up in the new block. This size is determined by the number of inputs and outputs and also by the address format used (page 192). However, each user can set the per-byte charge according to how fast one needs to write the transaction. Miners then write transactions with higher fees (higher cost per byte) first based on their own motivation.

> **The amount of transaction fees** for Bit-coin is usually quoted in the form of satoshi per byte (sat/B). The sender does not specify the amount of fees specifically for the entire transaction (e.g. 10,000 satoshi), but only for one byte of memory that your transaction will occupy in the block (e.g. 50 satoshi per 1 byte). The byte, abbreviated as B, is a basic unit of computer memory capacity and computer data volume in computer science. One byte equals 8 bits.

When sending a transaction consisting of many UTXOs, a problem may occur: the more input and output UTXO records a transaction has, the more space (bytes) is needed to write it and the more expensive it is. If you send too small amounts to your wallet, payments sent that are composed of many UTXOs may incur high fees.

In general, this issue can also be perceived in such a way that a fee is paid for the entry of each UTXO both at the input and at the output. On entry, the fee is paid by the person sending the transaction, but if you are sending the transaction out of the exchange yourself, you are the one who is paying the fee. If you're going to buy on exchanges in small amounts, then send transactions to your wallet that are ideally in the order of 0.01 BTC and above. You shouldn't create too low balances on your addresses, as sending transactions could become more expensive in

> **Dust** is essentially a non-spendable UTXO whose size is so small that the fee for writing it would be higher than the balance of the UTXO. What is and is not dust depends on the current level of fees and may change over time.

the future—especially when per byte fees rise. Very low balances, called dust, may even result in them no longer being usable. Use the Lightning Network (page 183) for small payments; this problem cannot occur there. If, however, you incur lower balances on some UTXOs over time as a result of the "change back" on payments you send, it is advisable to consolidate these balances. This can be done simply by sending selected UTXOs—some wallets offer this—or even the entire balance to yourself. The result will be that all UTXOs entered will be combined into one UTXO, which will contain the total balance less the transaction fee. Therefore, it is very important that you perform this consolidation transaction at a time when the network is not very busy (byte fees are low), and at the same time set a longer write time for the transaction (for example, 24 hours or more). In this case, you can achieve very low if not almost negligible fees. However, it should be noted that there may be privacy implications associated with the UTXO connection. You must keep in mind that if you combine too large an amount into one UTXO, the recipient of the next transaction may find out what funds you have within the UTXO used. It is also important to evaluate whether you are linking UTXOs from multiple sources that you do not want to link. For these cases, transaction labeling and coin control (more on page 297) are good helpers. Both tools can be found in the Trezor Suite interface for working with the Trezor hardware wallet, among other things.

To make it all look easy, some wallets, like the aforementioned Trezor, have add-on features that make it simpler to work with balances and send transactions. For example, in addition to calculating the transaction size, they also offer you processing time options—which can range from ten minutes to twenty-four hours. For these options, they can map your network load and suggest a fee level that will not overcharge the miner unnecessarily, while at the same time give you a good chance that your transaction will be posted within the time period you choose. The longer the time slot you choose, the cheaper the transaction fee will be.

Proof of Work versus Proof of Stake

Proof of Work (PoW)

As we discussed with Bitcoin, the Proof of Work method requires a lot of computing power, which consumes electricity.

It would be great to use supercomputers to mine bitcoins.
Instead of controlling humanity.

The first person to find a random number (nonce) by trial and error is entitled to create a block and collect the block reward plus transaction fees. However, it should be reiterated that it is the **proof of the work done** that not only guarantees the security of the ledger but, above all, gives value to the currency in question. In Book One, we defined a basic economic lesson in our discussion of the Yap Island Rocks: value is dependent on scarcity, and scarcity is dependent on effort and work done. Through investments in hardware and electricity, miners transfer real value from the physical world to the digital one. They must therefore raise the funds for mining by creating other benefits—good deeds—for society. This gives value to the coins mined. Some opponents of this technology believe that this method of securing the blockchain and transferring utility from the real world to the digital one is unsustainable in the long term. However, there are projects emerging around the world where bitcoin mining helps reduce CO_2 emissions, stores surplus electricity from renewable sources and, in generating heat using electricity, significantly reduces the cost of consumption in the form of mined bitcoins. Any opponent should also consider the fact that operating this independent global money network consumes far less electricity than operating banking systems, mining gold, running clothes dryers, or even forgetting to turn off the lights in your home (more on this issue on page 186).

Proof of Stake (PoS)

This is a completely different concept of creating a blockchain and it is the lack of proof of work that is often criticized by PoW proponents. In the Proof of Stake method, miners are replaced by validators (verifiers). In order to become a validator, you must pledge a set amount of the cryptocurrency in question, which you will not have access to while acting as a validator. Validators use this deposit to prove to the network that they have an interest in the correct creation of the ledger. The selection of validators to validate transactions and create a new block is usually done through a random selection whose algorithm is determined by the established rules of a given blockchain. The likelihood that you will be permitted to add a block to the blockchain and receive the block reward in addition to transaction fees rises based on certain criteria, such as the duration of your participation or the amount of cryptocurrency you hold or stake. Validators verify that the transaction is legitimate and add it to the blockchain. In this case, we say that the selected validators have reached consensus, and the PoS uses a **consensus algorithm**. However, if you validate bad or fraudulent data, you will incur penalties based on the protocol rules of the relevant cryptocurrency; your deposit may be downgraded or even sent to an inaccessible "dead" address that no one can access.

Comparison of Proof of Work and Proof of Stake

In PoW, the security of a given blockchain is maintained by preventing double spending or other fraudulent behavior through actual computing power, and the value of the currency serves as proof of the work done. For a 51% attack that could take centralized control of a given blockchain, it would be necessary to provide a technique that outperforms honest miners in performance. Furthermore, the attacker would have to provide sufficient electrical power for this technique. No power plant in the world can produce that amount of energy at once, and purchasing the required technology is beyond the means of nations and large corporations—both in terms of price and availability. Anyone can become a miner by acquiring the appropriate hardware and consuming the cheapest possible energy. You do not need to own the cryptocurrency in question, nor do you need to hold it on an ongoing basis.

In contrast, PoS is less energy-intensive, and the validator must own a specific number or multiples of a given currency's coins. Coin holders who lock in their funds are advantaged and have a much greater chance of profiting from transaction validation. To prevent a 51% attack, a high market capitalization is required. Therefore, the PoS method is not suitable for fledgling cryptocurrencies. Validators who hold large amounts of a given cryptocurrency may have an undue influence on the Proof of Stake system. However, the largest validators are centralized exchanges that must obey regulators, and there is a risk of censorship and influence. Other centralized entities behind the stablecoins used on a given blockchain can have a significant—and sometimes even decisive—influence in the case of hard forks. These stablecoins are enclosed in individual contracts, and when a blockchain forks, the company behind the stablecoin must decide which branch to recognize as the successor. Failure to comply would lead to a doubling of that stablecoin's amount, and the company guarantees the liquidity by ensuring it can be sold at a precise price. Anyone would surely understand that this is not possible.

The decision to adopt a successor blockchain—the one with the most validators and users—will no longer be purely a community decision, but will be heavily influenced by the politics of these big players. Users who do not adopt this branch would lose their locked resources. This situation has not yet occurred, but it will probably happen in the future. Further, some PoS blockchains could be vulnerable to other types of attacks than PoW. These could be, for example, **bribery attacks**, which in this case do not require a large upfront investment.

> **Bribery attacks** assume that at least some validators in the blockchain can act rationally. These validators may accept bribes from attackers to maximize their profit. If an attacker manages to obtain a high percentage of such validators, they may be able to successfully carry out an attack such as a double spend. The reward for a successful attack could be paid, for example, based on a smart contract only after such an attack is successfully performed.

Moreover, the functioning of PoS blockchains or blockchain bridges between them is heavily dependent on smart contracts, which may not always be sufficiently verified and may contain errors. This has happened several times in history. The susceptibility to attacks reduces the potential security of these blockchains. Thus, Proof of Stake is not as thoroughly vetted as Proof of Work, which has secured billions of dollars worth of blockchains for many years. However, it may be a very promising way of operating some blockchains in the future. It requires thorough testing of all protocols, including smart contracts and interconnected platforms.

Staking: income from holding

This is one of the ways to create passive income from owned cryptocurrencies. Staking is a process whereby cryptocurrency holders are rewarded for pledging a given cryptocurrency for a predetermined period of time. This process can be likened to a bank time deposit, where if you deposit money for a predetermined period of time, you will earn a higher interest rate than you would in a checking account. Staking can be done in two ways, where holders can choose to become validators or delegators.

- The first way is to pledge cryptocurrencies for a period of time, thus becoming a validator and earning interest for checking transactions on the blockchain.

- The second way is to gain delegate status after you deposit a portion of your cryptocurrencies into one of the staking pools for a predetermined period of time. This gives the validator, who is the operator of the staking pool, enough resources to have a higher chance of writing blocks to the blockchain. Each staking pool has its own terms of participation. In this case, you are not involved directly in creating blocks and writing transactions. Cryptocurrencies like bitcoin, which are not designed for staking, can still be staked on certain exchanges through a process known as off-chain staking. In this method, the coins are stored with a specific operator outside the actual blockchain, and the operator uses them as they see fit. Typically, the operators of these staking pools, who are usually cryptocurrency exchanges, specify which cryptocurrencies can be staked with them.

Lending: cryptocurrency lending

In the case of lending, the cryptocurrencies in question are made available for use by others on the basis of smart contracts in return for a reward.

ICO: Initial Coin Offering

The term Initial Coin Offering (ICO) is based on the financial term Initial Public Offering (IPO). An IPO is an initial public offering in which shares of a new company or new shares resulting from a capital raise are offered on the market. An ICO involves the issuance of coins of a new cryptocurrency in exchange for another cryptocurrency or fiat.

Airdrop: money from the air

In an airdrop, coins of a given cryptocurrency are distributed for free. As a rule, these are marketing campaigns, which can take various forms. For example, an airdrop may involve asking participants to fill in several online forms. In this way, customer data can be collected. In the case of certain airdrops, the project requires promotion on social media. For other types of airdrops, either participants already using the platform or a select group meeting specific conditions or chosen by lottery will receive coins of a particular cryptocurrency as a change.

DEX: decentralized exchange(s)

It is a place or service where a buyer can anonymously purchase cryptocurrencies that are available on a given exchange in liquidity pools managed by an Automated Market Maker (AMM). This is programmed to automate all DEX activities. It offers interested parties cryptocurrencies from a pool of liquidity that other users have made available for a specific period of time. Fiat currencies cannot be traded in a DEX, but stablecoins can substitute them. A DEX does not require users to deposit funds for trading, nor does it hold users' funds. It does not require users to register, nor does it require their email. Users trade directly from their wallets. A DEX will tell you the price, and if you approve it, it will execute the transaction. It deducts some fees from trading for the services provided. The AMM splits these fees between the various liquidity providers and developers who maintain and develop its protocol.

Liquidity mining and its possible extension with yield farming superstructure

These are two other possible ways of creating passive income from owned cryptocurrencies. DEXs need to fill liquidity pools in order to function. Into these pools, people provide their cryptocurrencies (liquidity) for a predetermined period of time so that ordinary users can trade them. This form of investing is called **liquidity mining**. The depositor is rewarded from the fees paid by the users who trade there. Cryptocurrencies—including stablecoins—must always form a pair. The formation of specific pairs is determined by the exchange. Every currency pair is one pool. The liquidity provider must always split the deposit in half so that the dollar value (price) of the two cryptocurrencies is always in a 50:50 ratio. However, when the price of a given cryptocurrency changes, the quantities of the two cryptocurrencies spill over each other so that the ratio of their dollar prices remains the same.. Unlike a scenario where a depositor simply holds a specific cryptocurrency, liquidity mining presents opportunities for both profit and risk for the depositor. One type of risk is known as an **impermanent loss** (IL) which is initially considered a temporary loss. However, this loss can become permanent if the price of one cryptocurrency rises or falls more rapidly than the other.

Example: cryptocurrency A against USDT (USDT is a stablecoin against USD):
At the beginning, the ratio of **1** coin **of cryptocurrency A** (worth $1,000 USD) : **1,000 USDT coins** (worth $1,000)

If the value of cryptocurrency A increases rapidly, there may be a 0.5:2,000 coin ratio, then 0.25:4,000, and so on. In this variant, you will make money, but if you only held the cryptocurrencies in question, you would make more. This is a better temporary loss (IL) option.

However, if the value of cryptocurrency A drops sharply, in an extreme case there may be a ratio of coins such as 1,000 A:1 USDT. In such a case, you may be left with hundreds or thousands of worthless coins backed by just a few USDT. In this case, the chosen cryptocurrency has probably collapsed and the temporary loss becomes permanent. The best way to prevent IL is to provide liquidity in pairs that are often correlated in price, but even this strategy is not 100%.

Yield farming was created as an incentive to provide liquidity to emerging cryptocurrencies. This could compensate for potential losses from impermanent loss, but more importantly, it aims to promote the spread of new cryptocurrencies into circulation and raise awareness. The entire mechanism operates by establishing a specific pool, or currency pair, for a new and unknown project. In exchange for the funds deposited, the validator receives both a token and trading fees. This token serves as a confirmation or receipt, verifying that the validator is actually providing liquidity to the pair. This token can then be staked and will receive rewards in the cryptocurrency of that new project. In this way, the new project spreads its own cryptocurrency into circulation—in addition to generating user awareness. The mechanism can thus be beneficial for all involved. These new projects offer a very high staking percentage at the beginning, which is very tempting. However, the yield is subsequently adjusted depending on how many depositors farm the cryptocurrency in question. As they increase, the percentage of return decreases.

Before starting farming, it is very important to check out every project that offers this possibility. In case the project is not successful or is not technically secure enough, the price of the cryptocurrency may drop dramatically and the depositor may lose the deposited funds.

Cryptocurrency capitalization: CoinMarketCap

What is CoinMarketCap?

It is a website that tracks a large number of cryptocurrencies that have already been listed on one of the many trusted exchanges. Important information can be found here, such as price history, trading volume, number of coins in circulation, and market capitalization size. It should be noted that this method of calculation can partially manipulate the market capitalization of some currencies that are not traded globally or in large volumes. For example, coins of a given cryptocurrency may be sold between related entities at an exorbitant price. In such a case, there may be a temporary multiple increase in price, which may affect the overall market capitalization at that point in time. The ranking of cryptocurrencies in both the top ten and the top 100 most capitalized cryptocurrencies changes dynamically—with the exception of bitcoin and ethereum. This shows how difficult it is to pick out currencies that will be worth their value in the long term.

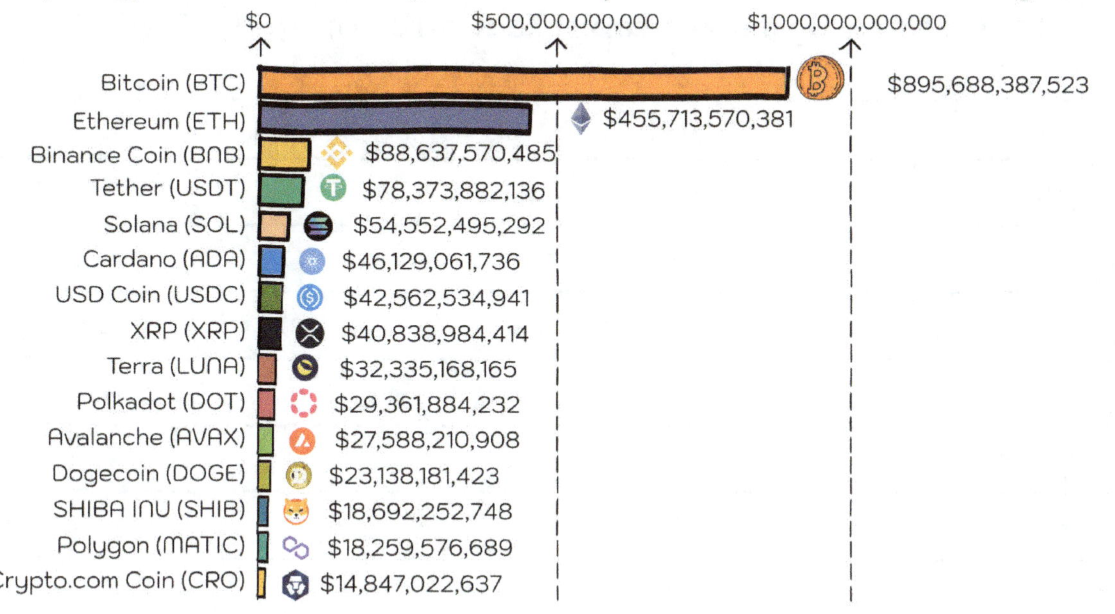

Data source (Statista):
https://www.consultancy-me.com/news/4692/determining-the-real-market-capitalization-of-crypto-assets

It will certainly be interesting to compare the currencies in the previous tables again in a few years and examine how their rankings have changed, how much each currency is worth, and what their market capitalization is.

Today's Cryptocurrency Prices by Market Cap via CoinMarketCap

What is market cap?

Market capitalization is used to compare various assets, including individual publicly traded companies, ETFs, and cryptocurrencies. Precious metals serve as examples of commodities whose prices are not seasonal and whose stock increases gradually without sharp fluctuations. Unlike these assets, market capitalization does not apply to fiat currencies. These currencies have a constantly growing money supply, which doesn't necessarily reflect their true value.

The following link provides a comparison of the following assets:

- publicly traded companies

- precious metals

- cryptocurrencies

- ETFs: publicly traded funds

Top 10 assets by market capitalization as of April 22, 2024

All assets, including public companies , precious metals , cryptocurrencies , ETFs

Rank	Name	Market Cap	Price	Today	Price (30 days)	Country
1	Gold — GOLD	$15.729 T	$2,342	-2.96%		
2	Microsoft — MSFT	$2.987 T	$402.01	0.72%		USA
3	Apple — AAPL	$2.572 T	$166.60	0.97%		USA
4	NVIDIA — NVDA	$1.994 T	$797.97	4.72%		USA
5	Alphabet (Google) — GOOG	$1.961 T	$158.64	1.88%		USA
6	Saudi Aramco — 2222.SR	$1.945 T	$8.04	0.33%		S. Arabia
7	Amazon — AMZN	$1.849 T	$177.76	1.80%		USA
8	Silver — SILVER	$1.534 T	$27.25	-5.53%		
9	Bitcoin — BTC	$1.307 T	$66,314	2.40%		
10	Meta Platforms (Facebook) — META	$1.232 T	$485.88	1.00%		USA

Top Assets by Market Cap via companiesmarketcap.com

At a price of around $30,000, Bitcoin would rank in the top ten of this list, while at around $20,000, it would be in the top twenty. Even at $10,000, it would still make the top 100 list of the world's most successful companies and major commodities. If considered as a commodity, Bitcoin would surpass silver in market capitalization at around $70,000, based on its price in November 2021. At approximately $600,000, it could even overtake gold, potentially becoming the most valuable and possibly the rarest commodity on Earth in terms of market capitalization. However, this projection assumes that the prices of precious metals will not experience a sharp increase.

CHAPTER 5 SUMMARY

- Few cryptocurrencies other than bitcoin make sense for holding long term.

- Most cryptocurrencies can have problems due to centralized administration, in which case the authorities may consider them to be shares subject to strict rules.

- Some bitcoin maximalists mean well and want to protect newcomers from financial losses.

- NFT is an interesting technology that is ripe for new applications, but be careful not to buy worthless rubbish.

- Stablecoins are needed by the crypto market, but they are not yet regulated. Holding them is not without risk.

- CBDC controlled by a state apparatus can mean an absolute loss of freedom.

- DeFi is the future, but not every smart contract is secure.

- Proof of Work is energy intensive, but it provides a global payment network. Banks, with their branches, data centers, and ATM networks, consume much more energy.

- Proof of Stake consumes less energy, but has not yet demonstrated long-term viability and may be susceptible to centralization.

- Passive income (interest on cryptocurrency holdings) staking is a smart thing to do, but not every platform providing these services is secure.

- Understanding the principles of cryptocurrencies and the techniques of their use requires a willingness and effort to continually educate oneself in the field.

- Beware of scams. The global crypto market is not a safe place for newcomers.

HOW TO INVEST IN CRYPTOCURRENCIES: IT TAKES A COOL HEAD AND STEADY HANDS

HOW TO INVEST IN CRYPTOCURRENCIES: IT TAKES A COOL HEAD AND STEADY HANDS

If you decide to put some of your funds into cryptocurrencies, you need to give thought to your approach. Many newbies make the fundamental mistake of investing their available funds in a lump sum, often driven by a fear of missing out on potential opportunities. This puts them at risk of sustaining significant losses for an extended period. If one invests in a cryptocurrency other than bitcoin, the loss may even be permanent. Of course, even with bitcoin, positive outcomes are not guaranteed. No one can give you unequivocally correct advice and certainly no one can make guarantees. We cannot see into the future and therefore everyone is just speculating. We must realize that the free market operates on the principle of real needs, but also on the principle of game theory. In this case, you, too, will become one of the hundreds of millions of players and will be part of this global game. The following chapter will explain the advantages and pitfalls of various approaches. Regardless of how you decide to proceed, study this information carefully and do not take unnecessary risks.

The moment you acquire cryptocurrencies, adhere to the principles outlined in this chapter. You'll learn how to store them safely and restore secure access to your funds should you lose your wallet. It's also vital to establish a way for your loved ones to access your funds in the event something happens to you. One significant advantage over the traditional banking system is that you alone own your funds. However, this comes with a downside: there is no intermediary to help you regain access should you lose your access keys. Nevertheless, by following these principles, you can achieve financial freedom and independence, a goal I personally consider very important.

PHILOSOPHY OF INVESTING IN CRYPTOCURRENCIES

Anyone who decides to acquire cryptocurrency should give consideration in advance as to why they are doing so and adjust their strategy accordingly. Yet determining the best strategy is often challenging because no one knows the outcome ahead of time.

No one should invest more in cryptocurrencies than they can afford to lose.

However, the same is true of other investments, with the possible exception of anti-inflationary government bonds—although the question remains how they would fare in periods of hyperinflation. In individual discussions, I usually do not provide specific guidelines and procedures. This information can be found on myriad websites, YouTube, and through various links in this book. In some cases, I include the link directly in the text. It is also important to note that the functionalities of individual interfaces and applications are constantly evolving, so there may be some differences in older tutorials compared to current versions. So let's go through the basic models of how investors enter the crypto market.

SPECULATION AND MARKET TIMING: QUICK PROFITS ARE RARE

Speculation is the most risky business and often results in a loss of part or all of the funds invested. Speculators oftentimes attempt to time the market in order to estimate how prices will vary. Newcomers often behave in this manner either because they receive advice from someone or because they conclude, based on sketchy information from the internet or social networks, that they can predict price movements. However, the market is a living organism made up of millions of other participants also trying to make a quick profit. The market can behave contrary to assumptions, and for a long time. If an investor needs to withdraw funds earlier than expected, they may lose a significant portion of the investment. Speculating on price movements and timing the market is risky, requires many years of experience in the environment, and is by no means recommended for inexperienced market participants or novices.

HOW TO MAKE A ONE-TIME PURCHASE: QUICK INVESTMENTS IN DIGITAL ASSETS

Most newcomers who decide to buy cryptocurrencies (digital assets) are prone to make a hasty one-time purchase. They tap into their savings, or simply utilize the money in their primary checking account, which is being devalued over time because of inflation. If they plan this purchase as a long-term investment (typically four years or more) and invest in bitcoin, then this purchase might not be that risky. In such a case, they need to take into account that they may be at a significant loss for some time. It is certainly more advisable to divide the amount of investment into several parts and to acquire crypto over time (more in the following paragraph on DCA). In case the price of bitcoin, which usually sets the market trend for other cryptocurrencies, is in a significant decline compared to the historical highs, it is possible to buy quicker and in larger amounts. In case bitcoin is trending upwards or approaching historical highs, it would be advisable to wait or split the acquisition into multiple amounts over a longer period (more than a year), as price declines can be expected. Of course, the inflation rate and the state of the markets must also be taken into account. When buying bitcoin in one go, there will likely come a point in time when it will hover in the red for several months or years. As long as investors hold onto their bitcoin, they are unlikely to incur a real loss. Over time, the market is likely to turn around, offering the potential for long-term profit.

People often accuse bitcoin of not even meeting inflation protection, let alone withstanding value maintenance. This is a short-term perspective. As we have already noted, humanity does not yet globally perceive bitcoin as a better money and value sustainer. Bitcoin is still in its infancy and its capitalization is still small in terms of money (not in terms of companies or commodities). Moreover, most investors see it as a speculative asset and move their capital into government bonds or real estate when markets fall, causing the price to plummet. This creates opportunities for new investors to buy at a discount, thereby creating much needed distribution among a larger population. New owners may no longer see bitcoin as just speculation and may want to hold it for other reasons. As the market capitalization gradually grows, price fluctuations will decrease and speculators will be replaced by people interested in saving for the long term. In the long run, bitcoin's price growth has always outpaced not only inflation, but also the rise in the prices of stocks, real estate, precious metals, and other commodities.

DOLLAR-COST AVERAGING AND SMART SHOPPING: HOW TO SAVE EFFICIENTLY

Dollar-Cost Averaging (DCA) is commonly used in stock investments, but it can be just as effective when applied to other assets like bitcoin. This strategy has gained increasing popularity for investing in volatile markets, including the cryptocurrency sector. The core idea is to invest smaller, preferably consistent, amounts in a specific asset on a **long-term, regular basis**. Doing so averages your purchase price. While a poorly timed purchase might coincide with a price peak, using DCA ensures you will also catch price dips. This increases your confidence that you're buying at an average price over the long term, resulting in a higher return when you eventually sell. Purchases can be made on a daily, weekly, or monthly schedule. Upon closer examination, the specific frequency tends not to make a significant difference in the long run. When choosing a cryptocurrency, it's important to consider its long-term viability, as many existing digital currencies may become obsolete and be replaced by others, leading to a potential loss of invested funds.

Choosing bitcoin or another flight-proven cryptocurrency is the safest and most responsible way to invest in digital assets. At the same time, DCA is suitable for newcomers and less experienced crypto market participants. With this method, you need to invest for a minimum of four to ten years, but preferably for the duration of your working life. This is a long-term savings strategy suitable for purposes such as retirement or providing a starting financial package for your children. It is crucial to begin as early as possible since the initial investments are likely to be the most valuable in the end.

Smart buying or buy the dip (BTD) is a well-known piece of investment wisdom that says that it is profitable to buy when there is a significant decline. Choosing to buy bitcoin with strategy can enhance the long-term profitability of DCA buying. The question is how to determine the right downside threshold. Generally speaking, the limit for bitcoin is when it drops tens of percentage points from its all-time high (ATH). At the current market capitalization, that's roughly a threshold of -30% to -70%, but as we've discussed, that threshold will decrease over time. During such a drop, it is advisable to temporarily increase the regular DCA savings amounts or to make a one-time purchase.

Prudent investors often implement a strategy to adjust their savings based on specific triggers in their investment plan (e.g., a 30% drop from the ATH results in a 10% increase in DCA contributions, with each additional 10% drop leading to another 10% increase in DCA). This approach typically involves incrementally increasing savings over a span of months, sometimes even tens of months, which may not be feasible for every investor. However, those on tighter budgets could opt for a strategy that only increases contributions when there is a 50%–70% drop from the ATH. Each

Retail refers to small-scale businesses that are the opposite of supermarkets or chain stores. Examples of retail stores include local shops, convenience stores, newsagents, and local hairdressers. In the contexts of banking and cryptocurrency, retail is used to describe small savers and ordinary investors.

investor must tailor these strategies to their own specific capabilities during any given period. Those with readily available cash often set stock orders in the 50%–90% range, depending on their pre-determined strategy, and wait to see if these orders get filled. In contrast, retail investors often behave counterproductively, purchasing when prices surge and showing disinterest when bitcoin experiences a significant decline.

Pro tips:

- Ideally, you should make your DCA investment as soon as you receive your salary. Studies show that people tend to spend more right after payday compared to other times of the month. If you postpone your DCA contribution, you might find you have nothing left to invest. Conversely, if you make it a habit to allocate the appropriate amount to your DCA investment immediately upon receiving your paycheck, you'll be better able to manage your remaining funds.

- Set up a standing transfer order, or ask your employer to send funds to your specified exchange on a regular basis. Learn more about preferred exchanges later in this chapter.

- Activate automatic purchasing (DCA bot).

- Make sure you regularly transfer cryptocurrency to your private wallet. Learn more about preferred crypto wallets later in this chapter.

Via the link below, you can see how your bitcoin investments would have appreciated over the years. The results are available for bitcoin only, as most currently relevant cryptocurrencies have not been on the market long enough.

Dollar Cost Averaging Bitcoin calculator

* Appreciation percentages do not depend on the currency used. Calculators may show differences due to different source data and exchange rate differences.

If you believe in the long-term growth of your chosen asset, this way of investing will put you in a perfect state of mental well-being. If the price of the asset is rising, you are happy that you are getting rich, and if the price is falling, you are happy that you are buying at a discount. However, the main point of DCA is that you are investing for the long term and over many years. Only then can you appreciate its true meaning. **This strategy is appropriate for assets with a proven multi-year track record and for investors who have a deep understanding of and belief in their future potential.**

TRADING, LEVERAGE, AND EMOTIONS: IT'S NOT FOR EVERYONE

By trading, we mean actively trading on the stock exchange to make a profit. The essence of trading is that traders try to time the market, which is exactly what I have tried to warn readers about. Trading is a discipline that some see as a gamble, while others see it as an easy path to wealth. But the reality is that long-term profitable trading is only possible based on multiple assumptions. Traders must have a thorough understanding of the market and understand how the price is formed on the stock exchange and what can affect it. At the same time, traders need to maintain a professional approach and learn to trade according to well-defined rules. The most important factors that fundamentally influence the path to success (roughly 80%) are mental control (calm and focused mind), discipline, patience, quick decision making, and emotional control. Another 10% of the path to success depends on proper money management (see the Basic Trader's Dictionary section that follows). The final 10% depends on the actual method used. Trading is a demanding discipline built on experience, humility, and discipline. A trader using only common sense, who has gained experience through hard work, can be much more successful than an egotistical genius.

General concepts and their explanations

Fear of missing out (FOMO): this is the fear or anxiety generated by a sense of missing an opportunity that others are experiencing. FOMO can occur when the price rises significantly, which can result subsequently in an exponential price spike. During this period it is usually too late to buy the asset because it is likely that the price will subsequently fall—allowing the market to correct itself. The larger the FOMO, the larger and longer the price decline can be.

Fear, uncertainty, doubt (FUD): these are news and events that cause panic in the market, such as black swan events (see page 180). Some of these messages recur over time, such as announcements of crypto-currency bans in China, India, Russia, and are often deliberately triggered by various sources including media, social networks, big players, and political lobbies to destabilize the market. Many investors, especially unsophisticated ones, subsequently succumb to these sentiments and divest their assets, often at a significant loss. Such news can trigger a cascading fall in prices.

Bull market: this is a period during which prices rise over a long period of time. There is an optimistic mood in the market and a general expectation that prices will rise permanently. It often occurs during periods of economic growth. Buyers—known as bulls, or optimists—outnumber sellers in the long term. Many buyers are under the influence of the FOMO effect. Experienced long-term investors are cautious and sell slowly in order to realize profits, rather than buying frantically. They are aware that over time the market will turn and prices will start to fall.

Bear market: this is a period during which prices decline over a long period of time. There is a pessimistic mood in the market, which occurs in times of economic downturn or because of negative news (FUD). Sellers—known as bears, or pessimists—prevail over buyers in the long term. Experienced long-term investors try to estimate the extent of the downturn and slowly buy in. They are aware that it is profitable to invest during a price decline and that eventually the market will turn around and prices will start to rise again.

All-Time High (ATH): means the highest value (price) ever achieved for a given asset.

Volatility: measures the fall or rise in price over a period of time and expresses the level of risk of an investment. When something has little volatility, it is stable. When something is highly volatile, then there is more fluctuation in price.

Basic trader's dictionary:

Trade: the act of buying, selling, or exchanging assets on an exchange.

Portfolio: originally this was the name for a portable document bag with various compartments. Today, the term is used in the investment industry to refer to a collection of different assets such as stocks, real estate, precious metals, cryptocurrencies, and cash. In our case, it means spreading the investment among different cryptocurrencies.

Candlesticks: are one of the options for displaying price development. It is a graphical representation that shows how the price has evolved over a selected time interval.

Order: a request made by a trader to buy or sell financial assets on an exchange.

Market order: a request that results in an immediate purchase or sale of a given asset at the current market price.

Limit order: a request to buy or sell a given asset at a specified price determined by the trader.

Indicator: a technical tool that uses mathematical calculations on past price data to project a curve onto a chart.

Setup: the strategy or investment plan by which a trader enters into a trade. Often used in conjunction with indicators, it helps determine the conditions under which it opens its position for entering a trade or placing an order to buy or sell.

Money management: is a plan for handling funds according to a trader's pre-established rules. The goal of money management is to minimize losses—even during the event of a series of losing trades. This protects the loss of capital and can subsequently lead to maximization of profits.

Target: a goal, intention, or specific price at which a trader takes profit and exits the trade.

Take profit: a pre-set price or place where a trader realizes a profit by selling a given asset. One target usually establishes multiple take profits at different levels. It is executed through a limit order.

Stop or stop loss: a pre-set price or place where a trader exits the trade if it does not go according to plan. Oftentimes, a loss is realized. It is executed through a limit order.

Long: a market condition where buyers dominate, leading to expectations of a price increase.

Short: a market condition where sellers dominate, leading to expectations of a price decrease.

Leverage: a strategy whereby assets can be purchased using a temporary loan. It brings great opportunities, but also great risks. Leverage allows the trader to create trades that are many times larger than the real deposit—creating an environment for potentially higher losses. It is a tool that can multiply the gains and losses from individual trades. Leverage should not be used by beginners and less-experienced traders under any circumstances.

Volume: the amount of orders that were traded at a specific price or price range.

Correlation: the identical or approximate chart trend between assets.

Liquidity: the ability of a given asset to meet supply and demand. This is particularly important if a trader wishes to sell an asset into a chosen currency.

Spike: rapid price movement in one direction.

Gap: this refers to the price difference for a specific asset, often observed between candles on a chart. In traditional stock markets, gaps can occur between the end and start of trading sessions. In the 24/7 crypto markets, hidden gaps may arise during sharp price movements (spikes) where minimal or no trading occurs between certain price levels. These gaps often get filled as the market eventually returns to them.

Main types of traders (trading styles)

High-frequency trader (HFT): In recent years, 60%–80% of all stock trades are executed by algorithms. HFT traders trade minimal price movements in the style of tens of thousands of transactions per day. They use various sophisticated mathematical models and artificial intelligence and trade according to order flow and liquidity.

Swing trader: seeks volatile market trends (short- or long-term), entering trades when anticipating a trend reversal. These traders utilize four-hour to one-day charts; the average trade length spans days, at most weeks.

Intraday trader, scalper: estimates price movements within minutes or hours. This trader utilizes tick, second, and minute charts, along with other intraday charts, and closes anywhere from a few to hundreds of trades within a single day.

Tick charts show the number of paired trades. One trade can contain a different number of contracts (volume charts show the number of paired contracts). For example, for a tick chart with a setting of 100, one line on the chart represents 100 trades executed.

Investment trader: generally trades with the trend rather than against it. This type of trader estimates market developments based on historical data, primarily using charts, often supplemented by fundamentals (see page 220), world events, and market sentiment. The trader monitors the positions of various market participants. They manage and execute trades based on daily or weekly charts. The average duration for an open trade ranges from weeks to months.

Main types of analysis (business methods)

There are hundreds of trading methods and strategies in the world. Every trader tries to find logic in the market and figure out how to make the stock market work. Along the way, a trader often goes from fundamental to technical analysis to various indicators such as signals, systems, or indicators. These indicators are themselves a broader topic and a trader can use a wide variety of them. These range from simple to complex, and can be based on artificial intelligence, advanced mathematics, or even astrology. It is impossible to trade on the stock exchange without a proper understanding and examination of possible price movements. That is why people use various methods of analyzing the market to help its participants predict with some probability what the market might do in the future. There are dozens of types of analyses and all of them must be considered only as supporting tools. They can be fundamentals, sentiment, news, inside information, or any data gathered from different types of charts. A trader makes a decision that may come from a combination of different analyses, but the final estimate of the market remains the trader's own choice. All analysis is fundamentally based on game theory and in effect attempts to predict the behavior of other players based on historical experience. There are hundreds of technical-analytical methods and every trader will go through a period of trying out many of these methods. Leaving aside the various fundamental, economic, and mathematical studies, the most used analyses in the stock market are:

Technical analysis and price action: a method of analyzing the price chart using various price formations and indicators. The analysis works only with data generated by the market. For example, it can be price, volume, volatility, or the number of open trades (orders).

Market and volume profile: a different graphical representation of the price chart, but with the addition of a representation of all trades executed at each price level. The method is based on the natural logic of market functioning.

Order flow and order stream: a method that utilizes both current and pending orders. Order flow provides detailed information on the number of contracts, stocks, or cryptocurrencies bought and sold at any given moment. Both order flow and order stream are primary methods used by all commercial traders and are also frequently used by other traders.

Business strategy

This is the investment plan according to which the trader enters into the trade.

- Each trader chooses a preferred trading style (see Main Trader Types) and a preferred trading method (see Main Analysis Types) based on their time, experience, and mental ability.

- Next, a trader decides whether to speculate on a rise or a fall in price at a given moment.

- A trader determines the amount of funds to be invested and how many trades (trading positions) to open.

- A trader selects specific cryptocurrencies and determines at what point they will enter the trade (open positions). Most traders use the aforementioned technical indicators and other supporting tools to determine this moment.

- A trader sets individual trading targets when they will gradually exit the open position (sell the asset with a predetermined profit).

- In the interest of money management, capital protection, and maximization, a trader sets the amounts they will trade and the maximum allowable loss for each trade. This involves setting up stop-loss measures for unfavorable price movements. When a stop-loss point is reached, the trader sells the asset at a predetermined loss, exiting the position and realizing the loss. If the price moves favorably, the stop-loss points are adjusted to a level where a loss would no longer occur.

Such a planned strategy is called an investment plan (setup). It depends on the discipline of the trader, their self confidence, and the investment plan. When trading, you are not dealing with the long-term development of the price of a given asset, but only speculating on the rise or fall of the price in the period you have chosen. It is common for some trades to end in a loss, but what is important is the overall result of all open trades over the selected time period. Most newcomers tend to change their predetermined investment plan on the fly, either based on euphoria or fear of the situation. In most cases, such actions result in chaos and a worse outcome than a well-thought-out and level-headed investment plan would provide.

Therefore, the success of trading depends mainly on the trader's approach, experience, and well-chosen strategy. In fact, it is the establishment and strict adherence to a good investment plan that separates the successful traders from the unsuccessful ones.

Various trading groups offer education to newcomers for a fee. However, it's crucial to find a group whose members genuinely understand the stock market, as opposed to being focused solely on marketing—which is unfortunately the case 90% of the time. Education groups are often run by people who don't have much more experience than beginners. Before joining such a group, it's best to contact the people in the group and check with appropriate questions that they really know what they're talking about. Avoid groups where it is not possible to trace several years of experience of the main players in these trading communities. Read reviews and use your own common sense, because even reviews are no guarantee of success. The moment the market grows, most of these groups can be successful. You only get to know the real quality traders when the markets are experiencing long term downturns. This is doubly true for crypto.

Usually, any newcomer who learns to look at a chart and logs on to one of the exchanges starts studying the past developments and it becomes immediately clear when it was profitable to sell and when to buy. This can lead to the conclusion trading is not as complicated as it is made out to be. This mindset usually results in a financial loss in the end. Only a few people in a thousand can make a successful living trading. However, if you enjoy the adrenaline rush and are aware that it is a big gamble, especially for the inexperienced, give it a try. Until you try it, you won't believe it anyway. Most newbies eventually can't resist trying to guess the price (market timing) despite the warnings. Greed and the prospect of potential profits will put you in a gambling mode and you'll think bitcoin is too expensive and try investing in another cryptocurrency you've read about or which has been recommended. Count on the fact that without a trading plan with strict rules for all trades, you are pretty much guaranteed to get burned and lose money. Always keep in mind that becoming a long-term profitable trader involves hundreds to thousands of hours of work. There is no way around this stage. The only thing that can help shorten the path is to find proven profitable traders and listen to their advice on exactly what to do. Learn it from them, understand the market, know yourself, and get the necessary experience, as cheaply as possible. Don't start trading money you can't afford to lose without experience and a plan in place. But try it, start on demo accounts, make one hundred trades without risk of big losses, and see for yourself. If you do well on the demos, put in less money. If after one hundred real trades with small money you are making money, up the risk and try to play a higher level.

Risk is profit, but don't be a sheep to the slaughter.

Chart types, candles, and their evaluation

There are many types of graphs, but we will mention only two basic ones in this book. The most common chart is the **line chart**. This chart records only the closing price for the selected period.

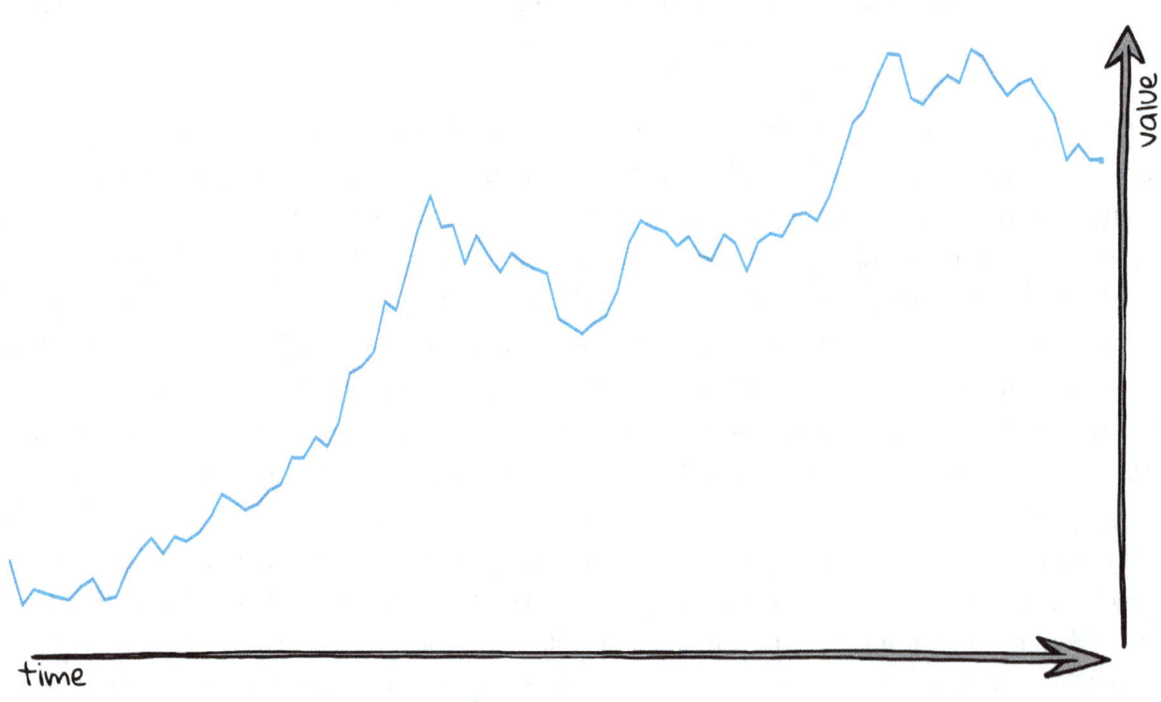

The second type is called a **candlestick chart.** Each candle shows the prices reached during a given time frame. The time frame—represented by individual candles—is selectable in intervals ranging from minutes, hours, days, weeks, months, and years.

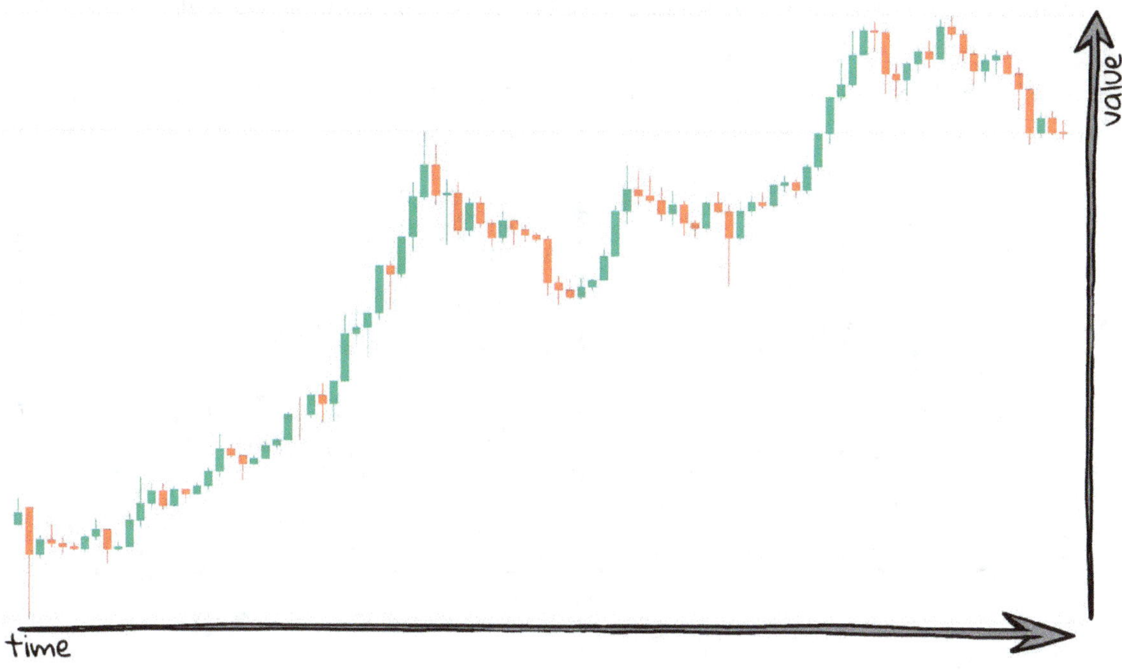

Each candle maps the price development in a given time frame and shows us the four basic values of the candle: the opening (**open**), closing (**close**), highest (**high**), lowest (**low**) price.

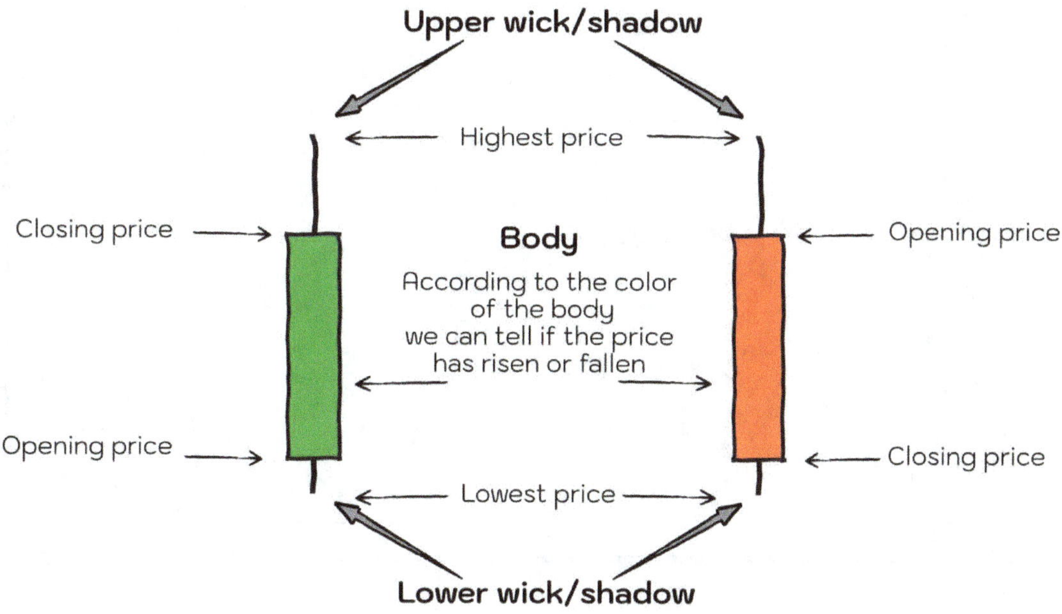

The **trend** tells us the mood of the market and shows us whether the price of a given asset tends to rise or fall. A period when the price of an asset is neither rising nor falling is called a sideways price movement or **range** (chop).

An **uptrend** (bullish trend) occurs once prices form higher lows and then higher highs.

A **downtrend** (bearish trend) is the opposite of an uptrend, where prices form lower highs and lower lows.

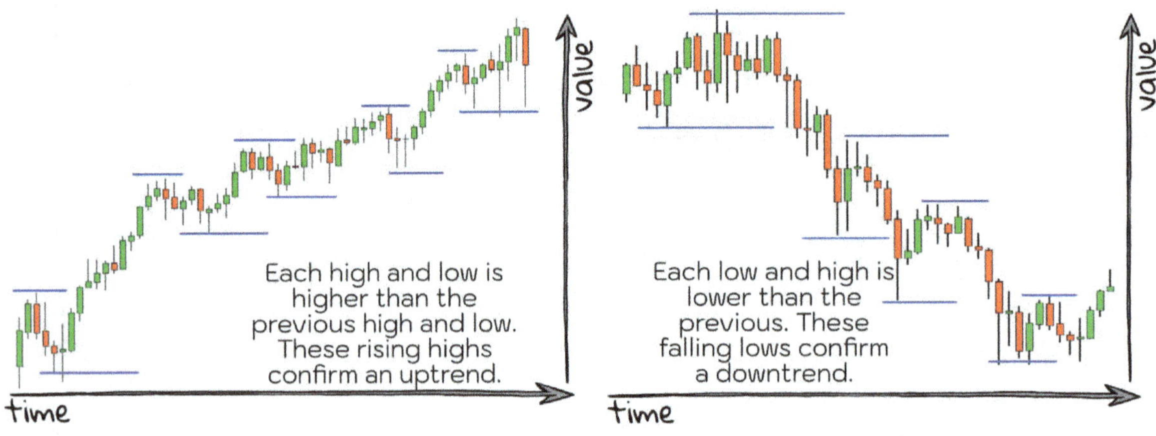

Support and resistance

Support and resistance lines are the individual levels where prices stop moving up or down. The support line is the level below which the price of an asset in a downtrend will not fall for some time. The resistance line is the level above which the price of an asset in an uptrend will not rise for some time. Support and resistance lines that run at a certain angle (not horizontal) are often referred to as **trend lines**.

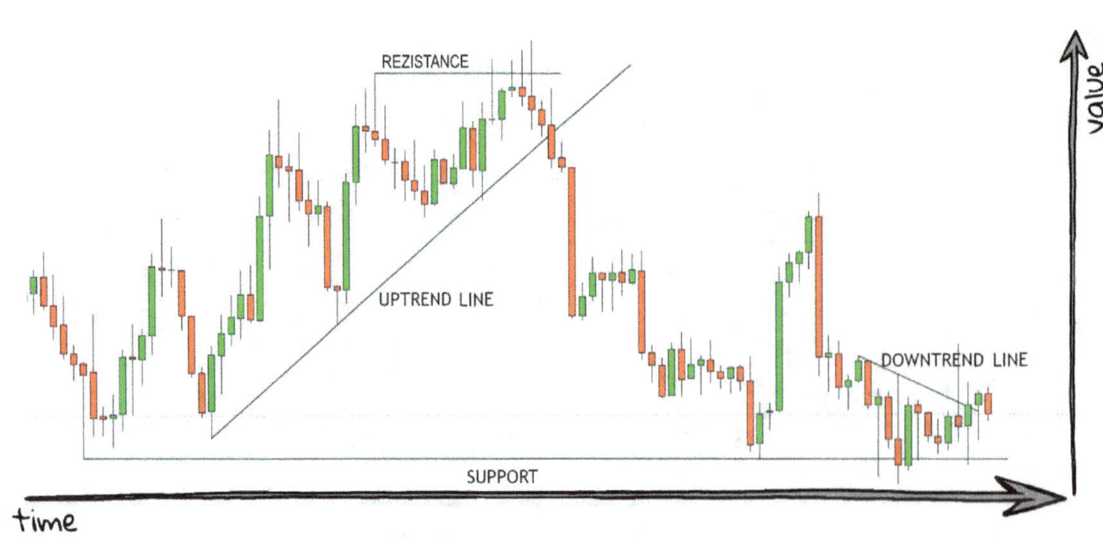

As the price drops towards the support level, buyers start buying more and sellers start holding on to their existing positions. The support line is the point where demand will peak above supply and price will not fall below this line.

In the case of resistance, it works the other way around. However, prices also often break the support and resistance lines. Breaking through resistance signals that the bulls (buyers) have won over the bears (sellers). The bulls have decided to push the asset price above the previous high. Once resistance is broken, another one is formed at a higher price level. For support, the opposite condition applies.

The support level can turn into resistance and vice versa. After the price breaks through support, market participants may try to limit their losses by selling, pushing the price back above the original support line, which will become resistance.

Pattern (candlestick pattern) refers to specific, recognizable formations created by price movements on the chart. These formations can be evaluated in two ways: either by assessing the individual candlesticks, where the importance of the body size is compared to the length of the wicks, or by evaluating candlestick formations over a set time period. It's worth noting that a single weekly candle might encompass a complete formation of four-hour candles, which will subsequently affect its appearance. These formations can be identified by combining closing prices or by examining price highs and lows over a period of time. Using these patterns, traders can make more accurate estimates of future price movements. While these formations are easily spotted on historical charts, trading them in real time can be challenging. There are dozens to hundreds of different types of formations.

CHART PATTERNS

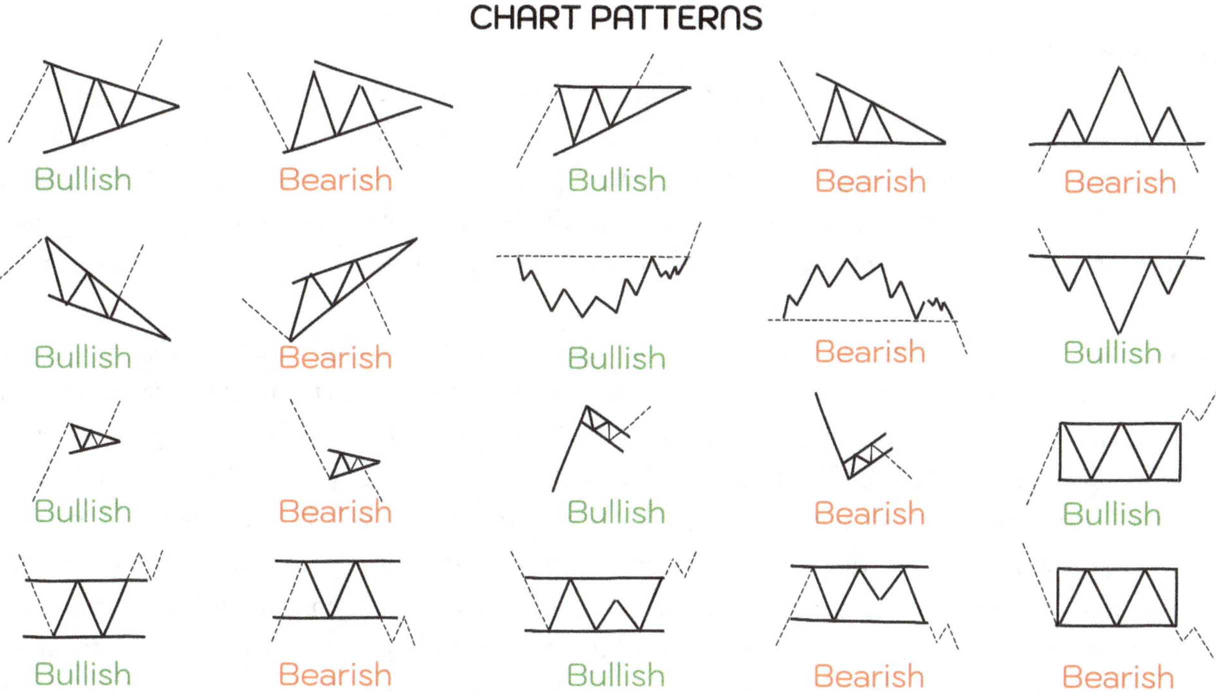

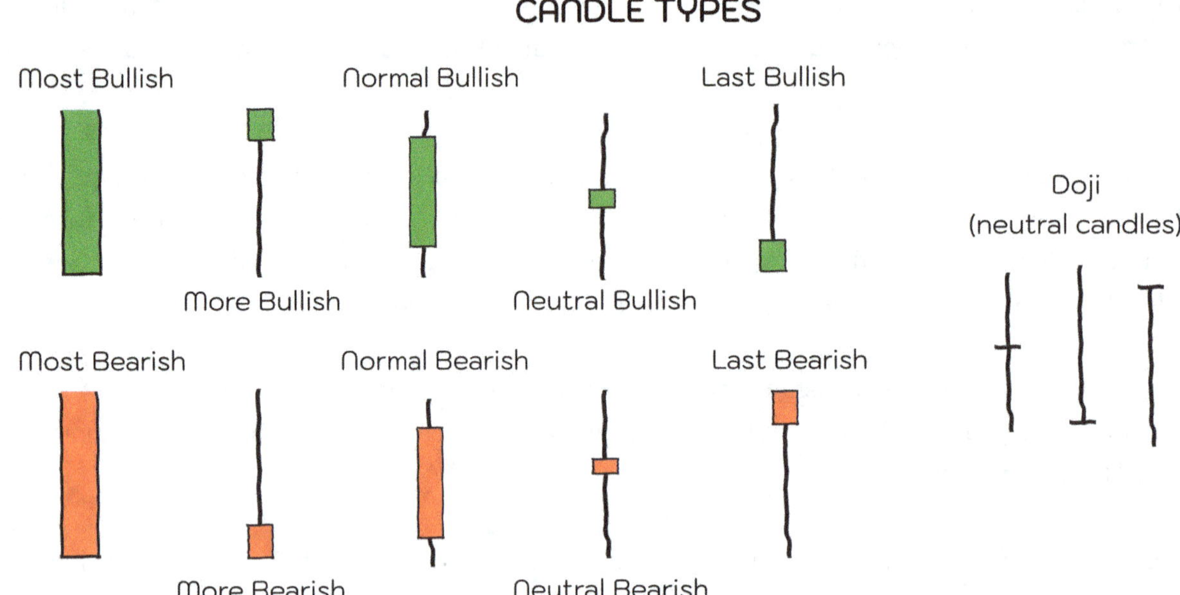

Let's take a look under the hood

For the purposes of this book, I asked professional trader Ludvík Turk to give us his perspective on the subject, to provide newcomers a hint of how the stock market works, and to gently reveal how a professional works. Ludvík is one of the most experienced traders in the Czech Republic, founder of czechwealth.cz, lecturer, consultant, and author of many books. He has been successfully trading on financial markets for more than twenty years. He lectures at professional conferences around the world and participates in international competitions. The following passages are summaries from the pen of Ludvík Turek.

Development of the trader

Trader development can be invaluable information for any beginner or intermediate trader, as it will help save a lot of time and money. Any successful trader who has managed to achieve consistently profitable trading and can take money out of the stock market on a regular basis has gone through three developmental stages. And since the first two phases are very stressful and also very expensive, it is important for traders to understand as early as possible that profitable trading is only possible in the third development phase.

The intuitive trader takes advice from experts, friends, television, newspapers, and draws information from wherever he can learn anything about the markets. He sometimes uses technical indicators, even if he doesn't understand their function properly, and loves the thrill of trading. He likes to brag about trading against the big investment banks and funds and changes his decisions to buy and sell stocks from minute to minute. These traders have no discipline and don't think they need any. Intuitive trading is, with few exceptions (these are intuitive traders who have been in the market for decades), a losing proposition. The intuitive trader will clear his account very soon, and when he loses all illusions of profitable trading, he will notice an ad in the local press "How to make a million dollars trading cryptocurrencies in a few weeks while working 5 minutes a day" and discover the world of price action, maybe a volume profile and other technical indicators.

A technical trader uses indicators from trading software, follows journals written by various experts and well-known analysts, and sometimes has some rules for entering and exiting the market. At this stage, traders read one website after another looking for the magic method, the indicator that will show them the way to riches. If we call understanding the market based on price action, volume profile, and order flow with a "magic indicator," it's only a small part of the puzzle, and if you don't have the rest of the puzzle, which is psychology and money management in a well-defined trading plan, no amount of "magic" will help. Technical traders usually don't get the point of these "magic methods" and even if they have the same things in front of them as pro traders, without a deep understanding of the market even using pro methods they are losing money. When even this doesn't help anymore, and yet the trader still has the will and patience to become a professional, they finally find a way to make money in the market and potentially get rich.

The strategic trader is born at the stage when the amateur trader has become a professional because he has understood the function of the market, has a precise strategy, knows the trading plan by heart, and enters and exits the market automatically with predefined rules. Using proper money management, he knows exactly what will happen with his money the moment he enters the market, why he has an open position, and when he will exit the trade. A strategic trader knows himself and knows where his weaknesses are, which he is constantly working to improve.

The main principle of the stock exchange

Every financial market operates on the basis of simple supply and demand, just like any other market. We have sellers on one side and buyers on the other. When buyers are more aggressive, the price goes up, when sellers are more aggressive, the price goes down. Banks and large financial institutions have to trade differently than retail traders because of their size. Simply put, they sell where retail buys, and they buy where retail sells. Let's remember that large institutions have unlimited resources and information. So they get into the market far before retail even has a clue that anything is going to happen. Thus, prices in the financial markets often move in anticipation of a move or just for pure manipulation to get big money to prepare ahead for an extreme move and liquidate positions therein. Retail often does not understand this and thus unwittingly does the opposite of big money with entries and exits exactly on trend reversals and exactly against the big money that de facto controls the price movement in the stock market.

Large market participants perceive the exchange by value, liquidity, trading volume, current situation, sentiment, and fundamentals, and use completely different methods and technologies to trade than the average retail trader. Large financial institutions trade according to a clear plan and clear rules. The traders who trade in these firms are selected and trained according to strict conditions and a predetermined psychological profile. This is a similar principle to the selection of air traffic controllers. If a retail trader wants to succeed, he must understand why and how the price moves on the stock market. They must try to trade like the big traders and understand their perceptions and approach to trading. Knowing that the big money manipulates prices to extremes, trading by structure, pure price chart, volume, and liquidity, I cannot trade by lagging indicators and lines that most retail traders use and then be surprised that 90% of them never succeed in the stock market.

How professional and institutional traders work

Commercial traders use a more comprehensive view of the chart than retail traders. The **market and volume profile chart** is the first of the charts used by professionals. It is a different representation and arrangement of candles, which are not drawn as candles but as columns, and these are then stacked rather than side by side. This then creates profiles on the charts, and in addition to this, the trade volumes executed at each price level are recorded from each candle. Thus, we get market profiles and volume profiles, according to which it is much easier to estimate the intention of the price development. In general, big money follows the areas with large trading volumes the most. Conversely, areas with the smallest trading volumes on the chart are watched for strong price movement through them and trend.

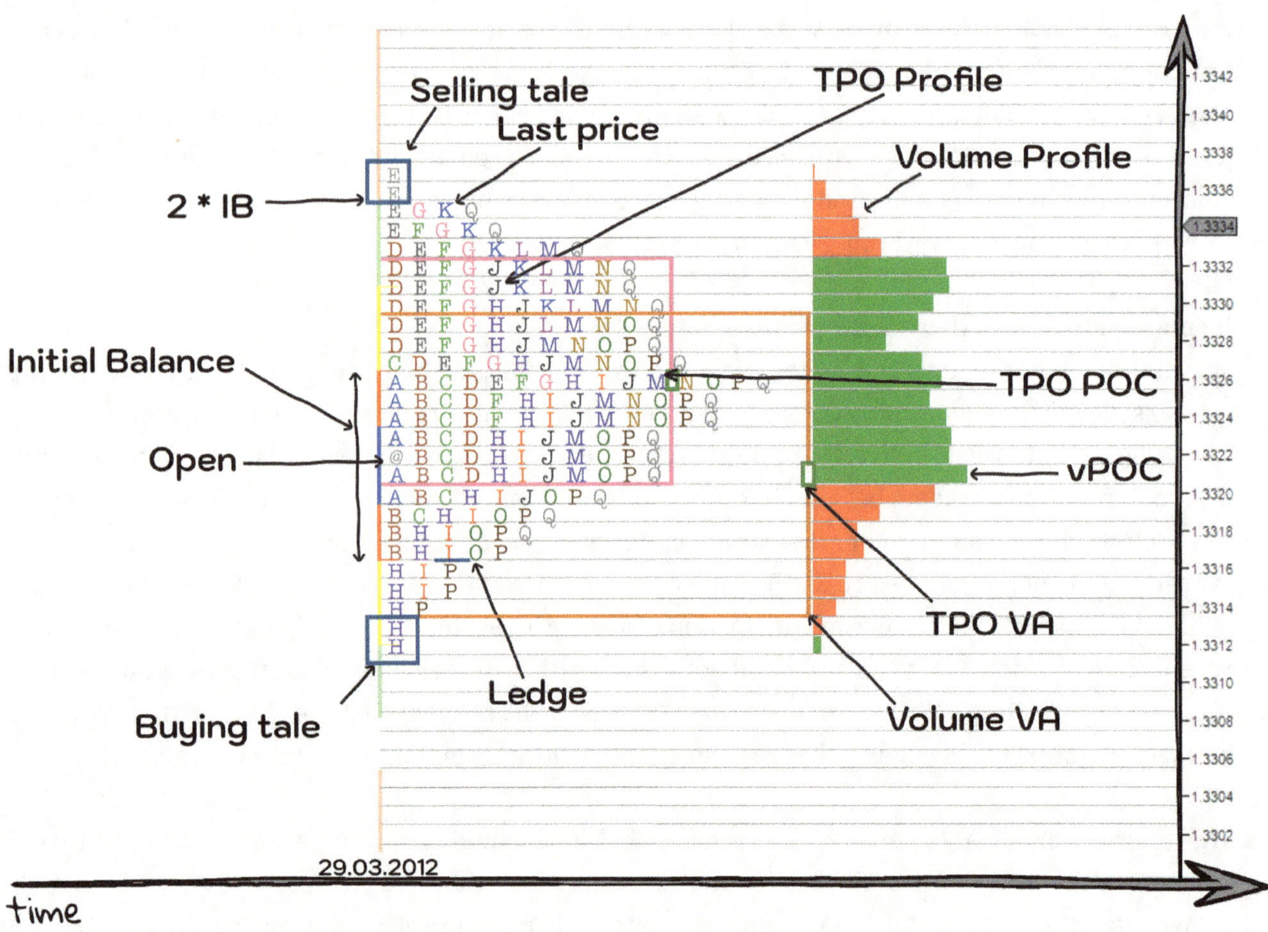

The order flow chart is the next most watched and often one of the few watched charts by commercial traders. From these charts, one can read exactly the number of all purchases and sales made over a selected period. Order flow charts provide a perfect view of the activity of all market participants, regardless of whether it is price manipulation, aggressive or passive buying or selling.

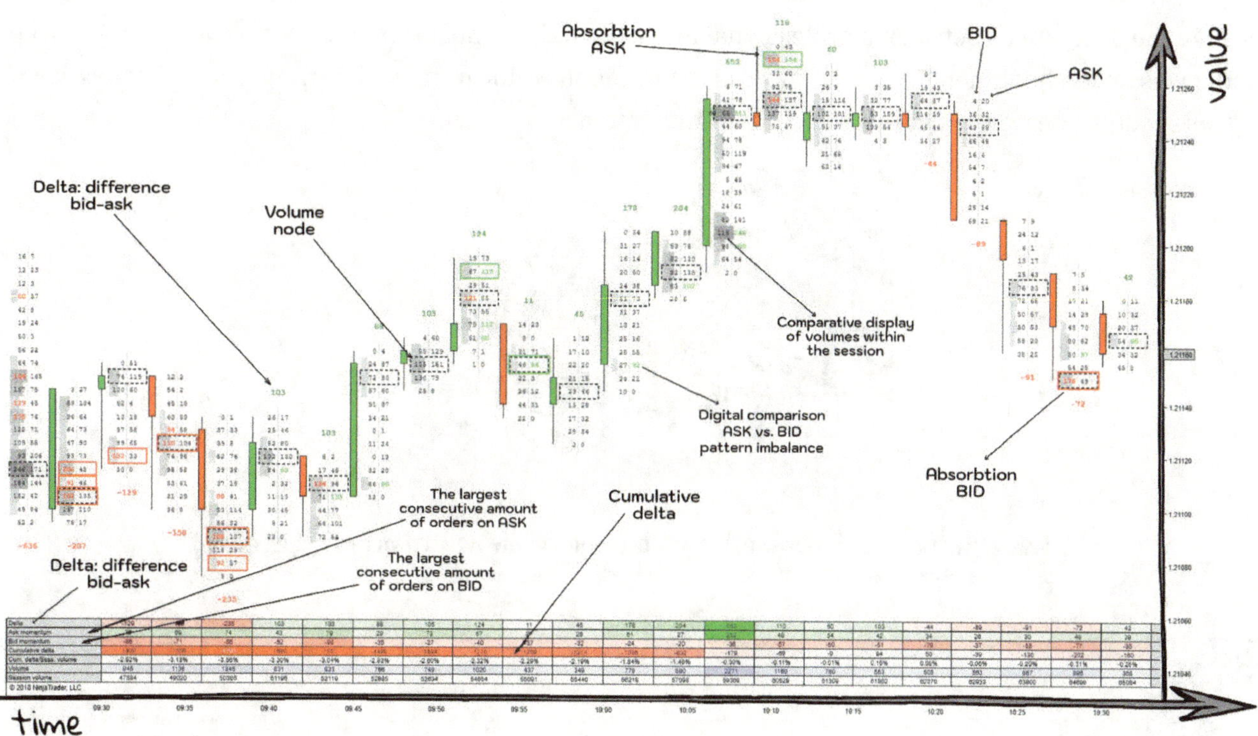

Any trader can trade according to simple rules and can use the same ideas and indicators used by traders in banks trading seven-digit dollar accounts. They just have to approach it responsibly, understanding that only people with a clearly defined trading plan and strict money management rules on the methods of institutional traders will succeed.

Thank you Ludvík for giving us a glimpse into the world of a professional trader. Whether it's chess, football, or stock trading, there is always a significant difference between seasoned professionals and those just starting out. Let's sum up these ideas with perspective and a dash of humor.

The difference between a professional trader and a novice can be compared to a game between an experienced chess player and a child who does not yet understand the rules of the game. A professional acts like a prudent scholar with extensive knowledge, keen judgment, and deep wisdom. The novice, on the other hand, resembles an excited puppy who curiously pounces on everything. The professional follows a carefully developed plan, analyses markets, and understands risk management. The novice, on the other hand, prefers to rely on all sorts of guaranteed tips from friends, information from discussions on social networks, and being influenced by dubious influencers. Their plan is based on the motto "buy cheap, sell at a big profit, and get rich quick." However, the opposite is usually true and the newcomer is then faced with a reality check, often accompanied by a significant financial loss. A professional trader can find balance between work and personal life. Meanwhile, a novice often falls victim to their own obsession. Their daily routine then consists of constantly checking charts, looking for new investment tips, and sleeping restlessly.

Despite the differences between a professional and a novice, we must remember that every experienced trader was once a beginner. The key to success is continuous improvement, learning from mistakes, keeping perspective, perseverance, self-discipline, and patience.

I have to say, I imagined this candlelit dinner a bit differently.

TradingView is among the most popular platforms for tracking charts. By registering with an email address, you gain access to a variety of charts—from commodities to stocks to cryptocurrencies—even with the free version.

HODL VS. TRADING

HODL is a slang term derived from the word "hold." HODLers, or diamond hands, refers to people who are willing to hold (not sell) their cryptocurrencies even during price drops because they believe that the price will eventually surpass historical highs again. Their opposite is weak hands, or paper hands. These are usually newcomers or inexperienced investors who get scared of a price drop and panic and dump their cryptocurrencies at a big loss. On the bitcointalk.org discussion forum on December 18, 2013, a drunken user, Game Kyuubi, made two posts where he wrote HODL instead of the intended word: HOLD.

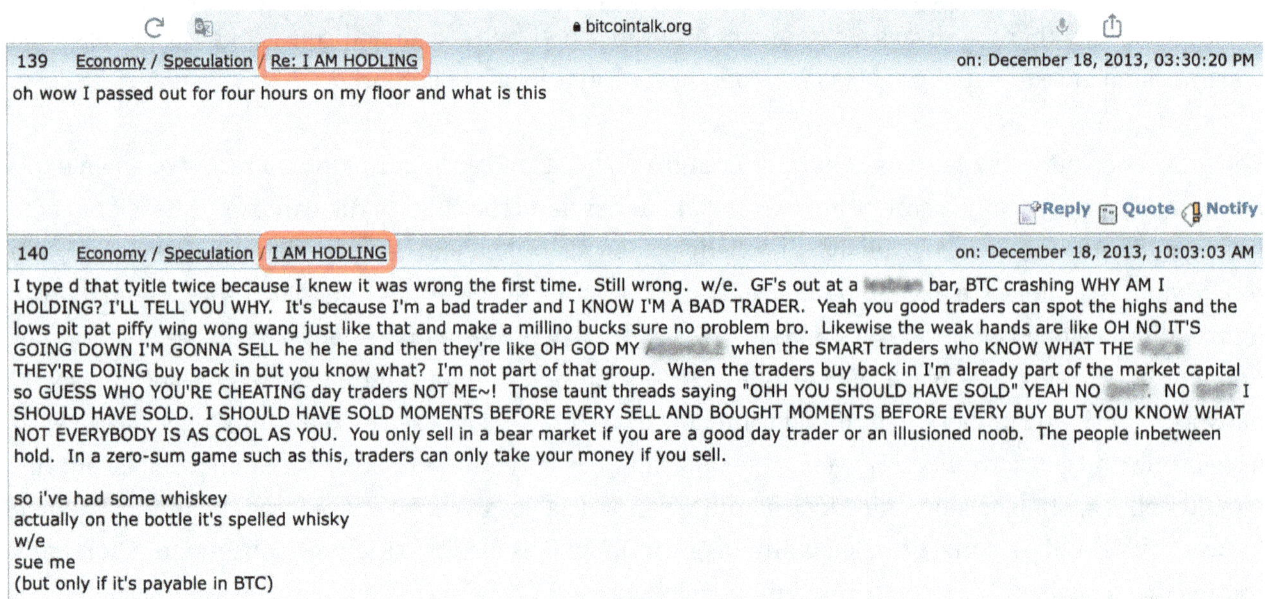

139	Economy / Speculation / Re: I AM HODLING	on: December 18, 2013, 03:30:20 PM

oh wow I passed out for four hours on my floor and what is this

Reply Quote Notify

140	Economy / Speculation / I AM HODLING	on: December 18, 2013, 10:03:03 AM

I type d that tyitle twice because I knew it was wrong the first time. Still wrong. w/e. GF's out at a ▓▓▓ bar, BTC crashing WHY AM I HOLDING? I'LL TELL YOU WHY. It's because I'm a bad trader and I KNOW I'M A BAD TRADER. Yeah you good traders can spot the highs and the lows pit pat piffy wing wong wang just like that and make a millino bucks sure no problem bro. Likewise the weak hands are like OH NO IT'S GOING DOWN I'M GONNA SELL he he he and then they're like OH GOD MY ▓▓▓▓▓▓ when the SMART traders who KNOW WHAT THE ▓▓▓▓ THEY'RE DOING buy back in but you know what? I'm not part of that group. When the traders buy back in I'm already part of the market capital so GUESS WHO YOU'RE CHEATING day traders NOT ME~! Those taunt threads saying "OHH YOU SHOULD HAVE SOLD" YEAH NO ▓▓▓▓. NO ▓▓▓▓ I SHOULD HAVE SOLD. I SHOULD HAVE SOLD MOMENTS BEFORE EVERY SELL AND BOUGHT MOMENTS BEFORE EVERY BUY BUT YOU KNOW WHAT NOT EVERYBODY IS AS COOL AS YOU. You only sell in a bear market if you are a good day trader or an illusioned noob. The people inbetween hold. In a zero-sum game such as this, traders can only take your money if you sell.

so i've had some whiskey
actually on the bottle it's spelled whisky
w/e
sue me
(but only if it's payable in BTC)

 The actual "I am hodling" post from GameKyuubi, originator of the word HODL via bitcointalk.org

 Various communication threads from GameKyuubi, originator of the word HODL via bitcointalk.org

The Bitcoin community caught on to this typo and the new word was subsequently used throughout the crypto space. The acronym was used by Michael Lewis five years later in his book on cryptocurrencies titled *HODL, Hold on for Dear Life: Getting Started in the Puzzling World of Cryptocurrency*. This gave the slang term the meaning of an acronym.

However, it is important to note that few cryptocurrencies are destined for long-term holding. Most cryptocurrencies will not recover from declines and therefore it makes no sense to buy them for long-term holding.

There is a fundamental difference between hodlers and traders:

Hodlers (long-term investors) buy a given asset for long-term holding or saving. Their time horizon is a minimum of four years, but they are often prepared to hold for decades. They only commit to proven currencies that they know and trust, primarily bitcoin. They mainly follow the fundamentals, take a detached view of events, do not deal with FUD, and are not concerned with FOMO. They don't sell in downturns, but rather buy in. They believe in the new ATH. They often consider traders as gamblers and look down on them. After a long time in the crypto market, they are already sufficiently hedged and take price drops with even more detachment. They sleep peacefully and don't have to keep an eye on charts. The most successful hodlers are those who have been in the market the longest. Anyone can be a good hodler right away. However, they have to follow the rules and have a strong hand during the dips. Most hodlers have tried trading as well, especially in the early days of their entry into the crypto market.

Traders trade at regular intervals with the aim of making profits. Unlike hodlers, traders are not so concerned with fundamentals, but prefer chart analysis. They only look at the market from a short-term perspective—a few months at most. They don't care if the market is rising or falling, but only feed on the success of their strategy. Trading is mentally demanding and time-consuming. Traders have to constantly monitor charts and often work at night. They look at hodlers as the simple investors who don't know how to trade and have to wait years for results—while they continuously make money in the meantime. They often can't find common ground with hodlers. For example, in medium downturns where the hodler is still talking about a bull market, the trader is already talking about a bear market. The most successful traders must have deep experience and a solid psyche. Only a few people out of a thousand will become successful traders. It takes many years of experience. Some traders drop out due to psychological stress or low success rate and some of them switch to HODL over time. Some traders actually maintain a HODL portfolio in parallel

HOW TO BUY CRYPTOCURRENCIES

There are a plethora of ways to buy cryptocurrency. These options change rapidly. Literally every month new services are being created and existing ones are being improved. It is not in my power to list all the options, let alone try to describe them in detail, not to mention that in a few months everything would be different anyway. I will attempt to categorize these methods and in each of them list at least one option that I consider optimal. Before buying cryptocurrency, you should obtain your own private wallet. Prior to diving into the purchase options, one more crucial consideration that divides cryptocurrency into two camps needs to be mentioned. This is because you need to think properly beforehand whether you will prefer the option of purchasing via KYC or, on the contrary, no KYC. Convinced anarchists and consistent advocates of freedom take the view that they never want to own any virtual coin that could potentially be linked to their identity. They don't trust the state and its powers and fear that one day someone may knock on their door and ask what they have done with their coins. The reasons can vary from confiscation to taxation. While the state cannot seize them, it can enforce a statement of the transactions and their justification. If holders cannot answer convincingly, they may face penalties or taxation. On the other hand, many people take the view that they are not criminals, have nothing to hide, and are not bothered by KYC. Therefore, everyone has to choose between the protection of privacy and the possible advantages or disadvantages of the solutions. Many people in the crypto community believe that the authorities are not yet able to effectively link information with individual institutions and blockchains. This is likely to change in the future. The authorities would then have the ability to examine your transactions well into the past and draw conclusions from them. Some users choose to go both ways for security, with some funds stored in KYC-linked addresses and some in non-KYC-linked addresses.

Do not leave your cryptocurrencies on exchanges. Consistently transfer them to your private wallet. Be aware that there are many scams in the cryptocurrency industry. Only trade with service providers that have a transparent history and numerous reviews. In a world where people don't know each other, reputation is a cornerstone. That's why the trust (or reputation) of participants is one of the main points emphasized in the Cryptoanarchist Manifesto.

KYC and AML

Know your customer (KYC) and anti-money laundering (AML) are regulations designed to combat money laundering, terrorist financing, and other illegal activities in the financial sector. These regulations require financial institutions to collect and verify information about their customers. This process is enshrined in international agreements, regulatory measures, and legislation. However, according to a recent assessment, AML has only about a 0.1% success rate globally, and it costs institutions a significant amount of money to implement.

The KYC process involves verifying your identity using official identification documents, as well as verifying your address, email, or phone number. In many cases the verifier asks you to upload copies of your documents to their system. Then, in the next step, using automated processes, it asks you to use the camera on your phone or computer to take a photo of yourself so that it may compare it with the documents you have submitted. As the data obtained is in the hands of other institutions, this process unfortunately carries the risk that your data or copies of documents may fall into unauthorized hands. If you are dealing with larger sums of money at the institution, you will probably be asked to prove your income or the origin of the money. Although KYC and AML are based on good intentions at their core, there is a possibility that these regulations could be misused as a basis for building an Orwellian state. If governments or other authorities start collecting and analyzing citizens' personal data beyond the scope of fighting criminal activities, this could lead to invasion of privacy, restriction of freedom, and abuse of power. It is important to strike the right balance between protecting society from illegal activities while maintaining respect for individual privacy and freedom. Transparency and democratic oversight of these processes are key to ensuring that KYC and AML do not cross the line and become tools of Orwellian control.

Is anonymity or confirmed identity better when buying cryptocurrencies?

Purchasing Cryptocurrencies: understanding the risks and benefits of KYC, no-KYC, mixers, and anonymous cryptocurrencies.

KYC benefits

- ✓ It is usually a more comfortable and less complicated way.

- ✓ You will probably always comply with the legislation, even in the future.

- ✓ You can better prove the origin of your funds.

- ✓ When you sell cryptocurrency and pay the appropriate taxes, you can then officially and legally use these funds through the fiat banking system, as well as for real-life purchases or acquiring other assets

- ✓ In countries where the time and value test applies, you are in a better position with regard to tax management.

KYC disadvantages

- ✗ There is a risk of data leakage from the service provider and the potential for its subsequent misuse.

- ✗ You lose privacy regarding the funds you purchase.

- ✗ The government or other institutions might request documentation of your transactions for taxation purposes or even attempt to seize funds. Although they can›t access your crypto without the private key or seed, they can try to compel you to release them by confiscating your tangible assets or using other methods.

No-KYC benefits

- ✓ You maintain anonymity to the outside world. However, be warned: your identity might be revealed if someone you transact with recognizes you.

- ✓ No one knows how much money you have.

- ✓ No government institution or thief will knock on your door—unless you tell someone about your cryptocurrencies.

No-KYC disadvantages

- ✗ This method often results in higher fees. It is also usually more complicated either technically or organizationally.

- ✗ Purchasing tends to be more complicated, either technically or organizationally.

- ✗ If necessary, you may not be able to prove the origin of the money.

If you decide to transfer funds from a KYC wallet to a no-KYC wallet over time, understand that this transition comes with its own set of benefits and drawbacks. Importantly, reversing this process won't necessarily legitimize your money. While there are two primary methods to execute such a transaction, remember that the original records from your KYC-verified exchange (or similar platform) will persist. As a result, you may still face government inquiries regarding the handling of these funds.

Subsequent anonymization of KYC coins using mixers (CoinJoin app)
To anonymize KYC coins you can use applications like CoinJoin for bitcoin. It ranks among the more modern, reliable, and secure apps—unlike older tools based on centralized mixing technology. These tools can be used to anonymously transfer a fixed value from a KYC wallet to a no-KYC wallet for a fee. This ensures that no one can trace where your funds have been sent, and the receiving wallet won't be able to identify the source of the funds. If you're choosing a mixing service, it's essential to consult discussion forums for user reviews of the mixer. Otherwise, you risk losing your funds or receiving tainted coins. Well-reviewed wallets, such as the Wasabi Wallet or Whirlpool (associated with the Samourai Wallet), are frequently used. The Lightning Network also offers a level of anonymity.

Many institutions and governments have raised concerns about mixing tools, citing AML regulations and potential abuses. However, a 2019 study by Chainanalysis found that only 2.7% of users used anonymizing apps for such purposes. The vast majority, 97.3%, were driven by a desire to preserve their financial privacy.

"Chainalysis Finds Mixed Bitcoin Aren't As Dirty as People Think" via Blockonomi

No one can see into the future or predict whether pressure from state institutions will force centralized exchanges to try to detect mixed coins and then reject or even seize them.

Subsequent anonymization of KYC coins using anonymous cryptocurrencies
You can purchase anonymous cryptocurrencies for long-term holding or to anonymize transactions when transferring from a KYC to a no-KYC wallet. Anonymization can be done by buying an anonymous cryptocurrency on one exchange and then sending it to another exchange that allows you to set up a no-account as long as you do not use fiat exchanges. Here, the anonymous cryptocurrency can be exchanged into the desired currency and sent to a no-KYC wallet address. Examples of anonymous cryptocurrencies include Monero and Zcash. These are cryptocurrencies technically designed to allow anonymous transactions with no traceable history.

However, regulation is advancing around the world. More often, exchanges have a KYC process in place. Retail exchanges are gradually removing anonymous cryptocurrencies from their offerings because they would experience AML-related complications and it would hurt their business. Some countries are talking about banning the use of cryptocurrencies entirely, but this is a cry in the dark because they cannot objectively enforce such a ban. Over time, it may therefore become more difficult to exchange anonymous cryptocurrencies for diat currencies through the various exchanges and bureaux de change.

Privacy is not a crime

When deciding which option to use, remember one crucial point: desiring privacy isn't a crime but a fundamental human right. This right is enshrined in the Universal Declaration of Human Rights, adopted by the United Nations on December 10, 1948. Specifically, Article 12 states: "No one shall be subjected to arbitrary interference with his privacy, family, home or correspondence, nor to attacks upon his honor and reputation."

If you choose to maintain your privacy and buy bitcoin without KYC, you must keep in mind that this is not enough. Your identity can be revealed, for example, through your IP address. You need to use tools such as Tor and VPNs to increase security.

WHERE TO BUY CRYPTOCURRENCIES

Let's dive into the specifics of where and under what conditions we can purchase bitcoin. While there are approximately 20,000 different cryptocurrencies, we'll focus on buying bitcoin due to its prominence and widespread availability. Most cryptocurrencies are primarily available through exchanges. Bitcoin ATMs and some other platforms offer a limited selection of cryptocurrencies besides bitcoin. Throughout this section, we'll frequently mention the Lightning Network. For more details on this, refer to page 183, also indexed in the Quick Reference as "LN."

The breakdown of fees is based on the following criteria:

Low	**0.1–1 %**
Middle	**1.5–3 %**
High	**4–8 %**

Official intermediaries

Increasingly, countries offer opportunities to invest in bitcoin through external service providers such as banks, investment funds, and brokers. These providers will establish an account for you, managing and storing your funds per your instructions. However, this approach does not circumvent KYC regulations, and because the funds are not in your direct possession, one of bitcoin's major advantages—ownership control—is lost. On the plus side, there is no risk of losing access to the funds you have deposited, and in the event of your death, your heirs will also gain access to them.

Nonetheless, it is important to verify the level of insurance on your deposits against potential theft (hacking) of the service provider. Some companies may only hold your cryptocurrencies virtually, meaning while you can convert them back into fiat currencies for a fee, transferring them to your private wallet is not an option. Crucially, it is essential that such an agent actually purchases the underlying asset, that is, the actual Bitcoin. Failure to do so can lead to a scenario akin to gold miners circulating gold certificates for gold they do not possess, leaving the agent unable to fulfill all clients' demands to transfer the underlying asset to a private wallet or exchange it for fiat.

Bitcoin Exchange Traded Fund (ETF)
Authentication: KYC / Complexity: MEDIUM / Fees: LOW / LN: NO

In a well-regulated environment a bitcoin ETF is a simple, cheap, and relatively safe way to have exposure to bitcoin through another entity. When you buy a bitcoin ETF, however, you only own a stake in a fund that replicates the value of bitcoin. Whereas if you buy bitcoin, you own the actual cryptocurrency.

Advantages:

✓ The ease of purchase and accessibility allows a wide array of traditional investors and institutions to trade bitcoin through a broker and traditional investment accounts, eliminating the need for direct purchase and management of the digital currency.

✓ The ease of holding means that the investor does not need to technically manage the Bitcoin holdings themselves; this responsibility is undertaken by the fund or the contracted asset manager. For institutions, this arrangement permits control over the invested funds in a conventional hierarchical manner, dictated by written mandates.

✓ With most ETFs, the deposit is insured up to a specified amount, providing an additional layer of security for investors.

✓ Regulation and oversight ensure that ETFs are regulated by the supervisory authorities of each country, offering some level of assurance that the fund will indeed purchase and back your deposit with actual bitcoin.

✓ On the tax side, legislation in some countries provides a tax advantage to those holding ETF shares as opposed to directly holding cryptocurrency.

✓ In terms of inheritance, your funds become part of the inheritance process, allowing heirs to access the funds even if they were unaware of the investment.

Disadvantages:

✗ Ownership is indirect; your funds are held by another entity, exposing you to potential risks of seizure, hacking, or the collapse of that agent or custodian. Furthermore, this arrangement precludes making full use of all bitcoin's technical features, including making payments with these funds.

✗ ETFs typically incur management fees annually for managing your funds, in addition to charges for deposits and withdrawals. In contrast, owning and holding funds in a bitcoin account is free, with only transaction fees applicable for transferring funds.

✗ The traded value of a bitcoin ETF may not accurately mirror the actual market price of bitcoin, potentially reacting more slowly to market price changes.

✗ ETFs do not trade round the clock; they are limited to trading hours, unlike bitcoin, which is traded 24/7.

✗ Purchasing ETFs requires undergoing the KYC process, necessitating client identification.

✗ In the context of inheritance, although your funds are included in the inheritance process, this can lead to a longer duration for the assets to be passed to survivors, along with the potential for additional fees.

The most famous bitcoin ETF:

- BlackRock iShares Bitcoin Trust (IBIT): BlackRock
- Grayscale Bitcoin Trust (GBTC): Grayscale
- Fidelity Wise Origin Bitcoin Trust (FBTC): Fidelity
- ARK 21Shares Bitcoin ETF (ARKB): Ark Invest/21Shares
- VanEck Bitcoin Trust (HODL): VanEck
- Valkyrie Bitcoin Fund (BRRR): Valkyrie
- Invesco Galaxy Bitcoin ETF (BTCO): Invesco/Galaxy
- Franklin Bitcoin ETF (EZBC): Franklin Templeton
- WisdomTree Bitcoin Fund (BTCW): WisdomTree

Bitcoin Exchange Traded Fund

Bitcoin ATMs and newsstands

Authentication: by operator (within USD/EUR 1,000 mostly NO KYC) Higher KYC amounts / Complexity: MEDIUM / Fees: in HIGH

The biggest advantage of bitcoin ATMs is anonymity when depositing or withdrawing smaller amounts, which is offset by higher fees. Along with the fees, you must also expect to pay a transaction fee, which depends on the amount of bitcoin mined. In some countries, even for smaller amounts, verification is required via email or phone. The convenience of purchasing from various ATMs extends beyond just the fees and presents significant challenges for comparison. With exchange rates in constant flux, each transaction is tied to a distinct exchange, each calculating transaction fees and the applicable exchange rates differently. Consequently, it's possible to find that, in some cases, a location with lower fees might actually result in a more expensive purchase than one with higher fees.

- To make a bitcoin purchase at enabled ATMs, first select the currency on the display, then click on the 'Make Purchase - Determine Limit' button. For higher amounts, scanning the receipts is required. Next, show the QR code of your address to the camera, and finally, insert the notes. The bitcoins will arrive in your wallet within tens of minutes or a few hours, depending on the transaction fees and the current network load..

- Withdrawing bitcoin at enabled ATMs involves two steps. First, determine the amount of cash you wish to use. The ATM will print a receipt containing a QR code that specifies the address to which and the amount of BTC you need to send. Then, wait for the transaction to complete—the time it takes for your payment to arrive in the ATM operator's wallet. Importantly, you are not required to wait at the ATM; you can retrieve your cash a few hours later or the next day. Upon the completion of your transaction, as indicated by the issued receipt, you can choose to withdraw the cash, and the ATM will dispense it.

Bitcoin ATMs and newsstands

Cryptocurrency exchange services

This phenomenon represents a revolutionary shift in the traditional landscape, operating globally and available 24/7. These platforms empower individuals to operate independently of banks and governmental oversight. Nonetheless, caution is advised: it's crucial to select reputable exchanges with positive references and avoid leaving cryptocurrencies in their custody.

These exchanges facilitate rapid transactions at predetermined rates, making them an ideal entry point for novices seeking their first bitcoin acquisition. Depending on the regulatory environment of their jurisdiction, some exchanges offer transactions up to approximately $1,000 USD without requiring KYC verification, provided the funds originate from a bank account. Conversely, others may impose KYC requirements for smaller amounts, motivated by the fear of account closure by commercial banks due to AML concerns. The KYC process may be required at the point of registration, prior to the initial transfer, or before transferring funds to a private wallet, potentially appearing as a barrier designed to permit purchases during volatile market conditions while delaying the withdrawal process until KYC verification is completed.

After registering on the exchange's platform, either through their website or app, users can transfer money to the exchange's bank account. Subsequently, the agreed amount of bitcoin is sent to the specified wallet. Transaction fees are moderate, typically ranging from 1.5% to 4%. Nevertheless, comparing exchange rates across different platforms is challenging due to their fluctuating nature, with each exchange applying its own methodology for calculating transaction fees and exchange rates. This variability can sometimes result in higher purchase costs, even at exchanges with lower fees.

In the passages that follow, I will list some of the exchanges and highlight their advantages.

Invity: currency exchange comparison engine
Authentication: KYC / Complexity: MEDIUM / Fees: MEDIUM

Invity strives to be a friendly and reliable guide in the journey towards financial independence, offering a safe and simple entry point into the world of cryptocurrencies. Founded in 2019 as part of the SatoshiLabs family, Invity is dedicated to empowering everyone to take control of their financial future. By focusing on simplicity, security, and accessibility, Invity makes the often complex world of crypto approachable through its user-friendly mobile app.

The Invity mobile app is designed specifically for those new to cryptocurrency, providing a straightforward and secure way to buy, sell, and save bitcoin. The app's intuitive interface, combined with in-app tips and top-notch security, ensures a smooth onboarding experience for beginners. With just a few taps, users can start buying, selling, and saving bitcoin.

A key feature of the Invity app is its dollar-cost averaging (DCA) functionality, allowing users to set up recurring bitcoin purchases easily. This approach helps minimize the impact of market fluctuations, enabling users to build their bitcoin savings gradually and securely. Users can also monitor their portfolio growth through a visual dashboard that provides a clear and easy-to-understand representation of their savings.

Along with offering a smooth transactional experience, Invity provides educational resources to help users better understand the process of entering the crypto space, enabling them to deepen their knowledge as they navigate their financial journey.

Invity

SIMPLECOIN

Authentication: KYC / Complexity: LOW / Fees: MEDIUM

Simplecoin is one of the oldest cryptocurrency exchange services in Europe. It entered the market in 2013 and has focused on three main pillars since the very beginning: simplicity, security and customer support. Simplecoin, with its many years of experience from the early days of the cryptocurrency market, offers users a truly simple way to acquire cryptocurrencies. While it primarily targets the European market, it has also gained the trust of customers from other parts of the world. As the name suggests, simplicity is its key advantage. From registration to buying or selling cryptocurrencies, everything follows the philosophy of maximum user-friendliness.

One of the essential aspects Simplecoin emphasizes is security. Since its inception, Simplecoin has proudly avoided any issues related to data breaches or customer asset losses. This commitment to privacy and security is one of the main reasons why it has gained the trust of thousands of users.

In the area of customer support, Simplecoin excels with its hotline, available daily from 9:00 AM to 9:00 PM CET. Customers can resolve their queries or issues directly with a team of experts, always ready to assist.

Moreover, Simplecoin is increasingly focusing on B2B collaboration. It offers the possibility of franchising its services and also a lucrative partnership program, opening doors to new business opportunities.

Simplecoin

FixedFloat

Authentication: NO KYC / Complexity: LOW / Fees: LOW

FixedFloat is an intriguing platform that facilitates the instant exchange of one cryptocurrency for another. However, it does not offer the option to exchange between cryptocurrencies and fiat currencies. It does enable the transfer of bitcoin (satoshi) between your bitcoin ledger (blockchain) wallets and the Lightning Network payment system—the second layer of the bitcoin blockchain known for fast and inexpensive transactions. Additional advantages include no requirement for registration, thus ensuring anonymity, and the fact that your funds are not stored with the service operators but remain in your own wallet. Launched in 2018 by a team of cryptocurrency enthusiasts with backgrounds in finance, web technology, and entrepreneurship, FixedFloat is an easy-to-use service that is well-suited for newcomers.

FixedFloat

A large number of internet exchange platforms are operating, with new ones launching continually. They strive to innovate, offering the best possible service and user interface, while also navigating an increasingly strict regulatory landscape. However, a critical rule remains: carefully vet the platform to which you send your money to avoid falling victim to scams. Additionally, it is prudent to regularly transfer your funds to your own wallet.

Centralized cryptocurrency exchange

All centralized exchanges require KYC compliance. Given their typically lower fees, buying cryptocurrencies through a centralize exchange tends to be more profitable (in terms of price) than the other options mentioned. Speculating on price movements allows for the acquisition of large quantities of cryptocurrencies. Although trading on these platforms is more complex than simple exchange services—necessitating an understanding of Limit and Market orders (refer to page 264) and the practice of withdrawing to one's own wallet—the benefits gradually become apparent. Many users, either out of convenience or lack of knowledge, leave their funds on the exchange for extended periods, not recognizing that these funds, effectively under the custody of an agent, may not be entirely secure. Such a stance exposes them to the risk of loss through theft, liquidity issues, or the collapse of the exchange. Historical precedents of such incidents exist.

Moreover, funds are vulnerable to seizure:

- in the event of international political shifts leading to sanctions (e.g., seizure or blocking of funds from Russian citizens).
- if there are changes in the political regime or laws within their home country.
- following a court decision.

Therefore, it is advisable to leave funds on the exchange only briefly, or as necessary for trading activities. Regularly withdraw the remaining funds to your private wallet.

Here are some recommendations for well-known exchanges by continent. In North America, Coinbase is a popular exchange, known for its user-friendliness and security. In Europe, one of the oldest American exchanges, Kraken, is widely used. However, the much younger DASE, which aims to target European countries, is also worth mentioning. In Asia, Binance is popular, being one of the largest exchanges in the world and offering extensive trading options. In Australia and Oceania, Independent Reserve is a reliable exchange that provides services not only to individuals but also to institutions. On the African continent, Luno is gaining popularity, supporting various fiat currencies and being easily accessible.

DASE
Authentication: KYC / Complexity: MEDIUM / Fees: LOW

The DASE exchange, set to launch in 2024, is a modern European cryptocurrency platform with aspirations to become the continent's largest exchange. It allows trading in cryptocurrencies using local European currencies, enhancing accessibility for regional users. DASE's strengths are rooted in its technological sophistication, innovative strategies, and adaptability to the evolving challenges of the cryptocurrency industry. It caters to both novice investors and seasoned traders, including institutional clients, with a range of basic to advanced trading features and products. It is governed by the European MiCA framework. The platform, developed in the Rust programming language without reliance on third-party solutions, enhances its security and reliability. It adheres to stringent security measures, including regular independent audits of client funds and penetration testing. From the inception of DASE, it has supported the use of the Lightning Network. Of course, there is also a mobile app. The exchange's developers are also the creators of Bitlifi, a popular Lightning Network wallet that enables users to send satoshi to phone numbers or convert them to on-chain transactions (see page 295).

DASE

There are many cryptocurrency exchanges around the world. Some disappear, while new ones emerge, competing with one another. If you plan to start buying cryptocurrencies on an exchange, it is important to check its references and reviews from both users and experts. The most important advice: never leave your cryptocurrencies on the exchange for long periods. After purchasing, transfer them as soon as possible to your hardware wallet.

Buying bitcoin for cash without KYC: over-the-counter purchases

It is not without reason that the saying "cash is king" persists. Utilizing cash is the most effective method for safeguarding your privacy since it leaves no trace of your transactions.

Buying bitcoins with cash is, in technical terms, quite straightforward. However, the organizational aspects present more complexity. Additionally, this method carries the risk of physical theft. One strategy is to purchase directly from miners. Another option involves utilizing the services of so-called 'ethical billers.' These individuals may have acquired their bitcoins clandestinely or might be connected to miners. They also might trade on decentralized exchanges. For a predetermined fee, along with a fixed or market rate, they will facilitate your cash transactions for buying and selling.

It's worth noting that it's not always necessary to engage in on-chain transactions. Alternatives include using the Lightning Network or conducting internal transfers of stablecoins and bitcoin on exchanges that do not require KYC compliance.

Those interested in either selling or buying cryptocurrencies typically form groups and coordinate using various communication tools, such as social networks (e.g., Facebook) and messaging apps (e.g., Telegram, Signal). Additionally, the actual contact details for these groups can be obtained through referrals within the cryptocurrency community.

This decentralized marketplace, where transactions can occur without the awareness of others, is referred to as over-the-counter (OTC). This term is also commonly used in the securities market. Furthermore, the Vexl app merits mention as it facilitates the purchase of bitcoin between specific individuals without the need for KYC compliance.

Vexl

Verification: NO KYC / Complexity: various / Fees: negotiable

Vexl is an open-source mobile application developed by SatoshiLabs. It provides users with the ability to buy or sell bitcoins in a manner consistent with the original vision outlined in the Bitcoin white paper: peer-to-peer and without going through any third party or financial institution.

The biggest innovation Vexl brings to the table is its unique reputation model. On Vexl's marketplace, you can only see offers from your friends and their friends. Offers are anonymized, but you always see how many common contacts you share with the counterparty, allowing you to easily assess the risks associated with your particular trade. Last but not least, if you're hesitant, you can mutually reveal identities in an end-to-end encrypted chat and verify the identity and credibility of the counterparty with your common contacts. Vexl's marketplace is dominated by offers for trading bitcoin for fiat and vice versa, but lately, there has been an increasing trend to trade goods and services as well. With Vexl's categories, communities can effectively form local circular bitcoin economies.

Vexl is non-profit, and using it is completely free—you don't need to pay any subscription fees or lock your bitcoin in escrow. The execution method for transactions—whether in-person exchanges, bank transfers, online payments, Lightning Network transactions, or on-chain transactions—is determined solely by mutual agreement between the parties involved. It is advisable, especially for newcomers, to start with smaller transactions.

This approach is considerably safer than the risks associated with engaging unknown individuals from groups on social networks like Facebook, Signal, or Telegram. Such groups often seek to recruit new members based on various recommendations, but thorough vetting is not always feasible, and the privacy of such trades is very limited—everyone in the group can see your offer, whether for fiat or Bitcoin. On Vexl, all of your activity is hidden from everyone except your counterparty, including service providers.

Finally, Vexl significantly simplifies the process of connecting with new bitcoiners, expanding your contact network, and integrating more seamlessly into the community, making the experience both easier and safer.

Vexl

Decentralized exchanges that accept fiat currencies

Authentication: NO KYC / Complexity: HIGH / Fees: LOW

A significant benefit of P2P exchanges is the heightened degree of anonymity they provide. However, as we will explore, this anonymity is not absolute. These platforms allow users to purchase bitcoin through bank transfers without the need for KYC procedures. Among the most reputable of these exchanges are Bisq and Hodl Hodl. Both offer remote trading capabilities that minimize the necessity of trust between parties.

One of the primary reasons decentralized exchanges can afford to operate without KYC requirements is that they do not hold customer funds. Instead, projects like Hodl Hodl and Bisq offer traders a protocol and code to facilitate transactions independently. To further reduce the risk of fraud, both exchanges employ a reputation system.

It's important to note that trading fees on these platforms typically range from 0.3% to 0.6% of the trade volume, in addition to transaction fees. However, it is crucial to recognize that remote fiat payments are not entirely anonymous. Transactions occur between identified bank accounts and, in many cases, are subject to regulatory scrutiny by banks obligated to report certain activities to authorities.

Other ways to obtain bitcoin

Income from an employer or your own business

Buying is not the only way to earn bitcoin. More and more people are trying to run their services directly with bitcoin or start a business in the crypto industry. Others are even looking for employers who will pay at least part of their salary in bitcoin. Web portals and apps that link supply and demand in the cryptocurrency reward labor market are also starting to appear.

Mining

Domestic mining has recently become less profitable as a method for acquiring cryptocurrencies. The primary challenge for most households is the lack of access to cheap, steady energy supplies. Additionally, the noise and heat generated by mining equipment are significant factors that must be considered. From a cost-effectiveness standpoint, it is often more viable to purchase bitcoin directly with the funds that would otherwise be spent on electricity and technology.

For many miners, the endeavor remains financially viable only because they relocate to areas with cheaper energy or find ways to utilize (or capitalize on) the heat produced by their mining operations. However, there are enthusiasts and advocates of personal freedom who may find value in domestic mining despite its limited profitability. Individuals with access to their own electricity, perhaps generated through home photovoltaic systems, and those able to make use of the excess heat may view mining as more than just an economic calculation.

For these individuals, mining serves as an automatic form of dollar-cost averaging (DCA) that avoids the need for KYC protocols, dealings with exchanges or ATMs, and interactions with traders. Despite the practical and financial challenges, this approach offers a hands-off way to gradually accumulate cryptocurrency.

Moreover, several companies now provide opportunities to invest in mining through a service model. These firms allow customers to purchase mining equipment and arrange for its installation in data centers worldwide, along with ongoing maintenance. One such company, 2Bminer.com, has even contributed to the support of this book. By contracting with these providers, individuals can participate in mining activities without managing the operational complexities themselves.

2Bminer.com

A global platform for cryptocurrency mining, headquartered in the heart of Europe—Prague—with hosting centers on four continents, allows retail customers easy and hassle-free access to mining through its proprietary software that monitors mining 24/7 and guarantees free repairs for the entire lifetime of the machine. With these conditions and a 95% annual uptime guarantee, this solution is attractive to a wide range of clients. The diversification of investment portfolios, the time investment required, and the detailed knowledge needed often make cryptocurrency mining challenging. 2Bminer is the gateway for new investors to easily enter the world of cryptocurrency. The company seeks out the most advantageous locations for its clients, focusing on stable geopolitical situations and low electricity prices, and it utilizes excess energy worldwide to ensure higher profitability for purchased equipment. Additionally, the bitcoins mined are regularly transferred to the customer's wallets. All machines are owned by the clients.

2Bminer

Shares in bitcoin-linked companies

If your interest in cryptocurrency is purely as an investment, and you have no inclination to possess physically volatile digital currencies, alternative avenues exist for investing in the cryptocurrency sector. Globally, numerous companies are engaging in cryptocurrency purchasing or are actively involved in the crypto industry. These entities include cryptocurrency exchanges and mining companies, among others. Investors have the option to buy shares in such companies, thereby gaining exposure to cryptocurrencies through the traditional stock market. A prime example of a well-known and substantial company that invests directly in bitcoin is Microstrategy.

MicroStrategy

Founded in 1989 by Michael J. Saylor, MicroStrategy is an American company that specializes in providing enterprise software solutions and cloud services. In recent years, the company has garnered attention for its aggressive investment strategy in bitcoin, emerging as a major corporate investor in the cryptocurrency sphere. Michael Saylor, the CEO, is a fervent advocate for bitcoin. He has steered MicroStrategy towards allocating the majority of its reserve assets into bitcoin, amassing tens of thousands of BTC in the process. This strategic move has transformed MicroStrategy into a de facto publicly traded "bitcoin company," with its stock value becoming increasingly intertwined with the fluctuations in bitcoin's price. Saylor's long-term optimistic outlook on bitcoin—anticipating it to play a pivotal role in the future financial system—underpins this distinctive investment philosophy. The company's pronounced exposure to bitcoin positions its stock as a compelling option for investors seeking to gain exposure to cryptocurrencies within the traditional equity markets.

MicroStrategy

Remember the tax man

If you plan to invest in cryptocurrencies on a large scale or on a regular basis, it is essential not to overlook the obligation to maintain accurate records and to report taxes properly on any profits earned. Additionally, many investors diversify their holdings across various exchanges and platforms, complicating the task of tracking investments and organizing supporting documents for accounting purposes. This process can be challenging and time-consuming. To alleviate these challenges, several companies have developed specialized software designed to streamline record-keeping. These applications can connect to most trading platforms via API, offering a clear and consolidated view of your transaction history. GENERAL BYTES, one of the world's largest manufacturers of cryptocurrency ATMs, has also ventured into this space with the development of the WhaleBooks platform.

WhaleBooks

This comprehensive platform helps individuals and businesses manage their cryptocurrency portfolios. It not only tracks your crypto assets but also prepares the necessary documents for taxation. The platform can retrieve transactions from exchanges and wallets and provides a detailed overview of your crypto holdings. It offers analytical tools to detect errors in input data and analyzes your entire crypto history to generate documents for tax returns. WhaleBooks also provides advanced accounting tools for working with your accountant and posting crypto transactions directly to your accounting software. Additionally, users have access to a network of professional accountants specializing in cryptocurrency taxation. Whale-Books offers its services in multiple languages to cater to a diverse client base.

Whalebooks

HOW TO STORE CRYPTOCURRENCIES

Cryptocurrencies are always stored in their blockchains, which usually operate on decentralized networks. Thousands of operators of a given blockchain around the world take care of the veracity, consistency, and backup of these blockchains, ensuring the operation of the network for other users. If you aim to maintain an updated ledger, operating your own full node is highly recommended. The process incurs minimal cost and requires some technical know-how. However, there are convenient ready-made solutions available for purchase that simply need to be plugged in and connected to the internet.

What is a crypto wallet and what is it for?

The idea that you can keep your coins in your own private wallet is a misconception. A private wallet only allows you to manage a set of your addresses on a given ledger. In other words, it stores your private keys, which you use to prove your authority to handle your funds. At the same time, it allows you to set up one or more accounts, an activity usually performed when you acquire it. You can manage one account from multiple wallets. Among other things, this allows you to deal with situations where you need multiple users to be able to receive payments into one account. Most wallets allow you to create new (different) addresses for a single account for added privacy. Thus, from the perspective of the wallet, you see all your funds in one account, but participants in the bitcoin network see separate transactions to different addresses. From this perspective, an account can also be seen as a set of multiple addresses.

Seed generation and preservation

The creation of a wallet, namely the generation of new private and public keys, is facilitated by what's known as a seed. This seed typically consists of twelve or twenty-four randomly chosen English words (or occasionally a QR code for software wallets). An algorithm employs this seed to create an extremely large random number with more potential combinations than there are atoms in the universe. This mechanism ensures that no two numbers are the same. You have to make a careful note of the seed words. An incorrect notation may mean that you cannot recreate your private keys in the future. The words are generated from a collection of 2048 words, and each word used in the seed can be accurately identified by its first four letters. If you lose your seed, you can generate a new wallet (new private keys) and if you have your original wallet and PIN, you can move your funds to this new wallet. How and where you store your seed is also very important. You must remember that if your wallet and seed are destroyed or lost, you will never be able to access your funds again. Let's go over some basic rules.

- You should keep your wallet and seed separate.
- If you also record your PIN, keep it separate from your wallet.
- If you use a passphrase (see below), keep it stored separate from the seed.
- Keep the seed stored so that no one else can get to it.
- However, think about the possibility of death so that your survivors can get the seed.
- NEVER take photos of seeds and store them on your computer, mobile phone, or other electronic devices, especially not on cloud services. If such a device or service is hacked, an attacker will immediately gain access to your funds.

- Record the seed on a medium that cannot be altered physically over time, such as by burning, getting wet, or fading. Physical backup elements designed for this purpose are commonly available on the market; they can be found by searching for "recovery seed" on the internet. These backups are typically made of stainless steel, a heat-resistant medium, onto which you can engrave or stamp the seed, or assemble it from stainless steel letters using the tools provided.

Access to the wallet is protected by a PIN and optionally by using a passphrase (see below). If you lose your wallet, you must regenerate your private keys on a new or different wallet using the seed.

If your wallet is stolen and your PIN is compromised, you will lose your funds. The same applies if your seed falls into unauthorized hands.

You should always maintain control of your cryptocurrencies. The cardinal rule in the world of cryptocurrencies is "**not your keys, not your coins.**" This means that if you don't own the seed (the private keys) to a given account (wallet), someone else is managing your funds. Consequently, you may face situations beyond your control and risk losing your funds. In other words, **if you don't have your own keys, they are not your coins.**

Multisig wallets

More advanced users can create multisig accounts in the bitcoin network. In this case, multiple signatures are needed in order to send funds from a given account. This is an optional functionality embedded in the bitcoin network via the bitcoin protocol. It can be utilized by an individual to enhance the security of their funds or by a group of people—such as an institution, company, public fundraiser, or family—as a safeguard against the misuse of power by any one participant. The number of signatures required to authorize a transaction from the total number of available signatures can be set according to preference. For instance, it can be stipulated that two out of three existing signatures, or three out of five existing signatures, are necessary to execute a transaction. Only certain bitcoin wallets, including BlueWallet, Electrum, Sparrow, and Trezor, support multisig technology.

Types of wallets

There are many types of wallets. In the following passages, we'll discuss the most basic divisions in order to give you a general idea.

Software wallets

A software wallet is an application for computers or mobile devices. These wallets are only as secure as the device they are installed on. Avoid sharing computers in workplaces or cafes. Always have up-to-date antivirus software on your computer. A wallet on your private mobile device is a little more secure, but keep in mind that even a mobile phone can be infected with a virus designed to steal your money.

Avoid storing large sums of money in software wallets and never input your hardware wallet's seed phrase into them.

In the case of bitcoin, wallets are further divided into on-chain and Lightning (explained earlier on page 183).

The division between non-custodial (sometimes also called self-custodial) and custodial wallets is very important. With a non-custodial wallet, you have exclusive control over your private keys; for instance, you own the seed or the QR code containing the seed. In this case, the funds are in your direct possession. With a **custodial** wallet, another party controls your private keys. Most custodial wallets today are found on exchanges or exchangers. Many users opt to store larger sums on the main bitcoin blockchain, which they access securely through their hardware wallet (see below), while transferring a smaller portion of their funds to the Lightning Network for quick, small payments, accessed via a custodial Lightning wallet.

Then there are specialized wallets, such as **MetaMask**.

MetaMask

The non-custodial wallet MetaMask is one of the most well-known and widely used since its inception in 2016. It is available on mobile phones with iOS and Android operating systems, but also works as a browser extension. Although MetaMask is a wallet designed exclusively for the Ethereum network, it supports the thousands of other cryptocurrencies functioning as ERC-20 tokens on this network, thereby accommodating a vast array of tokens. MetaMask can also be connected to other selected blockchains via extension services. It represents a certain standard through which you can connect and use the vast majority of DeFi projects, such as decentralized exchanges (DEX). Although it is a proven wallet full of useful features, it will never be as secure as hardware wallets.

BlueWallet

This wallet serves as the ideal tool for exploring the fundamentals of bitcoin addresses and transactions. It enables users to create a new wallet, generates a seed, and supports the use of a passphrase (refer to page 297 for more details). For practical experience, you might consider sending a small amount of money from an ATM, a stock exchange, or a currency exchange to test the wallet's capabilities for receiving and sending funds. Known for its ease of use, this wallet also boasts several interesting features.

- It is a non-custodial wallet that is designed for bitcoin only and has a proven track record based on the number of users.

- It supports iOS, Android, and desktop devices.

- It has simple and easy to understand controls.

- It is simple to switch between accounts in bitcoin, satoshi, and your chosen currency.

- It allows you to manage multiple separate accounts (wallets), both on the bitcoin network (on-chain transactions) and on the

- Lightning Network.

BlueWallet offers a range of advanced features that, while not immediately necessary, could prove beneficial over time. Among these is the option to set up a watch-only wallet. This feature enables you to sync balances and addresses from an account managed by a hardware wallet to BlueWallet's software wallet using a public key. Consequently, you can generate new addresses for your hardware wallet and monitor your balances within BlueWallet. Crucially, private keys are not stored in the software wallet, meaning you cannot initiate payments directly from it. However, this setup allows you to receive both operational and unscheduled payments when you do not have access to your hardware wallet and the computer it connects to. This functionality is especially useful for accepting payments directly from a bitcoin machine into an account controlled by your hardware wallet, eliminating the need to prepare a QR code beforehand. Additionally, BlueWallet facilitates the creation of extra addresses for any given account, mirroring the privacy-enhancing feature of your hardware wallet. The + (add wallet) button further extends BlueWallet's capabilities, enabling the creation of a secure multisig repository that requires multiple signatures for payment authorization, enhancing security (see above).

I strongly recommend making and maintaining a backup for each wallet—a feature available in each wallet's menu—in case you need to reinstall the app, such as after losing your device.

Bitlifi

Bitlifi revolutionizes access to bitcoin as a custodial Lightning wallet, streamlining the process for users, particularly beginners averse to the technicalities of creating a node and establishing payment channels. Its standout feature is the ability to send bitcoins (satoshi) via SMS to any phone number, eliminating the need for recipients to have the app installed beforehand. Should the recipient download Bitlifi after receiving the message, all received satoshi will be accessible in their account, facilitating immediate engagement with the Bitcoin Lightning Network without requiring prior knowledge or registration.

Bitlifi's simplicity, security, and speed make it an excellent option for those new to cryptocurrencies, offering a hassle-free introduction. Additional features include transferring funds from the main bitcoin blockchain to the Lightning Network and integrating with a Bolt card. Plans are in place for Bitlifi to support enhancements to your bitcoin balance via ApplePay and GooglePay shortly. Given its custodial nature, it is advisable to store only a portion of your total balances within the wallet for added security.

Bitlifi

Wallet of Satoshi

The Wallet of Satoshi offers a straightforward option for bitcoin transactions via the Lightning Network, presenting itself as a custodial wallet with a user-friendly interface. It facilitates the easy purchase of satoshi with fiat currency through bank cards, ApplePay, or GooglePay, without necessitating identification documents for small transactions. However, users should note that the fees for these transactions can be quite high. Additionally, Wallet of Satoshi enables the movement of funds in both directions between the Lightning Network and the bitcoin blockchain for a fee, and it offers several advanced features. It is advisable, though, not to store large amounts of funds in this wallet.

For those seeking non-custodial options that provide complete control over fund management, wallets like Zeus, Phoenix, Muun, Electrum, Wasabi, Samourai Wallet, Trust Wallet, Coinomi, BRD, Exodus, and others are popular choices. I encourage you to investigate the wide array of available wallets to find one that best meets your needs, whether that be specific features or support for certain cryptocurrencies.

Hardware wallets

These wallets—also known as cold wallets—store your private keys in a hardware device disconnected from the network. This method is much more secure than software wallets.

- To make transactions, you must always have another device—such as a computer, tablet, or phone—to which you temporarily connect the wallet via a USB port or, occasionally, Bluetooth.

- Unlike a software wallet, it is immune to computer viruses.

- The private keys are securely encrypted within it.

- Access to the wallet and confirmation of transactions are authorized directly by a PIN.

- Up-to-date antivirus software should be installed on the connected device.

- It is always important to verify the recipient's address with the address on the wallet display prior to confirming payment! The wallet cannot verify the correct address for you. A virus on your computer may purposely confuse this address and send the transaction to someone else instead of the recipient.

Among the most widely used and proven wallets are the Trezor, Jade, and Ledger wallets.

Trezor hardware wallets

Trezor ranks as one of the most secure and best-selling hardware wallets globally. The Trezor Model One went into mass production in 2014, making it the world's first hardware wallet. This device is a creation of the Czech company, SatoshiLabs. Presently, there are four devices available. The Trezor Model One offers an affordable option, with a 0.96" Monochromatic OLED screen, two-button pad, and a design that has stood the test of time. Following this is the Trezor Model T, with a vivid 1.54" Color LCD Touchscreen for on-device transaction confirmation, wider cryptocurrency support than its predecessor, and is notable for being the first hardware wallet to implement the SLIP-39 security standard known as Multi-share Backup (Shamir Backup). The Trezor Safe 3 was then introduced as the first member of the Trezor Safe family. Designed with everyday usability in mind, the Safe 3 has a clear OLED display and simple two-button controls, support for Multi-share Backup, and a dedicated Secure Element for protection against sophisticated attacks. The latest addition to the Trezor lineup is the Trezor Safe 5, which is the ultimate hardware wallet for crypto users who demand the highest level of security and seamless usability. It has a vibrant 1.54" color touchscreen complete with Gorilla Glass protection, a dedicated Secure Element for enhanced security, and tactile feedback provided via the Trezor Touch haptic engine.

Trezor Suite is an application that provides you with an interface to control Trezor hardware wallets. It is available for download for Windows, MacOS, and Linux. Trezor Suite provides you with security, a robust user interface, and many useful features for managing your cryptocurrencies. The web interface offers similar capabilities, but the desktop application provides greater functionality than the web app.

Labels in Trezor Suite, are tools that help you monitor your funds. You can label your wallets, accounts, addresses, and individual transactions. Additionally, you can annotate individual transactions to record the sender and note whether they are KYC-compliant or not. This practice helps prevent the linking of UTXOs that you prefer to keep separate when sending money. For enhanced privacy, consider segregating UTXOs from anonymous sources into a distinct account or wallet—created using a passphrase (see below)—to ensure they do not mix with others.

Accounts offer another method to organize your funds effectively. They enable you to segregate funds for various purposes, such as different events, family members, or to distinctly separate KYC and non-KYC coins. Each account can utilize a unique type of bitcoin address and possesses a distinct public key, functioning to a degree as an individual wallet.

Coin control (also known as coin management or UTXO management) in Trezor Suite is an advanced feature that allows you to select specific UTXOs to spend in a transaction. Proper use of coin control can enhance your privacy. Normally, when making a payment, your wallet may need to combine several UTXOs, and without coin control, it will automatically choose UTXOs, often opting for the least expensive ones to spend. Each UTXO has a history of previous transactions, some of which may be tied to KYC regulations or may contain information you prefer not to disclose to the recipient. To safeguard your privacy, you can activate the coin control feature and designate the particular UTXOs for use in your transaction. The selected UTXOs will then be shown as the input values for the transaction.

A passphrase can be used to increase the security of your assets by creating unique 'hidden' wallets, helping to protect your accounts from unauthorized access. Each passphrase functions like an extra word or phrase (in any language) added to your wallet backup, which commonly consists of 12, 20, or 24 words. These characters are appended to the original wallet backup (recovery seed) to generate a completely new set of private and public keys (including xpriv and xpub), which have no association with the original addresses and keys. This allows for the creation of multiple independent 'hidden' wallets within your device, enabling you to segregate wallets linked to KYC from those that are not.

The passphrase is notable for two key features.

- It's not stored anywhere. While your recovery seed is stored on your Trezor hardware wallet, you must enter the passphrase every time you wish to access that specific hidden wallet.

- It may be of any length and include any characters, with distinctions made for spaces and capitalization.

Changing a single character will cause a completely new and, of course, empty account to be generated. In order to discover your passphrase-protected funds, you must type the exact passphrase used to safeguard them; otherwise, you will create a new, empty wallet with every incorrect attempt.

Passphrase is an advanced feature that can significantly increase the security of your funds. However, it needs to be safely backed up and stored just like a recovery seed. Remember, losing access to a passphrase means losing access to the associated funds, so they must be handled very carefully.

Multi-share Backup (previously known as Shamir Backup) was first introduced on the Trezor Model T, and can also be used for the Trezor Safe 3 and Safe 5. The advantage of Multi-share Backup is that it generates between three and sixteen separate shares, rather than a single wallet backup (recovery seed). These shares are automatically created using a specific list of 1024 words, with each share consisting of either 20 or 33 words. This word list is distinct from the one used for standard backups, meaning some words are exclusive to Multi-share Backup. You decide the number of shares required to recover your wallet, effectively setting the 'composition' of the seed. For instance, a three-out-of-five scheme means that the wallet can be restored even if two shares are lost. To a potential attacker, individual shares are useless unless they obtain the critical number needed for restoration, which in this example is three. You can secure the generated seed shares by storing them in multiple locations or entrusting them to reliable individuals. This security method addresses issues such as inheritance management and access to corporate cryptocurrencies, while also offering protection against robbery or extortion. If you lose or have some shares stolen—fewer than the number required for recovery—your funds remain safe, as attackers cannot reconstruct the private keys or access your cryptocurrencies. However, if the number of lost or stolen shares exceeds the threshold for recovery, you will be unable to regenerate your seed. Consequently, if you also lose your wallet or access PIN, you will permanently lose access to your funds. Conversely, an attacker with the requisite number of shares could potentially steal your funds.

I recommend buying a hardware wallet directly on the manufacturer's website, because the availability is usually much better than through e-shops. Card and bitcoin payments are accepted.

 Trezor e-shop

 Trezor YouTube

Hardware wallet Jade

The Jade hardware wallet, developed by Blockstream, is an open-source solution designed to cater to both beginners and advanced users. It integrates with the Blockstream Green app on both mobile devices and computers, facilitating smooth, guided onboarding. For more experienced users, Jade includes a built-in camera that supports transactions through the air-gap principle, enhancing security by minimizing direct connections.

Jade is specifically compatible with Bitcoin and Liquid Bitcoins, a second-layer solution built on top of the Bitcoin network. The innovative use of the Jade camera enables a unique method of communication with its companion app. Rather than relying on USB or Bluetooth for message transfers, Jade and the app exchange information via QR codes scanned from each other's screens. For instance, to confirm a transaction, the companion app generates a QR code displaying transaction details, which Jade scans with its camera. After Jade signs the transaction, it presents a QR code reflecting the result, which the companion app scans and subsequently broadcasts. This process ensures users maintain physical control over data transmission, significantly bolstering security.

Jade

CHAPTER SUMMARY

- Bitcoin is different from other altcoins for many reasons and is suitable for long-term investments.

- Speculation and market timing often do not pay off. Trading is not a discipline for everyone.

- Saving in bitcoin on the principles of DCA, HODL and buy the dip is the way to sleep well and perhaps even to secure a better life in the future.

- Everyone should choose between KYC and no-KYC options based on personal preferences and allocate resources accordingly.

- Bitcoin purchasing options can be ranked by technical proficiency, ranging from the simplest to the most complex.

  - Bitcoin ETFs provide a very simple option for gaining bitcoin exposure, requiring Know Your Customer (KYC) procedures.

  - Bitcoin ATMs and software wallets like Bitlifi or Wallet of Satoshi involve higher fees but offer no-KYC transactions for smaller amounts.

  - Currency exchanges offer a user-friendly interface with medium fees, allowing no-KYC transactions for smaller amounts.

  - Exchanges are suited for intermediate users, featuring low fees and requiring KYC. These platforms allow for the placement of exchange orders.

- Mining is a venture best suited for large investors with access to inexpensive energy and the ability to repurpose the heat generated, or for technical enthusiasts who are not focused on immediate profits.

- For the long-term storage of substantial sums, it is advisable to use only a hardware wallet.

- If you lose your wallet or PIN, you will not be able to regain access to your funds without a seed.

- Never show the seed to anyone, do not store it on electronic devices, and keep it safe.

- Taxes on the sale or purchase of cryptocurrencies should be paid or there may be problems in the future.

- Follow the basic rules of internet safety.

Use antivirus software, change your password, don't share intimate photos, and most importantly… never take pictures of shiny things while naked.

CHAPTER 7

GLOBAL PERSPECTIVES ON CRYPTOCURRENCIES AND THE ROAD AHEAD

GLOBAL PERSPECTIVES ON CRYPTOCURRENCIES AND THE ROAD AHEAD

We are approaching the end of the book. I hope you have learned new information and gained a comprehensive view of both bitcoin and the crypto market as a whole. Related, I believe it's crucial for everyone to observe the broader context of how cryptocurrencies are gaining momentum across various countries. Since 2021, I've observed a growing polarization worldwide. Countries and their leaders are increasingly taking definitive stances on bitcoin and other cryptocurrencies. Some see it as a fair tool and an alternative for the free choices of ordinary people. They advocate for sensible regulations that would prevent fraud and create a stable environment for entrepreneurs in the sector. Others fear losing the ability to manage the economy and the capacity to claim a portion of each citizen's labor (good deeds) through deliberate inflation.

By the time you read this, the situation will certainly be much further along than it is at the time I write these lines. In light of the changing landscape, in this chapter I aim to provide a simplified overview of the current state of cryptocurrencies in the world. Additionally, I provide links to relevant resources so that you can make your own decisions about cryptocurrencies and focus on the particular aspects that interest you most. How the world perceives cryptocurrencies is important and will have a major impact on the further development of the (r)evolution, which has already begun. Once again, this is closely tied to game theory, which predicts that individual states will compete to determine whether the drive to advance their own interests or the ambition to seize opportunities and get ahead of others will prevail.

Reading this book is a great first step, but becoming an experienced market participant requires you to engage with various procedures and gain personal experience. It is important to refresh your thinking and continuously invest in self-education. This approach alone can unveil new opportunities and ensure that you are better prepared than others for a potential global economic crisis.

Know that fortune favors the prepared, and everyone is the author of their own destiny.

SHOULD A MODERN AND DEMOCRATIC STATE BE AFRAID OF CRYPTOCURRENCIES?

The rise of cryptocurrencies can no longer be overlooked and is gradually becoming an important topic at both state and political levels. Some countries have banned cryptocurrencies or their mining, while others are attempting to regulate them or embrace them as an opportunity for innovation. It's likely that an increasing number of countries will seek to reduce their dependence on the US dollar or find alternatives for their inflation-prone currencies. Eventually, some may adopt an independent currency, attracted by the additional benefits it offers. In just a few years it all could be markedly different.

Truly democratic states cannot be threatened by bitcoin.
But it could threaten ours.

Imagine if there was a global currency independent of political pressures. Such a global currency could be important for trade and travel, but it could also help maintain the quality of other national currencies. If we had an accepted global currency, all other currencies would be compared to it. If a national currency was not strong or stable enough, people would have less incentive to use it. This could push governments to maintain responsible financial policies and keep inflation low.

In his 1997 lecture on ideal money, Nobel Prize winner John Nash tried to define the view of money:

- Money is a service that mediates the transfer of benefits (good deeds) to people. This makes the money itself useful and thereby acquires value.

- According to him, the ideal money should be completely non-inflationary. Inflation erodes the value of our hard-earned achievements, diminishing the worth of the good deeds we've accomplished with significant effort.

- Money should be perceived as a public service and its quality should be evaluated in terms of the quality of service of the supplier (the state).

- The quality of money varies from country to country.

- People may not be concerned about whether the future quality of the currency is actually assured, or if it instead depends on the unpredictable nature of political decisions or the potentially arbitrary actions of bureaucratic officials.

- In the context of global competition between currencies, people should have the alternative of deciding for themselves where to place their savings.

- "Ideal money" should be completely free of inflation . It should be a global benchmark for other currencies. This could lead to pressure for better quality of other currencies.

But all the countries of the world can probably never voluntarily agree on a common currency, because each country defends its own economic and political interests. Geopolitical tensions and rivalries between major powers are likely to complicate any efforts to create a universal global currency. Although a global currency could bring enormous benefits, divergent interests and priorities of states will hinder its implementation.

In the event that there is an unmanaged, decentralized currency that is universally accepted, this could be a natural and non-violent solution. Individual countries, especially innovative and democratic ones, could gradually start to use it in different ways. Such an approach could lead to increased economic stability, which, by reducing dependence on traditional currencies, could reduce the risk of inflation and financial crises. The use of a global currency would facilitate international transactions and eliminate the need for currency conversions, which would promote trade, travel, and overall economic growth. Moreover, such countries would not be exposed to political decisions and manipulations of traditional currencies. This would give them independence from domestic and geopolitical pressures. A decentralized currency would provide greater financial freedom and access to financial services for all citizens. Countries that implement a global currency would be seen as pioneers and leaders in a new economic era. They would also gain a considerable lead over other countries, giving them a competitive advantage in the international market and strengthening their position in the global economy.

Political parties rapidly advance their electoral programs and make numerous promises, yet they seldom deliver on these commitments. Consequently, an increasing number of voters find these programs confusing and irrelevant, leading them to base their votes on the personas and performances of political representatives, rather than on the actual content of their platforms. In fact, many voters do not fully understand these programs or the direct impact they might have on their lives.

Don't ask me for a comment.
I'm a political scientist, while this is more about religion.

However, the more people encounter the rapidly growing crypto industry in their daily lives, and eventually own some cryptocurrency, the more they will be interested in how the nation is approaching this topic. There will soon be a time when political parties that are friendly towards cryptocurrencies will be able to appeal to voters who have skin in the game. These voters may show as much, if not more, interest in this issue as they do in infrastructure construction, education and healthcare concepts, pension pillars, or national budget policy. Traditional issues usually end up in the category of unfulfilled promises because political consensus or funding cannot be found for them. In numerous countries globally, cryptocurrencies are gaining significance, and politicians are increasingly clarifying their positions on this matter. Over time, the issue of the quality of national currency and access to cryptocurrencies can be expected to move into the spotlight. It will remain up to the electorate as to whether or not they can break away from convention and push for the possibility of using better money.

We live in an environment of excessive bureaucracy, where important matters are often decided by officials who have no idea what the crypto-industry is about and on what principles it operates. Unfortunately, opponents of cryptocurrencies are also represented in international institutions, governments, and central banks around the world. The question is whether the decisions of these officials and institutions are superior to our collective future and freedom. Many global and political analysts predict that the adoption of cryptocurrencies will significantly influence political election debates in the years to come.

Every country has a type of government that at least 51% of the voters deserve.

The crypto-industry requires no incentives or subsidies from governments. Instead, it needs the establishment of clear laws that protect both citizens and entrepreneurs, while also ensuring no discrimination against other countries worldwide. Cryptocurrencies are not a threat to the economy or financial stability. On the contrary, they are a wonderful opportunity for entrepreneurs, a great hope for citizens and perhaps the future engine of our economy.

Currently, the major barriers to wider adoption include outdated laws leading to legal uncertainty, the prevalence of fraud in the unregulated market, a lack of awareness, limited financial literacy regarding cryptocurrencies, and their inherent high volatility, which poses a significant obstacle for standard retail investors and some other investors.

A nation that champions innovation, democracy, freedom, and human rights should not restrict its citizens' choice of currency for financial transactions. This is particularly crucial at a time when modern monetary policies are increasing the debt burden on future generations, rendering the state incapable of protecting its citizens from inflation or ensuring adequate pension provisions.

GLOBAL POLARIZATION: ARE REGULATIONS A THREAT?

The crypto industry is among the world's fastest-growing sectors. Currently, the global community is determining its stance on cryptocurrencies. Hesitating could result in missing irreversible opportunities. Cryptocurrencies offer significant potential but also present regulatory challenges and complexities. As cryptocurrency technology evolves and becomes increasingly popular, governments around the world are targeting the push for regulation and oversight of the sector. However, bureaucratic processes have mostly failed to keep up with this pace. Regulatory rules and restrictions will arise and govern other areas in the coming years. They will also be continuously changed and refined. These regulations particularly affect areas such as payments, investments, the banking sector, currencies, stablecoins, taxation, and the monitoring of financial flows in relation to money laundering and terrorist financing.

In today's rapidly evolving financial landscape, we are witnessing a clash between two ideologies. On one side are traditional financial institutions that depend on centrally managed and politically influenced currencies. On the other side stands the vision of Bitcoin, symbolizing decentralization, freedom, and peer-to-peer (p2p) payment systems. The contrast between these two worlds is stark and evident. Traditional institutions seek to maintain control over the flow of money, and often rely on regulations like AML and KYC to achieve this goal. In contrast, bitcoin and its supporters believe in freedom and autonomy, where the currency is not in the hands of any central authority, and where payments cannot be censored or blocked. However, a decentralized currency also solves some of the economic problems that plague our society today more than ever.

You can still open an account for whomever you want. We just make sure you won't want to open accounts for certain clients.

The traditional financial sector is currently facing similar dilemmas as governments. Some banks view cryptocurrencies as a threat or risk, often citing unclear regulations. Conversely, other banks are exploring ways to use cryptocurrencies in their business, and some have already incorporated cryptocurrencies into their services. Banks that open up to cryptocurrencies early may gain a competitive advantage. Particularly in countries with a planned transition to Central Bank Digital Currency, cryptocurrencies may offer banks a new business model, especially if they were to lose the market for loans and mortgages.

As we have noted in the previous chapters, bitcoin is at the level of an innovation gap that, once crossed, could see a substantial increase in its adoption. This also applies to some altcoins. As adoption grows, there will be an influx of new participants from both retail and institutional sectors. This is already attracting the attention of some banking institutions, large corporations, and technology companies that are looking to incorporate the new technology into their solutions.

If "free money" were to become a kind of standard or independent global alternative to state currencies, it could have a huge global impact. International transactions would be faster and cheaper, while many isolated and disadvantaged communities would have better access to financial services. However, this freedom would bring its own challenges. Governments could lose opportunities to fund their projects by printing new money. This could lead to a reduction in social security for certain groups or a reduction in some public services. These areas would then most likely be taken over by commercial or non-profit organizations. People would have more power over their assets, which would mean more personal responsibility and self-management for them and theirs. This development could subsequently lead to a realignment of the world's wealth, the emergence of new investment opportunities, and possible changes in perceptions of the value of money. Bitcoin and other cryptocurrencies represent a new era in the evolution of money. Although the future is uncertain, one thing is clear. The idea of free money that bitcoin represents has the potential to profoundly change the world as we know it.

IS A BLANKET BAN ON CRYPTOCURRENCIES IMMINENT?

In recent years, cryptocurrencies have become an integral part of the global financial market. What would the implications be of banning the use of cryptocurrencies, or making the conversion between fiat currencies and cryptocurrencies impossible?

If key powers were to impose drastic restrictions on cryptocurrencies, it could cause panic in the market. The value of many cryptocurrencies would likely fall, which would likely impact the sentiment of investors. Many of the technological innovations and investments that are centered around the cryptocurrency sector would be redirected elsewhere or disappear altogether. Many startups and businesses currently operating in the cryptocurrency space would likely face financial challenges. Restricting access to cryptocurrencies would likely lead to greater use of decentralized exchanges and peer-to-peer platforms. These would largely allow trading outside the traditional financial system, making it impossible for states to effectively supervise and regulate. States would face significant challenges in enforcing such bans. In today's digitized age, it would be extremely challenging, if not impossible, to monitor, regulate, and block all cryptocurrency-related transactions. Moreover, such measures would likely lead to the increased popularity of cryptocurrencies such as Monero or Zcash, which offer anonymous transactions.

However, other consequences would be much more complex. Cryptocurrencies, and bitcoin in particular, were founded on the idea of decentralization and offering an alternative to the traditional financial system. On a social and political level, restrictions on access to cryptocurrencies could spark significant protests. Many people could perceive this move as a restriction of freedom and an attempt by nations to establish an authoritarian or totalitarian regime. Furthermore, nations implementing such measures would need to justify to their citizens and major investors why their actions have undermined previously lawful investments.

Responsible nations must approach cryptocurrency regulation with caution, understanding, and respect for the innovations these technologies offer.

It is also important to note that it is highly unlikely that all countries in the world will ban cryptocurrencies. Some countries see cryptocurrencies as an innovation and a tool for economic growth. Other countries are more skeptical about them because of the potential impact on their monetary policy or because of the complexity of monitoring and censoring transactions. Geopolitical differences, economic interests and ideological perspectives are likely to lead to different national attitudes on the international stage. Countries that consider taking the extreme step of banning bitcoin, for example, would face a significant challenge. Once an innovation like Bitcoin has been created and widely adopted, it cannot simply be erased or undone. Even if such a ban were implemented at an official level, the extensive community of supporters behind Bitcoin, and the decentralized nature of the technology, mean that many individuals would likely continue to use it outside the boundaries of state control and oversight. The result would be an underground economy where bitcoin and other cryptocurrencies would play a key role.

Historically, we have observed that despite prohibitions, desired items or concepts, such as alcohol during the Prohibition era in the US or banned literature in totalitarian regimes, have always found a way to reach people. If the gray economy begins to expand and bitcoin demonstrates resilience against state prohibitions, this could ignite renewed interest in its use. Consequently, its value and appeal might start to increase once again. Countries that choose not to ban bitcoin or even encourage its adoption could benefit from this growth and become global hubs for cryptocurrency innovation. In the long run, countries that initially ban cryptocurrencies might face the realization of economic and technological benefits they missed out on, as seen in other countries that adopted these technologies. Consequently, they may recognize that imposing a strict ban was counterproductive, leading to a lag in international competitiveness. Such a situation could lead to a reconsideration of bans and a relaxation of regulations. History shows us that meaningful innovation, supported by strong citizen interest and community effort, almost always finds a way to survive and thrive despite regulatory barriers.

The global crypto landscape

Let's take a look at where countries stand in terms of access to cryptocurrencies. In general, we can say that many democratic countries with developed economies are trying to regulate cryptocurrencies and integrate them into their financial systems to ensure transparency and consumer protection. These countries often see the potential of cryptocurrencies, but also want to avoid the possible risks associated with money laundering and terrorist financing. On the other hand, some totalitarian regimes or authoritarian governments may ban cryptocurrencies because of the potential threat to their power, control over the economy, or lack of regulation.

The European Union is the furthest along with across-the-board regulation. In 2023, the European Parliament ratified the Markets in Crypto-Assets Regulation (MiCA), which establishes uniform market rules across the EU. This regulation applies to crypto-assets that are not currently regulated by existing financial services legislation. It defines key provisions for entities that issue or trade in crypto-assets. In particular, the provisions relate to transparency, disclosure, authorization and supervision of transactions. Member

States should adapt these provisions and ensure their implementation by 2026 at the latest. MiCA thus represents a revolution for the world of crypto-assets and the EU has, for example, overtaken the US in terms of clearly defined legislation.

 "Cryptocurrency Regulations by Country" via Thomson Reuters

 PwC Global Crypto Regulation Report 2023

 Global Cryptocurrency Regulations via Freeman Law

 "From the U.S. to Japan, Regulators Are Beginning to Embrace Crypto" via Cointelegraph

 "7 Crypto-Friendly Countries You Need to Know About in 2023" via Binance

 "Swiss Crypto Valley at the Heart of the Global Blockchain Economy" via finance.swiss

 "Development in Crypto Valley Remains Stable" via liechtenstein.li

 Top 10 Crypto-Friendly Countries

Examples of countries where cryptocurrencies are legal and where they are seeking to incorporate them through regulation

North America: Canada, United States of America

Caribbean and Atlantic Islands: Bahamas, Bermuda, Cayman Islands

South America: Argentina, Brazil, Chile, El Salvador, Peru, Uruguay, Venezuela

Europe: Austria, Belgium, Czech Republic, Denmark, Estonia, Finland, France, Germany, Greece, Greenland, Hungary, Ireland, Italy, Latvia, Liechtenstein, Lithuania, Netherlands, Norway, Poland, Portugal, Spain, Sweden, Switzerland, Ukraine, United Kingdom (including Bailiwick of Guernsey, Bailiwick of Jersey, Isle of Man, and Gibraltar)

Asia: Australia, Hong Kong, Indonesia, Japan, Malaysia, Philippines, Singapore, South Korea, Taiwan, Thailand

Oceania: New Zealand

Middle East: Israel, Saudi Arabia, United Arab Emirates

Africa: Kenya, Nigeria, South Africa

Countries lacking regulatory clarity

Ecuador, India, Mexico, Russia

Countries where cryptocurrencies are banned

Algeria, Bangladesh, Bolivia, China, Colombia, Egypt, Iran, Morocco, North Korea, Turkey.

We recognize that creating new money makes the situation worse. But the end of fiat currencies is definitely not imminent until we complete the transformation of our portfolios into bitcoin.

INDUSTRY VISIONARIES

This book would not be complete without casting a spotlight on some of the key individuals whose profound insights and innovations have shaped the bitcoin landscape and, by extension, the world. These visionaries have educated both the general public and governments, playing pivotal roles since the inception of bitcoin or soon recognizing its potential to enhance global freedom and equity.

Adam Back

Adam Back, a British cryptographer and cypherpunk, implemented Hashcash, which is now integral to the Bitcoin mining process. He has corresponded with Satoshi Nakamoto regarding the foundational concepts of bitcoin and co-founded Blockstream, a company that develops technologies for managing digital assets. Back continues to devote significant energy and resources to promoting and educating about bitcoin.

Blockstream

Marek 'Sush' Palatinus and Pavol 'Stick' Rusnák

Marek Palatinus, known as Slush, founded the world's first mining pool—today's Braiins pool—and, together with Pavol Rusnák, also known as Stick, launched the world's first hardware wallet. They pioneered the existing seed concept for creating and storing private keys. In an effort to preserve bitcoin's essence as peer-to-peer money, they funded the creation of Vexl, a social network-based application that facilitates the anonymous and direct trading of bitcoin, bypassing KYC-regulated exchanges.

Trezor fundamentals

Michael Saylor

Michael Saylor is one of the most prominent advocates of bitcoin, viewing it as an independent global currency. His company, MicroStrategy, holds the distinction of being the largest institutional holder of bitcoin worldwide.

Michael J. Saylor

Saifedean Ammous

Saifedean Ammous, a professor of economics, is the author of The Bitcoin Standard, a best-seller published in 37 languages. He teaches courses on bitcoin and economics in the tradition of the Austrian School and hosts podcasts on the topic.

Dr. Saifedean Ammous

Samson Mow

Samson Mow, CEO of JAN3, a Bitcoin technology company, is best known for his involvement with El Salvador's Bitcoin initiatives. His efforts are crucial in promoting the adoption of Bitcoin by nation-states around the world.

Jan3

THE CASE FOR HOLDING BITCOIN: OPPORTUNITIES AND CAUTIONS

- Investors face risks such as the loss of private keys, the irreversibility of transactions, and challenges in transferring assets upon death.

- Non-investors risk missing opportunities, facing hyperinflation, nationalization, and asset seizure.

- While bitcoin itself remains largely unchanged, the ecosystem surrounding it is evolving progressively.

- Learning the basics of bitcoin from a savings perspective can provide a solid foundation for future investment strategies.

- I commit to a minimum investment horizon of four years when buying bitcoin.

- My investment strategy is cautious: as a beginner, I invest 1%–3% of my assets, and as an experienced investor, 3%–10%.

- My investment decisions are guided by my understanding and belief in the potential of the investment.

- For long-term security, I exclusively store bitcoin in my own hardware wallet.

- I ensure my seed is securely stored and never disclosed to anyone under any circumstances.

- I maintain privacy about the amount of satoshi I own.

- I have arranged for the transfer of my seed in the event of my death.

- I adopt a mindset that is unaffected by price fluctuations, focusing instead on strategic buying.

- Owning bitcoin provides a significant advantage in emergencies, such as natural disasters, wars, political regime changes, or threats to personal freedom, allowing me control over my resources and ease of global payment and transport.

- Consider the future implications of bitcoin investment; just as people today regret not buying bitcoin in 2011 for $0.3, future generations may regret not purchasing satoshi in 2022 when 1,000 satoshi cost less than $0.1.

Are you asleep?

Imagine if we'd started buying Bitcoin in 2011.

HOW BITCOIN RESHAPED MY PERSPECTIVE AND THE IMPORTANCE OF SELF-EDUCATION

Many people view their surroundings optimistically, trusting the government to provide for them, while others see only negativity, feeling powerless to effect positive change. However, it's crucial for everyone to recognize their personal responsibility in shaping their lives. As discussed in the introduction of this book, topics like saving, investing, and deferring consumption are vital. Some may argue they lack funds to invest, but investment isn't solely about money. One can invest in education, and this doesn't necessarily mean engaging in lengthy or costly academic pursuits. It's about staying informed and understanding the issues that directly impact us. Grasping the fundamentals of money creation, its functions, and related matters is essential for everyone.

Cryptocurrencies represent a significant innovation, providing an alternative to traditional state currencies. Currently, many people consider bitcoin primarily as an investment asset, with a substantial number of users engaging in speculation. In reality, however, it may be the non-state money of the future. It can be seen as a Plan B for humanity or as a hedge against inflation and monetary experimentation. It can also be seen as "digital gold" or as one of the tools for the separation of money and the state. Bitcoin guarantees you freedom and control over your own funds. You can decide according to your needs and wishes and no one can stop you. Once acquired, bitcoins belong to you unquestionably and no one has the power to take them away from you. Let's get out of the Matrix of state fiat money and take responsibility for our own lives.

However, anyone who decides to invest some money in cryptocurrencies should know what they are doing, understand the basic principles, and know the possible risks. Everyone has the opportunity to benefit significantly in the future by staying ahead of the curve. It's crucial to remain engaged with current events and pursue ongoing self-education. Those who adapt their thinking, breaking free from conventional patterns and accepted norms, will find themselves at a considerable advantage.

Over the course of humanity's existence, both money and payment methods have evolved. Many currencies have disappeared precisely because they failed to be scarce, and thus failed to perform the basic functions of money. Nor will the current monetary experiment of state fiat currencies be around forever. This money will disappear and be replaced by something new. Hand in hand with this reality will probably be a redistribution of the world's wealth. The prepared will be at a considerable advantage. Whether this innovation will be free bitcoin or exploitable CBDC, no one knows. We have already explained that the world has long been moving towards the need for a central money. If this money is controlled by some nations, they will face difficulties in coordination and cooperation. It is very likely that, despite the potential benefits of a common global currency, nations will not be able to come into agreement. This is due to the divergence of economic and political interests between countries.

Bitcoin, as a decentralized and globally recognized cryptocurrency, operates independently without needing to negotiate with any entity. It's anticipated that various countries will increasingly seek to harness its potential benefits. These include providing universal financial access to citizens in all types of nations, enhancing tourism, facilitating international trade, and contributing to financial stability and economic growth. Simplified, cost-effective, and swift international transactions could foster economic integration and expansion. Additionally, bitcoin's reduced currency risk and independence from national currencies might boost investor confidence and international investments. Its autonomy from central authorities and privacy features are appealing for those wary of political interference or skeptical of the current monetary and banking systems. Whether bitcoin will outpace the emerging Central Bank Digital Currencies in the race for global monetary dominance remains uncertain, leaving individuals to form their own opinions.

Open your mind, shift your perspective, and dedicate time to self-education. If you've read this book, I hope it has enlightened you and that your time was well spent. However, your journey of personal growth shouldn't stop here. There's a wealth of resources available, including literature—much of which is free—and numerous online platforms and YouTube channels focused on this subject. There's no excuse not to continue learning. I wish you great success and will be cheering you on.

Digital currencies won't catch on. People like being able to touch their money. And we're even happier when we can touch their money.

EDUCATIONAL AND OTHER INTERESTING LINKS

Education and the pursuit of knowledge are central themes of this book, and how you engage with this message is a personal choice. Whether you prefer reading, listening to audiobooks and podcasts, or watching YouTube videos, the choice is yours. The following links are provided to guide you in the right direction. Think of this as an investment in your future and potentially that of your children.

BITCOIN TOOLS

 Bitcoin network status

 Bitcoin fee calculator

 Mempool explorer

 Blockstream Explorer

NEWS AND ONLINE RESOURCES

 CoinDesk

 Cointelegraph

 Unchained Crypto

 Decript

 Bitcoin Optech

 Jameson Lopp - Bitc oin

YOUTUBE CHANNELS AND PODCASTS

 BTC Sessions

 Stephan Livera

 Bitcoin Audible by Guy Swann

 What Bitcoin Did by Peter McCormack

BOOKS

 The Bitcoin Standard: *The Decentralized Alternative to Central Banking* by Saifedean Ammous

 *Digital Gold: The Untold Story of Bitcoin* by Nathaniel Popper

 *Mastering Bitcoin: Unlocking Digital Cryptocurrencies* by Andreas M. Antonopoulos

 *Cryptoeconomics: Fundamental Principles of Bitcoin* by Eric Voksuil

 *The Little Bitcoin Book*

 *21 Lessons* by GiGi

 *Broken Money* by Lyn Alden

 *Bitcoin is Venice*

 The Second Realm

 *A Lodging of Wayfaring Men* by Paul Rosenberg

 *The Sovereign Individual* by James Dale Davidson & Lord William Rees-Mogg

 *The Bitcoin Bookshop*

CONCLUSION

Congratulations on completing this book. Having learned about the workings of bitcoin, its acquisition, and secure storage, you are likely eager to begin using this innovative currency for your purchases and transactions. I invite you to explore a website dedicated to listing merchants accepting bitcoin payments. The links provided will guide you to various global locations where bitcoin is accepted.

 Bitcoin Map

 Coinmap

I'd like to offer one final suggestion. Around the world, there are numerous fascinating conferences focused on bitcoin and cryptocurrencies. Attending these events presents a chance to learn about the technology, network with industry professionals, discover new products, and gain fresh insights. Typically, these conferences feature vendors selling merchandise and refreshments for cryptocurrencies, making them ideal venues to experiment with this payment method. They also provide an opportunity to meet a community of enthusiasts eager to share their experiences and offer valuable advice. Below, I have listed some noteworthy conferences that you might consider attending.

I wish you great success and enjoyment in incorporating bitcoin into your daily life. I am confident that you will have a rewarding experience with this cutting-edge technology and that it will become a staple in your financial activities.

Dear Readers,

I extend my heartfelt gratitude for your interest in my book. It's an honor to know you've dedicated time to reading it, and I hope it has provided you with valuable information and practical advice.

My goal is to make this book available to as wide a readership as possible. Within my limited means, I am trying to make copies available to schools and public libraries. At the same time, I would also like to translate the book into other languages. However, preparing such a large work—including translation, licensing of comic illustrations and images, graphic design, and typesetting of individual pages—is resource-intensive and costly. For this global edition English translation, funding has been obtained from sponsors in addition to my own resources.

If you would like to support the goal, I would be grateful for any contribution. Below you will find various methods for sending a contribution of your choice. Please don't hesitate to reach out to me.

Here's to **Plan B**!

—Kamil Bouška

BIBLIOGRAPHY

As part of my self-study, I drew information from the following sources:

Ammous, Saifedean. The Bitcoin Standard: The Decentralized Alternative to Central Banking. John Wiley & Sons Inc, 2018.

https://www.wiley.com/en-hk/The+Bitcoin+Standard:+The+Decentralized+Alternative+to+Central+Banking-p-9781119473862

Karpiš, Juraj. Zlé Peniaze: Sprievodca Krízou [Bad Money; A Guide to the Crisis]. INESS, 2015.

https://www.databazeknih.cz/knihy/zle-peniaze-272713

Plachetka, Jiří. Velká encyklopedie citátů a přísloví [The Great Encyclopedia of Quotes and Proverbs]. Knižní klub, 1996.

https://www.databazeknih.cz/nakladatelstvi/knizni-klub-96

Pritzker, Yan. Inventing Bitcoin: The Technology Behind The First Truly Scarce and Decentralized Money Explained. Self-published, 2019.

https://www.swanbitcoin.com/inventing-bitcoin/

Tětek, Josef. Separation of Money from the State. Braiins Insights, 2023.

https://braiins.com/books/bitcoin-separation-of-money-and-state

BIBLIOGRAPHY

ADDITIONAL SOURCES

"Bitcoin.org." https://www.bitcoin.org/en.

"Bitcoinforum." https://www.bitcoinforum.com.

"Bitcoin Magazine." https://www.bitcoinmagazine.com.

"Bitcointalk." https://www.bitcointalk.org.

"Coindesk." https://www.coindesk.com.

"Cointelegraph." https://www.cointelegraph.com.

"Wikipedia." https://www.wikipedia.org

Infographics inspired by @anilsaidso via X.

This time capsule will make someone very happy a hundred years from now. We put bitcoin in it.

INDEX

A

abstraction   34, 36–37, 108

altcoins   237–238

Amar's Law   207

anarcho-capitalism   99

antifragility   179–180

antoninianus   65–66

asset   22–23, 33, 49, 61, 64, 87–91, 223, 240–242, 260, 262

ATH (all-time high)   261, 264

aureus   67–68, 157

Austrian School of Economics   60, 100, 102–106

B

barter   26, 28, 33

Big Brother   139, 142

Binance   286, 310

Bisq   289

Bitcoin

    address   181, 190, 246, 294, 297

    Core   174, 182

    function   180, 188

    network operators   174, 177–178

    protocol   133, 145–147, 171–173, 176–178, 182–184, 236

    predecessors   134–135, 150

    whitepaper   135, 143, 147, 149, 153–155, 159, 171

bitcoin

    acquisition   260, 284, 286

    ATM   223, 281, 283, 290–291, 294

    commodity   254, 260

    grammar   133

bitcoinization   85–86

bitcoin.org   144–145, 170, 240

black swan   180

blockchain   133, 144–145, 147, 171, 175, 178, 183–184, 192, 237, 240–241, 243–246, 249–251, 292, 294, 310

B-money   135, 155, 156

Bretton Woods Agreement   50–52

Bridging the Gap   203, 220

Byzantine General's Problem   147, 154, 177

C

Cantillon Effect   61–62, 72, 118, 185

capital   23, 39, 87, 103, 260, 264, 267, 326

capitalization   85, 132, 224, 252–253, 260

CBDC   34, 243–244, 316

CeFi   245

central bank   47–48, 50–52, 54–55, 58–62, 70, 82–85, 89, 93, 96, 100–101, 143–144, 226, 243, 305

commodities   47, 77, 88, 90, 118, 218, 224–225, 253–254

computing power   173, 178, 248–249

    (see also hash rate)

crypto anarchy   140

chart

    candle 268–269, 271–272, 274–275

    line 268

    tick 265

D

darknet market   223

DCA (dollar-cost averaging)   260–262, 284, 290

decentralization   169, 171, 173–174, 184, 307–308

decree   33, 37, 54

DeFi   188, 237, 245, 294

denarius   65–67

DEX   190, 251, 294

dust   247

KAMIL BOUŠKA

THE BIG BOOK ABOUT BITCOIN
AND CRYPTOCURRENCIES
financial literacy for everyone